Methodological Challenges and New Approaches to
Research in International Development

Methodological Challenges and New Approaches to Research in International Development

Edited by

Laura Camfield
Senior Lecturer, School of International Development, University of East Anglia, UK

First published 2014 by
PALGRAVE MACMILLAN

Palgrave Macmillan in the UK is an imprint of Macmillan Publishers Limited,
registered in England, company number 785998, of Houndmills, Basingstoke,
Hampshire RG21 6XS.

Palgrave Macmillan in the US is a division of St Martin's Press LLC,
175 Fifth Avenue, New York, NY 10010.

Palgrave Macmillan is the global academic imprint of the above companies
and has companies and representatives throughout the world.

Palgrave® and Macmillan® are registered trademarks in the United States,
the United Kingdom, Europe and other countries.

ISBN 978–1–137–29361–9

This book is printed on paper suitable for recycling and made from fully
managed and sustained forest sources. Logging, pulping and manufacturing
processes are expected to conform to the environmental regulations of the
country of origin.

A catalogue record for this book is available from the British Library.

A catalog record for this book is available from the Library of Congress.

Typeset by MPS Limited, Chennai, India.

Contents

List of Tables, Figures, and Maps

Tables

Figures

Map

Acknowledgements

Thanks to my collaborator at the University of East Anglia (UEA), Richard Palmer-Jones, who co-organized the "As well as the subject" seminar series (www.uea.ac.uk/dev/ethicalanalysis) where many of these papers were first presented. His critical eye and impressive development knowledge has pushed me to go further in my analyses. Thanks too to seminar participants, colleagues, and students at UEA whose penetrating questions have also shaped my thinking. Other colleagues generously gave time in peer review and Hannah Green patiently checked through the references. My time was funded by an ESRC Methods for Comparative Cross-national Research Initiative grant (RES-239-25-0006) for which I am extremely grateful.

Notes on Contributors

Malin Arvidson is Lecturer at the Department of Social Work, Lund University, Sweden. Prior to this she was Research Fellow at the Third Sector Research Centre, Southampton University, UK. Her primary research interest is the role and behaviour of third-sector organizations, and how such organizations are involved in alternative ways of organizing the provision of welfare services. She recently participated in a longitudinal qualitative study of these organizations in England, and is presently involved in a Swedish study focusing on the changing role and positions of third sector organizations in relation to the welfare state. She has also been involved with research in Bangladesh (participation, empowerment, water and sanitation, health, and education) since 1998, including the five-year-long qualitative study Reality Check Bangladesh. Having worked with longitudinal, qualitative methods, Malin also has an interest in methodological issues.

Dominique Béhague is Associate Professor of Medicine, Health and Society and affiliated faculty in the Anthropology Department at Vanderbilt University. She received a BA and MA in Social Anthropology from Bryn Mawr College in the US and a PhD in Anthropology and Social Studies of Medicine from McGill University in Canada (2004). From 2005 to 2010 she was Wellcome Trust Postdoctoral Fellow at the London School of Hygiene and Tropical Medicine (LSHTM), where she completed an MSc in Epidemiology in 2009 and is currently Honorary Lecturer. With grants from the US National Science Foundation, the Fulbright Foundation, the World Health Organization, the UK Economic and Social Research Council, amongst others, her research has led to over 25 book chapters and journal articles on the anthropology of psychiatry, reproductive health and adolescent mental health in Brazil, and on the politics of the evidence-based movement in global health. She is currently developing a new project on the role of evidence in global mental health together with colleagues at Vanderbilt, the LSHTM and King's College London, where she also holds a yearly summer appointment as Senior Lecturer.

Philippa Bevan is a sociologist who was employed as a university researcher and lecturer at the universities of Oxford and Bath between 1993 and 2006. During this time, in addition to university and occasional practitioner teaching, she conducted empirical research in Ethiopia and Uganda and published related papers. She also produced theoretical articles and chapters on conceptualizing and studying multidimensional poverty, African welfare regimes, macro–meso–micro linkages in developing countries, well-being research, and the use of case-based methods in development research. Since 2006 she has worked as an independent development research sociologist and since 2009 as a consultant to a joint donor-government group in Ethiopia. She is currently working with colleagues on a study of the long-term impacts of development interventions in rural Ethiopia since the mid-1990s using a mix of qualitative and survey fieldwork undertaken in 20 exemplar rural communities in 1994/1995 (WIDE1), 2003 (WIDE2), 2004–2005, 2007, and 2009–2013 (WIDE3). The Ethiopia Longitudinal Community Study has generated policy-relevant conclusions in all areas of rural development and numerous academic outputs including the one in this book. This sets out how complexity-informed sociological theory, case-based methods, and qualitative software, can produce research findings of practical use to country-level policy designers and implementers. The author can be reached at pbevan@mokoro.co.uk.

Joanna Bornat is Emeritus Professor at the Open University, Faculty of Health and Social Care. She has a long-standing interest and involvement in oral history and biographical research methods. She is a joint editor of the journal *Oral History* and a committee member of the Oral History Society. Using an oral history approach she has researched and published on topics including labour and women's history, stepfamilies and ageing, older people's remembering, learning in later life, South Asian doctors and the development of geriatric medicine, the secondary analysis of archived interviews, and, most recently, the use of comparative oral history in relation to religious and secular ceremonies in three European countries. Amongst her publications are *Reminiscence Reviewed, The Turn to Biographical Methods in Social Science* (with Prue Chamberlayne and Tom Wengraf), *Oral History Health and Welfare* (with Rob Perks, Paul Thompson, and Jan Walmsley), *Biographical Methods and Professional Practice* (with Prue Chamberlayne and Ursula Apitzsch), and *Ageing, Ritual and Social Change* (with Peter Coleman and Daniela Koleva).

Laura Camfield trained as an anthropologist, but now works collaboratively using qualitative and quantitative methods and training others in their use, most recently with the DFID-funded Young Lives longitudinal research study in Ethiopia. Her current research focus is on enhancing the quality of cross-national methodologies used to collect qualitative and quantitative data on poverty and vulnerability throughout the life course (funded by an ESRC Comparative Cross-national research grant). At UEA she directs postgraduate research within the department for international development, convenes the main research training module for masters' students, and teaches on courses in impact evaluation and ethnography. She has published widely on methodology, specifically in relation to mixing methods to improve the quality of surveys and measures.

Sarah Coulthard has worked in International Development and the Environment for over ten years. She has a particular interest in reconciling environmental conservation with human welfare objectives, especially where people are heavily dependent upon natural resources for their livelihoods. Her recent research has questioned how a deeper understanding of social well-being and human behaviour can be applied to inform better governance, and creative solutions, within global fisheries, a sector in which conservation and livelihood conflicts are widespread. She has worked in fisheries throughout South Asia and Africa, and currently lectures at Northumbria University in the UK.

Graham Crow is Professor of Sociology and Methodology at the University of Edinburgh where he took up the role of Director of the Scottish Graduate School of Social Science in 2013. Prior to this he worked at the University of Southampton for 30 years. He has also been Deputy Director of the ESRC National Centre for Research Methods since 2006. His research interests include research methods (including research ethics), interdisciplinarity, comparative sociology and social theory, and the sociology of families and communities. He has published a number of articles and books on community studies and re-studies including *Community Life* (1994, with Graham Allan) and is currently principal investigator of an interdisciplinary consortium funded under the Connected Communities programme to investigate how change in community relationships is imagined and how it comes about.

Graham Davis is Professor of Economics and Business at the Colorado School of Mines, where he has taught and researched mineral and energy economics for 25 years. Prior to joining academia he worked for several years as a metallurgical engineer at mines in Canada and Namibia. He holds a BS in Metallurgical Engineering from Queen's University in Canada, an MBA from the University of Cape Town, and a PhD in Mineral Economics from the Pennsylvania State University. His research includes the impact of mineral extraction on developing economies, with an emphasis on growth and poverty outcomes. Work in this area has been funded by the National Science Foundation, the Inter-American Development Bank, the United Nations Industrial Development Organization, the World Trade Organization, and the International Council on Mining and Metals. Since 2007 he has served on the Editorial Board of *Resources Policy*, an international journal devoted to minerals policy and economics.

Peter Davis is a social researcher and consultant who works on social policy, development practice, and research training in developing countries. He has taught international development in UK universities and has conducted development research in collaboration with leading research and international development organizations including The World Bank, The Department for International Development, The International Food Policy Research Institute, The Economic and Social Research Council, and the International Labour Organization. His research into poverty and social policy in Bangladesh is internationally recognized and published in leading development studies journals and books.

Maren Duvendack is Lecturer in the School of International Development at the University of East Anglia (UEA), UK where she is involved in the MSc programme "Impact Evaluation for International Development." She has a PhD in Development Economics from UEA. After completing her PhD she joined the International Food Policy Research Institute in Washington DC as a Postdoctoral Fellow before joining the Overseas Development Institute in London as a Research Fellow in evaluation and impact assessment. Her key research areas cover development economics, applied micro-econometrics, impact evaluation, microfinance, replication and reproduction of quantitative analyses as well as research ethics. Maren has worked extensively on microfinance impact evaluations in India and Bangladesh. She is particularly interested in the link between microfinance, empowerment, and reproductive health. She has more recently worked on evaluations for the World Food Programme and the Gates Foundation and is currently evaluating the impact of AusAid-funded public works programmes in Ethiopia and Kenya. Maren's contributions appeared in a number of academic journals (*Journal of Development Studies, Journals of Development Effectiveness and Progress in Development Studies*) and she regularly presents her work at international conferences and frequently engages with the media.

Sian Floyd is Senior Lecturer in Epidemiology and Statistics at the London School of Hygiene and Tropical Medicine. She obtained an MSc in Biometry from Reading University in 1993, and then worked as a biometrician in the agricultural and natural resources sector for four years, first in the Caribbean and then in the UK. In addition to teaching Sian works as a statistician/epidemiologist on a range of different projects including the Karonga Prevention Study, which is based in northern Malawi and HPTN 071, "Population Effects of Antiretroviral Therapy to Reduce HIV Transmission (PopART): A cluster-randomized trial of the impact of a combination prevention package on population-level HIV incidence in Zambia and South Africa."

Dilanthi Koralgama is Lecturer at Ruhuna University and a current PhD scholar at University of Amsterdam, Netherlands.

Rob Macmillan is Research Fellow at the Third Sector Research Centre based at the University of Birmingham. He coordinated the "Real Times" qualitative longitudinal study of third sector organizations, which involved in-depth case study research following the fortunes, strategies, challenges and performance of a diverse group of third sector organizations and activities over time. Rob's main research interests are around the changing support needs of voluntary organizations and community groups and the role of capacity-building and infrastructure in meeting these needs, as well as competition and the construction of markets in the third sector.

Pamela Nasirumbi is Research Data Manager and Statistician in the Centre for Sexual Health and HIV Research at University College London. She is completing her PhD in Epidemiology at the London School of Hygiene and Tropical Medicine. She is a statistician and data manager, involved in the use of large data sets from population and business censuses and in medical research. This has included data management as well as the application of research techniques and statistical methods.

Richard Palmer-Jones is a development economist with more than 45 years' experience in South Asia, Sub-Saharan Africa, and Latin America. He obtained his PhD in Agricultural Economics from the Reading University in 1974. He has conducted extensive field research and analysis of secondary data, focusing on agricultural research, irrigation and water markets, natural resource and environmental political ecology, peasant economy, poverty, inequality, well-being, gender, nutrition, health, and education, and, most recently impact evaluation, systematic review and meta-analysis.

Nasheera Paranamana is Postgraduate Research Scholar based at Ruhuna University, Matara, Sri Lanka, and was employed as a full-time researcher for the ESRC WellFish Project.

Keetie Roelen is Research Fellow at the Institute of Development Studies in Brighton, UK and a member of the Centre for Social Protection. She is a development economist by training and her research interests include the dynamics of (child) poverty, social protection, and the linkages between child protection and social protection. Her research's geographical focus is on Sub-Saharan Africa and South East Asia, and the majority of the research uses mixed methods. In addition, Keetie has worked with many international organizations and NGOs such as UNICEF, Concern and Family for Every Child for research, evaluation and policy advice. Her work has been published in the form of peer-reviewed journal publications and book chapters, working papers, and project reports.

Lahiru Sandaruwan is Postgraduate Research Scholar based at Ruhuna University, Matara, Sri Lanka, and was employed as a full-time researcher for the ESRC WellFish Project.

Janet Seeley has been actively engaged in research on HIV and AIDS since the late-1980s, including four years with Medical Research Council in Uganda 1989–1993 when she was responsible for setting up what was to become the social science programme in the multi-disciplinary MRC/UVRI Unit on AIDS, the programme for which she returned to Uganda to head in 2008. She is currently also Professor of International Development at University of East Anglia, UK.

Andri Soteri-Proctor worked as Research Fellow at the Third Sector Research Centre (TSRC), University of Birmingham until August 2013. At TSRC she was part of the Real Times team and also undertook a micro-mapping project for the Below-the-Radar work stream. Prior to this she held ESRC Postdoctoral Fellowship at the University of Manchester. She has also carried out various projects on the UK's voluntary sector and is a member of the Voluntary Sector Studies Network (VSSN).

Katerini Storeng is Postdoctoral Fellow at the Centre for Development and the Environment and the Institute of Health and Society, University of Oslo, and Honorary Lecturer at the London School of Hygiene and Tropical Medicine. Her research interests include the anthropology of public health, reproductive health, and the history and politics of global health research and policymaking. Her doctoral thesis was an ethnography of the international Safe Motherhood Initiative's struggle to continually reposition itself with the competitive global health arena, building on research conducted with Dominique Béhague on how maternal health experts produce and use diverse forms of evidence as a tool in global socio-political negotiations. Katerini's postdoctoral research examines shifting meanings of "health systems strengthening" within the history of international health, focusing on the way pub-lic–private global health initiatives have appropriated, and redefined, this notion within their disease-specific agendas and business-oriented ethos. Over the past decade, Katerini has also conducted ethnographic research on social, economic, and policy-related aspects on reproductive health in Burkina Faso as part of several large multidisciplinary research projects on reproductive health in low-income countries.

Rebecca Taylor is Research Fellow at the Third Sector Research Centre (TSRC) based at the University of Birmingham. She has researched and published on various aspects of the third sector and its institutions and is a member of the Real Times project team exploring third sector organizations over time. Her interests also include cross-sectoral com-parative perspectives on workforce issues; paid and unpaid (voluntary) work; and the boundaries between different forms of work. She has considerable experience of qualitative longitudinal (QL) methodology and has recently been co-investigator on an NCRM Network led by the University of Sussex; New frontiers in qualitative longitudinal research: definition, design and display.

Simon Teasdale is Senior Lecturer in social business at the Glasgow Caledonian University. His research explores the intersection between social and public policies, discourses and organizational behaviour. He has published in a wide range of journals including Economy and Society, Housing Studies and Public Money and Management. In 2013 he won best paper award at EMES – the international social enterprise research conference. He is Associate Editor of Social Enterprise Journal, a peer reviewer and rapporteur for the ESRC and has sat on national and European level government committees.

1
Introduction

Laura Camfield

1.1 Background

When leading UK politicians commit to spending 0.7 per cent of Gross National Income on overseas aid from 2013 and the main distributor of this, the UK Department for International Development (DFID), states its commitment to the "three pillars" of research, evidence and evaluation, surely there has never been a better time to be a development researcher? Yet while in the UK and North America there is increasing demand for research presented in the form of "evidence" or "key messages" and pressure on researchers to demonstrate their policy "impact," what is the quality of the research that underpins their claims? The chapters in this volume recognize that research quality may be compromised by donor interests, short timescales, and limited reflection (Humphrey, 2007; Behague and Storeng, this volume). They present conceptual frameworks and methodologies that represent new directions for development research, alongside examples of good practice in other fields such as sociology and anthropology (for example, qualitative secondary data analysis and "revisits," Bornat and Crow this volume). By bringing together scholarship from the Global North and South, the contributors challenge the assumed separation between developed and developing countries (cf. Humble and Smith, 2007). These examples are valuable to development researchers since there is a growing expectation that data will be available for analysis/re-analysis and that development policy will be based on evidence of all types, appropriately assessed for quality.

The volume arises from a concern with the quality of data and its interpretation, which is framed around a discussion of the relationships involved in gathering data, analysing them, and addressing particular audiences. For example, the relationship of the development researcher to the people they research, the people they work with (peers, students, etc.), the people who fund them (donors, tax payers, etc.), and the people who use their analyses (policymakers, practitioners, activists, journalists, etc.). In thinking about what constitutes quality in terms of data and analysis, or how relationships shape research, we see three main challenges: maintaining research relationships and developing appropriate methodologies for studying the relational dimensions of poverty (Section I); time and changes over time (Section II); and analysis and representation (Section III). Section I looks primarily at research relationships, drawing on papers by Arvidson, Taylor et al. and Crow, but also at how the relational dimensions of poverty can be taken into account in resource-poor communities (Coulthard et al.). Section II addresses longitudinal studies at individual, household and community levels and the particular challenges posed by changes in the object of study as households disperse and reform (Nasirumbi et al., P. Davis), communities change in response to policy and intervention (Bevan) and children develop (Roelen). Finally, Section III focuses on analysis and representation, exploring the implications of the growth in data deposit, which enables secondary data analysis and re-analysis/replication of influential analyses, and the power of evidence derived from Randomised Controlled Trials.

1.2   Quality of research in international development

In the remainder of the introduction I describe problems particularly apparent in development research (aka the "global poverty research industry," Green and Hulme, 2005). These include the absence of theorization (Harriss-White, 2007) and challenges in establishing the quality of research due to lack of methodological documentation and access to datasets (Camfield and Palmer-Jones, 2013). I then outline the contents of the chapters in more detail. I argue that the problems I describe arise from the funding and structure of development research and are common to both applied and basic research. They include neglect of the researcher's positionality (Lewis and Opoku-Mensah, 2006; Bakewell, 2007), unreflective assumptions about the quality of large datasets (see Duvendack and Palmer-Jones, this volume) or the (in)completeness of interview transcripts (Jackson, 2012), failure to acknowledge the mediating effects of transcription and translation (Temple et al., 2006), and disconnects between data production, analysis and theorization. These problems could be treated as a social fact that needs to be located in a deeper understanding of how the development sector works (e.g. Behague and Storeng, this volume, ask whose interests are served by particular epistemological standpoints). However, it may also be possible to treat them as a practical problem that can be partially addressed using some of the approaches outlined in this volume. For example, Baillie-Smith and Jenkins (2012, p. 75) propose "considering the potential contribution that emotional methodologies may make to generating alternative knowledges of development" through "key concepts of responsibility and solidarity," building on earlier work on the "boundaries and borders" that are negotiated in doing qualitative research on development (Smith, 2007). For this reason the volume has dual and potentially competing goals – both doing development research better and seeing the field of knowledge in development as telling us something about that world and the interests that define what is important or understandable in it.

My discussion of the background to these problems is informed by Bourdieu's concept of "epistemic reflexivity" (Bourdieu and Wacquant, 1992), which extends from the individual researcher to encompass scientific practice and the organization of disciplines and fields. Bourdieu argues that a rigorous approach to social science requires us to "constantly scrutinize ... the collective scientific unconscious embedded in the theories, problems, and ... categories of scholarly judgment" (ibid., p. 40). This involves not only reflecting on our practice as development researchers, but also understanding the social and economic forces within and outside our field that shape categories of thought and action, including "the constructed and highly political nature of the boundaries, borders and identities on which the development project and idea has rested" (Smith, 2007, p. 3) (see also Duvendack and Palmer-Jones and Behague and Storeng, this volume). The relevance of these points will become apparent in the next section as I discuss the problems evident in development research.

The quality of research in international development, as in many applied fields, is extremely variable. There often seems to be an inverse relationship between the strength of the evidence base and the vehemence with which findings are asserted. This point is made respectively by Duvendack and Palmer-Jones in relation to micro-finance, G. Davis on governance, and Behague and Storeng on emergency obstetric care (this volume). These disconnects reflect the political economy of research in international development (Mohan and Wilson, 2005; Bakewell, 2007; Harriss-White, 2007) (for example, the particular nexus between DFID, the World Bank[1] and research in some UK universities).

A similar critique is made of US poverty research in O'Connor (2001) who suggests that its professionalization in the latter half of the 20th century moved it further away from the experience of poverty and closer to the interests of national government and private foundations such as Rockefeller. This change was signalled by its increased dependence on human capital theory, econometric methods, large datasets, and experimental programme designs, which has resonances with contemporary development studies. Harriss-White (2007, p. 48) sees a similar rationale behind the increase in commissioned policy research due to the outsourcing of core policy functions by bureaucracies such as DFID. This creates "commodified policy," "result[ing] both in a decline in the quality of evidence used in policymaking and in an increase in the difficulty with which the residual bureaucracy processes and interprets the outcome of this process." The increase in funding for commissioned research, at a time when research councils and universities are reducing their expenditure on research, has supported an exponential expansion of consultancies and self-funding research institutes in developed and developing countries (Lewis and Opoku-Mensah, 2006, p. 669). Due to the competitiveness of the sector there is little coordination between funders or researchers, which can lead to multiple simultaneous evaluations of high profile programmes with no collaboration or data sharing (Jones and Young, 2007). Harriss-White (2007, p. 48) argues that "what is most striking about the lists [of research topics generated in the plenary of the IDS 40th anniversary conference] is that these are themes in search of theories. Development studies is increasingly defining itself in relation to policy ... and it is the impetus coming from policy that makes us define development problems as themes rather than as problems for theory" (see also Lewis and Opoku-Mensah, 2006, p. 671). In another paper she expresses concern that the emphasis on "relevance" by research funders constrains the types of research that can be done as what is considered relevant reflects "cyclical fashions" among policymakers and entrenched local interests (Harriss-White and Harriss, 2007, p. 20). These problems are known and structural, so this volume is intended as a constructive engagement with those involved in data collection and analysis.

As discussed above, there are strong incentives for development researchers to "present a smooth ex post account of research methods (often airbrushing dead ends and false starts)" (Prowse, 2010, p. 211), although this phenmenon is not confined to development. Prowse suggests that these accounts do a disservice to policymakers as well as other researchers because fully describing the context of primary research (for example, the way the research team was structured) and its philosophical standpoint "can help to explain how research findings are generated, how robust findings are, and how findings can or cannot be extrapolated" (ibid., p. 211; see also Crow and Bornat, this volume). Sumner (2012) makes a similar point in his blog in relation to the depoliticization of mainstream poverty research which he says cannot be blamed on the "measurement obsession," but relates instead to a reluctance to "embed poverty research within an analysis that includes distribution, social differentiation and the process of economic development – in short the political economy of poverty." The examples he gives are lack of attention to inequality (for example, failing to ask "'who are the rich?' and 'why are they rich?'") and a tendency to treat poverty as a residual rather than a structural outcome.

So what is going wrong? Giri and Van Ufford (2004) suggest there is a clear distinction between the research priorities of what they call the "world of action," where manageability is the central concern of those commissioning development research (e.g. the results-based management agenda, critiqued in Eyben, 2013), and the "world of reflection" (academia). They suggest this distinction is relatively recent as "in the past development sociologists and anthropologists had stressed the importance of their academic research for improving development interventions. But now critical scholars tend to focus on analysing the hegemonic relations which development entailed" (ibid., p. 8). The result of this is that "the domains of critical understanding and developmental action became increasingly separated from each other" and researchers engage in "sustained scientific criticism ... not accompanied by a passion of reconstructive responsibility" (ibid., p. 3).

One example of this tension was the reception of David Mosse's account of his experiences working with a rural development programme in India, which Eyben (2009) suggests illustrate some of the fundamental differences between academic research and consultancy. Ex-colleagues of Mosse felt they could ask for changes in the typescript because they saw the book as a form of project report, i.e. a consensus document that aimed to define "the truth" of what the project was about. The ensuing debate (see Mosse, 2006; Sridhar, 2005) supported Eyben's (2009) conclusion that "development organisations may be particularly competent at exercising the privileges of power ... because of their quasi-religious function whereby power is legitimated by reference to 'the poor' for whose sake the organisation exists" (pp. 93–4).

Although Giri and Van Ufford (2004) distinguish between applied and basic or "pure" research, Harriss-White and Harriss (2007) argue persuasively that no research is "pure" and well-funded research centres face many of the same pressures, in addition to challenges that relate to the way development research is structured. For example, as I discuss later, research centres frequently operate with a "data extraction" model where data are collected in the study countries and analysed in the UK. There is little support given to the professional development of junior researchers in country teams and limited space and resources for more senior researchers in country to analyse the data they have collected. Norton (2012) suggests in his blog that this relates to a lack of research capacity (or incentives to develop it) "with southern researchers pulled into consultancy for aid agencies or advising wealthy businesses how to make higher profits" (a point also made by Lewis and Opoku-Mensah (2006) in relation to NGO research). He argues that "serious capacity building [in the social sciences] will need significant support from development partners ... a major initiative and not sticking plasters."

But while social sciences departments in African universities undoubtedly receive little financial support, and the support they do receive is often tied to other people's agendas and/or framings of problems, this does not let individual research programmes off the hook. The same separation of data production/ management and analysis can be seen within UK teams and UK-based projects, which maps to hierarchies within research teams and the social science more broadly. Mauthner and Doucet (2008) suggest that collaborative and team-based research "relies on a division of labour that creates divisions and hierarchies of knowledge, particularly between researchers who gather embodied and contextual knowledge 'in the field' and those who produce textual knowledge 'in the office'" (p. 971). Textual knowledge is seen as more objective and thus has higher status than knowledge gained through participating in fieldwork and is rewarded accordingly. However, by focusing solely on the interview transcript and demoting the embodied knowledge of the fieldworker to "background information" much of the context that gives meaning to the transcript, and that the interviewer would be aware of, is lost. As Bourdieu et al. (1999 in Mauthner and Doucet, 2008, p. 976) suggest "everything that came up in the interview – which cannot be reduced to what is actually recorded on the tape recorder ... tends to be stripped away by writing ... everything that often gives the real meaning and the real interest."

The dependency on survey and transcribed interview data is particularly common in development research where there is a stark separation between field workers (contract researchers and/or students in the study country who carry out the fieldwork), field researchers (typically

UK-based contract researchers, who manage the fieldwork and the data), and academic researchers (UK-based grant holders, who play a more strategic role in the management of the research and often write the papers). These hierarchies are justified by a perception that field-work is "a technical activity that can be done by anyone, rather than an intellectual process in which meaning and knowledge are being shaped and created by subjective researchers" (Mauthner and Doucet, 2008, p. 979). Recognizing field staff as "intellectual partners ... equally engaged in the production entails a radical shift in power relations and dynamics within research teams" (ibid.). While this would be a radical shift in development research practice, the debates around the viability of secondary analysis of qualitative data – see Bornat, this volume – suggest that the "cultural habitus" acquired through partici-pating in fieldwork is essential to data analysis. Without it researchers can succumb to what Mauthner et al. (1998) call "naive realism" where transcripts or extracts of multiple transcripts coded in a qualitative data analysis programme become the data, divorced from both fieldwork-ers and respondents. There are clear limits to the interpretations that can be made from these data and these cannot be easily circumvented. Decontextualization is not inevitable as some UK-based studies also draw on detailed field notes and/or oral or written debriefings, although these require a different relationship with field workers, as described in Bevan, this volume. These data provide some of the specificity of the encounter between interviewer and respondent and the knowl-edge gained through actually being present, which allows for a more nuanced and delimited approach to data analysis.

Further mediation of the data by transcription and translation is often overlooked, even though Temple et al. (2006) argue that the double removal of the analyst from the data by not participating in its produc-tion and not understanding the language in which it was produced effec-tively makes it "tertiary" rather than "secondary" data analysis. Given that most development researchers are not anthropologists and have experience of multiple countries, use of translators is common, whether this involves translating a questionnaire or a narrative. Maclean (2007) draws on her work on citizenship in Bolivia to argue that "translation of others' words without understanding the way in which they are embedded in their linguistic, social, and cultural context perpetuates privileged theories and concepts" (p. 768). In Maclean's case this applies to both translating loaded concepts such as citizenship into Spanish and Aymara and translating respondents' accounts into other languages for analysis. She suggests that unless this process is problematized, and used as a source of data in itself, the subtlety, ambiguity, and sense of how a particular word relates to other words will be lost. Further distortion in meaning can occur due to the convention of producing what Temple et al. (2006) call "easy to read English texts in which the process of production is not apparent" (i.e. the "translatese" derided by Gayatri Chakravorty Spivak). While many researchers would feel uncomfortable with the position advocated by Venuti (1998) of having translations that are "estranging" in style and draw attention to their own production, alternatives would be including words in the source language, maintaining the same sentence structure, and using notes to discuss possible meanings.

Foregrounding the presence of the translator in this way brings us back to the earlier discussion of the structure of research teams and whether one could give appropriate weight to the roles of participant, researcher, interpreter, translator, and in many cases transcriber (Davidson, 2009), as well as the author, in the production of the final text.[2] Unfortunately the "Fordist" research model of many research centres involves specialization and separation of different roles so it is not uncommon for three or four different people to collect the data, transcribe, and translate them, with little interaction between them, or with the people who then analyse the data and write about them. This process can produce data that are light on context, history, and politics, as Rademacher and Patel (2002, pp. 180–1) claimed was case with the World Bank's "Consultations with the Poor" project.[3] Paradoxically this may make it easier for the findings to speak to an international audience, even if it does not actually say very much.

Even though most development research is essentially secondary analysis (the analysis of data collected by others), there is a great reluctance to deposit qualitative data for others' use (and in some case quantitative datasets, see Duvendack and Palmer-Jones, this volume). This may reflect what Lewis (2009, p. 33) describes as the tendency of development to live in the "perpetual present." It could imply a different relationship to data, for example, seeing them as support for recommendations that may have been drafted before the fieldwork started, rather than a public good that could be productively re-analysed by future researchers. More cynically, it might indicate a reluctance to expose fragile data to public scrutiny – as McCullough et al. (2006, p. 1093 in Davis, 2013) observe in relation to the lack of enthusiasm for replication among economists: "If Pons and Fleischman had published their cold fusion results in an economics journal, the world would still be awaiting lower utility bills." The main reason given for failure to archive is lack of resources. However, while producing archival quality data is a resource-intensive activity, it can be accomplished with sufficient planning and acknowledgement of the potential burden that can fall on early career researchers, as well as researchers in the countries where fieldwork took place (Bishop, 2011).

The failure to archive data prompted one of the main recommendations of the DFID (2012) report on understanding poverty and well-being which is related to the availability of high quality data, specifically longitudinal qualitative and quantitative datasets. Panel data offer great potential for studying poverty dynamics, experiences across the life course, and the impact of interventions (see Roelen and Nasirumbi et al., this volume), however, its collection presents many challenges. As Ellis (2012) observes in a different context, "there are many poor countries that have difficulty producing routine household income and expenditure surveys on a regular basis, let alone going the extra mile to ensure that these comply with panel data requirements." As I discuss in the concluding chapter, cost and technical expertise are probably the main constraints as few funders are able to make investments of this size and duration in a panel dataset. Other challenges are the initial country and site selection, as donors' priorities shift[4] but panel studies cannot.

Panel studies also suffer from problems common to all survey research, summarized in Harriss-White and Harriss (2007). For example, the instability of both the term "household" and actual households which split and reform in new configurations (see Nasirumbi et al., this volume), the lack of reliable sample frames, and the organization of research where "surveys by hierarchically organised paid field assistance face problems of supervision, of incentives and of closed, a priorism in institutionalised enquiries" (Harriss-White and Harriss, p. 17). Harriss-White and Harriss observe that survey research gives a misleading impression of rigour by "making the complicit or selective responses of informants harder to recognise, a point revealed most clearly by innocent-looking but sensitive questions about gender relations and demography [or] about savings and credit" (p. 21). This sleight of hand causes readers to forget that "even large databases have microfoundations" (ibid., p. 21).

My final point in this section relates to a common criticism of development research: lack of theorization. This is due to both the failure of mainstream theories to explain many of the changes of the past 20 years (Martinussen, 1997) and a "theory-lag between development studies and social science" (Nederveen Pieterse, 2001, p. 4 in Mohan and Wilson, 2005). I draw on Green and Hulme (2005) to consider whether the methodological innovation in poverty research, some of which is celebrated in this volume, has concealed a lack of theorization and encouraged a focus on the effects of poverty rather than the causes. Green and Hulme (2005) claim that poverty is currently represented "as an entity to be attacked external to the social relations that generate it" (p. 868) with a focus on the characteristics of the poor rather than on the relations in which they are embedded (for example, concentration on the proximal causes of poverty at individual and household levels rather than national or global causes and a near-pornographic attention to the experience of poverty). This tendency persists in mainstream writing on poverty despite a growing emphasis on people's relationships (Coulthard, this volume) and other structural forms of disadvantage, for example, power relations based on class and gender (Bevan, this volume). By seeing poverty in political as well as economic terms and recognizing how social relations are "contingent on specific and culturally diverse notions about the social constitutions of different categories of persons, about the boundaries of the social and of the kinds of obligations toward others entailed by this positioning" (Green and Hulme, 2005, p. 870), it is possible to explain why, for example, being a widow is more problematic for women in South Asia than in Tanzania. This is the approach taken by chapters in the second section of this volume on understanding poverty over time, which propose "middle range" theories as an alternative to the "grand narratives" critiqued by Martinussen (1997) (see Bevan, P. Davis, this volume).

1.3   Chapter outlines

The first chapter in the section on "relationships" draws on the author's experiences as a qualitative researcher in a Reality Check Approach longitudinal study in Bangladesh. The Reality Check Approach foregrounds intimacy, immersion, and consensus in order to build ethical relationships and "give voice" to people living in poverty. The chapter explores the challenges experienced in translating these principles and ideals to practice. The second chapter by Taylor et al. continues the theme of maintaining relationships over time by describing the process of recruiting 15 UK third sector organizations to a qualitative longitudinal study, which took place over three years of government cutbacks. They explore the challenges posed in recruiting organizations, retaining participants, and navigating changing organizational structures, which will be familiar to students of the NGO sector in developing countries. Perhaps surprisingly they found that ease of initial recruitment was not a guide to the quality of the relationship overtime. In fact the hardest organization to access initially could be the most rewarding as they had carefully thought through the implications of their participation, underlining the importance of genuinely informed consent. Return visits highlighted how recruitment was not a "stage" but an ongoing process, especially when key personnel changed. The chapter by Crow describes how restudies of communities in the global North and South provide disconcerting information to researchers about the way in which participants' understandings and expectations of research differ from their own and consequently how their efforts are perceived. While researchers restudying communities may be able to repair relationships, participants' perceptions that they and their communities have been exposed to external scrutiny and their trust betrayed – perhaps because expectations of material benefit raised by the researcher's visit were not then met – colour future interactions, making it harder for other researchers to engage them. Crow's account reinforces the impression given by Arvidson (this volume) of the "ethical precariousness" inherent in the role of researcher, regardless of where they are located (Staples, 2007). The final chapter in this section by Coulthard et al. addresses the implications of using a "three-dimensional wellbeing approach," which looks at material, relational, and subjective factors, to understand the impact of the global crisis in fisheries management on a Sri Lankan fishing community. The authors contrast the abstract notion of sustainability with the daily efforts of fishers and their families to sustain their livelihoods and explore the structures and relationships that support and constrain them.

The second section in the volume looks at time and changes over time, starting with a detailed description of a longitudinal study of 20 Ethiopian communities which focuses on change and the impact of development in relation to this (Bevan). The study is framed within a complex realist ontology that recognizes communities as dynamic open complex and nested social systems, which are best studied using a comparative, case-based, longitudinal research approach. Davis's study of socio-economic mobility in rural Bangladesh focuses instead on individuals and their households, drawing data from life histories that explore interactions between endowments (assets, capabilities, liabilities, and disabilities) and life events (upward opportunities and downward pressures). The life-history interviews show how – not unexpectedly – people with low levels of key endowments were less able to cope with common downward pressures or exploit opportunities and were more likely to employ destructive coping strategies such as selling land. In

Nasirumbi et al.'s study the longitudinal dimension comes not from self-report, but from repeated surveys of a population cohort in Masaka District, Uganda, which was established in 1989 to study the epidemiology of the HIV epidemic. In 1991 the cohort data provided a sampling frame for the purposive selection of 27 households to study their lives and livelihoods using qualitative methods. Data collection began by monthly visits to household members over the course of one year from local people trained in participant observation. The cohort was followed up using similar methods in 2006–2007. This chapter examines how the qualitative data collected through the two year-long studies illuminate the quantitative data from the annual surveys and in particular the methodological problem of defining households and tracking them over time. Finally, Roelen shifts our focus from the household to the children within it and the question of how to create durable measures of child well-being across the life course. The chapter uses case studies from Vietnam and Ethiopia to argue that the combination of qualitative and quantitative panel data is crucial in gaining insight into the dynamics of child poverty, their underlying mechanisms and the potential to break such mechanisms. The case studies also highlight challenges in measuring children's well-being over time and across different stages of childhood.

The final section on analysis and representation begins with a chapter by Bornat on secondary analysis of qualitative data. This is both a new area for development practitioners (Lewis, 2009) and commissioned researchers and a perennial problem for large-scale studies where research design and analysis are separated from data collection. Archiving of interview data opens up exciting possibilities for qualitative researchers, if they can get access to them; for example, new empirical enquiries, theorization, and methodological scrutiny (assuming that the data have been archived in a form that enables engagement with the practice, mindsets, and biographies of previous researchers). Nonetheless, this practice presents epistemological and ethical debates and dilemmas, many of which will be familiar to development researchers, for example, the knowability of context. The following two chapters focus on economic replication, providing both an overview (Duvendack and Palmer-Jones) and a detailed example of what is involved (G. Davis).

The conditions under which knowledge is constructed and the influence of both the subjectivity of the researcher and the institutions of which they are a part are an important theme for Duvendack and Palmer-Jones who look at replication of authoritative quantitative works in development studies. They set this in the context of increased adoption of medical models of development policy research – a theme also addressed in the last chapter in this section – and explore the paradox that while replication has been widely advocated to strengthen our knowledge of what works in development, replications remain very limited and sporadic. They explain this through an analysis of the sociological features of quantitative social science, which include lack of incentives to undertake replications related to the role of "original" journal publications in academic careers and disincentives to challenge professional peers. The chapter by G. Davis extends the argument for the benefits of replication by describing in detail how he replicated (or failed to replicate) Sachs and Warner's influential paper on growth in Africa. He argues persuasively that their attribution of Africa's slow growth to poor economic policies rather than to geographic or health effects misdirected the attention of funders and may have paradoxically further slowed growth.

The final chapter in this section by Behague and Storeng draw together all the questions raised in this section, and in the volume as a whole, by looking at how evidence is used within the sub-field of maternal health. Behague and Storeng echo du Toit's (2012) proposal that to understand the role of evidence in development we need to look at how it is used or ignored. The example du Toit gives is of Mbeki's articulation of the "two economies" doctrine in South Africa, which allowed the African National Congress to "reframe" key social facts (e.g. rising inequality) and make it possible for these facts to be read in a new way. The result was that "evidence that previously had been awkward, dangerous, or not 'useful' in the discussion of possible policy changes could now be invoked, and valuable political space was created for formulating policies that sought to engage with the ways in which central processes and institutions in the core economy worked to marginalise poor and powerless people" (ibid., p. 8). In Behague and Storeng's example, the growing demand for experimentally derived evidence of the impact and cost-effectiveness of proposed interventions appears to be undermining one of epidemiology's core strengths, namely the interest in multivariate understandings of the interconnected biological, social, political, and economic determinants of health. However, others recognize its strategic importance, even though the interventions prescribed by this form of evidence tend to be technocratic, single component, and divorced from influential social and economic contexts. Behague and Storeng attribute this shift to the infiltration of neoliberal market principles in global public health over the past 20–30 years and the need for major donors to more accurately calculate the "returns" from their investment. This language will be familiar to "British taxpayers" who have heard the current Secretary of State for International Development promise that he will "squeeze every last ounce of value from [every penny of every pound of your money]" and demand "hard evidence of the impact your money makes" (A. Mitchell, 2010).

Notes

1. One of the largest actors in development research is the World Bank, which presents itself as a "knowledge bank" and perhaps understandably wishes to construct this knowledge in ways that represent its own interest (Mosse, 2004, Bayliss et al., 2011, see also Wade, 2002, p. 233 in Duvendack and Palmer-Jones, this volume). Toye (2009, p. 302), for example, notes that "[while] international public organizations can become powerful propagators of ideas, if they invest sufficiently in the mechanisms of intellectual propagation ... it is almost impossible for them to operate successfully as creative intellectual actors in areas where their managers are already committed to maintaining an economic doctrine."
2. The limited role of those closest to the data in its analysis is often overlooked as there is little information about how researchers do research and analysis, either individually or as a team, and little guidance from funding agencies or disciplinary organizations on appropriate practice.
3. "The very act of transferring PPA [Participatory Poverty Assessment] findings from a local to a global scale lends an external ordering that contains the political [and] decontextualises voices and experience ... the differences between local reports and the global synthesis reveal as much about the institution and the confines within which it can digest knowledge, as they do about human suffering and its causes."
4. For example, countries become less interesting as they develop – see the 2011 revision of the list of DFID's priority countries.

References

Baillie-Smith, M. and Jenkins, K. (2012). Editorial: Emotional methodologies – the emotional spaces of international development. *Emotion, Space and Society*, 5:75–77.

Bakewell, O. (2007). Breaching the borders between research and practice: Development NGOs and qualitative data. In: Smith, M. (ed.). *Negotiating Boundaries and Borders* (Studies in Qualitative Methodology, Volume 8). UK: Emerald Group Publishing Limited, pp. 217–238.

Bayliss, K., Fine, B., and Van Waeyenberge, E. (2011). *The Political Economy of Development: The World Bank, Neoliberalism and Development Research*. UK: Pluto Press.

Bishop, E. (2011). Challenges in archiving qualitative longitudinal data: Lessons from Timescapes, Presentation, "As well as the subject" seminar series, UEA-London.

Bourdieu, P. and Loïc J. D. W. (1992). *An Invitation to Reflexive Sociology*. Chicago: The University of Chicago Press.

Camfield, L. and Palmer-Jones, R. (2013). Editorial: As well as the subject: Additional dimensions in development research ethics. *Progress in Development Studies*, 13(4): 255–65.

Davidson, C. (2009). Transcription: Imperatives for qualitative research. *International Journal of Qualitative Methods*, 8(2): 1–52.

Davis, G. (2013). Replicating Sachs and Warner' Working papers on the resource curse. *The Journal of Development Studies*, 49(12): 1615–1630.

DFID (2012). Understanding poverty and wellbeing: A note with implications for research and policy. Unpublished report.

Du Toit, A. (2012). Making sense of "Evidence." Notes on the discursive politics of research and pro-poor policy making. PLAAS Working Paper No. 21.

Ellis, F. (2012). Book review: Tackling chronic poverty: The policy implications of research on chronic poverty and poverty dynamics. *Progress in Development Studies*, 12: 86–88.

Eyben, R. (2009). Hovering on the threshold: Challenges and opportunities for critical and reflexive ethnographic research in support of international aid practice. In: Hagberg, S. and Widmark, C. (eds, 2009). *Ethnographic Practice and Public Aid. Methods and Meanings in Development Cooperation.* Sweden: University of Uppsala.

Eyben, R. (2013). Uncovering the politics of evidence and results: A framing paper for development practitioners, http://bigpushforward.net/wp-content/uploads/2011/01/Uncovering-the-Politics-of-Evidence-and-Results-by-Rosalind-Eyben.pdf, downloaded 24/08/13.

Giri, A.K. and van Ufford, Q. (2004). A moral critique of development: Ethics, aesthetics and responsibility. Working Paper No. 128, Research Center on Development and International Relations.

Green, M. and Hulme, D. (2005). From correlates and characteristics to causes: Thinking about poverty from a chronic poverty perspective. *World Development*, 33(6): 867–879.

Harriss-White, B. and Harriss, J. (2007). Green revolution and after: The "North Arcot Papers" and long-term studies of the political economy of rural development in South India. QEH Working Paper No. 146.

Harriss-White, B. (2007). Development research and action: Four approaches. *IDS Bulletin*, 38(2): 46–50.

Humble, D. and Smith, M. (2007). What counts as development research? In: Smith, M. (ed.). *Negotiating Boundaries and Borders: Qualitative Methodology and Development Research.* Oxford: Elsevier, pp. 13–34.

Humphrey, J. (2007). Forty years of development research: Transformations and reformations. *IDS Bulletin*, 38(2): 14–19.

Jackson, C. (2012). Speech, gender and power: Beyond testimony. *Development and Change*, 43(5): 999–1023.

Jones, N. and Young, J. (2007). Setting the scene: Situating DFID's Research Funding Policy and Practice in an International Comparative Perspective. A scoping study commissioned by DFID Central Research Department. Overseas Development Institute, London, UK.

Lewis, D. (2009). International development and the "perpetual present": Anthropological approaches to the re-historicization of policy. *European Journal of Development Research*, 21(1): 32–46.

Lewis, D. and Opoku-Mensah, P. (2006). Moving forward research agendas on international NGOs: Theory, agency and context. *Journal of International Development*, 18: 665–675.

Maclean, K. (2007). Translation in cross-cultural research: An example from Bolivia. *Development in Practice*, 17(6): 784–790.

Martinussen, J. (1997). *Society, State and Market: A Guide to Competing Theories of Development.* Halifax: Fernwood Books.

Mauthner, N. S. and Doucet, A. (2008). "Knowledge once divided can be hard to put together again": An epistemological critique of collaborative and team-based research practices. *Sociology*, 42(5): 971–985.

Mauthner, N., Parry, O., and Backett-Milburn, K. (1998). The data are out there, or are they? Implications for archiving and revisiting qualtative data. *Sociology*, 32(4): 733–745.

Mitchell, A. (2010). 'Giving UK taxpayers value for money in aid', https://www.gov.uk/government/news/mitchell-full-transparency-and-new-independent-watchdog, downloaded 07/03/14.

Mohan, G. and Wilson, G. (2005). The antagonistic relevance of development studies. *Progress in Development Studies*, 5: 261–277.

Mosse, D. (2006). Anti-social anthropology? Objectivity, objection, and the ethnography of public policy and professional communities. *Journal of the Royal Anthropological Institute* (N.S.), 12: 935–956.

Mosse, D. (2004). Social analysis as product development: Anthropologists at work in the World Bank. In: Giri, A. K., van Harskamp, A., and Salemink, O. (eds). *The Development of Religion/the Religion of Development*, Delft: Eburon, pp. 77–88.

Norton, A. (2012). http://www.odi.org.uk/opinion/6511-poverty-research-well being-poverty-dynamics-andrew-norton.

O'Connor, A. (2001). *Poverty Knowledge*. Princeton: Princeton University Press.

Oyen, E. (2005). The polyscopic landscape of poverty research. Report prepared for the Research Council of Norway.

Prowse, M. (2010). Integrating reflexivity into livelihoods research. *Progress in Development Studies*, 10: 211–231.

Rademacher, A. and Patel, R. (2002). Creating Global Poverty – Reading Local Experiences, Creating Global Discourse: Reflections on Re-Contextualizing Participatory Research Data for Global Policy. In: Brock, K. and McGee, R. (eds). *Knowing Poverty: Critical Reflections on Participatory Research and Policy*, London: Earthscan.

Smith, M. (2007). Negotiating Boundaries and Borders: Qualitative Methodology and Development Research. UK: Emerald Group Publishing Limited.

Staples, J. (2007). When things are not as they seem: Untangling the webs of a South Indian NGO. In: Smith, M. (ed.). *Negotiating Boundaries and Borders: Qualitative Methodology and Development Research*. Oxford: Elsevier, pp. 131–153.

Sridhar, D. (2005). Ethics and development: Some concerns with David Mosse's "Cultivating Development."*Anthropology Today*, 21(6): 7–19.

Sumner (2012). Deprivation, distribution and the political economy of poverty: Is poverty research about the non-poor as much as the poor?. http://www.ids.ac.uk/news/deprivation-distribution-and-the-political-economy-of-poverty-is-poverty-research-about-the-non-poor-as-much-as-the-poor, downloaded 02/02/14.

Temple, B., Edwards, R., and Alexander, C. (2006). Grasping at context: Cross language qualitative research as secondary qualitative data analysis. *FQS*, 7(4) art. 10.

Toye, J. (2009). Social knowledge and international policymaking at the World Bank. *Progress in Development Studies*, 9: 297–310.

Venuti, L. (1998). *The Scandals of Translation: Towards an Ethics of Difference*. London: Routledge.

Section I
Relationships

2
Ethics, Intimacy, and Distance in Longitudinal, Qualitative Research: Experiences from Reality Check Bangladesh

Malin Arvidson

2.1 Introduction

This chapter originates from the experience of working as a researcher with a longitudinal study, the Reality Check Approach (RCA) in Bangladesh. The approach puts intimacy, immersion, and consensus at its core. These concepts signify an ethically motivated approach that aims to "give voice" to people living in poverty. They also describe an ideal research relationship assumed as the basis for good quality data. The chapter examines some difficulties encountered in the field and it aims to contribute to our understanding of the various dilemmas researchers, and practitioners, may experience when research principles and ideals are transferred to practice.

Debates in qualitative research encourage a more public reflection on research experiences (Knowles 2006; Mauthner et al. 2002). They argue that it is important to go beyond the methodological rhetoric and recognize the ethical and methodological dilemmas that qualitative research practice generates (Karnieli-Miller et al. 2009). These debates have clear relevance to international development research and practice today. Over the last couple of decades a string of participatory-based approaches have appeared as a result of a conceptual shift that emphasizes agency as opposed to an assumption that people living in poverty are passive, powerless, and lacking in initiative (Lister 2004). Examples of such approaches include appreciative inquiry (Ludema et al. 2001), most significant change (Davies and Dart 2005), Action Learning and Planning System (ALPS) by Action Aid International (2006), and a plethora of participatory-based tools (ranking, mapping, etc.) that have come to influence small, local as well as large, international organizations, and academic research alike. New methodological frameworks are continu-ously launched for use in both academic research and evaluation studies carried out by practitioners. While this suggests a great appetite for inno-vation there is also a penchant for moving on from one approach to the next. Although much has been written on "the tyranny of participation" (e.g. Cook and Kothari 2001; Hickey and Mohan 2004) these accounts primarily concern the values underpinning and processes within devel-opment interventions, and offer less reflection on research methodology and the experience from a researcher's point of view.

A related conceptual shift in development studies towards seeing people living in poverty as active agents has resulted in methodolo-gies that seek more subjective descriptions to complement objective ones produced by the researcher (Hulme 2004). This shift emphasizes qualitative approaches and integration with communities as the basis for understanding, and with this follows challenges and dilemmas related to relations in the field. While aimed at being more inclusive, for exam-ple, it "simultaneously risk[s] excluding" individuals and communities that are hard to reach and to integrate with (Simpson 2007: 156). It also raises questions about the roles and position of the researcher: in a development context researchers often find themselves presented with opportunities and/or expectations to act as agents of change, which may conflict with the intentions and skills of the researcher and puts ethical guidelines to the test (Mellor 2007). Some of these debates build on long-standing discussions in anthropology and ethnography that address the nature, content, and analysis of ethnographic work, and its relation to other methodological approaches (see, for example, Atkinson and Hammersley 1994). But while there is indeed a wealth of discussions around the value and nature of this type of qualitative work, there may also be a tendency "to portray qualitative inquiry as inherently ethical" (Brinkmann and Kvale 2005: 157, 162) and thereby overlook ethical and methodological dilemmas provoked by close interactions between the researcher and the researched.

Based on the author's experience from a longitudinal study in Bangladesh, called the RCA, the chapter illustrates and examines ethical dilemmas and methodological insights and shortcomings of the RCA study in Bangladesh. It describes how dilemmas arise when ethical research guidelines come into conflict with realms of ethics that call for care and reciprocity between the researcher and the researched. The analysis uses the concept of intimacy as point of departure for a critical examination of the RCA. The concept suitably describes what the RCA aspires to create in the field and convey through reports. The concept is also useful for elaborating on three particular sources of tension experienced during the fieldwork: (1) intimacy as ethically motivated and intimacy as tool; (2) how the striving for intimacy makes research ethics clash with other ethical realms, such as friendship, and community norms; and (3) intimacy and assumptions about how such research relationships will generate good quality data. The latter refers specifically to RCA being a listening study, and its assumptions about "giving voice." These three areas will be discussed in turn, after a brief description of RCA, using reflections from the field experience and references to ongoing debates in qualitative research.

2.2   Reality Check Bangladesh

In 2007 the Swedish International Development Cooperation Agency (Sida) initiated a qualitative longitudinal study in Bangladesh aimed at investigating the implementation and impact of interventions to improve services in primary health care and primary education (GRM International 2011; Sida 2011). Sida is part of a donor consortium supporting two nationwide government-lead programmes which were implemented initially over a five-year period, but have since been extended. The RCA comes from an identified need for better information about the use and experiences of primary health and education services, and what was happening at community level as a result of these large-scale reforms. Questions that were guiding this initiative were whether user needs correspond with the policies underlying the two programmes, and to what extent knowledge and local interpretations of interventions correspond with their intended purposes.

The aim of RCA is to provide people-centred information. It places the voices of users at its core to address what is seen as weaknesses in conventional evaluation methods in capturing how people experience and interpret change induced by development interventions. The intent is to convey agency as expressed by people at community level, and thereby improve policymakers' understanding of how large-scale interventions translate to practice on the ground.

2.2.1   The RCA principles

RCA is based on a set of principles intended to guide the fieldwork to ascertain that this agency can be better understood. Firstly, the approach is based on the idea of *living with rather than visiting*: each year team members spend four days and four nights with selected host households, and each year, for five consecutive years, the teams return to the same households. Secondly, the approach is focused on *conversations rather than interviews*: this is based on the assumption that conversations would have advantages over formal interviews and some participatory-based approaches (focus groups, ranking exercises, etc.) since they are more two-way, relaxed, and informal. The conversations were guided by scripts rather than conventional interview guides. Thirdly, the approach emphasizes *learning rather than finding out*: again this contrasts with methods that see data as something to be "accessed" or "extracted" from the field. The principle of learning is phrased as a rhetorical device for the researcher, a reminder that the researcher takes a step back, rather than as a method as such. This is closely linked to RCA being framed as a *"listening study,"* which requires the researcher to listen effectively to other people's views and perspectives. They should refrain from using pre-defined questions, and be wary of implying that certain knowledge and viewpoints are preferred over others (see, for example, Wright et al. 2006). The intent is to prevent polite but limited answers, and encourage people to share their views and interpretations of their worlds. "Listening" is of course also linked to the notion of "giving voice" to people living in poverty (Chambers 2005; Collins et al. 2009) which is in line with the "Voices of the Poor" project initiated by the World Bank in the late 1990s (Narayan et al. 1999; World Bank 2008). Fourth, the approach highlights *inclusion* as an essential ingredient: this implies a behaviour that is sensitive to gender- and age-based differences that may lead to (self)exclusion, something that is found as a weakness in, for example, focus group discussions, public meetings, and other forms of participatory rapid appraisals. Finally, the approach advises that, being set in the context of development intervention, the researchers interact with frontline staff, in this case, from primary health and educational services. Exploring this side of service provision serves as an important point of reference, or triangulation, that can support more probing conversations about programme activities.

The RCA is not an action-based study that aims at instigating change, or advising people about rights, opportunities, and new services. Rather than facilitating the two programmes our intention was to listen to people's views about them and to observe their effects. We foresaw that by staying with families living in poverty we may encounter situations that would prompt our direct intervention, for example, requirements to give advice, or to give practical support in situations of conflict or perhaps medical emergencies. For these reasons the approach prescribes a passive, low-key role for the researcher. This was motivated by ethical guidelines used in qualitative research with the intent to "protect all groups involved in research" (ESRC 2012). Taking action in situations of emergencies, for example, could jeopardize the safety of both researcher and researched. Taking on a passive role was also based on an understanding that should we become "advisors," i.e. some kind of authoritative voice, we may enter into roles that would preclude people from sharing their own views and talking about their own actions.

The reflections in this chapter are based on my experience as one of three team leaders, and my interpretations and practice of RCA. As a sociologist with experience from ethnographic work, interviews, and surveys, I chose to emphasize particular aspects of the RCA based on a wish to bring out what in my view seemed to be distinctive about RCA. These distinctive aspects were to listen, to take time, and be patient. This meant waiting for conversations rather than setting up scenarios with the intent to encourage debate, hence I consciously distanced myself from using conventional participatory-based tools. The emphasis on conversations and listening meant leaving behind tools that are often used to facilitate staged conversations, such as mapping, ranking, and focus group discussions.

My team of three and I worked on being low key, a steady but non-disturbing presence. The idea was initially to emphasize our role as listeners, and to see the researched as the ones to take initiatives. The slow-paced, longitudinal study would eventually yield the relations and information that we sought. We envisioned that with a short but still shared history developed through our consecutive visits, our conversations would change in character based on firstly an aim to get to know each other to later an appetite to learn and probe into stories together. Within my team we discussed our method of working and how we experienced our interactions in the field on a daily basis. Our discussions related to the dilemmas, emotions, and frustrations that are examined in this chapter, although they reflect my interpretations alone.

2.3   Intimacy in qualitative research and in RCA

The concept of intimacy captures what the RCA is striving to achieve. The idea of placing intimacy at the core of qualitative research comes from a feminist tradition, signifying what can be described as an ideal research relationship. It is based on a critique of positivist research that is characterized by power-distance, hierarchy, and expertise (Duncombe and Jessop 2002). It comes from a wish to move away from an emphasis on objectivity, gained partly through the researcher taking on a detached role in relation to the researched, which in turn (unintentionally) fosters power-distance and hierarchies. A relationship based on intimacy includes qualities of "mutual care and friendship as well as revelation of, and respect for, personal vulnerabilities" (Busier et al. 1997: 165). To achieve such a relationship qualitative researchers direct their attention to both initial rapport and the continuing maintenance of good relationships, and this involves "self-examination, sharing, and self-disclosure" (Dickson-Swift et al. 2006: 856). In RCA the researchers aim to build rapport and trust with households and communities. We worked towards creating space for conversations in order to understand needs and experiences as expressed by people not heard or listened to. "Space" is here not seen as geographical but as a relationship, an "affective space" (Jensen 2012) where there is trust and empathy and the individuals can express mutual care.

2.3.1   Reflections from the field – building rapport

The team's arrival was carefully prepared for by visits from one of our team members. He tried to ascertain that the chosen host households,[1] neighbours, and key individuals in the community had been informed about the intention of our visits, and had had the chance to ask questions and give consent. We tried to ensure that no special arrangements were made to accommodate us, and that we did not disrupt normal activities. Initially, we "stripped off" visual attributes that could get in the way of open and non-judgemental conversations, and "put on" features appropriate for the position we aspired to take on, that is as members of the community instead of outsiders, researchers. We changed urban and western clothes for a more modest dress, adhering to Muslim dress codes. We left behind research tools such as pen and paper, recorder, and list of questions (although we later used notebooks). Sharing time and space, day and night, paved the way for trust: we exposed ourselves for others to see us as normal people with shared needs, rather than outsiders with unknown habits. Time turned out to be an essential ingredient. The longitudinal aspect of the study played to our advantage, an experience that echoes other longitudinal work (Thomson and Holland 2003). During our fifth year, for example, we were told by some that "I actually lied to you last time we spoke." Our revisits built trust that we had a genuine interest in understanding practice on the ground, and that talking to us would not result in negative repercussions (Lewis 2012).

2.3.2   Trust and intimacy in the field

While trust was gained at a community level, closeness and intimacy were established with particular individuals and families. We immersed ourselves in family life, sharing space, meals, and time with all family members. As the only non-Bangla-speaking team member,[2] I often took on a quiet role verbally, and used body language to engage in conversations and to invite people to share space. Often we gathered in small rooms, with little other furniture than a bed where we would sit, adults and children together, talking and playing. We came to understand how intimacy grew not only, or even primarily, through talking, but also through understanding mundane things related to, for example, eating. We felt intimacy and closeness tacitly expressed through knowledge of how we take our tea, how much salt we use with our food, or us saving particular food items for the children to enjoy. Silent nods of understanding and care were shared during mealtimes, in the morning and at bedtime; that is at hours when researchers would not normally be present.

In qualitative research intimacy is promoted as a unique way of learning, and closeness in research relationships is essential to gain insight into an understanding of our world and those around us (Busier et al. 1997). While on the one hand intimate research relationships are described as egalitarian, authentic, and characterized by honesty (Duncombe and Jessop 2002; Hewitt 2007), it is difficult to get away from the notion that power remains with the researcher. Glesne argues that "rapport is a trust-building mechanism that primarily serves the interests of the researcher" (1989: 45) as it is used as a means "to attain ends shaped by their own needs" (ibid.: 46). Furthermore our view on intimacy as an end goal (ethically and/or politically motivated) or a means to an end (instrumentally motivated) may change during the course of the research. Relationships are not static and the researched has "options for countercontrol" vis-à-vis the researcher (Brinkmann and Kvale 2005: 165), which in turn encourages the researcher to review strategies to maintain relationships and to preserve an "affective space" in order to maintain a level of control. So while the "building of rapport" and "intimacy" are primarily interpreted as ethically informed approaches, they have become commodified and professionalized, and are now part of any sociologist's toolkit (Duncombe and Jessop 2002). Behind the RCA principles we find both an ethical and an instrumental motivation for an intimacy-based approach. RCA addresses problems of an ethical character that have political and policy implications, such as exclusion caused by power-distance, by focusing on immersion, learning, and listening. At the same time this is also seen as the basis for a "relaxed and trusted context for conversations that can lead to enhanced understanding" (Reality Check Approach 2010–2013). This dual meaning/function of intimacy in research relationships opens up tensions: what is initially presented as an ethically motivated approach can suddenly appear as unethical practice, which is captured in a string of words used by Duncombe and Jessop (2002) when describing the "ethics of faking friendship" as phoney, inauthentic, and insincere. The ambiguous meaning and use of rapport and closeness can be experienced with great discomfort by the researcher (Pitts and Miller-Day 2007). Although engaging in intimacy and closeness can be seen as a process that takes the researcher to a place where we are out of control and power, it can also be "interpreted as a mask for some type of manipulation or exploitation carried out to obtain data needed for the study" (Karnieli-Miller et al. 2009: 283). In RCA intimacy is gained through physical presence (immersion) and a mind set (to learn and listen). This has only meaning for the research task at hand if it is translated to real relations in the field. Our initial visits were filled with rituals familiar to many other social contexts. We used our social skills (as opposed to, for example, a questionnaire) to explore family histories, recent local and national events, and so on. As our research progressed over time generic research instruments were turned into individually based tools adapted for our purpose: we used our increasingly specific and situational knowledge of our host families to bond and to fit in. The term "social skills" graduated from having a broad and non-specific meaning, to becoming an act based on personal relations.

2.4   Intimacy and competing realms of ethics

As described above, intimacy has a dual meaning in research. Furthermore, intimacy also brings the research-participants to positions where roles are not well defined. "The rapport building process can require a merging of boundaries between researcher and participant," writes Dickson-Swift et al. (2006: 856). This may be desirable, and seen as "benign" but can also expose and exploit the researched with unforeseen results (ibid.). The blurring of boundaries may be the result of longitudinal work, and is the "unintended consequence of growing emotional intimacy" (Hewitt 2007: 1152) between the researcher and the researched (see also Kleinman and Copp 1993; Watson 2012).

There are two issues to consider here: firstly, the role of emotions in qualitative research and secondly, the implications of this blurring of boundaries. The two issues are closely related. As discussed earlier, the aspiration to create intimacy in research means bringing care, empathy, and vulnerability into the research relationship. The blurring of boundaries between a research relationship and friendship leads all involved to new emotional territories.[3] For the researcher the idea may have been to create a controlled affective space where important research material can be gained. While emotions may be placed at the core of producing and constructing knowledge, there are also requirements that we should remain distanced from emotions (Watson 2012). When analysing material we can distance ourselves from emotions experienced in the field and this is important for the credibility of our research in the eyes of an academic audience and policymakers (Harrington 2002; Watson 2012). Emotional distance can also be achieved in the field by adapting a "detached concern" approach, by applying "the right amount of empathy": enough to bond and create trust, but not so much that we get carried away by empathy and lose sight of our research focus (Kleinman and Copp 1993). The blurring of boundaries, closeness, and emotions lead to "concern over roles" and "all add additional stress to research work" (Dickson-Swift et al. 2006). The similarities of "rapport-building behaviour to friendship-developing behaviour" (Glesne 1989: 45) presumably prevents the researcher from being in control and from maintaining distance. Glesne (1989) contends that for this reason we must avoid friendship in research situations, and others warn against being unprepared for what research-based friendship may bring in terms of dilemmas (Brinkmann and Kvale 2005; Dickson-Swift et al. 2006).

Working with intimacy as a core idea in qualitative research, the field may present us with a reality where emotions cannot be controlled. Watson describes how while doing ethnographic research she became overwhelmed by emotions, which in her mind contradicted the way she intended and was expected to behave, i.e. she "crashed the boat and wept" (2012). It was unprofessional, she felt, but eventually made her consider the role of emotional attachment in how she came to understand the community she had immersed herself in as a researcher. Knowles (2006) describes how "emotional baggage" caused her to exclude certain research subjects. An emotionally charged event in the field made her confront her own prejudices, and they opened up surprising and important research results. Emotions cause problems as well as support our strivings to understand our research subjects.

Although equipped with the RCA principles and aims, and with a clear understanding of ethical research guidelines that prescribe informed consent, respectful relations, and the protection of individuals and organizations from any threat to their well-being (ESRC 2012), the evolving character of our research presented us with real dilemmas related to emotions, roles, and relations in the field. The dilemmas were caused by sudden events and by emerging emotional attachment to individuals. In the two following scenarios I describe how, based on emotional attachment and blurred boundaries between research process and friendship, the principles guiding our research came to conflict with expectations and roles as we entered positions as friends and members of the community.

2.4.1 Reflections from the field – intimacy, emotions, and ethics of care

During the first year we made friends with a young mother, only 16 years old, who had lost her husband and been expelled with her then two-month-old son from her in-laws' house. Since then she had been residing with relatives. We spent a lot of time together and she often followed us around, introducing us to people and places. On our third visit her situation had changed: when her relatives were in dire straits she was forced to move out and find a job. Dressed in rags, looking tired and unwell she mostly shied away from us, and chose to talk to us only when no one else was present. She explained how she was under great pressure to pay back a debt to a local snack-shop owner. Things were not looking good: she was vulnerable and exposed to some unpleasant forces in the community.

On our departure after our third year's stay, the young mother stayed in the background of well-wishers waving goodbye. I was suddenly overwhelmed with emotions: looking at the young woman with her son, in distress, and recognizing that I know her and care about her – should I not also care *for* her? Should I take on a "detached observer" position, hoping to learn from her destiny? Or should I take on my role as a friend, a role that I had instigated, and accept responsibility that comes with this? In the crowded space it was difficult to smuggle a rolled-up stack of notes to her without attracting attention but I also considered the consequences of doing so. As tears began to cover my face a teenage boy took my hand and whisked me away from the crowd. I left without acting on my emotions.

I hesitated to extend my relationship from empathic to actively caring. Financially supporting a person who is also being "researched" could mean the motivation for people's interest in us would change radically, and it would undermine our aim to overcome expectations of us as potential donors. Also, our providing resources would highlight power-distance, and may put the receiver of money in a position of indebtedness. It would, in other words, be inappropriate ethically as well as instrumentally. This event took only ten minutes but the emotional reaction that came from my concern for the young mother, and the unease over my inability to support her, stayed with me. It was a relief when we saw her in better shape the following year, with support from relatives and a job to pay for her expenses. But should my decision not to support her be judged on the fact that, in the end, she did well all by herself?

The emphasis on "living with rather than visiting" in the RCA principles takes the researcher to positions that bring new expectations and obligations. This resulted in ethical dilemmas as we as researchers felt ourselves caught between research ethics that prescribed a passive role in situations of emergency as well as general needs, and ethics related to general community courtesy. The care expressed in research ethics – to protect all those involved in research – takes on an elusive meaning and does not provide much by way of guidance when intimacy brings the reality of the researched close to the researcher. What would "protect" imply in the situation described above, where norms of friendship would prescribe action that may contradict our principles of not getting actively involved? On several occasions our team felt we were presented with opportunities to practise norms related to patronage that prescribe actions that confirm power and status. But following these norms would not, we reasoned, result in power-*distance* but rather in closeness based on recognition of how support and care are expressed in the community. The following vignette will illustrate this further.

2.4.2 Experience from the field – norms and expectations of patronage

We arrived at our peri-urban site for our second year's fieldwork just after Ramadan. Shortly after our first stay here, the area had been struck by a major cyclone. Several of our host families had suffered severely as a consequence. In one case the house, already in very poor condition, was damaged, as well as furniture, courtyard, fishing net, and boat. My colleague was torn: as an accepted member of this Muslim community, and being a Muslim himself, he felt obliged to help the family to recover. Through simple means he could provide support to the family taking a definitive step out of a disastrous situation. Again, we were faced with different normative fields, prescribing different sets of behaviour all with reference to what would be ethically right. As a friend of this family my colleague *wanted* to help them, as a community member of considerable status due he was *expected* to do so. My colleague felt that by ignoring expectations, although not verbally expressed, community members saw him more as an outsider than an insider.

Apart from the tearful episode in the first scenario described above, I managed to maintain a "detached concern" position, adhering to our ethically based principles of not getting involved through monetary or any other such support. While I saw my ability to largely remain detached in action (if not emotionally) as a strength, I also felt it disturbing. I considered whether moving from a principle-based approach, that suggested I adhere to our principles, to a care-based (Hewitt 2007) approach, suggesting I followed my emotions, would have solved the ethical dilemma? Supporting the young mother could have compromised our relationship through emphasizing power-distance and causing feelings of shame and indebtedness towards me. It may also have compromised our position in the community at large: there is no end to people in need, and one of our priorities was to avoid an authoritative, need-based relationship. A care-based approach to practising ethics may resolve an urgent emotional need, but such an action does not take long-term relations and unintended consequences into account. The dilemma confronted in the second scenario relates to how research ethics and RCA principles come to conflict with community norms of support and reciprocity. This clash reveals cultural and political implications of the RCA principles that we had not considered. The principles are based on the idea that by reducing power-distance we would be able to establish closeness. This principle was also grounded in the aim to provide room for the often excluded and marginalized to make their voices heard. Although we did not act on the norms prescribed by patronage, we had to imagine and recognize how closeness, and thereby access to people's voice, may be established through the practising of norms based on hierarchy, status, and power.

2.5   Intimacy, distance, and voice

The third and last point to address in relation to ethics and intimacy in the RC approach concerns assumptions regarding the quality and type of material this approach is expected to yield. I will pay particular attention to the idea of *having conversations*, and RCA as a *listening* study. This was formulated with an understanding that structured interviews undertaken in formal settings would not be suitable. Our intention was to address distance and lack of empathy that can come as result of such interviews (Brinkmann and Kvale 2005; Mellor 2007; Mizen and Ofosu-Kusi 2007; Simpson 2007) and instead create space for voices, and affective space – intimacy – in order to develop an understanding based on shared experiences and empathy. The reflections here concern qualitative research and assumptions about data quality, highlighted through the concepts of consensus/conflict, unobtrusive/obtrusive, and intimacy/distance. I also consider how "giving voice" requires a range of different audiences.

The in-depth interview is often assumed to be a consensual dialogue, and this consensus-driven approach is seen as key to "yielding good quality data" (Knowles 2006: 394). It is through relationships signified by consensual conversations and intimacy that we can gain "richness of the research data" (Karnieli-Miller et al. 2009: 280). Although research relations are key, the nature of relations in the field is seldom discussed other than through references to informed consent. In books on methodology we are often presented with idealized images of research relations as consensual and part of collaborative projects of knowledge production through language that emphasizes "genuine rapport, honesty, and emotional closeness" (Hewitt 2007; 1155). Knowles argues that the fixation on consensus and intimacy in the field has led to a naivety and neglect of the role of conflict in research: "sociologists have trapped themselves inside a 'research imagination' that fails to present the actors concerned in all their shades of color and circumstances" (2006: 394) (see also Crow, this volume). Knowles draws on her own experience of unintentionally facing a conflictual situation during her fieldwork, and she argues that conflicts can reveal prejudices and assumptions held by the researcher, and lead to important research findings.

Similar to the consensus/conflict dichotomy, Harrington (2002) raises issues around the ideal image of the researcher as unobtrusive as opposed to obtrusive. The emphasis on an unobtrusive position stems from an ethnographic approach that sees the researcher immersed with the field. Subsequent accounts of and analysis from the fieldwork will gain credibility from such an immersion. Harrington, however, provides examples of how credibility and insight can be gained at the point of "subverting methodological rules about avoiding obtrusive research techniques" (2002: 50). She describes how being provocative can serve important purposes: it can be used as a method to gain insights and can be seen as "constructive engagement" or "critical imperative" that creates opportunities for better understanding of people's views. This can occur either in individual conversations or in group settings, where a provocative comment can be followed by debates between the group participants that would normally not have taken place. Harrington concludes that "if researchers accept that most participant-observers are obtrusive to some degree, unavoidably altering the data by their very presence, it might be constructive to consider how to maximize the potential inherent in the situation" (2002: 61). In revising the relationship between consensus/conflict, unobtrusive/obtrusive, we can imagine a continuum of positions that the researcher can take during the course of a research project ranging from "fly-on-the-wall" participant observer, to being actively engaged in change, from working towards conforming and blending in, to refusing to accept certain aspects of or events in a research relationship. One position does not need to exclude the other. The following vignette illustrates how, in RCA, I came to reconsider my role as passive and conforming.

2.5.1   Reflections from the field – reinventing "distance"

Alia, the wife of our urban-host household, had presented us with a life trajectory filled with drama and events that stood out from most others'. Her daughter eloped for a love marriage, and once back in the community a bitter feud erupted between Alia's family and her son-in-law's caused by arguments about dowry and the mother-in-law physically assaulting her daughter-in-law. Later on, Alia's son got heavily engaged with politics and drugs, resulting in him losing his business, causing financial loss and great distress as the family tried to find a remedy for his addiction (he later recovered). As each year passed, we saw how these events took their toll on Alia's well-being. During our fourth and fifth year, our intimate relationship with Alia was mainly evident by the fact that she did not feel compelled to look after us as guests, but got on with her very busy life while we could sit in her home and exchange a few sentences with her now and then as she passed us between her tiny kitchen and the little tea stall they were running at the front of the house. Although her very relaxed and inviting manner made our stay emotionally comfortable it no longer provided us with much by way of conversations. In fact, we were ready to listen, but she had not much to say, or so it seemed. Frustrated by a situation that provided little by way of insightful conversations I decided to change tactics. I explored how we could use "distance" through the establishment of new roles to enhance our conversation, which meant relaxing our aim to erase boundaries. Although a guest in her home I arranged a formal meeting with her. My research colleague and I turned up for our meeting, with pen and paper in hand, and with a large sheet of paper with her recent life history illustrated, and a grid spanning the five years we had been there, with seven pre-defined topics to discuss. We were well aware that this may present Alia with a challenging situation: we were to present her with her life, as we saw it. This tactic meant we were somewhat going against the principles of the RCA.

We entered a new territory with our relationship, one we had not explored before. Alia smiled hesitantly, sat down, and looked slightly embarrassed, and so were we. A detailed conversation (or was it interview?) followed around the seven topics. A clear distance was established between us through the large sheet of paper, our questions, and interruptions in Alia's story-telling. As we talked a less eventful trajectory began to unravel than the one we had pictured initially, a story that ran parallel to the drama we had been witnessing and that included Alia's very individual perspectives on well-being and what makes for a good life. This meeting resulted in new and very important insights, in terms of how we understood Alia. It also led to a new kind of closeness in our relationship, which to me illustrated that closeness and intimacy are gained through a variety of routes. Creating distance through re-positioning myself as a researcher, with pen and paper in hand, questions ready, did not only present me with a role in which I felt more confident, but also Alia with a position of clear purpose, and with a worthy audience. She engaged fully with this new setting.

The naive assumptions made in RCA are similar to those described in research settings aspiring to instigate change through action research (David 2002; Greene 1988; Simpson 2007): there is no guarantee that people are interested in participating. Reflecting on the meaning of "speech" and assumptions about "voice" Jackson argues that, in development studies, empowerment and participation initiatives have been preoccupied with the practice of "giving voice" but have not paid much attention to the meaning of voice and "the 'how' of speech" or the role of listeners (2012: 1). Jackson argues that a voice needs a worthy audience, and "talk always needs triangulation with observation and other evidence" (ibid.: 14). In our work, "listening" meant hearing what was said and pairing this with knowledge gained through experiences and observations. The experience in the field showed I needed to take on various, sometimes conflicting roles as a researcher to provide a good and worthy audience. Jackson argues that "social inequalities are widely assumed to be based on speech deficits" and consequently "the social inclusion agenda is implemented through building voice through talk and testimony" (ibid.: 1). In RCA "listening" was primarily linked to providing space for voices, without considering the role of an audience. The audience/ researcher came, in my case, to take on a passive role. This was based on a striving to achieve a relaxed and non-threatening atmosphere, and us steering away from taking authoritative and advisory roles. The implications of such friend-like, consensus-based positions may be a researcher "censoring questions in order to avoid alienation" (Glesne 1989: 52). Being scared of interrupting a smooth relationship may lead the researcher to "assume a nonreactive presence" (ibid.). In this context, taking on an unobtrusive position, and practising "friendship" in fieldwork over a period of time, presented us with frustrations. This reveals some naivety in the RCA: the focus on listening, coupled with a researcher taking an unobtrusive position, meant we failed to recognize that as listeners we must be prepared to take on active roles because an approach based on a speaker relies on an audience that is interactive. The story above reveals that it is through interchangeably using intimacy and distance that revealing conversations can be encouraged. This is perhaps particularly important as we aimed at going beyond the outstanding and dramatic events that may be easy to outline, to understanding their implications and relations to longer trajectories.

2.6   Concluding remarks

The RCA is now being replicated around the world, and great interest has been shown in RCA by international development actors. It is hence both timely and important to reflect on the approach, and in so doing contribute to ongoing debates about ethical and methodological dilemmas in the field. Qualitative research is "a compromising experience" (de Laine 2000: 2). In understanding what compromises are being made it can be useful to make a distinction between dilemmas and shortcomings: while the former highlights a need for reflection, the latter implies a critique of the approach. The dilemmas examined here refer to how the principles are ethically and instrumentally motivated, illustrated by the difficulties in finding a balance between the idea of "giving people space to talk" with the need to "make people talk." The dilemmas also concern ethics in different types of relationships, where a balance between principle-based action and action based on emotions and care can come into conflict. There are no recipes for resolving such dilemmas: they are inherent in qualitative field research. By examining these dilemmas in detail, the analysis shows that they are intimately linked to assumptions that underpin methodology. These include tacit views of what constitutes good research relationships and how this is linked with good quality data. The analysis suggests that we reconsider concepts such as intimacy/distance, consensus/conflict, and unobtrusive/obtrusive as dynamic complementary pairs rather than dichotomies. This is well illustrated through the case of RCA being framed as a listening study: in order to facilitate the "giving voice" we must pay attention not only to space (a relaxed and non-threatening atmosphere) but also to audience. The role of the researcher should be allowed many characters: intimate as well as distant, unobtrusive as well as obtrusive.

The future success of RCA and similar approaches cannot rely on rhetorical presentations that hold them as ethically right, framed as responses to what is seen as previously flawed evaluation techniques, policymakers with a preference for quantifiable data, or research that favours objective reporting as opposed to analysis based on empathy and immersion. This implicit comparison inadvertently leads to dilemmas and methodological ambiguities being brushed aside, and as a consequence the meaning and value of the findings cannot be fully understood. Here it is also important to consider the impact of general ethical guidelines that perhaps unintentionally show a preference for consensus and conflict avoidance. The analysis of RCA shows that this kind of approach calls for an understanding of the complex nature of research relationships, which requires that we allow for a variety of positions, including distance, conflict-based, and the researcher as obtrusive.

Notes

1. Our host households were chosen based on poverty level. The definition of "poor" was based as far as possible on contextual indicators, including occupation, ownership of productive and household assets, and type and structure of housing. Although this was our intention we did not always manage to realize this. On some occasions our hosts had been rearranged when we arrived for our fieldwork. On other occasions our host families had been so badly affected by natural disasters (cyclones, flooding) that they could no longer host us and we resided with their better-off relatives.
2. My spoken Bangla is very limited but I understand Bangla and could, with help from my colleague, follow and engage with conversations.
3. Here, I consider the researchers' position rather than that of the researched. The experience of the latter is of course important too. After the fifth and final year of the RCA study, a small group representing the three research teams visited the communities and families where we had stayed, to ask how they had experienced the study. The findings are presented in a forthcoming report, which also includes findings from interviews with policymakers on how they made use of the information generated and shared through RCA Annual Reports (see Lewis 2012).

References

Action Aid International (2006) ALPS. *Accountability, Learning and Planning System*, http://www.actionaid.org.uk/sites/default/files/doc_lib/alpsfinal2006. pdf, [Accessed 13 August 2013].

Atkinson, P. and Hammersley, M. (1994) "Ethnography and participant observation." In: Denzin N. K and Lincoln Y. S. (eds) *Handbook of Qualitative Research* (Thousand Oaks, CA, UK: Sage Publications), pp. 248–261.

Brinkmann, S. and Kvale, S. (2005) Confronting the ethics of qualitative research, *Journal of Constructivist Psychology*, 18: 157–181.

Busier, H-L., Clark, K., Esch, R., Glesne, C., Pigeon, Y., and Tarule, J. (1997) Intimacy in research, *International Journal of Qualitative Studies in Education*, 10(2): 165–170.

Chambers, R. (2005) *Ideas for Development* (London: Earthscan).

Collins, D., Morduch, J., Rutherford, S., and Ruthven, O. (2009) *Portfolios of the Poor* (Princeton, NJ: Princeton University Press).

Cook, B. and Kothari, U. (eds) (2001) *Participation: The New Tyranny?* (London: Zed Books).

David, M. (2002) Problems of participation: The limits of action research, *International Journal of Social Research Methodology*, 5(1): 37–41.

Davies, R. and Dart, J. (2005) *The "Most Significant Change" (MSC) Technique: A Guide to its Use*, ISBN-10: 0955549809, http://www.mande.co.uk/docs/MSCGuide.pdf, [Accessed 13 August 2013].

De Laine, M. (2000) *Fieldwork, Participation and Practice. Ethics and Dilemmas in Qualitative Research* (London: Sage).

Dickson-Swift, V., James, E. L., Kippen, S., and Liamputtong, P. (2006) Blurring boundaries in qualitative health research on sensitive topics, *Qualitative Health Research*, 16: 853–871.

Duncombe, J. and Jessop, J. (2002) "'Doing rapport' and the ethics of 'faking friendship.'" In: Hammersley, M. and Traianou, A. (eds) *Ethics in qualitative research* (London: SAGE Publications), pp. 107–122.

ESRC (2012) Framework for Research Ethics (FRE) 2010 Updated September 2012, http://www.esrc.ac.uk/_images/Framework-for-Research-Ethics_tcm8-4586.pdf, [Accessed 13 August 2013].

Greene, J. (1988) Stakeholder participation and utilization in program evaluation, *Evaluation Review*, 12(2): 91–116.

Glesne, C. (1989) Rapport and friendship in ethnographic research, *Qualitative Studies in Education*, 2(1): 45–54.

GRM International (2011) *Reality Check Bangladesh 2010: Listening to Poor People's Realities about Primary Health Care and Primary Education*, Year 4. (Sweden: Sida).

Harrington, B. (2002) Obtrusiveness as strategy in ethnographic research, *Qualitative sociology*, 25(1): 49–61.

Hewitt, J. (2007) Ethical components of researcher-researched relationships in qualitative interviewing, *Journal of Qualitative Health Research*, 18: 1149.

Hickey, S. and Mohan, G. (eds) (2004) *Participation – From Tyranny to Transformation. Exploring New Approaches to Participation in Development* (London: Zed Books).

Hulme, D. (2004) Thinking small and the understanding of poverty: Maymana and Mofizul's story, *Journal of Human Development and Capabilities*, 5(2): 161–176.

Jackson, C. (2012) Speech, gender and power: Beyond testimony, *Development and Change*, 43(5): 999–1023.

Jensen, H. J. (2012) Emotions on the move: Mobile motions among train commuters in the South East of Denmark, *Emotions, Space and Society*, 5: 201–206.

Karnieli-Miller, O., Strier, R., and Pessach, L. (2009) Power relations in qualitative research, *Qualitative Health Research*, 19(2): 279–89.

Kleinman, S. and Copp, M. A. (1993) *Emotions and Fieldwork*, Qualitative Research Methods Series, no. 28: Sage University Paper.

Knowles, C. (2006) Handling your baggage in the field reflections on research relationships, *International Journal of Social Research Methodology*, 9(5): 393–404.

Lewis, D. (2012) *Reality Check Reflection Report* (May 2012, draft).

Lister, R. (2004) *Poverty* (Cambridge: Polity Press).

Ludema, J. D., Cooperider, D., and Barret, F. J. (2001) "Appreciative inquiry: The power of the positive questions." In: Reason, P. and Bradburg, H. (eds) *Handbook of Action Research* (London: Sage), pp. 155–174.

Mauthner, M., Birch, M., Jessop, J., and Miller, T. (2002) *Ethics in Qualitative Research* (London: Sage).

Mellor, M. (2007) "Researching for change." In: Smith, M. (ed.) *Negotiating Boundaries and Borders, Studies in Qualitative Methodology*, Volume 8 (Bingley: Emerald Group Publishing Limited), pp. 177,195.

Mizen, P. and Ofosu-Kusi, Y. (2007) "Researching with, not on: Using photography in researching street children in Accra, Ghana." In: Smith, M. (ed.) *Negotiating Boundaries and Borders, Studies in Qualitative Methodology*, Volume 8 (Bingley: Emerald Group Publishing Limited), pp. 57–81.

Narayan, D., Patel, R., Schafft, K., Rademacher, A., and Koch-Schulte, S. (1999) *Can Anyone Hear Us? Voices from 47 Countries* (Washington DC: World Bank).

Pitts, M. J. and Miller-Day, J. (2007) Upward turning points and positive rapport-development across time in researcher – participant relationships, *Qualitative Research*, 7(2): 177–201.

Reality Check Approach (2010–2013) http://reality-check-approach.com/approach, [Accessed 13 August 2013].

Sida (2011) *Reality Check Bangladesh. Listening to Poor People's Realities about Primary Healthcare and Primary Education*. Year 5. http://reality-check-approach.com/download/view_document/21-sida-bd-reality-check-2011, [Accesses 13 August 2013].

Simpson, K. (2007) "Hearing voices? Negotiating multiple ethical commitments in development research." In: Smith, M. (ed.) *Negotiating Boundaries and Borders, Studies in Qualitative Methodology*, Volume 8 (Bingley: Emerald Group Publishing Limited), pp. 177–195.

Thomson, R. and Holland, J. (2003) Hindsight, foresight and insight: The challenges of longitudinal qualitative research, *International Journal of Social Research Methodology*, 3(6): 233–244.

Watson, A. (2012) I crashed the boat and wept: Localizing the "field" in critical geographical practice, *Emotion, Space and Society*, 5: 192–200.

World Bank (2008) *Whispers to Voices: Gender and Social Transformation in Bangladesh*. Bangladesh Development Series, No. 22 (Washington DC: World Bank).

Wright, D., Corner, J., Hopkinson, J., and Foster, C. (2006) Listening to the views of people affected by cancer about cancer research, *Health Expectations*, 9(1): 3–12.

3
What's in it for us? Consent, Access, and the Meaning of Research in a Qualitative Longitudinal Study

Rebecca Taylor, Malin Arvidson, Rob Macmillan,
Andri Soteri–Proctor, and Simon Teasdale

3.1 Introduction

Recruiting third sector organizations (TSOs) to a qualitative longitudinal (QL) study turned out to be in some cases a time-consuming and challenging process, and in others a little too easy. The governance structures of the organizations approached were not always simple to navigate with some organizations in a state of flux. Stakeholders' different understandings of the meaning of research created tensions around anonymity. Establishing meaningful consent was not a straightforward process: who has the authority to grant "organizational" consent? This chapter explores the process of gaining consent and access, and maintaining relationships with research participants in "Real Times"; a study of TSOs and activities over three years. By third sector we refer to a range of non-governmental organizations and activities, including voluntary organizations, community groups, and social enterprises. Whilst the study is concerned with UK-focused organizations the issues raised can be seen to have direct relevance to the NGO sector and NGO scholarship more generally. Drawing on researchers' field notes on the recruitment process, and interviews with the research team a year into the project conducted by one member of the team, we unpack some of the practical and ethical challenges of undertaking QL research in organizations.

The chapter begins by describing the Real Times study and its methodology, the ethical protocols we adopted around consent and anonymity, and the recruitment process. This is followed by a review of methodological debates and literatures, including that of international

38

development, that help to shed light on the particular issues raised by the study. The chapter then explores the researchers' experiences in some depth. The first part looks at the initial recruitment process; why some cases were quick and easy to recruit and others long and time-consuming and how informed consent was negotiated. The second part, drawing on researchers' reflections on returning to the field for subsequent waves of data collection, highlights how recruitment was not a stage but an ongoing process. Consent, it turned out, did not guarantee access and was often partial. Maintaining relationships with our cases meant ongoing navigation of shifting organizational structures and internal dynamics, while the different meaning of research for different stakeholders continued to cause tensions. The chapter concludes with a discussion of how our reflections on the recruitment process, the maintaining of relationships with cases, and navigating chaining organizational structures provides important insights. In particular, it provides insights on the organization itself, its practices and ways of relating and the core issues that the Real Times project sets out to explore; leadership governance and the management of change. These themes have much wider relevance to those seeking to better understand organizational change and the operation of NGOs. Lewis for example flags up the need to "better analyse stakeholder dynamics at the organizational and intra-sectoral levels including the management, funding, governance and staffing" (Lewis 2006, p. 189).

3.2   Real Times: project methodology and ethical practice

The Real Times research project is a longitudinal study of 15 TSOs and activities. Its longitudinal case study design entails following organizations in "real time" over a period of three years. It aims to contribute to a theoretically informed and dynamic account of the third sector. The sector is notoriously hard to define and scholarly attempts to understand it refer to "blurred boundaries" (Alcock and Kendall 2011), hybridization (Billis 2010), and contested terrain (Alcock 2010). Further, many studies of the sector have taken single "snapshots" of organizations (Alcock et al. 1999; Scott et al. 2000) and there is a tendency for some of these to be normative and lack a critical dimension (Di Maggio and Anheier 1990). Broader debates in organizational studies, particularly framed by New Institutionalism, have offered potential insights to the study of TSOs. These have suggested the importance of understanding institutional logics, power relations between organizations in a field giving rise to processes of isomorphism and hybridization (Di Maggio and Powell 1983),

Table 3.1   The case study organizations

Ash	A large housing association
Cedar	A consortium of third-sector organizations
Fir	A cooperative sports club
Mimosa	A local mental health charity
Indigo	A local charity supporting ethnic minority older people
Beech	A local environmental social enterprise
Cherry	A medium size campaigning organization
Hawthorn	A small local parenting charity
Mulberry	A community centre in a deprived neighbourhood
Sycamore	An affluent village in the south of England
Birch	A large advice agency
Fig	A national charity delivering services to families
Larch	A village in the north of England
Pine	A resource centre in a multicultural community
Teak	A large social enterprise focusing on regeneration

and institutional entrepreneurship (see overview by Suddaby 2010). Yet these tend to be viewed at a macro level and less is known about TSOs' practices and behaviours, how they respond to challenging contexts, and how and why they survive and change. "Real Times" aims to gain a more in-depth and realistic understanding of how TSOs, groups, and activities operate in practice over time.

The 15 "cases" followed over three years were selected to capture a diverse range of organizations, groups, and activities, based on characteristics such as organization size, age, and field of work, and on different aspects of the setting in which cases operate such as, for example, urban and rural, relative affluence and deprivation, and local political context. The final selection included large national charities-delivering services, social enterprises, and two contrasting villages which enabled us to capture and explore the range of less formal groups and activities that operate "below the radar"; outside formal organizational structures. See Table 3.1 for a summary of the cases anonymized using pseudonyms of tree names.

The study has involved five "waves" of fieldwork from Spring 2010 to Spring 2013 taking place roughly every eight months. Each wave combined three data-generating methods:

1. interviewing people associated with each case study: paid staff, unpaid volunteers, community activists, and governing body members.
2. observing activities in each case study: attending specific events, service-related activities, board or staff meetings, Annual General Meetings, and meetings with funders or collaborative partners.

3. reading documents produced by and about the organization or its locality: annual reports, financial statements and management accounts, marketing and publicity material, project reports and evaluations, and minutes of meetings.

Ethical review for the project was carried out as part of a broader university procedure to gain ethical approval for the work of Third Sector Research Centre (TSRC) where Real Times is based. This review was undertaken following guidance set out by the Economic and Social Research Council (ESRC) in its Framework of Research Ethics. In addition TSRC had agreed to archive its data with the UK Data Archive (UKDA), giving rise to a further layer of complexity and scrutiny of the project's ethical practice. A number of ethical principles and practices for the study were agreed during early project meetings. Anonymization of cases and individuals was central to these discussions.

An important aspect of the study was its potential to provide an independent and critical view of TSOs: the "warts 'n all" account. This aim could not be taken for granted in a context where the project's multiple stakeholders (policymakers, funders, academics, and participants) had particular expectations of research and claims to its outputs. Anonymization was viewed as essential by the research team for two reasons. Firstly it was crucial that staff in our cases felt they could talk freely without fear that they exposed the organization or themselves in any way. Secondly it was essential to minimize harm to the organization that might result from publishing something that risked damage to an organization's reputation with funders, members, or the public. Anonymization was built into the research process from the onset with pseudonyms given to cases at the transcription stage.

A second key aspect of the ethical process was informed consent. It was decided that consent would be sought at both organizational and individual levels. The former meant obtaining signed consent from a senior staff member who would effectively authorize the organization's participation including in the more fluid observation activities. The latter entailed consent forms signed by each individual staff member interviewed that aimed to ensure that staff understood the implications of their individual participation in the study. Information sheets provided details of the project, including digital recording, anonymity, data archiving, and ability to withdraw at any time. A linked consent form asked the participant to sign to confirm they had read and understood the information sheet. In practice, as we go on to show, these processes were not straightforward; gaining written organizational consent was not always feasible and researchers relied on ongoing verbal agreements. Nor did consent necessarily involve the whole organization or adequately cover the variety of data-gathering techniques we were using, particularly in the case of observation of meetings.

3.3   The literature: access, consent, gatekeepers, and politics

Methodological discussions about recruiting organizations to QL studies are scarce. The QL literature focuses on retention of participants and strategies for maintaining contact (Harocopos and Dennis 2003; Thomson and Holland 2003). The unit of analysis is almost always the individual. There are few QL studies of organizations and those that exist do not always define themselves as such or explore the particular issues longitudinality raises. However, insightful and useful debates reflecting the issues raised by Real Times can be found across a range of disciplines: health care research in institutions such as hospitals and care homes where stringent ethical review processes have made access and consent issues particularly pressing; organizational ethnographies in a range of workplaces and institutions that provide inside views on organizational life; and international development where increasingly studies inspired by an ethnographic approach illuminate issues around relationships and tensions between the researcher and the researched. We draw on these sources in the following discussion and explore several issues that are highly pertinent to understanding the recruitment of the issues raised by the Real Times cases: gaining informed consent, the role of contacts and gatekeepers, "creating access," the process of navigating organizational hierarchies and politics, and the emotional labour entailed by "access work."

Texts focusing on the doing of organizational research (Burgess 1984; Bryman 1989; Grey 2009) have long reflected on what are termed "the problems of access." Bryman (1989) suggests that "the bounded nature of organizations imposes an additional layer between organizational researchers and their subjects" (p. 2).There is acknowledgement that organizations are complex structures, often internally contested, and those in charge can be guarded about practices and protective of their staff and their public profile, all of which can make access and relationship building a delicate operation. For example a study of work–life balance in one ethically oriented, brand-driven clothing company highlighted the intensely time-consuming process of gaining access. The researchers describe how "a series of email and phone conversations over six months before finally being granted permission" resulted in only two days allowed for fieldwork. These difficulties, the authors suggest, reflect the organization's desire "to maintain or protect valuable brand identity" (Land and Taylor 2010: 401–402).

For the majority of the Real Times cases the researchers sought access through the most senior member of staff, usually the Chief Executive Officer (CEO) but also coordinators or managers, and in the village cases through a visible and active group of residents. The senior staff and sometimes their personal assistants became gatekeepers or champions for the research, positions which the literature reminds us have implications. Sanghera and Thapar-Björkert (2008) note that the researcher needs to be "vigilant" about the ways in which the relationship with gatekeepers "may facilitate, constrain or transform the research process by opening and/or closing the gate" (p. 543). They use the concept of "positionality" to explore how researchers may come to be strongly associated with the gatekeeper and how this "governs the 'tone' of the research" (ibid., p. 553). The international development literature identifies similar issues. During Hilhorst's ethnographic research in a Philippine NGO, she describes how "actors knew about the nature of my research" and made assumptions about her positionality in relation to contested, local political discourses, and this had implications for who and how people approached her, or indeed chose to avoid her (Hilhorst 2000, p. 72).

Once organizations have agreed in principle to participating there is still the formal process of informed consent to navigate. Discussion of the process of gaining formal consent has focused on research with individuals, particularly vulnerable groups (Heath et al. 2007). Concerns are raised about the bureaucratic load consent processes place on participants; the risk is that this will overburden them, reducing participation of more marginal groups and ultimately resulting in poorer quality data (Crow et al. 2006). Franklin et al. (2012) note that in health research vulnerable participants are the main focus of ethical concerns around consent rather than medical professionals who are "construed as powerful and by definition able to make 'rational informed choices'" (p. 1731). Yet this group, they argue, also raises issues for the consent process, some of which only become apparent as the research gets underway; they may be over-researched or facing organizational restructuring for example. These discussions highlight the salient issue for Real Times where organizations may not be obviously "vulnerable," namely that the dynamics of consent vary for different types of participant. The diversity of our cases implies the necessity of a degree of flexibility and context sensitivity in the informed consent process.

The most fruitful and relevant discussion in the literature was about "access" which, in studies of organizations, is less about formal agreement for the organization to participate in the study and more about the process of recruiting staff to be interviewed once consent is secured. Indeed we would argue that it is important to distinguish between gaining formal consent and a more fluid practice of "creating access" with the latter a feature of the whole research process. For the researcher it is work that can involve educating, familiarizing, and even selling the research to staff who are prospective participants. The health research literature provides some interesting examples of this process. Franklin et al. (2012) describe a range of strategies that researchers undertook including presenting to groups of staff in the hospitals where their research was based. In another study of health care workers researchers describe providing a free lunch in an easily accessible conference room for open forum discussions during workers' 30-minute lunch breaks (Mawn et al. 2010, p. 77). Broyles et al. (2011) similarly advocate for "multimodal recruitment strategies" to maximize participation of staff in health care settings. As our Real Times cases demonstrate "creating access" and building relationship with staff required creative, flexible, and ongoing strategies on the part of researchers.

However, the literature also highlights how not all strategies for creating access can overcome sensitivities, crises, and political issues that structure practices and priorities in institutions and workplaces. The effects of restructuring or other crises in an organization can push participation in a research project to the bottom of an organizational agenda (Mawn et al. 2010; Franklin et al. 2012). Organizations may participate but remain wary of the impact of potential findings. Mawn et al. (2010) found it difficult to gain direct access to workers and saw several agencies withdraw in the early stages of their study. One agency was concerned that published study findings could be used to organize the agency's employees into a union (ibid., p. 73). Again these issues chimed with our experiences in accessing Real Times cases where certain cases went through a period of crisis or upheaval that changed the relationship between the case and the research team and the nature of access.

The implications of the "work" of creating accessing and building relationships for the researchers themselves are a crucial element of the discussion. Carmel (2011) explores what it means to "gain and retain social access" in workplace ethnography arguing that the intense emotional labour involved in the "active creation and maintenance of personal relationships" is integral to the process since friendly relationships in the field are vital for ethnographic work (Carmel 2011, p. 552, see also Arvidson, this volume). Whilst Real Times is not an ethnography the high levels of engagement with organizations meant that researchers described similarly intense and sometimes difficult moments in the building and maintaining of relationships with their cases. In particular power relations come into play here since these relationships are often being built with senior staff in large organizations, effectively elites.

The tensions involved in establishing and maintaining relationships with research participants are also explored in the international development literature. These studies detail the negotiations and compromises involved, at personal as well as organizational levels, in "doing development" (Arvidson 2008; Fechter 2012). Focus is on informal, unscripted roles and unofficial interpretations of development work (Mosse 2011b). When the researcher follows a "long-term academic anthropological concern with the contradictions between what is said and what is done in development" (Lewis and Mosse 2006, p. 2) it is at odds with the self-presentation offered by organizations and their members. This, argues Mosse (2011a, 2011b), lies at the heart of tensions between the researcher and the researched, leading to organizations being guarded and defensive and causing "rupture" in relations. Again, for Real Times these issues of tensions between researcher and participant in terms of interpretation and presentation underscored relationships in several of the cases.

Perhaps the most important point and one which structures our concluding discussion is what reflecting on the recruitment process and accessing of cases and participants tells us about those cases. Similar points have been made by ethnographers and anthropologists who note the connection between research process and research data. As Carmel (2011) argues, "an analytical separation of 'access' from other ethnographic data could be seen as contrary to the spirit of the enterprise" (p. 552). He adds that where the primary aim is cultural interpretation "the very processes of gaining access are likely to demonstrate aspects of the culture being studied, and analysis of access processes is rightly included as part of the analysis of the culture itself" (ibid.). Mosse (2011b), in reflecting on the source and meaning of the controversies surrounding the publication of his study of a development project in India, aims to generate insights regarding the characteristics of organizations, projects, and professional identities.

These diverse discussions offer valuable insights into the issues for Real Times and other QL studies of organizations. They highlight how the problematic nature of access, consent, and building relationships over time are not in any sense confined to QL studies but that these issues can be seen as being amplified and extended by the methodology (Mcleod and Thomson 2009, p. 167) effectively because they play out over a longer period of time. In the empirical sections that follow we draw on researchers' field notes and interviews to explore the issues in more depth, focusing first on the initial recruitment process and secondly on what became apparent as we went back into the field for subsequent waves of fieldwork.

3.4 Recruiting the cases

Case study recruitment started in December 2009 and merged with Wave 1 of the fieldwork, which ran until summer 2010. Each member of the team was responsible for recruiting and working with a particular group of cases. These were selected based on the criteria outlined in the methodology section above, however an additional strategy had been to canvas researchers and colleagues at TSRC for knowledge of and contacts at organizations that fitted the categories. This meant that in many of the 15 cases researchers had prior knowledge of the case or had been introduced to the case by a contact and this facilitated initial access. Potential cases were mainly approached through an email to the CEO, director, or other senior member of the organization.

Of the 16 cases initially selected two declined immediately. In a third case the researcher abandoned recruitment following difficulty establishing contact of any kind and in a fourth case we decided to pull out after some extended negotiation which showed no sign of resolution. All four were cases where we had no prior contacts. Three were successfully replaced with similar organizations leaving us with 15 case studies. However, the fact that 15 organizations eventually said yes belies the considerable time and resources that went into securing the participation of some. In one case the whole process took just under six months. Yet in other organizations it was quick and seemingly uncomplicated; they signed up by return email or during a short phone call following the initial email. In fact given what was being asked of organizations the speed with which some agreed to participate is perhaps more surprising than the fact that some deliberated for a considerable time.

The research programme described to them was a three-year study with two yearly researcher visits including interviews with staff in different roles, observations of meetings, and access to documents. This implied a burden on organizations in terms of staff time spent managing and participating in the research process but also an expectation that organizations expose their internal processes to external scrutiny. We explore the process in more detail looking at what made some organizations time-consuming to recruit and others apparently quick and easy and we highlight how obtaining formal organizational consent for participation in the study raised some unanticipated challenges.

3.4.1 Long and time-consuming

In five of the organizations we approached recruitment involved a slow and in some cases time-consuming and lengthy dialogue between the organization and the researchers over a period of weeks and months. Emails, phone calls, and visits were interspersed with "long waits" and periods of uncertainty. In some cases it was not always apparent who would be able to give consent. Staff turnover meant initial contacts moved on. During the six months it took to recruit Cedar the organization saw the exit of an interim CEO and the appointment of a new one. The researcher describes a catalogue of unreturned calls and being passed around the organization without finding anyone who was able to accept the authority either to give consent to participation or conversely to say no.

Consultation with staff and boards of trustees, whilst important for the consent process, was time-consuming and could take several weeks or even months, particularly as trustees might only meet quarterly. In one case the trustees failed to agree at the first meeting and discussion continued at the next meeting. In the case of Cherry, the researcher was required to take a substantial role in the consultation process and presented on the Real Times study to both senior management and wider staff groups. However, staff were not always immediately receptive to the study and even where there was support and interest these meetings could involve some difficult questions asked of the researchers. A particular challenge was how to respond to the common question that several potential cases raised; "what's in it for us?". One researcher recalls feeling very demoralized after one of the meetings which she described as "a grilling": "I just thought there's no way they're going to let us in, it was very much 'what are we going to get out of this', that was the focus." Another described how the Head of Policy had been rather quiet during a meeting "she had her arms folded and was sort of leaning back in her chair [...] and her immediate response was 'I can't see what in it for us, what use will the research make for us? I'm going to have to manage the PR for this.'"

In these cases the researcher found there were tensions between different understandings of the meaning and purpose of research. The issue of case anonymity which had been a central priority for researchers was viewed critically by organizations thinking about participating in the study. Where their previous experience of research had been action research or research which they could use to promote their services they were uncertain what the rewards were for participating anonymously. They saw the research as potentially raising their profile and questioned why they could not tell their funders they were part of the study, talk about their participation in the project in funding bids, or put links to the study on their website. One researcher recounted how "there's a moment at which they say, 'Could we do a press release about being involved in the research?'"

For the researchers these requests could not be met within the parameters of an anonymized study designed to enable a more critical understanding of the sector. The challenge for them in these particular cases became one of attempting to persuade the staff to forgo the publicity and legitimization that they felt participation conferred for less tangible rewards around the greater long-term good of the sector and the value of academic research. One researcher described it as "trying to market the longitudinal project and its value in and of itself." Researchers were ambivalent about this "selling" of research in order to gain access. Whilst being a necessary part of the recruitment process in several cases, it generated feelings of being underprepared and vulnerable in their negotiations with potential cases particularly where these were often conducted with senior and powerful figures in the organization.

3.4.2   Quick and easy

Recruitment in the majority of the 15 cases was deemed "fairly straightforward" by the researchers. It was clear that approaching cases where we had pre-existing contacts or introductions facilitated the recruitment process. For example, Ash was suggested by a TSRC staff member who knew the CEO. His name was mentioned in the initial email and the CEO was immediately interested. The whole process was described by the researcher as "very quick and very smooth." Similarly the CEO of Birch had been prepared for the initial approach by an informal chat with a colleague at an event. When the researcher phoned to arrange a meeting she said "I've been waiting for your call."

What defined the quick and easy cases was not only the existence of prior knowledge or introductions but that the staff approached asked very few questions about the research and did not consult widely with other staff or trustees. The cofounder of Beech replied to the initial email saying "no problem that's fine." In the case of Indigo, the researcher had interviewed the CEO for a previous project and arranged a visit to talk about the possibility of participating in the Real Time study. The CEO agreed there and then.

> There was virtually no need to go to Management Committee according to her. She said she'll just mention it to them, which I was a bit anxious about but she would say no, no, I'll tell them and that's fine.

Several of these cases were, like Indigo, relatively small community organizations with just one or two senior staff members which reduced the possibility for consultation. Unlike the process of "selling" the research in the long and time-consuming cases, researchers described finding people were not particularly interested in hearing about the study or asking questions. A researcher recalls how in one case the manager interrupted her when she was "halfway through the spiel." He said, "yeah that's great" "and then started talking about himself." Whilst these organizations were apparently easier to recruit these different levels of information provision and engagement with the study raised questions about how complete and informed the consent was in these cases.

3.4.3 Formal consent

The process of obtaining some kind of organizational consent at the start of the project (rather than consent by individual staff members to be interviewed during the fieldwork itself) raised a number of issues. The detailed project-based guidelines for researchers on recruitment, did not specify how and when to introduce this formal part of consent-giving. Researchers had different understandings of consent (Wiles et al. 2007) and used different strategies in particular in relation to when and how they introduced the process and the forms to their cases.

The consent process in the two villages was necessarily different because it had been acknowledged that "whole village" consent was not possible; it needed to be more incremental and flexible. Instead the researcher identified a key individual who could provide an entry point to a prominent group of active residents. In both villages he was invited to an informal meeting with this group of village residents to speak to them about the study. Both meetings ended in a show of hands or nods of agreement to the question "so, do we want to go ahead with this?" However the researcher notes this was not so much consent as "permission to carry on with the research." It served simply as a starting point for gaining wider access.

Even amongst the organizations the consent forms were perceived quite differently. One researcher noted the contrast between two of her cases in terms of the ways in which they engaged with the consent process. In one, a small charity, she felt both the language barriers and the lack of experience of formal research processes meant they would have not understood or engaged with the consent form and she found herself reluctant to broach it with them. On the other hand in another, a large charity, she noted that "process" was very important and the consent form, as part of a formal recruitment process "made sense" to them and she had no difficulty getting it signed.

In practice whilst all the organizations had agreed to participate and some had undergone lengthy negotiation to establish this agreement, signed organizational consent forms were only obtained for half the organizations. Instead researchers felt they were operating with what one researcher called "workable consent," "enough for us to be going on with." This highlighted something that became more apparent as the project went on, that whatever forms had been signed at the outset, consent was in reality an ongoing negotiated process.

3.5 Reflecting on recruitment and building relationships

In this section we shed further light on the recruitment process reflecting on what happened when we went back to our cases for Waves 2 and 3 of the fieldwork. In several of our organizations this served to reframe our understanding of the initial process. More generally the longitudinal perspective enabled an exploration of how building and maintaining relationships with cases are ongoing processes over the life of the project.

3.5.1 Partial consent and partial access

In subsequent waves of fieldwork it became apparent that in some cases initial permission only constituted partial consent. As we noted earlier the process of obtaining organizational consent from senior staff had not necessarily involved consulting or communicating with others in the organization about Real Times. Researchers noted "awkwardness" at Wave 1 when those they approached did not know anything about the study. In Birch, for example, the CEO had apparently taken a unilateral decision to participate and when the researcher went to observe a board meeting no one knew who she was or anything about the research. The result was the researcher "really had to do a selling job there and then about the research and what it involved." The researcher in Mimosa felt involvement had probably been presented as a "fait accompli" to the board and at Wave 1 found very little enthusiasm or interest from other staff. She remembers introducing the project at a senior managers meeting and asking if there were questions: "they all looked rather stone-faced, ... didn't show any emotions, didn't sort of say 'Oh my god just another thing we have to do.'" More problematically in another case the researcher found herself observing a meeting with users of the service who had clearly not been informed about the study or asked about their willingness to participate, albeit indirectly.

Returning to organizations, researchers also found that certain parts of the organization were closed off to them. In Cedar the researcher felt he had gained a "foothold" at Wave 1 with senior staff interviewed and "signed up," but he also noted that he had not yet been allowed to observe a board meeting or to look at paperwork and this blocking of access continued until Wave 3. The closing off of parts of the organization to the research process was also a product of how much information individuals were prepared to divulge in practice during interviews. While the CEO of Indigo had been happy to participate in the study initially, in subsequent waves of fieldwork the researcher found it very hard to arrange interviews with her or when she had, to elicit much information, particularly about the financial situation of the organization. The CEO deferred to the management committee and committee members deferred to the CEO meaning that effectively no one would take responsibility for describing this aspect of the organization's functioning. One interpretation of this might be that the understanding of staff of what participation entailed developed during the research process itself rather than at the consent stage and they simply avoided the elements they were less comfortable with.

However where limited access was ongoing it could seriously undermine the position of the case in the study. In Pine, a local resource centre for community groups, the researcher found it difficult to set up interviews with the manager who never responded to emails. As he was one of the only paid staff (a "one man band" as the researcher put it) and there was no board of trustees, it was difficult to gain any overview of how the organization worked without his contribution. The organization had not pulled out of the study but the issue around access raised questions about the extent to which their data was comparable in scope and depth with other cases.

3.5.2 Shifting organizational structures

Access difficulties at subsequent waves also occurred when the researcher returned to find the organization had changed; sometimes through an organizational restructuring, a turnover of personnel, or the exit of a CEO. These scenarios required work navigating the new terrain and rebuilding relationships. In Cedar for example the end of Wave 3 saw the exit of the chief executive who had signed the organization up to the research rendering Real Times' future in the organization again uncertain. Sometimes these changes were planned and anticipated but they could also be quite sudden. At one organization, a local parenting project, the researcher arrived for the Wave 1 interviews to find no one to meet him at the station as arranged. Further investigation revealed an internal crisis involving the dismissal of the original coordinator that could have signalled the end of the organization and certainly its participation in the research. The chair was keen to stay involved, and following time to resolve the crisis the research eventually went ahead. The researcher, however, remembers being worried about renegotiating access with the new coordinator who might not understand the study.

Researchers did not always feel their position was more vulnerable as a result of changing staff, particularly if these events happened in later waves when trust and relationships had been established. In Mimosa, where there has also been a high turnover of CEOs over the course of the study, the researcher describes much stronger relationships with staff at Wave 3 but also a level of organizational understanding that made her position more secure; "I had seen three chief executives and suddenly I had perhaps a better grasp of where the organization came from than the newly appointed CEO."

3.5.3   Internal politics and researcher positionality

In some organizations the internal structures were relatively stable but negotiating access at subsequent fieldwork waves meant navigating internal politics or researcher positionality. For example in trying to recruit Fir, the researcher, getting no response to an email to one of the directors, followed up a contact who introduced him to the general manager. The manager signed up immediately but six weeks later the director finally replied suggesting the proposal would need to go to the board. This put both the researcher and the general manager in an awkward position and had implications for later access to the board. Similarly in a small social enterprise the researcher had initially approached the founder who agreed to participate without consulting the director who had a more central role. This caused some tensions that needed to be resolved by the researcher: "I realised by going to her that, not upset him, but put his nose a bit out of joint."

The issue of researcher positionality arose in relation to the use of contacts and introductions in recruiting cases. One of the community organizations, for example, was known to other researchers at the university who were still researching the organization and the manager frequently referred to Real Times and the other study as if they were the same one. In another case the researcher was introduced to the case study organization by a contact from an infrastructure group with a particular focus on cooperatives. He noted that it took some time before the case's coordinator stopped assuming the Real Times study was about cooperatives.

Again these issues did not always have negative impacts on the process. Organizational dynamics could sometimes make it easier to access staff. In Teak the researcher described board members queuing up to be interviewed in what he described as competitive research participation: "they all think their voice is equally important." A similar dynamic happened in one of the villages where members of the group of active residents emailed the researcher to ask when they would be interviewed. Individuals wanted their voice and views to be heard although this raised other issues about who was not being interviewed and whose voices were not represented in the cases.

3.5.4 The meaning of research and anonymity

Once the fieldwork was fully underway there were fewer "what's in it for us?"-type discussions. Questions about the overall benefits to the organization receded replaced by the practicalities of organizing interviews and discussions about what had happened since the last visit. When the researcher offered to provide feedback on the study to the staff in Cherry the coordinator suggested that it was not really a good time with redundancy notices about to go out. However the different meanings of research for the participants and the researchers continued to infuse relationships in subsequent waves of fieldwork. In some cases individuals began to understand the need for anonymity during the interview process as they realized the sensitive nature of the material they were discussing. One researcher noted how the CEO in one of his cases had been very bullish about having "nothing to hide" in the initial meeting but changed his mind during the first interview following a rather probing question.

> I think I asked him, "How much autonomy do you have in relation to your board," I can't remember the exact question. And he said, "Ah now I can see why it's anonymous" and proceeded to tell me that his board just rubberstamps decisions.

However others were still keen to publicize their participation in the project during later waves and in one case had independently created links to the Real Times website despite the discussions around anonymity during the consent process. Building relationships with organizations and their staff meant researchers gained a sense of how an organization's previous experience of research coloured their engagement with and expectations of Real Times. This researcher noted a particular example of the wider research context for one of his cases where a local university had found them some funding which provided a rather different research experience to participation in Real Times.

> [local university] tell them how brilliant they are and then [name of case study] get to say how brilliant they are and that it's been independently verified. So for me to come along and ask slightly awkward questions is unusual and they wonder what I'm doing.

In a small number of cases the researchers found it difficult to penetrate organizational rhetoric. This was particularly true in the social enterprises which were skilled at self-promotion and navigating the media and engaged with the research in the same way. The researcher describes one CEO:

> He is on the television and in the newspapers a lot, he's so used to being interviewed and carefully media trained not to say the wrong thing. I'm finding it very difficult to get too much out of them.

However researchers also noted that the advantage of the longitudinal study was that it provided time for them to excavate some of the more formalized organizational narratives that were presented initially and uncover the practices and tensions beneath.

3.6 Discussion and conclusions

The preceding empirical sections have shown how the recruitment process can be long and time-consuming or quick and easy depending on a whole range of factors such as whether existing contacts were used in approaching cases, the extent to which staff and board members were consulted, whether there is someone with the authority to grant consent, and of course the organization's understanding of what was in it for them (the meaning of research and the rationale for anonymity). The consent process that had been designed at the start of the study required some flexibility in implementation and tailoring to specific organizational contexts. Yet as our relationship with the cases developed over subsequent waves of fieldwork we also learned that those initial experiences masked other complexities in the process. Some of those quick and easy cases, where gaining organizational agreement to proceed took a matter of days, were cases where we struggled to get data in the longer term. Organizations signed up without fully understanding what was involved, despite the best efforts of the researcher. On the other hand some cases that were long and time-consuming to recruit, where researchers were given "a grilling," resulted in open and privileged access to all aspects of the organizations in the longer term. Issues we thought we had left behind at the end of the recruitment phase including navigating organizational structures, tensions around anonymity, and gaining consent all turned out to be ongoing processes. These processes were part of the work that we have called "creating access"; maintaining navigating and building relationships over the lifetime of the project.

Many of these issues are illuminated by discussion in the literature outlined early in the chapter. Exploring the role of gatekeepers provided insight into the implications of our use of existing contacts to provide the basis for research engagement. Initially using contacts and introductions seemed to be a highly successful strategy, particularly when organizations that declined were those where we had no existing knowledge or relationships. Yet these relationships influence how researchers are viewed and thus who is willing to engage. The notion of positionality (Sanghera and Thapar-Björkert 2008) provides insights into the way introductions created obligations that pre-empted full understanding of what was involved or alignments within organizations that hindered other relationships being formed.

Texts that explore the consent and access process were also illuminating. Whilst Real Times was not engaging with obviously vulnerable groups the diversity of cases meant consent needed to be achieved in different ways and tailored to the setting. However as we showed, the degree to which cases were always fully informed is arguable. At the same time, gaining formal consent in whatever form was not the final stage in the recruitment process but rather a beginning. Reflections in the literature on the process of building relationship within organizations and institutions were also insightful. In the Real Times project access was not gained but rather created in a continuous process. Mawn et al.'s (2010) and Franklin et al.'s (2012) descriptions of strategies for recruiting hospital staff to long-term research projects formalize some of the activities that Real Times researchers undertook in a more ad hoc and spontaneous way. The difficult meetings and long waits can be seen as embedded in and central to the process of "creating access" in organizational research.

While we describe the process of building relationships and negotiating access as challenging, the benefit of longitudinal research is that the nurturing and maintaining of relationships does get easier over the course of the study. Trust was built up and a web of relationships was established within and around the organizations that mitigated against the impact of CEOs leaving, structures shifting, and crises taking place, that otherwise may have jeopardized the project. Perhaps importantly, by Wave 4 all 15 cases were still participating in the study. Instead we found the quality of the data to be different between cases that were fully engaged and others that were signed up but where relationships and access had been harder to create and maintain. Texts by Mosse (2011b) and Carmel (2011) were useful in shedding light on personal and emotional aspects of the process from the perspective of the researcher.

Perhaps the most important insight here is that researcher reflexivity about the recruitment process, the maintaining of relationships, negotiating consent, creating access, and managing expectations provided the study with important data in itself. Reflexive data provides insights into the nature and culture of the organization, particularly in relation to the core research questions that the Real Times project set out to explore: leadership, governance, and the management of change. In observing how organizations responded to approaches by researchers, and how they engaged in the relationship with an external body, we can begin to understand the organization's practices, priorities, internal tensions, and power dynamics and we can see these change over time. This is data that is not easy to gain directly from interviews but constitutes tacit knowledge that researchers gain about their cases.

For example recruiting Cedar was a long and labour-intensive process involving many phone calls, long waits, and being passed around to various people, none of whom were in a position to agree to participate. Yet these difficulties provide insight into the workings of a very young organization with infighting and conflicts between and within senior staff and the board about the organization's purpose and direction. That no one could agree to participation in the research reflected a vacuum in leadership caused by the rapid turnover of CEOs and other staff. The partial access was testimony to the tensions between different parts of the organization and some unwillingness of senior staff to make internal divisions public.

A contrasting example, Indigo, was relatively easy to gain consent from, yet one of the harder to access. The CEO was reluctant to be interviewed or talk freely about the organization. These difficulties concealed an organization that was fragmented, with a flat structure, where different parts of the organization operated fairly autonomously and few decisions were made jointly. There were no group meetings and thus no "organizational perspective" or strategizing. The researcher reflected that in this organization there was no route down from the top: creating access had to happen from the bottom up, by speaking to those on the ground.

This chapter has sought to explore the diversity of the access and consent issues in the Real Times project and touched on how these illuminate the organizations' structures and cultures. Real Times, as a QL study of TSOs and activities, has given rise to a particular web of methodological issues and questions that have much broader relevance to international development and NGO scholarship. Here we have started the process of untangling them and we look forward to further opportunities to explore our methodology and practices and enrich our understanding of doing longitudinal research in organizations.

References

Alcock, P. (2010) "A Strategic Unity: Defining the Third Sector in the UK," *Voluntary Sector Review*, 1(1): 5–24.

Alcock, P., Harrow, J., Mcmillan, R. (1999) Making funding work: Funding regimes and local voluntary organisations York: Joseph Rowntree Foundation.

Alcock, P. and Kendall, J. (2011) "Constituting the Third Sector: Processes of Decontestation and Contention under the UK Labour Governments in England," *Voluntas: International Journal of Voluntary and Nonprofit Organizations*, 22(3): 450–469.

Arvidson, M. (2008) "Contradictions and Confusion in Development Work: Exploring the Realities of Bangladeshi NGOs," *Journal of South Asian Development*, 3(1): 109–134.

Billis, D. (2010) "From Welfare Bureaucracies to Welfare Hybrids," in Billis, D. (ed.) *Hybrid Organizations and the Third Sector* (Basingstoke: Palgrave Macmillan).

Broyles, L. M., Rodriguez, K. L., Price, P. A., Bayliss, N. K., Sevick, M. A., Broyles, L. M., and Rodriguez, K. L. (2011) "Overcoming Barriers to the Recruitment of Nurses as Participants in Health Care Research," *Qualitative Health Research*, 21: 1705–1718.

Bryman A. (1989) *Research Methods and Organization Studies* (London: Routledge).

Burgess R. G. (1984) *In the Field: An Introduction to Field Research* (London: Routledge).

Carmel, S. (2011) "Social Access in the Workplace: Are Ethnographer's Gossips?," *Work, Employment and Society*, 25(3): 551–560.

Crow, G., Wiles, R., Heath, S., and Charles, V. (2006) "Research Ethics and Data Quality: The Implications of Informed Consent," *International Journal of Social Research Methodology*, 9(2): 83–95.

Di Maggio, P. and Anheir, H. (1990) "The Sociology of Nonprofit Organisations and Sectors," *Annual Review of Sociology*, 16: 137–159.

Di Maggio, P. and Powell, W. (1983) "The Iron Cage Revisited, Institutional Isomorphism and Collective Rationality in Organizational Fields," *American Sociological Review*, 48(2): 147–160.

Fechter, A. M. (2012) "The Personal and the Professional: Aid Workers' Relationships and Values in the Development Process," *Third World Quarterly*, 33(8): 1387–1404.

Franklin, P., Rowland, E., Fox, R., and Nicolson, P. (2012) "Research Ethics in Accessing Hospital Staff and Securing Informed Consent," *Qualitative health research*, 22: 1727–1738.

Grey, C. (2009) *A Very Short Fairly Interesting and Reasonably Cheap Book About Studying Organizations* (London: Sage Publications).

Harocopos, A. and Dennis, D. (2003) "Maintaining Contact with Drug Users over an 18-month Period," *International Journal of Social Research Methodology*, 6(3): 261–265.

Heath, S., Charles, V., Crow, G., and Wiles, R. (2007) "Informed Consent, Gatekeepers and Go-betweens: Negotiating Consent in Child- and Youth-orientated Institutions," *British Educational Research Journal*, 3(33): 403–417.

Hilhorst, D. (2000) *Records and reputations: Everyday politics of a Phillipine development NGO* (Wagening: Wagening University).

Land, C. and Taylor, S. (2010) "Surf's Up: Work, Life, Balance and Brand in a New Age Capitalist Organisation," *Sociology*, 44(3): 395–413.

Lewis, D. (2006) "Issues and Priorities in Non-governmental Organisational Research," *Journal of Health Management*, 8: 181.

Lewis, D. and Mosse, D. (2006) "Encountering Order and Disjuncture: Contemporary Anthropological Perspectives on the Organization of Development," *Oxford Development Studies*, 34(1): 1–13.

Mawn, B., Siqueira, E., Koren, A., Slatin, C., Melillo, K. D., Pearce, C., and Hoff, L. A. (2010) "Health Disparities Among Health Care Workers," *Qualitative health research*, 20(1): 68–80.

McLeod, J. and Thomson, R. (2009) *Researching Social Change* (London: Sage).

Mosse, D. (2011a) "Introduction: The Anthropology of Expertise and Professionals in International Development," in Mosse, D. (ed.) *Adventures in Aidland. The Anthropology of Professionals in International Development* (New York: Berghahn Books).

Mosse, D. (2011b) "Policies and Ethics: Ethnographies of expert knowledge and professional identities," in Shore, C., Wright, S., and Pero, D. (eds) *Policy Worlds: Anthropology and Analysis of Contemporary Power* (New York: Berghahn Books).

Sanghera, G. S. and Thapar-Björkert, S. (2008) "Methodological dilemmas: Gatekeepers and positionality in Bradford," *Ethnic and Racial Studies*, 31(3): 543–562.

Scott, D., Alock, P., Russell, L., and Macmillan, R. (2000) *Moving Pictures: Realities of Voluntary Action* (Bristol: Policy Press).

Suddaby, R. (2010) "Challenges for Institutional Theory," *Journal of Management Inquiry*, 19: 14.

Thomson, R. and Holland, J. (2003) "Hindsight, Foresight and Insight: The Challenges of Longitudinal Qualitative Research," *International Journal of Social Research Methodology*, 6(3): 233–244.

Wiles, R., Crow, G., Charles, V., and Heath, S. (2007) "Informed Consent and the Research Process: Following Rules or Striking Balances?," *Sociological Research Online*, 12(2).

4
Going Back to Re-study Communities: Challenges and Opportunities

Graham Crow

4.1 Introduction

This chapter addresses the issue of what can be learned about how research on communities is received through projects in which research is undertaken in communities that have been researched previously. It does so by first considering what researchers in the field of re-studies have reported in terms of their rationales for revisiting communities and the problems that they have encountered in relation to the reception of previous work. These problems are outlined and then five sources of such problems are identified and discussed: researchers responding to academic criticisms of romanticism; researcher misrepresentation; media misrepresentation; researcher overpromising; and mutual misunderstanding. The chapter then concludes by considering various strategies that are available to reduce these problems so that the benefits that community research (including re-studies of communities) has the potential to provide may continue to be available.

4.2 Problems in the field

Undertaking community re-studies has a number of rationales, the most important of which is that they have the potential to shed light on the social change that has taken place in that community in the intervening period. As Jan Breman has put it, "Returning to a location that has earlier been subjected research offers an excellent opportunity to check the pace, direction and effects of social change" (1997: 53). In addition, re-studies allow the findings of the original study and its underlying assumptions to be re-examined (Burawoy 2003; Crow 2012; Kloos 1997; Seale 1999: ch.10). In general, re-studies are undertaken at least a decade after the original research was conducted, allowing long-term processes of social change such as modernization, urbanization, and changing gender relations that are the subject of macro-level theorizing to be explored in a community context. In some cases the gap between the original study and the re-study amounts to several decades, and in such circumstances the likelihood is greater that differences in findings will be attributable at least in part to changes in the research perspectives adopted. Thus Göran Djurfeldt et al., returning to India a quarter of a century on from their original fieldwork which had been conducted at the end of the 1960s reflected that they had moved away from their earlier thinking that had been framed in terms of dependency theory: "Twenty five years is more than half the working lifetime of a researcher, and it is not only the village and the villagers that have changed, but so have we" (1997: 177). In undertaking such research, many things have come to light about the reception of the original researcher and his or her (or, in the case of research teams, their) research outputs. This reception may be positive, as in the case of Djurfeldt et al., who refer to villagers who spoke to them as "our friends" (1997: 182), but it can also be hostile. In cases where re-studies are undertaken by the original researcher, the reception that they receive can be intensely personal.

Returning to the site of her investigations in the west of Ireland a quarter of a century on from her original fieldwork, Nancy Scheper-Hughes (2000: 324) was not welcomed by all community members and was subjected to "drumming out of the village" by some. Several locals had not taken kindly to her study, *Saints, Scholars and Schizophrenics*, published first in 1977, for its sympathetic yet critical analysis of community decline framed in terms of her understanding of how social relations in small, tight-knit communities can be oppressive to individuals by virtue of the scrutiny to which community members are subject. Her return was prompted in part by a sense that her approach may have led her to "an overly critical view of village life in the mid-1970s" (Scheper-Hughes 2000: 320), but she found that time had not yet been "a great healer" (ibid.: 328). Her book had clearly touched a nerve.

Half a century earlier, Art Gallaher returned to "Plainville," Missouri, which had been studied by James West 15 years previously (West 1945). West told Gallaher that "to the best of his knowledge, with one outstanding exception most Plainvillers had taken his report 'with relative composure.'" But Gallaher had people saying to him, "I certainly hope you are not here to do the same thing that feller West did a few years ago ... Folks here are mighty unhappy with him ... Some would like to lynch him." Their accounts of their dissatisfaction were expressed in the language of betrayal of trust. Even residents who were more favourably disposed were unsure. For one, West was "A nice guy, *but he asked a hell of a lot of questions*" (Gallaher 1971: 286, 288–9, emphasis in original). Members of the community had hosted West so that he could conduct his research, and had implicitly expected and trusted him to do something other than he actually did, which in their view was to concentrate in his book on the negative aspects of the community. With this in mind, Gallaher included in his book "A Note to Plainvillers" expressing his hope that they would appreciate that "no analysis of community life can be completely pleasing and still be honest" (1961: xiv).

In "Springdale," New York State, no one dared attempt a re-study after publication of Arthur Vidich and Joseph Bensman's *Small Town in a Mass Society* in 1958 led to the authors being hanged in effigy by the townspeople and cast as "manure spreaders." The authors "had expected that Springdale 'rightly' would be scandalised by our analysis," which (amongst other things) failed to achieve anonymization. They had knowingly engaged in providing reassurances in pursuit of good "community relations" between the project and the townspeople, promising "a positive approach" from which they consciously deviated in writing the book in which they highlighted the town's parochialism. Vidich declined an invitation to go back, even though this was many years later, saying he "lacked the inclination and emotional stamina" (2000: xxxii, 448, 491). The project has become a textbook case of how relations between communities and researchers, and also research organizations, can go awry (Bell and Newby 1971: 116ff.). It serves as an extreme case, about which it is useful to know so that the difficulties encountered might be anticipated and avoided by researchers preparing to enter the field of community research.

4.2.1   Sources of fieldwork problems: researchers responding to academic criticisms of romanticism

A first reason why reports on communities may not meet with favour by members of those communities is that researchers have been at pains to avoid suggestions of romanticism or failing to acknowledge the heterogeneity of communities (Guijt and Shah 1998), a criticism that has some foundations. Geoff Payne once asked why monographs in the community studies tradition are typically so full of "nice" people. Having reviewed the accumulated literature, Payne was led to the conclusion that "the main impression generated is one of a world populated with pleasant, likeable people" (1996: 21). This ran counter to his experience: "In the course of fieldwork in several locations in the past half a dozen years, I have encountered people whom I did not like, and situations that felt most unpleasant ... The people in community studies are too 'nice'" (ibid.: 22). The explanation for what have come to be considered as rather romanticized accounts of community in which accounts of social life are too good to be true relates to problems of selective sampling and of "selective reporting" (ibid.: 23). Through these processes, less likeable people and unhappier experiences may be screened out from research, leaving a sanitized account of local social relationships. There is a parallel between this argument and Derek Freeman's critique of Margaret Mead's classic study of Samoan culture, in which he relates how many educated Samoans familiar with Mead's work entreated him "to correct her mistaken depiction of the Samoan ethos" (1984: xv) and to provide instead a less romanticized account.

The criticism of community research presenting romanticized accounts has been levelled at the work of the Institute of Community Studies by Jocelyn Cornwell, whose selection of East London as the location of her research led her to reflect on how previous analyses of community there had contributed to "the post-war myth of Bethnal Green as the model of urban village life." Her distinction between public and private accounts that people provide of their lives allows the argument to be made that "public accounts are selective and partial," and that a more rounded portrayal of community life requires penetration beyond this public face in order to access "those parts of people's experience and opinions that might be considered unacceptable and not respectable" (1984: 24, 205). In her own research, the ideas of her participants about blame for ill-health that were contained in their private accounts are indeed uncomfortable when compared to the less judgemental views expressed in their public accounts, but the book is all the better as a work of social science for the inclusion of both. Community researchers are committed to doing more than descriptively reproducing public accounts built around mythical conceptions of harmonious communities, even where these are generated by ostensibly participatory processes.

The susceptibility of Michael Young and Peter Willmott's work on Bethnal Green to romanticism relates to a methodological problem of which they were well aware. In writing *Family and Kinship in East London*, they noted that although they had supplemented their interviews with ethnographic observations, it remained true "that for the most part we can only report what people say they do, which is not necessarily the same as what they actually do" (1962: 14). They were as researchers cut from a different cloth to James West, whose conduct in Plainville earned him a reputation as an aggressive interviewer; as one community member put it, "he didn't care if you didn't want to answer questions, he just kept asking them anyway" (Gallaher 1971: 294). By contrast, Young and Willmott were concerned not "to create discord between our informants" (1962: 26), and as a result dropped potentially contentious questions about earnings. Their general approach has been taken to task for its lack of rigour, a criticism connected to their "desire to popularize" (Platt 1971: 137). Mindful of such criticisms, social scientists have sought to go beyond the public face that community members present to outsiders. Ken Dempsey's study of "Smalltown" in Australia is a good example of this. He shows that the notion of community members being like "one big happy family" with which he was presented was at odds with the realities of the stigmatization and social exclusion of marginal groups in the community. Nonetheless, he found ways of sustaining a productive working relationship with members of the community over the best part of two decades while developing such analyses. The fact that "Smalltownites are pragmatists who are sceptical about the value of all academic activities" (Dempsey 1990: ch.4, ix) will doubtless have helped in this process of accommodation. Other re-studies also indicate that people studied may exhibit a degree of indifference to what researchers say about them, preoccupied as they are with "getting on with their lives" (Bryson and Winter 1999: 6). In addition, some members of communities that have been studied will be persuaded by the core argument that many of them make about diversity within communities, including diversity of perceptions. As Jan Breman and his co-editors express it, "The village is not the same village for all its inhabitants" (1997: 5), echoing in an Asian context the point made about British research by Ray Pahl regarding how one group's "village in the mind" (1968: 271) can be quite at odds with that of another group, even though they both inhabit the same place.

4.2.2 Sources of fieldwork problems: researcher misrepresentation

Community researchers are, then, under pressure from their academic peers to question stories of local social life presented to them by community members because such narratives have a tendency to embody romanticized elements that are at odds with reality. The sociologist Norbert Elias would have had his own published work on community in mind when he described the role of the sociologist as "a destroyer of myths" (1978: ch.2), because that research revolved around the (in Elias's view questionable) attitude among some community members that they were "*better* than the others." Elias saw it as his role to interpret such thinking as the stuff of "fantasies" (Elias and Scotson

1994: xv, xliii, emphasis in original), based as it is on the development of stereotypes in which key characteristics are exaggerated to implausible lengths. From this point of view, social scientists coming to a community from outside may be better placed to develop an analysis of relationships within that community than that based on community members' conceptions of themselves.

Elias and Scotson do not record how well their interpretation of local social relationships was received by members of the community that they studied, although they report that many participants in the study "took a cheerful and encouraging interest in the research" (1994: xiii), without which the project would not have been possible. A similar recognition of the debt owed by researchers to members of communities being studied can be found in the acknowledgements of Norman Dennis et al.'s classic study of a Yorkshire coal-mining village *Coal Is Our Life*. These are worth quoting quite extensively because their tone is at odds with the views expressed to Dennis Warwick and Gary Littlejohn by townspeople when they returned to undertake a re-study some three decades later. The original research team had written that their "greatest debt without question is to the people of Ashton. They have neither resented nor rejected our prying into their affairs. Whenever there was an opportunity for co-operation this has been extended to us. Although they remain anonymous, this is their book" (Dennis et al. 1969: 6). This account runs counter to the sense of betrayal by the authors of the original study that Warwick and Littlejohn had expressed to them. Several inhabitants told Warwick and Littlejohn that "outsiders continually get the place and its people all wrong," which raises the question of how community research might accommodate local people's views. Put bluntly, "Can a community study ever be a negotiated product in which sociologists are not the only definers of the situation?" (1992: 33). This issue will be returned to in the conclusion.

An important lesson of the study and re-study of Featherstone (the real name of the place given the pseudonym "Ashton") is that memories of previous research can endure, especially if local people feel that trust has been betrayed by researchers who use the opportunity to portray their community in a negative light, although others with more positive evaluations of *Coal Is Our Life* were among those of the re-study interviewees who remembered it. Among the critics, some linked their objections to the arguments developed in the original study with comments on what they regarded as poor research practice that had been at the root of the community being misrepresented. Thus one of Warwick and Littlejohn's participants "also thought it bad because it gave a thoroughly distorted picture of the town. Some aspects of life were over-emphasized, even caricatured, some hardly alluded to or even ignored completely. He considered it a bad piece of research. The researchers, in his view, had come with firmly fixed stereotypes in their heads and with preconceived ideas. They had looked only for evidence which would support these stereotypes and preconceived ideas, and of course had not failed to find them." For another interviewee the problem lay in over-reliance on older miners in pubs as sources, one of whom was "able to keep up an endless stream of anecdotes and information, so long as the beer flowed." The over-reliance of the original research team on talking to men has also been identified as a source of bias and misrepresentation, and Warwick and Littlejohn's decision "to give priority to women as respondents" (1992: 32, 73) in their re-study was a conscious response to this.

4.2.3   Sources of fieldwork problems: media misrepresentation

One of the reasons why so many Featherstone residents were able to recall the original study after three decades may be the extensive coverage that the book received in the Yorkshire Post on its publication. This media coverage had portrayed the study as one that had "an emphasis on the seamy side of life" (Warwick and Littlejohn 1992: 32), but to the authors this misunderstood their purpose of seeking to expose "the cultural poverty and isolation imposed on the working-class community" by material deprivation. Reflecting on the book's reception more than a decade after its publication, Fernando Henriques rejected the view that he and his co-authors had been driven by "a somewhat morbid preoccupation with the miners' past," arguing that the realism of their analysis had been vindicated by the failure of more optimistic scenarios that accompanied the nationalization of the coal industry and the development of the modern welfare state around the middle of the 20th century. That said, it is understandable how reproducing the view of outsiders of Ashton as "that dirty hole" (Dennis et al. 1969: 8, 12) would be met by mixed emotions among the people whose village is so described.

Another example of the role of the mass media in influencing the reception of community research is provided by Margaret Stacey's first (1960) study of Banbury, which had its discussion of social status represented in the press as a description of "a place pulsating with snobbery and riddled with class distinction." This made it a challenge to meet the requirement of the re-study's funders "that there should be evidence that the study would be welcome in the town," and the problem was compounded when an open meeting to publicize the re-study project was covered in the Oxford Mail under the headline "New Probe Into 'Snob

Town'" (Bell 1977: 58, 57, 58). Colin Bell implies that such coverage was unfair because although the original study was "not an affectionate book," it was also not one that involved "disparagement of the place." Bell's memories of working with Stacey on the re-study were that "She loved being there. She really liked being in the town and liked the work, liked the people" (2008: 114); she had no intention of belittling them. A key lesson of this case is that academic discussions of social scientific concepts like status consciousness do not translate unproblematically into journalistic coverage of research.

We should be wary, however, of blaming the mass media entirely for instances of poor reception of research publications by the people about whom they have been written. It has been said that once a book is published "its authors lose control over how it is to be understood, misunderstood, interpreted, and misinterpreted," a comment made by Vidich and Bensman whose book's hostile reception has been mentioned above. But the genuineness of their claimed "bemusement" must be questionable, since in the first edition of the book they noted how the local newspaper "always emphasises the positive side of life; it never reports local arrests, shotgun weddings, mortgage foreclosures, lawsuits, bitter exchanges in public meetings, suicides, or any other unpleasant happenings." It reproduces Springdale's "image of itself" as "Just Plain Folks," and epitomizes the outlook in which "A challenge to the image of Springdale as a preferred place cuts deep" (Vidich and Bensman 2000: xxv, 31, 29, 31). Thus just as Dempsey courted disfavour by writing about outsider groups in Smalltown such as the "blockies" (people living in poor-quality accommodation on the margins of the community) and the "no-hopers" (1990: 45, 43) because their presence ran counter to the ideology of Smalltownites comprising one big happy family, so too did Vidich and Bensman for their explicit discussion of "the shack people." By drawing attention to this deviant group about whom "in the course of ordinary activities ... there appears to be a tacit agreement not to rec-ognise or mention their existence" (2000: 69, 70), they must have known the risk of becoming unpopular that they were taking by breaching this arrangement.

4.2.4   Sources of fieldwork problems: researcher overpromising

The hostile reception of community members to the publication of Vidich and Bensman's book has another dimension to it relating to the authors promising more than they delivered. Expectations of the sort of report on Springdale that they would produce were shaped by their responses during the period of fieldwork to questions about their purpose. When they were (reasonably enough) "pressed by the community to tell what the study was about, who it included, what its purpose was, and what kind of book would be written" the project team developed what they called "a line" that included various reassuring statements: "We are not interested in the negative features of the town ... A positive approach is needed ... We are interested in constructive activities because from this we feel we can help other people in other communities to live better lives. Springdale is a laboratory which may help us find important solutions ... We have to get back to the older values of the individual, neighboring and the neighborhood, and Springdale seems to provide an opportune setting for this. We enlist your cooperation in helping us to solve this scientific problem." Vidich and Bensman go on to say that "these commitments were made as a way of selling the project to the townspeople at a time when no one knew what the project would be studying," but to characterize the townspeople as overly "sensitive" (2000: 447, 431) is to pay too little heed to the research team's responsibility for the ultimately disappointed expectations that they generated through overpromising regarding what their research would be like. This can also be a problem within participatory, action, or even applied research in development where the explicit or implicit promise is that participation will lead to (positive) change.

A particularly important aspect of overpromising by researchers relates to assurances about participants remaining anonymous. In the Springdale case, the research team responded to concerns about being identified as the sources of quotations through the reassurance that they were "doing only a statistical report," and when the book turned out to include (in the words of Vidich and Bensman's critics) "clearly recognisable Springdale individuals" (2000: 448, 449), the defence on which they fell back, the use of pseudonyms (for place and individuals) as standard practice in community research, predictably failed to appease. The promise of anonymization may be hard to deliver even if greater care is taken over it than Vidich and Bensman did. According to Gallaher, "A well-thumbed copy of *Plainville, U.S.A.* in the local library has the real names carefully pencilled by the pseudonyms invented by West" (1971: 292). An almost identical story is told about the first Banbury study by Bell, although he adds that in this case the pseudonyms that "have names of real people written against them" have had this done "in many cases wrongly" (2008: 114). Even so, the point remains that anonymity among fellow members of a community being studied is difficult to achieve. It is virtually impossible in smaller communities where the teacher or doctor of a particular village can be only one person.

Overpromising can also occur in relation to what is said, or at least implied, about the benefits of research for members of communities being studied. Oscar Lewis called meetings as part of his re-study of the Mexican village of Tepoztlán and reported how at a particular event "One dignified, elderly Tepoztecan rose and said, 'Many people have come here to study us, but not one of them has helped us'" (1963: xv). Mindful of such expectations that research will produce tangible benefits, Gallaher was aware of the possibility that a researcher can, intentionally or otherwise, give "the impression that he can determine the answers to all of a community's problems … Some Plainvillers, at least for a time, viewed me as such a resource person, and there was the uncomfortable problem of having to convince them to the contrary" (1971: 296). The existence of numerous variations on these themes led Karen O'Reilly to conclude that researchers will search in vain for easy answers to the ethical issues that are raised when people invited to participate in research "might give consent based on false hopes (that you might do some good for them or for the wider community)" (2012: 66). The purpose of research that does not have such benefits, of research that is purely "academic," will not be immediately grasped by everyone. Community members may well reply to requests to participate in research with the question "Is it worth it?" (Clark 2008: 958), especially if their previous experiences are of research that has not produced positive change. That said, Caroline Humphrey's experiences in Siberia provide some reassurance for researchers who feel that the generosity of people being researched far outweighs any benefits that they may receive. Suspected on her first visit in the 1960s of being a spy, over time she earned the farmers' trust and reports how she found it "very moving to be surrounded with the warmth of people to whom one can give so little in return" (1998: xix). Her acknowledgement (1998: xviii) of local people's ability to do better than she had done when constructing genealogies in the first edition of her study (Humphrey 1983) says a good deal about effective ways of tapping into local knowledge.

4.2.5 Sources of fieldwork problems: mutual misunderstanding about the purpose of research

The conclusion to which Vidich and Bensman were led about the controversy that followed the publication of their book was that it encapsulated the tension that exists for researchers between following scientific procedure and pursuing the maintenance of good community relations. Vidich wrote that "the obligation to do scientific justice to one's findings quite often conflicts with the social obligation to please all objects of research." His pejorative description of the practice of modifying information about people in order to secure their anonymity as "fixing" (in Vidich and Bensman 2000: 429) data sets him apart from many other researchers, but his concerns about investigators on projects doing things in order to keep community members happy do have echoes elsewhere. Robert Moore, for example, prefaces his monograph on Peterhead with the warning that "What I have to say in this book will not please everyone" (1982: x), mindful no doubt of the reception of his previous research (with John Rex) into race and housing in Birmingham which some community members felt had "amplified their problems" (Rex and Moore 1981: xvi). The commitment to portray something as it is has the potential to cause friction through the telling of uncomfortable truths. Srinivas et al., refer to the tension inherent in the research situation in which the researcher is interested in the community members' "dirty linen, which he cannot expect them to wash before him" (2002: 5). Research extends to areas that people whose communities are being researched may prefer to keep private.

An important dimension of this issue relates to the status of knowledge about secrets and private matters. Many researchers have lamented their exclusion from communities that they were seeking to study on the grounds that they were suspected of being spies or government investigators (Crow and Pope 2008; Frankenberg 1990: 174; West 1945: ix), or at least of wanting to find out more than is appropriate about matters that are regarded as private by the people they are seeking to research. Frankenberg's sense of being on the outside is neatly captured in his account of how "In my early days in the village I would often climb a hill and look sadly down upon the rows of houses on the housing estate and wonder what went on inside them" (Frankenberg 1969: 16), and it was only after he gained the trust of the villagers that he made headway with his research. Such success in turn generates other concerns amongst researchers. Pierre Bourdieu's *The Weight of the World* begins with his doubts about the consequences of being trusted: "How can we not feel anxious about making *private* words *public*, revealing confidential statements made in the context of a relationship based on trust ... True, everyone we talked to agreed to let us use their statements as we saw fit. But no contract carries as many unspoken conditions as one based on trust" (1999: 1, emphases in original). Different understandings about the purposes to which things said to a researcher will be put underlie many of the cases of dissatisfaction with what researchers do with community members' words.

Another aspect of mutual misunderstanding concerns fieldwork encounters in which the purpose of some research questions is not always

apparent. Mike Savage et al., have described how in their research conducted in Greater Manchester some of their white respondents struggled
with being asked about whether they saw themselves as belonging to a
particular ethnic group. Responses included "A strange question that! ...
I'm not sure about the reasoning around that question" and "What a
bizarre question" (Savage et al. 2005: 184), and sometimes, on the basis
of how the interview had progressed up to that point leading to a hostile
response being anticipated, the question was not asked at all. Similar
experiences of questions being regarded as "strange" have been reported
by other community researchers (Neal and Walters 2006), and in the
light of such experiences West's reputation among Plainville residents
as an aggressive interviewer may be reconsidered. To pursue a question
with research participants who do not see the point of asking it could be
interpreted by interviewees as inappropriately pushy and intrusive and
contravening local norms of politeness which the researcher may not
completely understand at the same time as it is felt by researchers to be
an important part of getting to the heart of the matter being investigated.

4.3 Conclusion

One of the purposes of reviewing the history of a field is that it confirms
that many of the problems encountered by contemporary researchers
are long-standing. This is demonstrated, for example, through Howard
Becker's observation that "Publication of field research findings often
poses ethical problems. The social scientist learns things about the people he studies that may harm them, if made public, either in fact or in
their belief" (1971: 267). The history of responses to such problems is
also instructive. One piece of advice offered by Warwick and Littlejohn
in the light of the reception of the Ashton study is that researchers
should heed the "warning to anyone who tries to comment without
first reaching some agreement with the subjects of the research as to the
appropriate framework of analysis" (1992: 33). This advice does not use
the language of the democratization of research, but it is in the spirit of
a trend in this direction that is embodied in the development of collaborative and participatory approaches to research. Reflecting on his own
and other people's research in Asian villages, Otto van den Muijzenberg
concluded that "new insights in anthropology call for a high degree of
involvement of those studied in the formulation of goals of research
and a stronger representation of their, as opposed to the researcher's,
interpretation" (1997: 344). This perspective involves a significant
change in thinking, away from the idea that "the anthropologist does

fieldwork to advance his career and not to benefit those whom he studies," prompted in part at least by a recognition among researchers that the development of such instrumental relations with informants can leave the latter feeling "sore" and used (Srinivas et al. 2002: 11). As Shah and Ramaswamy note, finding new and more effective ways of "listening to the voices from below" (2002: vii) has been a particularly important innovation in how research in the field is conducted. As people being researched achieve greater voice and have their points of view heard more clearly, the possibility arises that if researched populations continue to feel badly treated, they may in increasing numbers decline invitations to participate in research in the future, or at least request substantial payments.

Among many examples of participatory work that could be cited in the field of community research, Eric Lassiter et al.'s (2004) collaborative ethnography *The Other Side of Middletown* is particularly appropriate to refer to here because it is a re-study for which the auspices were by no means favourable. The community being researched (Muncie, Indiana) had been extensively studied previously over the course of the best part of a century starting with Robert and Helen Lynd's (1929) original *Middletown*, but over that period the town's African American members remained more or less invisible in the many publications that researchers produced. In one way or another they had been edited out. The fact that in collaborative ethnography "ethnographers work with local communities to construct their texts" (Lassiter et al. 2004: 19) means that researchers cannot publish reports on their research that is at variance with community members' understandings in the way that much previous work in the field has been, and in this case it meant that Muncie's African Americans could not be overlooked. It also means that reports on how research has been received by community members can be more readily accepted in this type of publication than those claims made about their reception by authors of more conventional monographs.

The research relationships developed in collaborative approaches have the potential to reduce misunderstandings about the nature and purpose of research. John Dollard's comment that "I expected to lose my friends in Southerntown when this book was published" rested on his belief that "Candid analysis cannot be combined with friendship either in life or social studies" (1957: vii). Dollard's view was that the development of friendships was a necessary part of establishing the trust necessary to gain access to data that would otherwise remain hidden, and it is for these reasons that Srinivas describes "winning the trust and friendship of the people being studied" as "crucial" (1992: 144; see also

Arvidson, this volume). The cultivation of positive relationships among members of the community being studied is a feature of many research reports (e.g. Breman 2007: xviii; Lewis 1976: 6). Gallaher, for example, mentions "withdrawing from a large number of very close friends" (1971: 300) when he left Plainville, and refers to the tension between publication of outputs that contain academic assessments of community life and doing the right thing by friends in that community who made such outputs possible. In his case he did not suffer the accusations of betraying the people of the town that his predecessor West had, but the expectation of loyalty from friends is always going to be tested by publication of analyses of information gathered through friendships. The statement of ethics produced as part of Lassiter et al.'s (2004: 20) research clarifies roles and responsibilities in the research process, and while such documents do not preclude friendships developing between researchers and members of communities being studied, they do make it clear that research relationships involve other, more formal elements than friendship.

Friendships with research participants are also mentioned by Scheper-Hughes, who became conscious of being regarded as a "species of traitor and friend" by some of her fieldwork participants. Her reflections following her return to the community suggest that part of the problem may lie in the practice of anonymization, since it "makes us forget that we owe our anthropological subjects the same degree of courtesy, empathy, and friendship in writing that we generally extend to them face to face in the field, where they are not our subjects but our companions." The "brutally frank sketches of other people's lives as we see them" (Scheper-Hughes 2000: 325, 12–13) are not magically sanitized and made acceptable by anonymization, because the issue at stake involves what is written as well as whether sources of information are identifiable. A further lesson of this and other studies is that there are varying levels of acceptability within communities. Publication of her book saw Scheper-Hughes lose some by no means all of her local friends; her return visit would not have been possible had that been the case. Warwick and Littlejohn (1992: 31) encountered not only critics of the original Ashton study but also people who defended it as an accurate portrayal of the town and its people. And alongside vociferous critics of West's book, Gallaher found other people whose view of it was that it "was *largely* correct as far as it went" (1971: 292, emphasis in original). This should not surprise us. Community research tells us that communities are not homogeneous entities, but are characterized by diversity, including diverse opinions about the value of social research.

References

Becker, H. (1971) "Problems in the publication of field studies," in Vidich, A., Bensman, J. and Stein, M. (eds) *Reflection on Community Studies* (New York: Harper and Row), pp. 267–84.

Bell, C. (1977) "Reflections on the Banbury restudy," in Bell, C. and Newby, H. (eds) *Doing Sociological Research* (London: George Allen and Unwin), pp. 47–62.

Bell, C. (2008) "The second Banbury study," *International Journal of Social Research Methodology*, 11(2): 113–6.

Bell, C. and Newby, H. (1971) *Community Studies* (London: George Allen and Unwin).

Bourdieu, P. (1999) *The Weight of the World: Social Suffering in Contemporary Society* (Cambridge: Polity Press).

Breman, J. (1997) "The village in focus," in Breman, J., Kloos, P. and Saith, A. (eds) *The Village in Asia Revisited* (Delhi: Oxford University Press), pp. 15–75.

Breman, J. (2007) *The Poverty Regime in Village India: Half a Century of Work and Life at the Bottom of the Rural Economy in South Gujarat* (New Delhi: Oxford University Press).

Breman, J., Kloos, P. and Saith, A. (1997) "Introduction," in Breman, J., Kloos, P. and Saith, A. (eds) *The Village in Asia Revisited* (Delhi: Oxford University Press), pp. 1–14.

Bryson, L. and Winter, I. (1999) *Social Change, Suburban Lives: An Australian Newtown 1960s to 1990s* (St Leonards NSW: Allen and Unwin).

Burawoy, M. (2003) "Revisits: An outline of a theory of reflexive ethnography," *American Sociological Review* 68: 645–79.

Clark, T. (2008) "We're over-researched here! Exploring accounts of research fatigue within qualitative research engagements," *Sociology*, 42(5): 953–70.

Cornwell, J. (1984) *Hard-Earned Lives: Accounts of Health and Illness from East London* (London: Tavistock).

Crow, G. (2012) "Community re-studies: Lessons and prospects," *Sociological Review*, 60(3): 405–20.

Crow, G. and Pope, C. (2008) "The future of the research relationship," *Sociology*, 42(5): 813–19.

Dempsey, K. (1990) *Smalltown: A Study of Social Inequality, Cohesion and Belonging* (Melbourne: Oxford University Press).

Dennis, N., Henriques, F. and Slaughter, C. (1969) *Coal Is Our Life: An Analysis of a Yorkshire Mining Community*, Second edition (London: Tavistock).

Djurfeldt, G., Lindberg, S. and Rajagopal, A. (1997) "Coming back to Thaiyur: Health and medicine in a twenty-five years perspective," in Breman, J., Kloos, P. and Saith, A. (eds) *The Village in Asia Revisited* (Delhi: Oxford University Press), pp. 175–98.

Dollard, J. (1957) *Caste and Class in a Southern Town*, Third edition (New York: Doubleday Anchor Books).

Elias, N. (1978) *What Is Sociology?* (London: Hutchinson).

Elias, N. and Scotson, J. (1994) *The Established and the Outsiders: A Sociological Enquiry into Community Problems* (London: Sage).

Frankenberg, R. (1969) *Communities in Britain* (Harmondsworth: Penguin).

Frankenberg, R. (1990) *Village on the Border: A Social Study of Religion, Politics and Football in a North Wales Community* (Prospect Heights, Illinois: Waveland Press).

Freeman, D. (1984) *Margaret Mead and Samoa: The Making and Unmaking of an Anthropological Myth* (Harmondsworth: Penguin).

Gallaher, A. (1961) *Plainville Fifteen Years Later* (New York: Columbia University Press).

Gallaher, A. (1971) "Plainville: The twice-studied town," in Vidich, A., Bensman, J. and Stein, M. (eds) *Reflections on Community Studies* (New York: Harper and Row), pp. 285–303.

Guijt, I. and Shah, M. (eds) (1998) The Myth of Community: Gender issues in participatory development. (Rugby: Intermediate Technology Publications Limited).

Humphrey, C. (1983) *Karl Marx Collective: Economy, Society and Religion in a Siberian Collective Farm* (Cambridge: Cambridge University Press).

Humphrey, C. (1998) *Marx Went Away – But Karl Stayed Behind* (Ann Arbor: University of Michigan Press).

Kloos, P. (1997) "Restudies in anthropology: Modalities, limitations and alternatives," in Breman, J., Kloos, P. and Saith, A. (eds) *The Village in Asia Revisited* (Delhi: Oxford University Press), pp. 229–46.

Lassiter, L., Goodall, H., Campbell, E. and Johnson, M. (eds) (2004) *The Other Side of Middletown: Exploring Muncie's African American Community* (Walnut Creek, CA: AltaMira Press).

Lewis, O. (1963) *Life in a Mexican Village: Tepoztlán Revisited* (Urbana: University of Illinois Press).

Lewis, O. (1976) *Five Families: Mexican Case Studies in the Culture of Poverty* (London: Souvenir Press).

Lynd, R. and Lynd, H. (1929) *Middletown: A Study in Contemporary American Culture* (New York: Harcourt Brace).

Moore, R. (1982) *The Social Impact of Oil: The Case of Peterhead* (London: Routledge and Kegan Paul).

Muijzenberg, O. Van Den (1997) "Philippine lowland villages revisited," in Breman, J., Kloos, P. and Saith, A. (eds) *The Village in Asia Revisited* (Delhi: Oxford University Press), pp. 313–52.

Neal, S. and Walters, S. (2006) "Strangers asking strange questions: A methodological narrative of researching belonging and identity in English rural communities," *Journal of Rural Studies*, 22: 177–89.

O'Reilly, K. (2012) *Ethnographic Methods*, Second edition (London: Routledge).

Pahl, R. E. (1968) "The rural-urban continuum," in Pahl, R. E. (ed.) *Readings in Urban Sociology* (Oxford: Pergamon), pp. 263–97.

Payne, G. (1996) "Imagining the community: Some reflections on the community study as a method," in Stina Lyon, E. and Busfield, J. (eds) *Methodological Imaginations* (Basingstoke: Macmillan), pp. 17–33.

Platt, J. (1971) *Social Research in Bethnal Green* (London: Macmillan).

Rex, J. and Moore, R. (1981) *Race, Community and Conflict: A study of Sparkbrook* (Oxford: Oxford University Press).

Savage, M., Bagnall, G. and Longhurst, B. (2005) *Globalization and Belonging* (London: Sage).

Scheper-Hughes, N. (2000) *Saints, Scholars and Schizophrenics: Mental Illness in Rural Ireland* (Berkeley: University of California Press).

Seale, C. (1999) *The Quality of Qualitative Research* (London: Sage).

Going Back to Re-study Communities 75

Shah, A. and Ramaswamy, E. (2002) "Preface to the second edition," in Srinivas, M., Shah, A. and Ramaswamy, E. (eds) *The Fieldworker and the Field: Problems and Challenges in Sociological Investigation*, Second edition (New Delhi: Oxford University Press), pp. v–x.

Srinivas, M. (1992) *On Living through a Revolution and Other Essays* (Delhi: Oxford University Press).

Srinivas, M., Shah, A. and Ramaswamy, E. (eds) (2002) *The Fieldworker and the Field: Problems and Challenges in Sociological Investigation*, Second edition (New Delhi: Oxford University Press).

Stacey, M. (1960) *Tradition and Change: A Study of Banbury* (Oxford: Oxford University Press).

Vidich, A. and Bensman, J. (2000) *Small Town in Mass Society: Class, Power and Religion in a Rural Community*, Revised edition (Urbana and Chicago: University of Illinois Press).

Warwick, D. and Littlejohn, G. (1992) *Coal, Capital and Culture: A Sociological Analysis of Mining Communities in West Yorkshire* (London: Routledge).

West, J. (1945) *Plainville, U.S.A.* (New York: Columbia University Press).

Young, M. and Willmott, P. (1962) *Family and Kinship in East London* (Harmondsworth: Penguin).

5

Taking a Well-being Approach to Fisheries Research: Insights from a Sri Lankan Fishing Village and Relevance for Sustainable Fisheries

Sarah Coulthard, Lahiru Sandaruwan, Nasheera Paranamana and Dilanthi Koralgama

5.1 Introduction – taking a well-being approach to fisheries research

Over the last decade, the concept of *well-being* has experienced a surge of interest in international development debate about how it might offer a holistic, people-centred, and perhaps more meaningful interpretation of development and progress, which moves us beyond narrow economic measures such as gross domestic product (GDP) (Gough and McGregor 2007; White 2010; NEF 2011). Bridging this interest with environmental concerns, debates have expanded to question how well-being might be relevant, and applicable, to natural resource management and environmental sustainability (Duraiappah 2004; Armitage et al. 2012). In 2005, the influential series of reports which formed the Millennium Ecosystem Assessment focussed international attention on the ways in which human well-being is dependent upon a functioning and productive natural environment, bringing the term "well-being" to the centre of sustainability debates. However, the reports also recognized that there is a significant gap in understanding around how ecosystem services, defined as the *benefits* derived from the environment (Millennium Ecosystem Assessment 2005), relate to the experience of human well-being, and how that experience itself might be understood (Carpenter et al. 2006, 2009).

Recognizing that the complexity and ambiguity of the term can make it difficult to put into practice (Gasper 2004; McGregor et al. 2009), substantial research efforts have sought to operationalize and practically apply the concept of well-being so that it is useful for a range of development and sustainability policies (Gough and McGregor 2007; Copestake

2008; Camfield and Guillen-Royo 2010; Coulthard 2012a). Debates on well-being have stimulated a rethinking of how poverty is experienced, and helped to create a space for people's own voices in shaping how their lives might be understood. For example, a well-being framing was used as part of the Young Lives project[1] to explore children's experiences of poverty across four different countries. By collecting information on children's values, aspirations, and their own understandings of well-being, the Young Lives project gained important insights such as the impact of poverty on feelings of self-esteem, respect, a sense of optimism, and social inclusion. Using Young Lives project data, Camfield and Tafere (2009) further describe significant differences in how children understand a "good life," in particular between girls and boys, and between children from rural and urban areas. These detailed understandings can provide important context-specific information to inform development interventions seeking to enhance children's well-being. Researching well-being amongst adults in Thailand, McGregor et al. (2009) devised individualized measures to capture a person's satisfaction with criteria for well-being that they report as being most important to them. The authors argue that measuring satisfaction with self-determined criteria for "living well" has capacity to contribute to more effective and democratic forms of governance in the development process. Progress too has been made with the evolution of well-being indicators capable of measuring a wide range of variables to monitor development progress, see for example the OECD's "Better Life Initiative."[2]

Within this flourishing research arena, a number of scholars have drawn on the context of sustainable fisheries as a useful bounded context within which to explore how marine resources relate to human well-being, and how a better understanding of that relationship might contribute to fisheries policy (Coulthard et al. 2011; Daw et al. 2011; Weeratunge et al. 2013). Coulthard (2012a) argues that the concept of well-being could contribute to the goal of sustainability in fisheries (and natural resource management more generally) in two ways: first, by providing a deeper form of social impact assessment, capable of illuminating some of the social and psychological impacts of fisheries decline on affected fishing communities, recognizing that these factors are often overlooked and usurped by economic and biological assessments (Symes and Phillipson 2009; Urquhart et al. 2011). Second, it may give new insights into human behaviour, if behaviour can be understood as the pursuit of well-being within the context of fishing, and the social values and meanings that frame fishing as an occupation. These two assessments of well-being – the extent to which it is experienced, and how the pursuit of it might shape behaviour – are different but closely connected. The former considers well-being as a measurable *outcome* for people; the latter recognizes well-being as a *process*, which emphasizes what people do, and the choices they make, in their pursuit of well-being outcomes (McGregor et al. 2007; Coulthard 2012a). Drawing from Dasgupta (1990) and Sen's (1999) discussions on well-being, McGregor et al. (2007) outline how these two assessments – outcomes and processes – represent two distinct ways of thinking about "the person" in social science literature. Outcomes place emphasis on "beings" – what a person can be – relating to welfare outcomes, life satisfaction, and happiness; Processes, on the other hand, emphasize "doings" – the freedoms and rights which people experience (or are denied) to make choices about how to live their lives, and what they are capable of doing with those freedoms, as articulated in Sen's discussions on capabilities (see Coulthard 2012a for further discussion). Underlying these debates is the implicit assumption that people do actually pursue well-being for themselves and their families and that this serves as a key influence on their behaviour (Deci and Ryan 2000; McGregor 2007). As McGregor and Sumner (2010: 1) posit: "How people relate to others and what people feel they can do or can be play a strong role in what people will actually do and be able to be." The assumption that people pursue well-being is a defining feature of a well-being perspective, and is based on the argument that people, even those living in dire circumstances with very little opportunity, are still conscious of how they are doing in life and have some capacity to achieve elements of well-being as they perceive it (Gough and Clark 2006; McGregor 2007). This focus on what people "can" have, do, and feel, rather than only what they lack (through poverty analysis for example), is arguably a more rounded and respectful approach (ibid., McGregor and Sumner 2010; White 2010) that explicitly addresses those factors which facilitate, and inhibit people's freedoms to choose, and capabilities to act (Sen 1999). This assumption is significant for fisheries management. As Coulthard (2012a) argues "If we frame what people do, and how they pursue their aspirations in terms of well-being, it broadens the range of motivating factors that become visible to us, as resource managers, who seek to understand and influence peoples' behaviour."

Within the context of fisheries, recent research has emphasized the need for conceptual and methodological innovation that can holistically capture and assess the full range of impacts of declining fisheries and management interventions which seek to stem the decline on those people who are most affected (Coulthard 2009; Urquhart et al. 2013). Ultimately, an understanding of the linkages between fisheries and well-being may enhance the scope for policymakers to integrate their concern for sustainable oceans with continued welfare of fisheries-dependent societies, contributing to long-standing calls for improved integration of conservation and poverty reduction agendas (Adams et al. 2004; Sachs et al. 2009).

In this chapter, we use a recently developed framework for *social well-being* which, we suggest, goes some way to meeting the methodological challenges described above. We begin with an outline of the three-dimensional well-being framework developed at the University of Bath, and then describe its empirical application as part of a recent research project, which sought to explore how fisheries relate to well-being in a Sri Lankan fishing community.[3] We detail methods used to explore each dimension of well-being and discuss preliminary data and findings. We conclude with a discussion of emerging insights, and suggest possible contributions to practical policy recommendations in Sri Lankan fisheries.

5.2 A three-dimensinal framework for researching well-being

The ESRC research group Wellbeing in Developing Countries (WeD),[4] based at the University of Bath until 2007, established a framework and suite of methods to explore both objective and subjective dimensions of well-being, arguing that both the objective circumstances of people along with their subjective evaluation of their quality of life are essential parts of a holistic vision of well-being (Gough, McGregor and Camfield 2007). Their framework also incorporates a strong social/relational dimension, recognizing that well-being is a dynamic phenomenon that is framed by complex and dynamic social relations with others (ibid., Gough and McGregor 2007; Camfield et al. 2009). Drawing from several theoretical frameworks, including Doyal and Gough's (1991) Theory of Human Need (THN), and various quality of life approaches (Camfield and Skevington 2008), a definition of well-being emerged as;

> a state of being with others, which arises where *human needs are met*, where one can *act meaningfully* to pursue one's goals, and where one can enjoy a satisfactory *quality of life*.
>
> (McGregor 2007)

In this definition, three interrelated dimensions are taken into account: (1) a *material* dimension which considers the *resources* people have and the extent to which their *human needs* are met; (2) a *relational* dimension to address how people act, through relationships with others, to pursue well-being; and (3) a *cognitive* dimension which accounts for the level of satisfaction with the quality of life they achieve (McGregor 2007: 317). All three of these dimensions must be considered in relation to each other to provide an adequate assessment of well-being (McGregor and Sumner 2010; CMEPSP 2009).

McGregor (2007: 317) breaks these dimensions down into three basic categories:

(1) what a person has and does not have;
(2) what they can and cannot do with what they have; and
(3) how they think and feel about what they have and can do.

The WeD group operationalized this framework for well-being through a comprehensive methods tool kit.[5] The remainder of this chapter details the adaptation and application of *three* of the available tools to a Sri Lankan fisheries context: (1) a *human needs assessment* which seeks to determine the extent to which human needs are being met, or denied; (2) a *Governance Relationship Assessment (GRA)*[6] which explores social relationships that are important (specifically) for fishing behaviour and the degree of satisfaction that people report with significant relationships; and (3) a *quality of life measure* which assesses the respondent's quality of life according to self-determined criteria. Since this research is still in the early stages of data analysis, we present only a small subsample of data collected under each method, all from male household heads.[7] We are therefore illustrative rather than conclusive in our interpretation of these initial findings, and only infer some of the possible emergent messages for fisheries management.

Our study area is Rekewa Lagoon, located in the Southern Province of Sri Lanka. Rekewa is home to several important boat-landing sites, where a mix of mechanized boats (with small outboard engines) and traditional (non-mechanized) craft operates (Community Profile Report (CP1 2012)[8]). Marine fishing and fish trading are the main sources of employment in the area, but additional livelihood opportunities are available from fishing in the lagoon, the growing tourism sector, turtle conservation initiatives, and vehicle hiring (three-wheelers) for transportation. Fishing is predominantly a male occupation, with women being involved in net repairing and cleaning, ornamental fish trade, handicrafts, and buffalo rearing to produce curd and fresh milk (ibid.).

5.3 Assessment of basic human needs

According to the WeD definition, the first component of well-being arises where *human needs are met.* Drawing from Doyal and Gough's THN (1991), basic human needs are defined as the life essentials which, if denied, will result in *serious harm,* of an "objective" kind, to the person. Gough (2003: 8) defines harm as "fundamental disablement in the pursuit of one's vision of the good" or "an impediment to successful social participation." The assessment of needs therefore provides a critical threshold point for assessing social impact – if there is evidence that needs are unmet, serious harm to the person will result. Doyal and Gough's (1991: 73) Theory of Human Need provides us with a universally applicable theory, which recognizes two *basic human needs* "health" and "personal autonomy." It emphasizes survival, human action, and social participation, which: "[all] humans must satisfy in order to avoid the serious harm of fundamentally impaired participation in their form of life." The two basic needs are fulfilled through satisfaction of *11 universal intermediate needs (or needs satisfiers)*: Adequate nutritional food and water; Adequate protective housing; A non-hazardous work environment; A non-hazardous physical environment; Appropriate health care; Security in childhood; Significant primary relationships; Physical security; Economic security; Safe birth control and child-bearing; and Basic education.

The THN establishes this set of intermediate needs as universal, and thus comparable between cultures, providing an "objective" indicator of welfare regardless of social and cultural relativism. In line with Nussbaum's work on universal capabilities (Nussbaum 2000), Doyal and Gough (1991) advocate that this universality of needs is powerful in that it contributes a set of "basic constitutional principles that should be respected and implemented by the governments of all nations, as a bare minimum of what respect for human dignity requires" (Nussbaum 2000: 5, as cited in Gough 2003: 5). THN goes on to state that whilst their list of intermediate needs provides a universalist framework, the ways in which needs are satisfied are indeed culturally variable (Gough 2004). For example, as Lavers (2007: 7) describes:

Although there are many different types of cuisine in different cultures that can satisfy the requirement for nutritional daily food, there is a universal satisfier characteristic of a minimum number of calories a day for a specified group of people required to avoid detrimental effects to an individual's health.

THN therefore creates "a conceptual space" where a universal list of needs is possible, but which recognizes the importance of cultural context in how those needs are met in practice: "The universal can guide but never dictate the local vision of what must be done to achieve well-being in specific contexts" (Gough and Clark 2006: 14).

5.4 Exploring needs and establishing thresholds

An adapted *Human Needs Assessment*[9] *survey* was administered to each household head, enquiring as to the experience of themselves and other household members with regard to their ability to meet basic needs. Questions were structured so as to capture information on actual experiences, how people had acted in response to that experience, and their reflections on future possibilities (see Figure 5.1 for an example). It is recognized that interviewing the (male) household head only is an insufficient way to assess the needs of an entire household. For example, women may be better placed to comment on whether a household is meeting its food security needs, whilst opinions on more psychological needs, such as feeling respected, can vary significantly between different household members and depend upon one's own individual reflection. Despite these short comings however, the needs assessment does provide an initial baseline data source about the household, which can be triangulated with other data (for example interviews with a wider range of household members). Careful attention was also given to ensure the questions could answer the criteria set by the needs *threshold determinants* (Figure 5.1).

Drawing from the THN, which provides universal categories for human needs assessment, the process of setting specific criteria to objectively

Economic Security.
[Experience]
During the last year, have you or any member of your household experienced an emergency or a major problem where you needed to borrow money?

Yes ☐ No ☐

[Action]
Were you able to borrow the money that you needed?

Yes ☐ No ☐

[Subjective assessment on future possibilities]
If, in the next year, you suddenly needed to borrow money for an emergency, how confident are you that you would be able to do so ?

It would not bepossible ☐
It might be possible ☐
It would be possible ☐

Figure 5.1 Needs category: economic security

assess whether a need is met, or unmet, takes account of social and cultural context. Table 5.1 illustrates the outcome of discussion with fishers and academics in Sri Lanka which established locally relevant criteria/ indicators by which needs could be defined as being unmet. Using a baseline threshold of "harm" for each needs category, a set of conditions was agreed upon when, if materialized, we would *reasonably expect* that a person would experience significant harm following Gough's definition outlined above. Hence, our understanding of harm thresholds emerges from a consensus generated by people living in the same social and cultural context in which the study was located, but is structured by the universal categories of basic human needs provided by the THN[10] (see McGregor, McKay and Velazco 2007 for a similar approach).

Whilst the results in Table 5.1 are based on a small sub-sample of the data, and are therefore only discussed here in an illustrative manner, there are several emergent findings worth noting. We can see, for example, a majority of households are reported as not meeting their basic need for *education*. Given the existence of free primary education for all in Sri Lanka and the availability of primary schools in the vicinity (CP1 2012), this result is initially surprising. However, within fishing communities, it is often documented that children skip school from an early age to start fishing with their fathers (Coulthard 2008; Maddox et al. 2009). This practice has sometimes resulted in an observably lower literacy rate in fishing communities compared with other occupational groups (George and Domi 2002) (although it should be noted that there is substantial variation in education levels in fishing communities (see Maddox 2006). Whilst further analysis of the data is required here, our results may signify the presence of other barriers to accessing school, or a lower prioritization of primary education amongst fishing families, perhaps replaced instead by values surrounding the importance of learning fishing skills, and contributing to household income from an early age (the age range of fishers interviewed spans from 13 to 80 years, n=150). Furthermore, cultural meanings attached to fishing, such as a coming of age, and being able to participate socially with other fishers, may also influence the start of fishing from an early age. Britton and Coulthard (2013), for example, describe how fishing from a young age in Northern Ireland was popular and considered an advantage or "step up" in life (at least, in the past when fisheries were profitable). As Westaway (2009: 84) notes from an exploration of formal schooling in Ugandan fishing communities:

> schooling does not necessarily mean success in a fishing community, and fishing communities remain places where people who are

Table 5.1 Percentage of sample with unmet needs in the different needs categories

Needs category	Needs indicators: *For each category, needs are defined as being "unmet" if the respondent reports one or more of the following situations.*	Percentage of sample with UNMET needs (n=20)
Economy security	No access to savings facility, No access to credit in an emergency	30
Food security	Suffered a shortage of staple food over the last year	5
Safe drinking water	An UNSAFE drinking water source	0
Sufficient housing	A house that doesn't provide protection from weather A house that doesn't provide security for persons and assets	0
Sufficient sanitation	No access to toilet facilities	0
Education	Household members over 16 years age who did not receive a full 10 years of schooling (6–16) Children under age of 16 are not attending school	80
Health	Having been ill/injured and DID NOT receive treatment when needed (due to lack of availability, cost, or inadequate knowledge) Did not receive basic vaccinations If the household has children but mothers did NOT receive any pre- or post-natal care	15
Physical security	Having been subject to physical violence	15
Emotional relationships	Having NO ONE to go to for help with a problem Having NO friends	0
Social participation	Having no involvement in social organizations Having not participated in ANY community activities	0
Respect	NO ONE comes to them for advice or help Holds no positions of responsibility Having no involvement in household decision-making Having no involvement in community decision-making	20

not formally educated come to find work. People's success is often determined by business acumen and hard work rather than by qualifications.

This initial finding speaks well to Sen's (1999: 74) writings on capabilities, in that well-being cannot be understood only in terms of the resources a person can access (a school in this case), but rather must be understood in terms of the choices that people make to live the life that they have reason to value. The focus, therefore, is placed on the freedoms that people can exercise (or are denied) in choosing to send their children to school. An alternative explanation may of course lie in the setting of the indicator criteria – in that all household members need to show a *minimum level* of 10 years of schooling for the need for education to be met. Many of the older household members may not meet this need, given that access to schooling has increased over the last 20 years in Sri Lanka and there have been changes in social values around primary education (Ministry of Education 2011). Hence, our current indicator set may not reflect recent changes around the value of education, and may need to disaggregate between the total number of household members who lack primary education, and the number of children currently not in school. Evidence to support this is found in Maddox's (2006) global review of literature on education in fishing communities, which noted that while formal schooling is often difficult to access, there are usually high levels of motivation amongst parents to send their children to school (see also Westaway et al. 2009).

The need for economic security, unmet by 30 per cent of household (HH) respondents is determined by two criteria – no access to savings and no access to credit in an emergency. Both criteria were deemed as being important to avoid harm and to achieve economic security, in the context of living with an unpredictable fishing income that is entirely dependent upon an unreliable (and often dwindling) catch. The need to access credit in an emergency is especially problematic. The lack of access to banking facilities among poor fishing households in particular opens up space for fish traders and other middlemen to establish credit services in exchange for long-term secured fish catches, which frequently can lead to "boat tying," a common practice in fisheries where a number of boats pledge their catch for a set price to a trader in return for a loan. Boat-tying agreements, and their associated debts, often lead to the exploitation of fishers who are frequently forced to sell their catches at a reduced market rate until the loan is repaid. This is discussed further in the next section of this chapter, where we triangulate with findings from the Governance

Relationship Assessment (GRA). Interestingly, the need for social participation and emotional relationships is met in all households within the sample, which may indicate the strong sense of community and social cohesion within fishing communities in Sri Lanka and more generally (Bavinck 2001), supported by a common identity and livelihood (all respondents are Sinhala and Buddhist fishers). For example, all respondents reported their involvement in temple activities, festivals, and holy days, which provide important opportunities for social participation.

5.5   Governance Relationship Assessment

The centrality of relationships to the experience of well-being is frequently highlighted (Gough and McGregor 2007; Devine et al. 2008; White 2009), and emphasizes well-being as a process: "something that happens in relationship – between the collective and the individual; the local and the global; the people and the state" (White 2010: 168). As White (2010) points out, this has implications for how development interventions are carried out, and necessitates a better understanding of how different relationships work to support, or deny, a person's experience of well-being (ibid.).

The GRA tool does not form part of the WeD toolkit, but is an adaptation of the WeD Quality of Life methodology (see Section 5) which was used in this research to identify the range of social relationships that are important in achieving well-being, with a particular focus on how relationships influence fishing behaviour. The term "relationship" is purposefully broad to capture any interaction that the interviewee perceives as having a significant influence over his/her fishing behaviour. Administered as part of a semi-structured interview, fishers were asked to identify the *"most important relationships with other people that affected their lives as a fisher,"* explaining each choice. After a few minutes of open response, fishers were also prompted using a "relational landscape tool" (Figure 5.2) which was effective in structuring the discussion and eliciting the wide range of different relationships that can influence people's lives. Once a list was exhausted, fishers were then asked to select the *top three most important relationships that influenced their fishing decisions*, again explaining each selection. Fishers were then asked to score their *level of satisfaction* with each relationship using a Likert scale of 1–5, where 1 is the worst they could imagine, and 5 is exactly as they would like it to be.

The development of the GRA stemmed from the relational component of well-being, which queries how people exert agency and "act meaningfully," or are restricted from acting, through relationships with others in

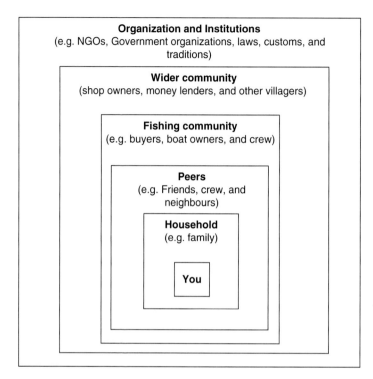

Figure 5.2   Relational landscape[11]

their pursuit of well-being. We use the term GRA drawing from Kooiman et al.'s (2005: 17) theory on *interactive governance* which places emphasis on "the whole of interactions taken to solve societal problems and to create societal opportunities" – or in other words, how relationships with others govern what people can do. It also relates to Giddens' (1984) and Long and van der Ploeg's (1994) debates around the social nature of agency, where agency is understood as the capability of a person to act and make a difference, which can only materialize through relationships with others (see also Coulthard 2012b for a discussion on agency and resilience in relation to fisheries). The GRA method facilitated an insightful understanding of the variety of relationships that affect fishing decisions. Documenting the level of satisfaction that people feel about significant relationships further unpacks the degree of control that people have in transforming their resource access into different well-being outcomes. Some relationships are positive, and can contribute to well-being through, for example, creating jobs and income, friendship and respect, whilst others are perceived as negative relationships, such as conflicted or exploitative interactions which instill a sense of injustice and anger. Figure 5.3 shows preliminary results taken from a sample of 10 fishermen.

Figure 5.3 gives a reminder of the wide range of different social relationships that can have an influence over a person's fishing behaviour. This, in itself, is useful for fisheries management which often primarily focusses on economic incentive and the size of catch to explain fisher decision-making and behaviour (Salas et al. 2004; Branch et al. 2006). Whilst financial drivers are of course important, they are not the complete story (see Nielsen and Mathiesen 2003). The GRA tool seems to offer a quick and direct means of gaining insight into which relationships matter the most, facilitating greater recognition of the complexity of social relationships that fishers themselves state influence their own behaviour.

Figure 5.3 shows that respondents reported a high (average) satisfaction score for relationships with crew, onshore workers, and family members. This is supported by comments made by fishermen, the first of which describes his satisfaction with his family and how it relates to his fishing, and the second hints at the importance of collective action amongst fishers:

> Unity and peace of the family is essential for a good life. Then only a fisher can do his work correctly. Fortunately I have a very good wife and mother in law. They help me lot.
>
> (Lahiru, Rekewa fisherman, July 2012[12])

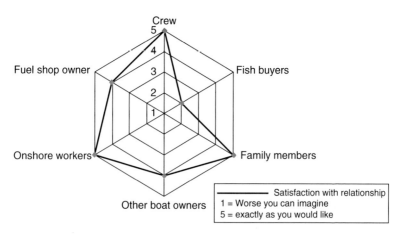

Figure 5.3   Relationships stated by fishermen as being important for fishing and average scored satisfaction (n=10)

Crew satisfaction is also of vital importance to fisher well-being, especially for boat owners who depend upon a reliable and trustworthy crew in order to function. Onshore workers play an essential role too in assisting in the landing of the boat. Since there is no harbour in Rekewa, fishers are entirely reliant on help from each other, and other onshore workers, to pull the boat on land, clean the nets, and to sort the catch. Onshore activities provide an important livelihood for many retired fishers and women and, as such, act as an important form of social security for the more vulnerable in society.

Lower satisfaction scores were found with "other boat owners" and "fish traders," which highlights an interesting conundrum facing many fishers in Rekewa. Other boat owners were often discussed in a positive light, in that there is a strong sense of congeniality at sea, where fishers look out for each other's safety and are reliant on good communication around possible hazards. However, this sense of collaboration is also marred by inevitable competition between boat owners and, in some cases, jealousy, secrecy, and conflict (especially between different fishing gear users), which may explain a lower satisfaction rating (see Figure 5.3). The relationship between fisher and fish traders is similarly double-edged. Traders are vital actors in the life of a fisher – they provide a market for catch once landed, and can provide important benefits such as access to credit (note that the need for economic security, indicated by "no access to credit in an emergency," is unmet in many of the households interviewed (see Table 5.1)). Traders are also frequently the first to raise the alarm when boats fail to return from a fishing trip, since they are onshore awaiting the produce. However, the relationship with traders can also be difficult and often exploitative. *Boat tying* is a practice common throughout fisheries (Amarasinghe 1989; Platteau 1992) where an advance loan is given by a trader in return for a pledged sale of the entire catch of a boat at a set price, for a period of time (often several years), or until the loan is repaid. The set price for fish is usually far below the market value, which can restrict the capacity of fishers to trade in a free market acquiring the best prices for their produce.

Within debates on sustainable fisheries, a great deal of interest revolves around what influences fisher decisions to exit beleaguered fisheries and take up alternative livelihoods (Cinner et al. 2008; Daw et al. 2012) and yet, the majority of efforts to reduce fishing capacity do not focus on the ways that social relationships enable or restrict exit from fisheries. Here, we can see how a range of relationships necessitate a fisher to keep fishing. Relationships of exploitation and indebtedness to fish traders dictate that a fisher must sell his catch until his debt to the trader is relieved; relationships of obligation to shore workers and crew may further influence a boat owner's decision to keep fishing, in light of the dependency of others (often relatives and friends) on his continued work. The GRA tool brings our attention to these significant influences and facilitates improved understanding of the viability of exit strategies and alternative livelihoods in particular contexts.

5.6   Measuring subjective well-being – the "Global Person Generated Index"

The third dimension of well-being "where one can enjoy a satisfactory *quality of life*" focusses on how people think and feel about the quality of life they are able to achieve. The WeD group adapted an existing method used in health studies to measure patient quality of life (QoL) (Ruta et al. 1994) to create the "Global Person Generated Index" (GPGI) – an "individualised" measure that uses a mix of open-ended questions and scoring to establish a person's satisfaction with the areas of life that are most important to them. In parallel with the GRA outlined above, it includes a process where respondents are asked to nominate up to five areas that they consider important to their lives and explain their importance, and to then score each to indicate their level of satisfaction (where 1 represents "the worst you can imagine" and 5 represents "exactly as you would like it to be"). Figure 5.4 highlights the well-being domains stated by fishermen in Rekewa lagoon as being important for living a good life, alongside average satisfaction scores.[13]

As Figure 5.4 shows, emerging important domains for life satisfaction, which fishers seem to be fairly satisfied with, include income, religious devotion, and having good neighbours. Religion is clearly an important part of Buddhist life and has been frequently linked to well-being (Ellison 1991; Jha 2011).

There was dissatisfaction with the domains of "community behaviour," "health," "fishing gears," and access to "vehicles/transportation." Explanations from the interviews (see below) suggest that dissatisfaction with community relates to a lack of respect from younger generations and community violence, which is often fuelled by alcohol abuse.

> Liquor addiction is a crucial factor that decides the direction of a fisher's life. Most of the fishers think liquor and drugs are essential items for their lives. They justify it, as drugs and liquor are mental and physical pain killers. They take liquor to forget their problems, but liquor and drugs decay their entire lives.
>
> (Buddhika, Rekewa Fisherman, July 2012)

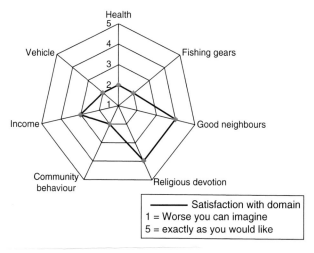

Figure 5.4 Well-being domains described by fishermen as being important for living well (n=10)

> Some fishers forget manners when they are intoxicated ... they make conflict with others, and the community do not respect non-decent members ... When people take liquor by exceeding their limit they forget manners and they do bad things for others – then he makes enemies.
>
> (Sanjeewa, Rekewa Fisherman, July 2012)

The problem of excessive alcohol consumption is common in fishing communities worldwide (Westaway et al. 2007; Busby 1999). These comments around alcohol and violence in Rekewa can also potentially be connected to findings in part 1 (Table 5.1) which demonstrates that people's basic need for physical security (indicated by experience of physical violence) is denied in a significant number of cases.

Dissatisfaction with access to vehicles and transportation reflects a lack of public transport options throughout Rekewa, which presents a significant barrier for transporting fish to market, as well as substantial transportation costs (hiring three-wheelers) for many households. Having a vehicle can open up opportunities to diversify from fishing into fish trading, and can also mean the avoidance of exploitation by middlemen traders.

Fishing gear inadequacy is another aspect of dissatisfaction. Many fishers (as is commonly found throughout fishing communities) aspire to enhanced fishing capacity; larger boats that can cover wide expanses of ocean and more efficient gears. Of most surprise, however, was the dissatisfaction with health, given that health care is relatively good in Sri Lanka, and the availability of nearby hospitals and free health care access. The poor *quality* of national health care services was sometimes mentioned in interviews, however, fishers in the area also suffer substantially from back pain and damage to limbs caused by the hauling of boats onto the beach (see excerpts below), and it is this aspect of ill-health which seems to dominate:

> In my young age I was not concerned about my health ... I would drag the boat to land without asking help of others. Due to this malpractice my vertebra column is now damaged and I have severe back pain. Therefore, I cannot fish in the deep sea. I cannot be satisfied about my health. I have to work at least twenty years more until my son can do a job. But already my strength has deteriorated and I have become a patient. Doctors advise me to take bed rest for at least six months. If I do that, no one will give money for my family. My family totally depend on me therefore I have to work hard continuously without concern of my pain.
>
> (Ishan, Rekewa fisherman, July 2012)

The significance of poor health was also a conclusion made by Eppinga (2009) from her research in the nearby Sri Lankan fishing community of Kalametiya, which found that fishing-related "back problems" were a major source of ill-being, and were in fact worsening since a higher volume of boats landing at the beach necessitated fishers to pull their boats further up the beach.

5.7   Linking well-being to fisheries policy

This chapter has outlined a range of findings and early interpretations that have emerged from applying a three-dimensional well-being approach to a Sri Lankan fishing community. The methods discussed unpack major components of well-being, defined as "a state of being with others, which arises where *human needs are met*, where one can *act meaningfully* to pursue one's goals, and where one can enjoy a satisfactory *quality of life*" (McGregor 2007).This focus on human needs and areas where they are being unmet (such as economic security and education), the range of relationships that can facilitate or restrict the pursuit of well-being (such as the complex role of fish traders), and subjective perspectives on well-being according to criteria set by fishermen themselves, provides a powerful multi-dimensional vision of a person's quality of life. Whilst well-being may at first appear an abstract concept, which is difficult to put into practice, our experience of discussing the nature of well-being with fishermen in Sri Lanka revealed that the concept was easily understood by respondents, and generally encouraged an engaging and fruitful debate. In particular, giving people the space to name their own criteria of assessment (in the GRA and GPGI tools) may help stimulate a sense of fuller participation than that provided by existing approaches that use predetermined well-being criteria (see, for example, Bavinck et al.'s (2012) research into job satisfaction and subjective well-being in fisheries).

Another strength of the well-being approach seems to be its capacity to highlight the *social* nature of well-being in fishing communities. We see the importance of social relationships with others in the achievement and denial of several well-being aspects – for example, the role of family relationships which support and enable a fisherman to do his work without worry when he is at sea (leaving his family onshore), and the interdependencies of fishermen in terms of reliable crew, safety at sea, and efficient working on shore (net mending and fish sorting). Even aspects of individual health can be strongly influenced by working with others, as we observe in the earlier comments of Ishan who describes how his back injuries might have been avoided had he asked the help of others to land his boat. We also gauge insight into the negative influence of relationships, particularly for those in debt and who are heavily reliant upon middlemen for the sale of their catch. The high value attributed to owning one's own vehicle is explained here, as it is not just an economic indicator but also provides a route to freedom to make decisions about how to market their catch.

Well-being approaches also have their risks and limitations. Inherent in methods which depend upon people's own subjective responses (such as the GPGI tool) are problems of ignorance, expectation, and adaptation. People may report themselves as feeling satisfied with conditions that objectively are undesirable, due to ignorance of any alternative way of being, or that they give a response that they feel is expected. For example, in this research, expectations seem to play a role in shaping some of the responses of people when scoring relationships with close family members, which may have been scored "satisfactory" due to a sense of duty to avoid portraying family members in a negative light. The problem of adaptation can also occur when people have managed to suppress their needs and desires in order to adapt to a particular hardship (Sen 1999; Clark 2007). As Sen (1999: 62) observes,

> Failure to account for adaptive preferences when assessing individual well-being can be deeply unfair to those who are persistently deprived … The deprived people tend to come to terms with their deprivation because of the sheer necessity of survival, and they may, as a result, lack the courage to demand any radical change, and may even adjust their desires and expectations to what they unambitiously see as feasible.

The problem of adaptation can lead to people reporting their situation as being better than what is objectively evident, hence obscuring the ways in which well-being can be subjectively assessed (Qizilbash 2006). A careful consideration of adaptation within subjectively reported data should form part of the data interpretation process. Nevertheless, within the WeD framework, the focus on "needs met" provides an objective indicator of a person's welfare, which can be correlated with his/her subjective reflection on life. This makes adaptation more visible through the analysis of gaps between the objective circumstances of a person and his/her subjective reflections on them, and reasserts the importance of considering objective and subjective measures of well-being together (Gough and McGregor 2007). As White (2010) warns, if the subjective element of well-being is allowed to be assessed in isolation from other dimensions it risks misuse, such as justifying the withdrawal of development support if people subjectively report themselves as being satisfied with life, in cases when objectively their needs remain unmet.

Notwithstanding this critique, a three-dimensional analysis of well-being has much to recommend it. Its application to a fisheries context illuminates clear areas of focus for development policy and provides a deeper understanding of some of the motivations behind human behaviour, which is useful for fisheries management. For example, dealing with the concerns of back injuries from landing boats could be tackled through better provision of boat-landing facilities, but with due attention to the concerns of other fishers in the area and beach users whose livelihoods may be disrupted by harbour development. Social well-being may also be supported by efforts to encourage reduced alcohol consumption, and to understand the impacts for the many affected victims of alcohol abuse and community violence such as women (see Paranamana et al. forthcoming). Whether or not these development activities are considered to fall within the remit of fisheries management remains to be seen, but an argument can be made that fisheries sustainability and poverty reduction can be mutual goals (Coulthard et al. 2011). Agendas of marine conservation (including substantial turtle conservation interests in the area) and fisheries sustainability might win greater buy-in and support from local fishers, if they can realign with improving the quality of people's lives as a whole, rather than solely focussing on the fish on which those lives depend.

Acknowledgements

Research presented in this chapter was carried out as part of the ESRC funded project Developing a social wellbeing approach for sustainable fisheries in South Asia (Well-Fish) 2011–2014.

Notes

1. Young Lives is a long-term international study of child poverty in India, Ethiopia, Peru, and Vietnam based at the University of Oxford, UK (see www.younglives.org.uk).
2. http://www.oecdbetterlifeindex.org/.
3. The research discussed in this chapter forms part of an ESRC-funded project: Developing a social well-being approach for sustainable fisheries in South Asia (Well-Fish), active between 2011 and 2014.
4. For further information on WeD outputs see Gough and McGregor 2007 and also a series of working papers available at www.welldev.org.uk.
5. See www.welldev.org.uk/research/methods-toobox/toolbox-intro.htm.
6. The GRA does not form part of the WeD tool kit – rather it is an adaptation of one of their quality of life measures (Global Person Generated Index GPGI), which emerged as part of a methods trialling period in Sri Lanka.
7. The WellFish project also conducted interviews with women regarding their well-being, see Paranamana et al. forthcoming.
8. The WellFish project produced a series of reports, which were derived from a six-month period of community profiling involving key person interviews, participatory mapping, and focus group discussions held with men and women from Rekewa lagoon in 2011.
9. For a detailed description of the original Resources and Needs Questionnaire as developed by WeD see www.welldev.org.uk/research/methods-toobox/ranq-toolbox.htm.
10. The needs categories used in Table 5.1 are slightly adapted to be more relevant to a fisheries context. They exclude the intermediate needs of "a non-hazardous work environment" and "a non-hazardous physical environment" on the grounds that fishers, living in the coastal zone, are exposed to substantial hazards both at work (when at sea) and in terms of the geography of where they live (in an exposed coastal zone vulnerable to cyclones and coastal flooding). We therefore know that fishers, worldwide, are likely to

fail in meeting these two needs due to the nature of their work. The list also expands to explicitly include indicators for social respect and participation.
11. See also Britton and Coulthard 2013.
12. To protect anonymity, all peoples' names used in this paper are pseudonyms.
13. Some broad re-categorization was carried out (as is detailed here) to reduce the number of factors illustrated in Figure 5.4 (which is illustrative of the method only, not the full data set): Health [personal health, strength to work, health of family members]; Fishing gears [having good boats, nets, owning a mechanised boat]; Good neighbours [helping each other, having friends, being respected by others, having generous neighbours]; Religious devotion [practicing religion, living without sin]; Community behaviour [community discipline, living without being a burden to others, avoiding alcohol and drugs]; Income [money, stable income, avoiding debt, having savings]; and Vehicle [having a truck, three wheeler].

References

Adams, W. M., Aveling, R., Brockington, D., Dickson. B., Elliott, J., Hutton, J., Roe, D., Vira, B., and Wolmer, W. (2004) Biodiversity conservation and the eradication of poverty, *Science*, 306 (5699): 1146–1149.
Amarasinghe, O. (1989) Technical change, transformation of risks and patronage relations in a fishing community of South Sri Lanka, *Development and Change*, 20: 701–733.
Armitage, D., Bene, C., Charles, A. T., Johnson, D., and Allison E. H. (2012) The interplay of wellbeing and resilience in applying a social-ecological perspective, *Ecology and Society*, 17(4): 15.
Bavinck, M. (2001) *Marine Resource Management. Conflict and Regulation in the Fisheries of the Coromandel Coast* (New Delhi: Sage).
Bavinck, M., Pollnac, R., Monnereau, I., and Failler, P. (2012) Introduction to the special issue on job satisfaction in fisheries in the global South, *Social indicators research*, 109(1): 1–10.
Branch, T. A., Hilborn, R., Haynie A. C., Branch, T. A., Hilborn, R., Haynie, A. C., Fay, G., Flynn, L., Griffiths, J., Marshall, K. N., Randall, J. K., Scheuerell, J. M., Ward, E. J., and Young, M. (2006) Fleet dynamics and fishermen behaviour: Lessons for fisheries managers, *Canadian Journal of Fisheries and Aquatic Sciences*, 63(7): 1647–1668.
Britton, E. and Coulthard, S. (2013) Assessing the social wellbeing of Northern Ireland's fishing society using a three-dimensional approach, *Marine Policy*, 37: 28–36.
Busby, C. (1999) Agency, power and personhood: Discourses of gender and violence in a fishing community in South India, *Critiques of Anthropology*, 19(3): 227–48.
Camfield, L. and Skevington, S. M. (2008) On subjective well-being and quality of life, *Journal of Health Psychology*, 13(6): 764–775.
Camfield, L., Choudhury, K., and Devine, J. (2009) Wellbeing, happiness, and why relationships matter, *Journal of Happiness Studies*, 10(1): 71–91.
Camfield, L. and Tafere, Y. (2009) Children with a good life *have* to have school bags: Diverse understandings of wellbeing among older children in three

Ethiopian communities. Working Paper No. 37, Young Lives, Department of International Development, University of Oxford.

Camfield, L. and Guillen-Royo, M. (2010) Wants, needs and satisfaction: A comparative study in Thailand and Bangladesh, *Social Indicators Research*, 96(2): 183–203.

Carpenter S. R., DeFries, R., and Dietz, T., Mooney, H. A., Polasky, S., Reid, W. V., and Scholes, R. J. (2006) Millennium ecosystem assessment: Research needs, *Science*, 314: 257–258.

Carpenter, S. R., Mooney, H. A., and Agard, J. (2009) Science for managing ecosystem services: Beyond the millennium ecosystem assessment, *Proceedings of the National Academy of Sciences*, 106(5): 1305–1312.

Cinner, J. E., Daw, T., and McClanahan, T. R. (2008) Socioeconomic factors that affect artisanal fishers' readiness to exit a declining fishery, *Conservation Biology*, 23(1): 124–130.

Clark, D. A. (2007) Adaptation, poverty and well-being: Some issues and observations with special reference to the capability approach and development studies. Working Paper GPRGWPS-081, Global Poverty Research Group, University of Manchester, UK.

Copestake, J. (ed.) (2008) *Wellbeing and Development in Peru* (New York: Palgrave Macmillan).

Coulthard, S. (2008) Adapting to environmental change in artisanal fisheries – insights from a South Indian lagoon, *Global Environmental Change*, 18(3): 479–489.

Coulthard, S. (2009) "Should we hang up our nets? Adaptation and conflict within fisheries – insights for living with climate change," in Adger, N. W., Lorenzoni, I., and O'Brien, K. (eds) *Adapting to climate change: Thresholds, values, governance* (Cambridge: Cambridge University Press), pp. 255–268.

Coulthard, S., Johnson, D., and McGregor, J. A. (2011) Poverty, sustainability and human wellbeing: A social wellbeing approach to the global fisheries crisis, *Global Environmental Change*, 21(2): 453–463.

Coulthard, S. (2012a) What does the debate around social wellbeing have to offer sustainable fisheries?, *Current Opinion in Environmental Sustainability*, 4(3): 358–363.

Coulthard, S. (2012b) Can we be both resilient and well, and what choices do people have – incorporating agency into the resilience debate from a fisheries perspective, *Ecology and Society*, 17(1): Article 4. http://dx.doi.org/10.5751/ES-04483-170104.

CPR1 (2012) Community Profiling Report 1 (unpublished report), WellFish Project, Northumbria University, UK.

Dasgupta, P. (1990) Well-being and the extent of its realisation in poor countries, *Economic Journal*, 100(supplement): 1–32.

Daw, T., Brown, K., Rosendo, S., and Pomeroy, R. (2011) Applying the ecosystem services concept to poverty alleviation: The need to disaggregate human wellbeing, *Environmental Conservation*, 38(4): 370–379.

Daw T., Cinner J. E., McClanahan T. R., Brown, K., Stead, S.M., Graham, N. A. J., and Maina, J. (2012) To fish or not to fish: Factors at multiple scales affecting artisanal fishers' readiness to exit a declining fishery, *PLoS ONE*, 7(2): e31460.

Deci, E. L. and Ryan, R. (2000) The "what" and "why" of goal pursuits: Human needs and the self-determination of behavior, *Psychological Inquiry*, 11: 227–268.

Devine, J., Camfield, L., and Gough, I. (2008) Autonomy or dependence – or both? Perspectives from Bangladesh, *Journal of Happiness Studies*, 9: 105–38.

Doyal, L. and Gough, I. (1991) *A Theory of Human Need* (New York: Palgrave Macmillan).

Ellison, C. G. (1991) Religious involvement and subjective well-being, *Journal of Health and Social Behavior*, 32(1): 80–99.

Duraiappah, A. K. (2004) *Exploring the Links: Human Well-being, Poverty and Ecosystem Services*. IISD, UNEP. http://www.iisd.org/pdf/2004/economics_exploring_the_links.pdf, [Accessed 14 May 2013].

Eppinga, R. (2009) Exploring a Wellbeing Approach to Connect People's Realities with Research, Policy and Practice: The Case of Youth in the Sri Lankan Fishing Villages of Kalametiya and their Perceptions of Wellbeing and Livelihood Aspirations, MSc Thesis Unpublished (Sussex: Institute for Development Studies).

Gasper, D. (2004) Subjective and objective well-being in relation to economic inputs: Puzzles and responses. *WeD* Working Paper No. 9, www.welldev.org.uk, [Accessed 1 May 2013].

George, M. K. and Domi, J. (2002) Residual illiteracy in a coastal village: Poovar Village of Thiruvananthapuram district, Discussion paper, Kerala Research Programme on Local Level Development, Centre for Development Studies, Thiruvananthapuram, India, http://www.cds.ac.in/krpcds/publication/downloads/w45.pdf.

Giddens, A. (1984) *The Constitution of Society: Outline of the Theory of Structuration* (Cambridge: Polity).

Gough, I. (2003) Lists and thresholds: Comparing the Doyal-Gough theory of human need with Nussbaum's capabilities approach. *WeD* Working Paper No. 01, www.welldev.org.uk, [Accessed 1 May 2013].

Gough, I. (2004) Human well-being and social structures: Relating the universal and the local, *Global Social Policy*, 4(3): 289–311.

Gough, I. and Clark, D. A. (2006) "Capabilities, needs and wellbeing: Relating the universal and the local," in Manderson, L. (ed.) *Rethinking Wellbeing* (Perth, Australia: API Network).

Gough, I. and McGregor, J. A. (eds) (2007) *Wellbeing in Developing Countries: From Theory to Research* (Cambridge: Cambridge University Press).

Gough, I., McGregor, J. A., and Camfield, L. (2007) "Theorizing wellbeing in international development," in Gough, I. and McGregor, J. A. (eds) *Wellbeing in Developing Countries: From Theory to Research* (Cambridge, UK: Cambridge University Press), pp. 3–44.

Jha, S. (2011) *Well-being and religion in India: A preliminary literature review.* Working Paper (Birmingham: University of Birmingham).

Kooiman, J., Bavinck, J. M., Jentoft, S., and Pullin, R. (eds) (2005) *Fish for life* (Amsterdam: Amsterdam University Press).

Lavers, T. (2007) Asking people what they want or telling them what they need? Contrasting a theory of human need with local expressions of goals. *WeD* Working Paper No. 28, www.welldev.org.uk, [Accessed 1 May 2013].

Long, N. and van der Ploeg. J. D. (1994) "Heterogeneity, actor and structure: Towards a reconstitution of the concept of structure." In: Booth, D. (ed.) *Rethinking Social development: Theory, Research and Practice* (Essex, UK: Longman Scientific and Technical).

Millennium Ecosystem Assessment (2005) *Ecosystems and Human Well-being: Synthesis* (Washington DC: Island Press).

Maddox, B. (2006) *Literacy in fishing communities. Sustainable Fisheries Livelihood Programme* (DFID/ FAO), ftp://ftp.fao.org/fi/document/sflp/SFLP_publications/English/Literacy_Maddox_2006_Final2007.pdf, [Accessed 1 May 2013].

Maddox, B., Allison, E. H., and Daw, T. M. (2009) Literacies, education and development in fishing-dependent communities, *Maritime Studies*, 8(2): 5–8.

McGregor, J. A. (2007) "Researching wellbeing: From concepts to methodology," in Gough, I. and McGregor, J. A. (eds) *Wellbeing in Developing Countries: From Theory to Research* (Cambridge: Cambridge University Press), pp. 316–350.

McGregor, J. A., McKay, A., and Velazco, J. (2007) Needs and resources in the investigation of well-being in developing countries: Illustrative evidence from Bangladesh and Peru, *Journal of Economic Methodology*, 14(1): 107–131.

McGregor, J. A., Camfield, L., and Woodcock, A. (2009) Needs, Wants and Goals: Wellbeing, Quality of Life and Public Policy, *Applied Research in Quality of Life*, 4(2): 135–154.

McGregor, J. A. and Sumner, A. (2010) Beyond business as usual: What might 3-D wellbeing contribute to MDG momentum?, *IDS Bulletin*, 41(1): 104–112.

Ministry of Education (2011) *Education for All: Monitoring and Evaluation* (Sri Lanka: Ministry of Education).

NEF [New Economics Foundation] (2011) *Measuring our Progress: The Power of Well-being*, www.neweconomics.org, [Accessed 23 April 2013].

Nielsen, J. R. and Mathiesen, C. (2003) Important factors influencing rule compliance in fisheries lessons from Denmark, *Marine Policy*, 27(5): 409–416.

Nussbaum, M. (2000) *Women and Human Development: The Capabilities Approach* (Cambridge: Cambridge University Press).

Paranamana, N., Coulthard, S., Amarasinghe, O., and Sandaruwan, L. (forthcoming) *Women's wellbeing in fisheries and the problem of alcoholism*, Paper presented at the 7th People and the Sea conference, University of Amsterdam, June 2013.

Platteau, J. P. (1992) "Small scale fisheries and the evolutionist theory," in Tvedten, I. and Hersoug, B. (eds) *Fishing for Development: Small Scale Fisheries in Africa* (Upsala, Sweeden: NordiskaAfrikainstitutet), pp. 91–114.

Qizilbash, M. (2006) Well-being, adaptation and human limitations, *Royal Institute of Philosophy Supplement*, 59: 83–110.

Ruta, D. A., Garratt, A. M., Leng, M., Russell, I. T., and MacDonald, L. M. (1994) A new approach to the measurement of quality of life: The patient-generated index, *Medical Care*, 11(1): 109–126.

Sachs, J. D., Baillie, J. E. M., Sutherland, W. J., Armsworth, P., Ash, N., Bateson, P., Beddington, J., Blackburn, T., and Collen, B. (2009) Biodiversity conservation and the Millennium Development Goals, *Science*, 325(5947): 1502–1503.

Salas, S., Sumaila, U. S., and Pitcher, T. (2004) Short-term decisions of small-scale fishers selecting alternative target species: A choice model, *Canadian Journal of Fisheries and Aquatic Sciences*, 61(3): 374–383.

Sen, A. (1999) *Development as Freedom* (New York: Knopf Press).

Symes, D. and Phillipson, J. (2009) Whatever became of social objectives in fisheries policy?, *Fisheries Research*, 95: 1–5.

UNEP [United Nations Environment Programme] (2006) *Marine and coastal ecosystems and human wellbeing: A synthesis report based on the findings of the*

Millennium Ecosystem Assessment, http://www.unep.org/pdf/Completev6_LR.pdf, [Accessed 3 November 2013].

Urquhart, J., Acott, T., Reed, M., and Courtney, P. (2011) Setting an agenda for social science research in fisheries policy in Northern Europe, *Fisheries Research*, 108: 240–247.

Urquhart, J., Acott, T., and Zhao, M. (2013) Introduction: Social and cultural impacts of marine fisheries, *Marine Policy*, 37: 1–2.

Weeratunge, N., Béné, C., Siriwardane, R., Charles, A., Johnson, D., Allison, E. H., Nayak, P. K., and Badjeck, M. C. (2013) Small-scale fisheries through the well-being lens, *Fish and Fisheries*, DOI: 10.1111/faf.1201.

Westaway, E., Seeley, J., and Allison, E. H. (2007) Feckless and reckless or forbearing and resourceful? Looking behind the stereotypes of HIV and AIDS in fishing communities, *African Affairs*, 106(425): 663–679.

Westaway, E., Barratt, C., and Seeley, J. (2009) Educational attainment and literacy in Ugandan fishing communities: Access for All?, *Maritime Studies*, 8(2): 73–97.

White, S.C. (2009) Bringing Wellbeing into Development Practice. *WeD* Working Paper No. 09, www.welldev.org.uk, [Accessed 1 May 2013].

White, S. C. (2010) Analysing wellbeing: A framework for development policy and practice, *Development in Practice*, 20(2): 158–172.

Section II
Time and Changes over Time

6

Researching Social Change and Continuity: A Complexity-Informed Study of Twenty Rural Community Cases in Ethiopia in 1994–2015

Philippa Bevan

6.1 Introduction

Since the turn of the millennium the pace of economic and social change in poor developing countries has accelerated considerably, eliciting a need for theoretical approaches and research methods appropriate for the empirical study of change. Complexity social science provides a paradigm for exploring both change and continuity, and when used with case-based methods, can lead to innovative and practical policy-relevant conclusions. Complexity frameworks for studying the dynamics underpinning social change and continuity are of increasing interest in the UK in the fields of management (Allen et al. 2011), social policy (Byrne 2011; Room 2011), and international development (Ramalingam and Jones 2008, Ramalingam 2013). In the complexity framework which underpins the study described here the communities are conceptualized as "dynamic open complex systems" co-evolving on path-dependent trajectories with internal sub-systems, for example households and people; overlapping contextual systems, for example wider clan and religious systems; and encompassing systems, for example the region and the country as a whole.

The chapter describes a longitudinal research programme which began in 1994 as a synchronic comparative study of fifteen rural communities which had been selected as exemplars of the main agriculturalist livelihood systems in Ethiopia by economists planning a panel household survey.[1] Parallel qualitative research using secondary sources, rapid assessment techniques, and protocol-guided semi-structured interviews produced fifteen "Ethiopian Village Studies" (Bevan and Pankhurst 1996) which later became known as *WIDE1* (Wellbeing and Illbeing Dynamics in Ethiopia). The WIDE acronym was introduced in 2003 when comparative qualitative fieldwork was undertaken in twenty communities (*WIDE2*[2]): the fifteen studied in 1994–1995, plus three agriculturalist sites which had been added to the Ethiopian Rural Household Survey community panel in 1999, and two pastoralist communities where Ph.D. research had taken place in the 1990s.

Between 2010 and 2013 a donor group in Addis Ababa[3] funded new fieldwork (*WIDE3*) in the twenty sites which has been conducted in three stages: Stage 1 in six sites in early 2010; Stage 2 in eight sites in late 2011; and Stage 3 in six sites in spring and autumn 2013.[4] The WIDE3 data are being used in two ways: to conduct comparative case analysis of the communities in 2010–2013, and, in conjunction with the WIDE1 and WIDE2 data, to investigate the longer term cumulative impacts of development interventions and wider modernization processes on the trajectories of the communities and the life qualities of their different kinds of member.

In what follows I describe the WIDE3 research process from philosophical assumptions to policy-relevant conclusions. The next section outlines the Foundations of Knowledge Framework (FoKF) (Bevan 2007, 2009) which identifies nine different linked aspects of knowledge generation which all empirical researchers ought to address transparently.[5] Section 6.3 describes the research domain and questions, Section 6.4 the approach to theory, Section 6.5 the research strategy, including the fieldwork process and interpretation and analysis, and Section 6.6 provides examples of the five different types of research "answer" we are producing. Section 6.7 outlines future directions for the research, Section 6.8 provides methodological reflections, and the concluding section on rhetoric and *praxis* describes how we have tried to bridge the disconnect between research and policy design and implementation by government and donors.

6.2 The Foundations of Knowledge Framework

Sound empirical research frameworks require transparent philosophical and methodological foundations and those designing research projects should be in a position to justify their choice of stance in nine scientific areas. These are:

1. Domain or focus of study: what exactly are you interested in?
2. Values/ideology: why are you interested?

3. Ontology: how do you understand the nature of reality?
4. Epistemology: how can you know about that reality?
5. Theory: how do you understand/explain your object of study?
6. Research strategies: how can you establish what is really happening?
7. Research answers: what (kinds of) conclusions do you want to draw from your research?
8. Rhetoric: how do you inform (which) others about your conclusions?
9. Praxis: what to do? who should do it?

The FoKF shows how these different knowledge areas are linked (Figure 6.1).

In the remainder of this section we very briefly describe the WIDE3 approach to each of these knowledge foundations, returning to the most interesting in greater depth in the remainder of the chapter.

6.2.1   Domain or focus of study

Our *research domain* is modernization and change in Ethiopia's rural communities since 1991 with a particular focus on the roles played by development interventions since 2003.

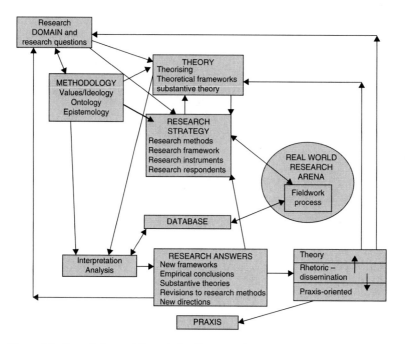

Figure 6.1   Foundations of Knowledge Framework

6.2.2   Values/ideology

Our *ideological* commitment is to empirical research that is (1) relevant for improving the life chances of the poorest and most vulnerable people; (2) scientifically important; and (3) helpful for well-motivated practitioners at all levels to understand how their area of intervention really works, including potential unintended consequences of their actions, in order that they can act more efficiently and equitably.

6.2.3   Ontology

Our complexity social science approach[6] pays attention to ontology–what is the world *really* like? Complexity scientists like Coveny and Highfield (1995) have provided much evidence that the world *really* is complex. "The story of the universe is one of unfolding complexity. [p. 328] ... Energy and chemical elements produced by the stars have led to the emergence of intricate structures as organised as crystals and human brains. [p. 10] ... Life is an emergent property which arises when physico-chemical systems are organised and interact in particular ways. ... A city is an emergent property of millions of human beings (p. 330)."

From complexity ontology we take a number of key messages. Parts are related, interdependent, and inter-act. Complex systems are characterized by emergence; the whole is more or less than the sum of the parts: "Emergence means that something new comes into being. We have a change of kind rather than just a change of degree [p. 13] ... Emergent phenomena are not explicable in terms of that from which they emerge [p. 18]" (Byrne 1998). A simple example is water – H_2O – a molecule emerging from a combination of hydrogen and oxygen atoms. Degrees of connectivity among parts vary across systems leading to differences in overall resilience and adaptability to external changes. Degrees of connectivity also vary across different areas within one system, affecting the intensity of (negative and positive) feedback processes. Degrees of connectivity change through time. Initial conditions matter and trajectories are path-dependent.

We conceptualize rural communities and their members as complex social and human systems which are open, as they depend on and interact with their environments, and dynamic as they are capable of non-linear changes. Complex social systems have material, technological, social, economic, political, and cultural dimensions and are constituted by elements in relationships. People are organized in unequally structured co-evolving systems which, in Ethiopia, include households, communities, kingroups, lineages, clans, other community-initiated organizations, formal and informal enterprises, NGOs, political parties, national and international donors, government, transnational companies, etc.

Social systems have nested sub-systems, are nested in larger "super-systems," and overlap with other systems. Interacting systems co-evolve: a change in a key aspect or parameter of one system is likely to lead to adaptation in others.

6.2.4 Epistemology

Knowledge is imbricated in historically changing complex systems, so that what we can know is contingent and provisional, pertaining to a certain context. However, this does not mean that "anything goes." We are committed to the institutionalized values and methodological rules of social science which include logical thinking and the testing of ideas against reality through rigorous and transparent empirical enquiry, including in this project establishing an Evidence Base to which we and others can turn if questions arise.

Complexity theory tells us a number of things of relevance about ways to know about complex systems. Research is usually exploratory, the aim being to identify (1) patterned similarities and differences among the complex systems under study and (2) common processes and mechanisms which play out differently in different contexts, rather than "laws" or generalizations. Frameworks and methods depend strongly on the research questions. There is continuous interaction and iteration between ideas and the field. As explained further below data are seen as "traces" of the passage of the communities and their sub-systems through time. Quantitative data tell you *how much* of the research object of interest there was at the time of measurement, while qualitative data tell you *what kind* of thing it was.

"More than one description of a complex system is possible. Different descriptions will decompose the system in different ways" (Cilliers 2005, p. 257). As shown below the adoption of a multiple perspectives framework each focusing on a different level of community structure and dynamics generates a rich structured dataset which can be used to establish how the system, parts, and context have worked together.

6.2.5 Theory

Theorizing uses the ideas and theories of other scholars; "building on the shoulders of giants." *Theoretical frameworks* are exploratory tools which clarify concepts and identify key processes linking them. The FoKF is one theoretical framework used in this chapter and some others are set out in Section 6.4. Examples from the development literature include livelihoods and well-being frameworks. They are developed through theorizing and in the dialogue between ideas and evidence and provide guides for the design of research instruments and the interpretation and analysis process. *Substantive theories* are to do with causal understanding or explanation. In complex social systems causation is complex; what happens is usually the result of the interaction of multiple internal and contextual causal mechanisms.

A fundamental theoretical framework for understanding longitudinal complexity-oriented research processes distinguishes between synchronic and diachronic analyses. Complex systems evolve through time and their past is co-responsible for their current state. "An analysis of a complex system that ignores the dimension of time is incomplete, or at most a synchronic snapshot of a diachronic process" (Cilliers 1998, p. 40). I describe in Section 6.4 how we are combining synchronic and diachronic analyses of our longitudinal data.

6.2.6   Research strategy

Our research strategy depends on *case-based methods* which fit well with the complexity paradigm since they do not depend on any assumption of linearity as most standard variable-based methods do. Also they can combine qualitative and case-based quantitative interpretation in an integrated fashion. Case-based quantitative analysis uses a conception of measurement that depends on *classification* which fits with the way in which people think. In everyday life we constantly use (stereo)typing to guide our responses to other people and their actions, events, and so on. A case-based quantitative approach is contrasted with a traditional quantitative approach where variables (particular features of cases, for example education, income etc) are seen as causal agents while cases (people, households, firms, countries) are seen simply as sites for measuring variables. Analysis of quantitative data becomes a contest between disembodied variables to see which are "significant."

Byrne argues that "integrated accounts constructed around a complexity frame offer the best narratives for describing change" (2001, p. 74). In order to achieve such accounts he advocates the use of four processes:

1. *Exploring*: descriptive measurement of variate traces (see 6.5.1) and examination of the patterns generated by the measurements in conjunction with exploration of qualitative materials (which might be texts, photos, artefacts, etc.)
2. *Classifying*: sorting of things into kinds on a prototypical basis (Bowker and Starr 1999) and (temporary) identification of meaningful boundaries of a system or ensemble of similar systems

3. *Interpreting*: measures and narratives in a search for meaning
4. *Ordering*: things sorted and positioned along the dimension of time and procedures for documenting changes and when they occurred.

The research process involves using the theoretical frameworks to develop a *research design* which identifies what to ask about; how to ask, including potentially surveys, protocols to guide semi-structured interviews, participation observation, photographs and the collection of documents; and who to ask.

In comparative community research such as this once the cases have been selected and the research instruments are designed the *fieldwork* process involves time planning, training of fieldworkers, field supervision, and planning and implementation of the data journey from fieldworker notes to the *database*. Comparative case-based analysis of qualitative data can take four forms (Tilly 1985). One case can be analysed in terms of (1) its location in a larger system or (2) its internal dynamics. Two or more cases can be compared in a search for (3) diversities and/or (4) regularities. We are using all four approaches:

- *Structural location*: communities are spatially, economically, politically, culturally, and historically located in wider complex systems. The relationships which each community has with these encompassing systems have a bearing on both the substance and the style of what happens.
- *Internal dynamics*: since communities are historically located each is on a trajectory constructed by the path-dependent actions and social interactions of the actors involved. Community trajectories can change direction as a result of internally initiated changes, linked internal and contextual changes, or big changes in context.
- *Diversities and regularities*: increasing interest in case-based research (e.g. George and Bennett 2005; Byrne and Ragin 2009[7]) has led to recommended procedures for different types of cross-case comparison to identify common causal mechanisms, produce descriptive typologies sorting cases into different kinds, and typological theory development.

6.2.7   Research answers, dissemination, and practice

There are five kinds of *research answer*: empirical conclusions, new theoretical frameworks, substantive theories, revisions to research methods, and new questions. Some examples from the WIDE3 research are described below.

6.2.8 Rhetoric

For *dissemination* these answers have to be presented in *rhetorical* styles appropriate to different kinds of audience; academics, government and donor development policy designers, implementers and evaluators, other practitioners, the communities under research, and the general public via various forms of media.

6.2.9 Praxis

The complexity social science framework is highly suitable for *praxis*[8]-related research. "Complexity is essentially a frame of reference – a way of understanding what things are like, how they work, and how they might be made to work" (Byrne 2002, p. 8). Policymakers should establish what is possible (and not possible) in the future for different kinds of system/case.

Having briefly outlined the knowledge underpinnings of the WIDE3 research, in the rest of the chapter we provide more details on particularly interesting aspects.

6.3 The WIDE3 research domain and research questions

Our *research domain* is modernization and change in Ethiopia's rural communities since 1991 with a particular focus on the roles played by development interventions since 2003. The WIDE3 *research questions* are:

1. In each community what were the *key features of the development situation* at the time of fieldwork?
2. In what ways have the development situations of the communities changed since the mid-1990s? What *modernization processes* were involved in each of *their trajectories*?
3. What *differences were made* to the trajectories and the communities by *development interventions* and the interactions among them since 2003?
4. What similarities and differences can we identify in these impacts? How did they *vary among different types of community* and what are the reasons?
5. How did what happened fit with *government and donor models* of how development *should* happen?
6. What do the *longer term trajectories* of these communities look like? Where have they come from and where might they be going in the next few years?
7. In what ways have recent *social interactions*, relationships and processes across the development interface between government and

community affected the *implementation and achievements* of the various government and donor programmes?

8. What have been the impacts of modernization as a whole, and recent development interventions in particular, on the *lives of the different kinds of people* who live in the communities?

The map locates (Map 6.1) the twenty WIDE3 communities and Table 6.1 sets out some key similarities and differences.

6.4 Theory

The distinction between three types of theory spelled out in Section 6.2 (theorizing, theoretical frameworks, and substantive propositions) and used in this section came from Mouzelis (1995). Little in the way of substantive theory emerged from the exploratory Stage 1 project. Towards the end of the Stage 2 analysis I developed a theory about drivers of change and continuity in rural communities which is described in Section 6.6.The complexity approach and theoretical frameworks are discussed in the following section. These have been developed through an ongoing process of interaction between ideas and evidence which started during the 1994 Village Studies. The search for sound knowledge foundations for the WeD research in Ethiopia in 2002 led me to explorations of "(critical) realism" (Pawson 1989; Archer 1995; Pawson and Tilly 1997; Sayer 2000) and "complexity theory" (Byrne 1998). These related emerging paradigms informed the development of the ontological, epistemological, and ideological foundations underlying the research (Bevan 2007, 2009).

We rely on complexity theorizing about how social continuity and change happen. During periods when complex social systems do not really change it is possible to identify *control parameters*– dominating aspects with a governing influence – which, through a complex set of feedback processes, ensure that the system reproduces itself in much the same way. For community systems on stable trajectories there are a number of ways in which change may eventually occur. One is a huge and sudden event or intervention from outside such as a war, land-grab, pandemic or the discovery of oil. At the other extreme myriad cumulative small changes in control parameters over a long period may, in complexity social science language, push the community further "from equilibrium" until it is ready to be sent in a new direction by a relatively small new event or intervention. In between, one or more meso changes may lead to relatively rapid moves towards disequilibrium and

112

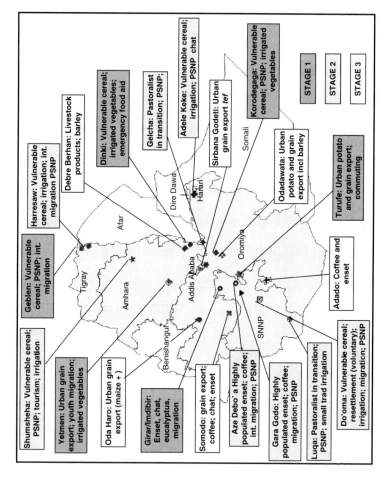

Map 6.1 WIDE3 research communities

Table 6.1 The WIDE communities – some key features

Community	Field work	Location	Livelihood base*	Identity groups	Region
			DROUGHT-PRONE AND REGULARLY DEPENDENT ON FOOD/CASH-FOR-WORK		
Gara Godo	Late 2011	Remotish but new municipality	Highly populated; gardens – cash-crop coffee, root crops, fruit and vegetables; other land grain; agricultural & urban migration; PSNP	1 ethnicity 2 religions	SNNP
Aze Debo'a	Late 2011	Near zone town but remotish	Highly populated; gardens – cash-crop coffee, root crops, fruit and vegetables; also grain; illegal migration[a] to South Africa; and PSNP	1 ethnicity 1 religion	SNNP
Luqa	Late 2011	Very remote	Pastoralist in transition + small irrigation + Emergency Food Aid (EFA)	1 ethnicity 2 religions	SNNP
Do'oma	Late 2011	Nr *wereda* town but very remote	Vulnerable cereal + some irrigation + agricultural and urban migration + PSNP	3 ethnicities 2 religions	SNNP
Adele Keke	Late 2011	Near Haramaya and on main road	Cash-crop *chat* [some exported to the Gulf] + vulnerable cereal; irrigation + PSNP; commuting for urban work	1 ethnicity 1 religion	Oromia
Gelcha	Late 2011	Near town and main road but remote	Pastoralist in transition + small irrigation + PSNP	3 ethnicities 2 religions	Oromia
Korodegaga	Early 2010	Remotish	Vulnerable cereal + some irrigation + migration + PSNP	1 ethnicity 1 religion	Oromia
Shumsheha	Late 2011	Near Lalibela town	Sorghum, teff, beans, cattle, shoats; some irrigation + migration + PSNP	1 ethnicity 2 religions	Amhara
Dinki	Early 2010	Quite remote	Vulnerable cereal + some irrigation + migration + EFA	2 ethnicities 2 religions	Amhara
Geblen	Early 2010	Quite remote	Vulnerable cereal + a little irrigation + migration + PSNP	2 ethnicities 2 religions	Tigray
Harresaw	Late 2011	Quite remote	Vulnerable cereal + some irrigation + illegal migration to Saudi Arabia[b] + PSNP	1 ethnicity 1 religion	Tigray

(continued)

Table 6.1 Continued

Community	Field work	Location	Livelihood base*	Identity groups	Region
			INDEPENDENT ECONOMIES IN AREAS WITH ADEQUATE RAIN		
Girar	Early 2010	Outskirts of *wereda* town but remotish	Highly populated; gardens – *enset* + cash-crop *chat* and eucalyptus + migration	1 ethnicity 4 religions	SNNP
Adado	2013	Remotish	[2003] Gardens: cash-crop coffee, *enset*, barley, maize	1 ethnicity 1+ religions	SNNP
Turufe	Early 2010	Increasingly near to expanding Shashemene	Food surplus and cash crop potatoes and grain; commuting for urban work	5+ ethnicities 4 religions	Oromia
SirbanaGodeti	2013	On main highway between Bishoftu and Mojo – 20km to each	[2003] Food surplus + cash crop grain (*tef*, wheat)	1 ethnicity; 3 religions	Oromia
Oda Dawata	2013	On main road between Adama and Asella	[2003] Food surplus + cash crop potatoes, irrigated vegetables and grain in 2003	1 ethnicity, 3 religions	Oromia
Oda Haro	2013	Remotish – 16 km east of Bako	[2003] Food surplus + cash crop grain (maize+), oilseed, peppers, *chat* in 2003	2+ ethnicities; 3 religions	Oromia
Somodo	2013	Remotish – 5 km from main road Jimma-Gambella; 20 km from *wereda* town	[2003] Food surplus + cash crop coffee, *chat*, and grain in 2003	2+ ethnicities; 5 religions	Oromia
Debre Berhan environs	2013	Near DebreBerhan town	[2003] In good years some crops sold for cash – barley, beans, wheat; livestock; dairy products; weather problem – frost; 1999–2003 regular food-for-work programme	1 ethnicity 1 religion	Amhara
Yetmen	Early 2010	On allweather road but remotish	Food surplus + cash crop grain; new irrigated vegetables; agricultural migration	1 ethnicity 1 religion	Amhara

aMigrants have no official papers and are smuggled across Ethiopian borders and on to South Africa where they mostly make a living selling goods on the streets with some graduating to ownership of small shops.

bThese migrants are mostly smuggled to Djibouti and taken across the Red Sea to Yemen in small boats; most travel on to Saudi Arabia.

*Enset (false banana) takes eight years to mature and is drought resistant; contents of stalk and stems are allowed to ferment and then used for food.

Tef is a grain endemic to Ethiopia used to make injera – a fermented pancake.

Chat is a narcotic plant whose fresh leaves are chewed.

change, for example green revolution changes combined with irrigation potential and increasing market demand or rapid urban expansion eating away at the borders of adjacent rural *kebeles.*[9]

6.4.1 Key theoretical frameworks

In this section we describe our synchronic–diachronic research framework in more detail, spell out the multiple perspectives we have taken on the communities, and describe two diachronic frameworks illustrating processes involved in community evolution and path-dependent trajectories.

6.4.1.1 The synchronic–diachronic research framework

Synchronic analyses of complex systems focus on a "point in time" and use an "all-at-once" logic to consider structures of systems. *Meaning* comes from difference and similarity and from (dis)connections and patterns.

Diachronic analyses follow the "sequential logic of a road" and can answer two questions: why a current state was born of a prior state and why a certain state progressed to some future state. The focus is on process and *meaning* comes from the narrative produced through the tracing of plot and sequence. Figure 6.2 shows how we can conduct comparative synchronic analyses of the communities in 1995, 2003, and 2010/11/13 and diachronic "process-tracing"[10] of the trends and events driving community trajectories between 1995 and 2003 and 2003 and 2010/11/13. We can also compare the three sets of WIDE3 communities in early 2010, later 2011, and spring 2013 to identify common trends and idiosyncratic changes over the three years 2010–2013.

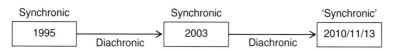

Figure 6.2 Synchronic and diachronic analyses

Using Cilliers' suggestion that more than one description of a complex system is possible we have looked at the communities from seven (synchronic) perspectives asking questions about (1) the community as a whole; (2) the community in its wider context; (3) household structures; (4) five domains of power/fields of action; (5) structures of inequality; (6) social interaction; and (7) types of social actor.

Perspective 1: The community in the wider context

Where is the community located in encompassing social, cultural, economic and political contexts?

Perspective 2: The community as a whole

What kind of community is it? How does it work as a whole? What are its main internal and contextual parameters? Which currently control its trajectory?

Perspective 3: Households

What is the local cultural ideal for household structures? What kinds of household structures actually exist? What are the important differences among households? How do households relate and interact with other households?

Perspective 4: Intermediate social organization – five domains of power/ fields of action

Community members are active in five institutional settings which are simultaneously domains of power and fields of action. These are:

The livelihood domain:

- smallholder agriculture and agricultural employment
- non-farm business and non-farm employment
- migration and remittances

The domain of human re/pro/duction:

- "producing" people: pregnancy, birth, child-rearing
- "producing" people: learning, training, formal education
- "reproducing" (maintaining) people: domestic work, food consumption
- "reproducing" people: housing, household assets, water, and sanitation
- "reducing" people: illness, conflict, ageing

The domain of social re/pro/duction

- social networks
- social institutions: marriage, circumcision, inheritance, land/labour/ oxen exchanges
- social organizations (including households)

The domain of community management

- community-initiated structures for decision-making and implementation
- *kebele* (community government) structures
- *wereda* (district) structures

The domain of ideas

- local customary repertoires
- local modern repertoires
- in-coming ideologies, religions, cultures and other ideas

Perspective 5: Community macro-organization – structures of inequality

How is the community structured in terms of class, wealth/poverty, and income? What forms do genderage[11] inequalities and relations take? What other community-specific status markers structure inequality? Who are the community elites?

Perspective 6: Social interactions

The community system is reproduced and changed through the day-to-day actions and interactions of its members and relevant outsiders. What kinds of people do what in the five domains of power? What kinds of social interactions are involved?

Perspective 7: Social actors

Each social actor has a genderage, class/wealth position, ethnicity, religion, maybe other community-relevant social statuses, a personality, accumulated human resources and liabilities, and a personal history. How are individuals constrained and enabled by their histories, the roles open to them in the different fields of action, and their relative power positions in local structures of inequality (Pankhurst, 2011)?

6.4.1.2   The community co-evolving with context and sub-systems

Figure 6.3 depicts a community co-evolving with its households and people and wider context. Communities do not have life cycles as households and people do. The trajectory followed by each community system is the result of interactions among (1) a stream of external happenings to which people organized in household sub-systems have to respond and (2) creative activities generated from within the community.

Households can be seen as involved in a "struggle for existence" through which they occupy an economic niche for longer or shorter periods. Those with greater wealth, status, and political connection are likely to do better in the competition for positional advantage and leverage; those that are poor, socially marginalized, and politically irrelevant are likely to remain excluded and/or adversely incorporated. However, given the uncertainties of rural life, customary institutional arrangements for co-operation, and the important contribution to

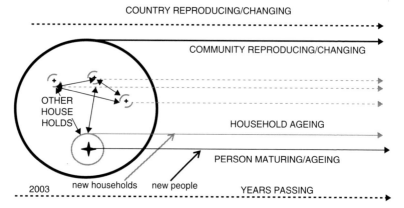

Figure 6.3   Co-evolution of communities, country, households, and people

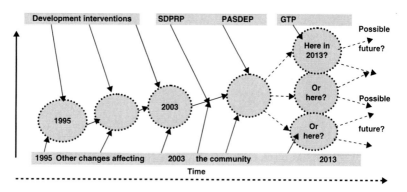

Figure 6.4   Community trajectories

success of individual character, motivation and skills, there are varying levels of intra-generational and inter-generational social mobility both upwards and downwards.

Men and women, and youth and children "co-evolving" with their communities and households are affected by what happens to each. Individual consequences depend on community trajectory, household trajectory, genderage, class-wealth, status, political connection, education, health, personal characteristics and chance. The complex of choices different kinds of people make in response to what happens to them also has consequences for the future trajectory of each community and, taking all communities together, for the country.

6.4.1.3 Community trajectories

What kind of trajectory is each community on? Where might each be heading? The framework in Figure 6.4 shows how development interventions related to government strategy plans (the SDPRP, the PASDEP and the GTP[12]) and wider changes in context have interacted with ongoing community processes since 1995.

6.5 Research strategy

6.5.1 Case-based research methods

In the original research design we chose as cases three kinds of open and dynamic complex social system: the communities and the households and people which constitute them.[13] As shown below this choice had implications for how we asked our questions and to whom we put them. We also had to choose the research topics and deconstruct them into manageable "variates" whose traces at the time of the research we would be measuring quantitatively or qualitatively. In conventional quantitative research these would be called "variables" but I have been persuaded by David Byrne's rallying cry "Death to the variable!" (2002, p. 29). Byrne argues that the term "variable" is often used in a way that implies that measurements, such as education measured by years of schooling or income, are substances or forces with causal powers. But variables are not real; "(w)hat exists are complex systems ... which involve both the social and the natural, and which are subject to modification on the basis of human action, both individual and social (ibid.: 31). What we measure are 'traces of the systems which make up reality" (ibid.: 32).

6.5.2 Research design – what to ask

We used the seven perspectives framework in a number of ways. For example, the "Modernisation variate master list,"[14] i.e. traces of modernization processes (Table 6.2), was used in Stage 2 to design questions and organize the Modernization Evidence Bases matrices for 1995, 2003, and 2011. The *community features* list relates to the community as a whole in its context; the *livelihoods* list to the livelihoods domain of power; the *lives* list to the human re/pro/duction domain; and the *society and government* list to the social re/pro/duction, community management, and ideas domains.

6.5.3 Research instruments – how to ask

The Research Officers were given Modules[15] (Table 6.3) to guide semi-structured interviews. They also observed and participated in community life to deepen their knowledge and understanding of the

Table 6.2 Research framework – modernization variate master list

Community features	Livelihoods	Lives	Society and government
Terrain	Local economy	Population	Elders roles and activities
Ecology and environment	Credit, saving, and debt	Household types and inequalities	Religious organizations and activities
Weather	Shocks and processes leading to food insecurity	Wealth differences	Other community-initiated organizations and activities
Land use	Land access	Social protection	Physical safety and security
Settlement pattern	Smallholder farming – crops	Class relationships	Group disagreements and conflicts
Urbanization + public buildings	Smallholder farming – livestock	Genderage differences: children	Justice
External relationships	Irrigation	Genderage differences: youth	Informal welfare regime
Electricity	Other farm technologies	Genderage differences: adults	Governance structures: *kebele* and sub-*kebele*
Communications	Inward investors	Genderage differences: elderly dependents	Community and *kebele* leadership
Roads and transport	Co-operative farming	Marriage, widowhood and divorce	Government–community relations
	Agriculture market linkages – upstream	Gender and inheritance	Community modern repertoire of ideas
	Agriculture market linkages – downstream	Gender relationships: nurturing, income-earning, power relations	Community conservative repertoire of ideas
	Prices and inflation	Inter-generational relationships	Incoming religious ideas
	Agricultural labour	Elite-mass differences	Incoming government ideas
	Labour-sharing/ co-operation	Vulnerability and social exclusion	Incoming urban ideas
	Diversification and non-farm activities	Other status differences and relationships	Incoming global ideas

(*continued*)

Table 6.2 Continued

Community features	Livelihoods	Lives	Society and government
	Migration	Social participation Deviance Housing Household assets Household expenditure Other consumer goods Domestic technologies Household work and workers Leisure activities Clothes Food, diet, and nutrition Drinking water Common illnesses and treatment-seeking Producing children Raising children: nurturing, socialization & non-formal learning Education generally	Key clashes of ideas

community and took a wide range of photographs. The contents of the research instruments responded to inputs from donor and research officer workshops. Phase 1 fieldwork reports informed the design of the Phase 2 modules.

6.5.4 Research respondents – who to ask

In each site male and female Research Officers conducted separate interviews. Women and girls were always interviewed by the women fieldworkers but, given that there were more questions for men due to their greater representation in official positions, the women also interviewed some men. Respondents included *wereda* officials, *kebele* officials, and

Table 6.3   The WIDE3 Stage 1 and Stage 2 research modules

	Stage 1	Stage 2	Stage 3
	Phase 1	**Phase 1**	**Phase 1**
M1	*Wereda* perspective 2003–2010 (1)	*Wereda* perspective 2003–2012	*Wereda* perspective
M2	*Kebele* perspective 2003–2010	Community trajectory 2003–2012	Community trajectory 2003–2013
M3	Community trajectory 2003–2010	*Kebele* perspective	*Kebele* perspective
M4	Community experiences of interventions	Experiences of recent interventions	Farming
	Phase 2	**Phase 2**	
M5	*Wereda* perspective (2)	Community organizations and leaders	Non-farming activities
M6	Interventions & households	Other community member vignettes	Young people's perspective
M7	Interventions and dependent adults	Households and interventions	Households and interventions
M8	Organizations& interventions	Marginalized people and interventions	Key informants' experiences and perspectives
			Phase 2
M9	Key development actors	Youth comparison	Site-specific gap-filling
M10	(i) Gender relations (ii) HIV/AIDS	PSNP	Site-specific follow-up
M11	Site-specific follow-up	Site-specific topics	Research Officer topics
M12	Research Officer topics	Research Officer topics	

others who were particularly knowledgeable about the community and its history. The same questions about interventions were put to rich, middle-wealth, and poor men and women and there were in-depth interviews in each community with four male household heads and their wives from households of different wealths, plus rich and poor women heading households. There were also interviews with government employees working in the *kebele*, government volunteers from the community holding *kebele* Cabinet, Council, Committee and other official positions, leaders of community-initiated organizations, elders, religious leaders, clan leaders, model farmers, investors, traders, other business people, skilled workers, daily labourers, returned migrants, ex-soldiers, traditional health workers, youth, and various kinds of vulnerable and excluded people.

6.6 Fieldwork process and the making of the database

The *fieldwork* has been conducted by trained Ethiopian social scientists; the WIDE1 fieldworkers were all male but in WIDE2 and WIDE 3 male and female researchers worked together in each site. By Stage 3 eleven of the twelve researchers had worked on a previous WIDE project and were familiar with the approach. They used the Modules to guide interviews during which they wrote field notes which were used to produce Report Documents paralleling the Modules. Figure 6.5 shows the journey which the Stage 2 data,[16] in the form of a narrative guided and set down by the Research Officer, made from the mouth of the interviewee to the database organized in the NVivo9 software package. Community lead researchers[17] loaded the Report Documents into NVivo.

6.7 Interpretation and analysis process

The interpretation and analysis process by the lead researchers began after the Phase 1 fieldwork with a Research Officer de-briefing workshop. This produced tentative findings which were shared with a network of people working for donors, NGOs or as researchers or consultants in a Rapid Briefing Note. In Stages 1 and 2 the feedback contributed to the design of the Phase 2 fieldwork which was followed by another de-briefing workshop and Rapid Briefing Note. The lead researchers then each wrote two *individual community case studies*. In Stage 3 which is still under way we are conducting most fieldwork in a longer Phase 1, then

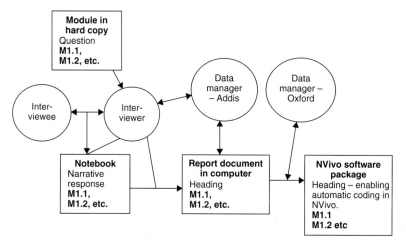

Figure 6.5 Data journey – from interviewee to NVivo software package

writing draft community reports, using a short Phase 2 to fill gaps and follow-up community-specific issues.

The community reports are organized under four main headings with detailed sub-headings: the community as a whole, households, structures of inequality, and fields of action/domains of power. They are revised following comments from the fieldworkers. They are book-length reports and a good read in their own right but they also form part of the evidence base for the Final Report.

The *synchronic comparative analysis process* began in the de-briefing workshops and was taken forward in dissemination workshops in Addis Ababa following completion of the community reports. During Stage 2 we made a clearer distinction than we had in Stage 1 between synchronic and *diachronic analyses*, with separate sections in the Summary Report on (1) what was happening in 2011 and (2) the trajectories of the eight communities. To support conclusions in both areas the community reports were used, along with return to the original data, and where appropriate the 1995 and 2003 databases, to construct four matrix-based Evidence Bases on modernization, community-government (dis) connects, the impacts of development interventions on different kinds of people, and the longer term impacts of development interventions. These four Evidence Bases were used with the community reports to write five related summarizing Annexes. These Annexes were then used to produce the Summary Report which underpinned a range of headline findings for policymakers, a few of which appear below.

The longitudinal data related to the eight Stage 2 communities were used to produce academic papers using *paired diachronic comparisons* (Bevan et al. 2012; Carter and Eyerusalem 2012; Dom 2012; Pankhurst 2012). These paper were presented in a panel at the International Conference on Ethiopian Studies in October 2012 alongside a paired comparison of two Stage 1 sites (Bevan et al. 2013) and a paper on one of the pastoralist sites written by two Research Officers (Tefera and Aster 2012).

6.8 Research answers

Here are examples of the five different types of research answer described above.

6.8.1 New frameworks

During the Stage 1 research we inductively developed three (synchronic) theoretical frameworks to show how macro-development interventions enter the rural communities they are designed to change. We used them to introduce new angles and questions in Stage 2.

6.8.1.1 The policy journey

Figure 6.6 shows how most development interventions are transmitted to Ethiopian rural communities and how information about their progress is relayed back to government. As policies travel down the government chain at each stage it is not possible to implement the policy as designed and officials at each level have to be creative in dealing with risks not anticipated in the policy design (Hirschman 1967). While our focus is on the *kebele* and its interactions with the *wereda* we are interested in how what happened compared with what federal and donor policymakers expected to happen.

6.8.1.2 Cultural disconnects

Development interventions are attempts to change the technological, institutional and "ideas" landscapes within which community systems

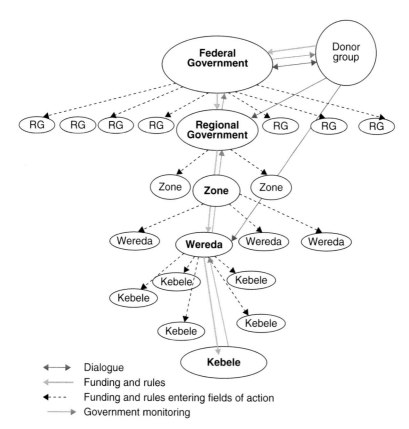

Figure 6.6 The policy journey

are working. Figure 6.7 depicts potential *synchronic* cultural disconnects between the aims and assumptions implicit in the mental models (ideas) and institutional designs (norms and rules) associated with top-down sector policies and programmes and local beliefs, values, norms and ways of doing things which we are calling cultural repertoires. A simple example is the clash between nationally designed school timetables and local daily and seasonal demands for household labour. This framework of cultural disconnects was used as one focus for a deeper exploration of sector interventions in Stage 2.

Taking a *diachronic perspective* on cultural change these communities have never been totally cut off from external influences though the degree to which such influences have entered over the years is related to levels of remoteness. Religious missionaries have operated in some

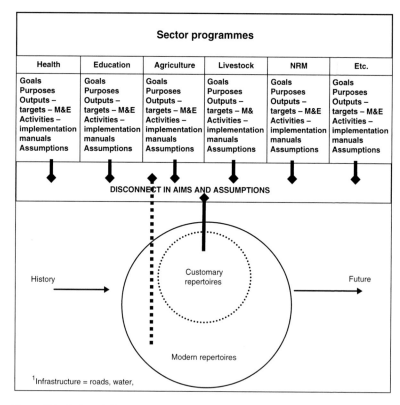

Figure 6.7   Cultural disconnects between top-down and local repertoires

parts of the country since the 19th century and since the fall of Haile Selassie local cultures have been increasingly penetrated by a number of different kinds of modern ideological repertoire. Through time aspects of these repertoires have fed into local repertoires in re-iterative processes of cultural "bricolage," a term that describes "the muddle" that happens when new rules and ideas meet long-standing ones (Pain and Cantor 2010, p. 34).

It is possible to look into the muddle and identify two ideal-type cultural repertoires available at any point in time: the local customary repertoires and local modern repertoires depicted in Figure 6.8. *Local customary repertoires* do adapt but they are slow to change. Given Ethiopia's cultural heterogeneity rural customary repertoires are diverse; however all contain traces of external values and beliefs which entered them during the Imperial era which ended in 1974, the military socialist regime of the *Derg* in power from 1974 to 1991, and the current EPRDF regime which came to power in 1991. *Local modern repertoires* contain the most up-to-date mental models and institutions accepted by community opinion leaders.

Local customary and modern repertoires are promulgated by cultural entrepreneurs, for example elders and teachers. People can pick and mix ideas from different repertoires and may also be influenced by incoming *ideological repertoires* and other "foreign" ideas diffused in less organized ways. In recent years local repertoires have come under increasing

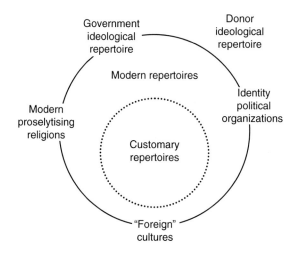

Figure 6.8   Customary cultural repertoires under pressure

pressure from incoming ideas associated with religion (Protestant, Muslim and Orthodox Christian), politics, urbanization, and globalization (see Figure 6.8).

6.8.1.3 Social interactions in the development interface space

The cultural contradictions between top-down and community development models are not easily resolved and they cause difficulties for those whose official positions require them to bridge the cultural divide.

Figure 6.9 shows the key development players in the *wereda*, *kebele*, and communities and identifies a set of "go-between" government employees who work in the development interface space interacting with *wereda* officials and community members (Dom, 2011). *Kebele* managers, Development Agents (Agriculture, Livestock and Natural Resources), Health Extension Workers and teachers mostly, though not always, come from outside the community. They are employed by the *wereda* and given performance objectives (targets) which, if not met, may have repercussions for their careers. A second set of "go-betweens" – *kebele* and sub-*kebele* officials and *kebele* Council members – are (s)elected from within the community and embedded in community networks and structures whilst by

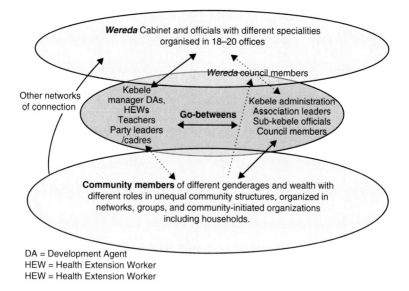

DA = Development Agent
HEW = Health Extension Worker
HEW = Health Extension Worker

Figure 6.9 Social interactions in the development interface

their function they are also linked to higher government structures and increasingly to party structures. They are unpaid "go-between" government volunteers. This framework was used in Stage 2 to design new questions and inform data interpretation.

There are four types of response that members of a community can make in the face of planned change from above: (1) exit, (2) voice, (3) loyalty, and (4) foot-dragging. We have started to explore these different responses.

6.8.2   Some empirical conclusions

6.8.2.1   The Stage 2 communities in late 2011

The headline findings from the Stage 2 Summary report ran to twelve pages. Here a small selection is presented.

- There were reports of *climate change* effects from all sites including increases in temperature, shorter rainy seasons, more erratic and intense rains, unseasonal rains which damaged crops, streams drying up, and decreasing levels of groundwater.
- *Urbanisation processes* had affected all communities: in one *kebele* a new highway was a growth point for a tiny town, in three *kebeles* small towns were growing fast, while four *kebele* centres were in commutable distance of growing towns.
- All communities had suffered *annual rain shortages* whose severity varied by year; all had suffered at least one severe drought since 2003. Nevertheless the six agriculturalist sites had experienced *economic growth* related to improvements in roads, increases in agricultural and non-farm incomes and the PSNP. There had been no equivalent economic development in the two pastoralist sites although there were signs of a possible take-off in the more remote one.
- *Landlessness* was a problem in all sites, especially for youth.
- A *richer farmer class* was solidifying in the agriculturalist sites with many diversifying into trade or other businesses.
- The main focus of *agricultural extension was cereals and fertiliser* and the *shift to higher-value* crops such as onions, peppers, spices, sesame, *chat*, coffee, and eucalyptus was *mainly farmer-led*.
- Not all government-provided fertiliser and seeds were suitable for local soils and climates.
- Only two *wereda* agricultural offices were actively promoting *irrigation*.
- Five of the sites had been affected by different kinds of *inward investment* involving loss of community land but also new employment opportunities.

- Few livelihood interventions focused on *women* and *youth* were sustained for any length of time.
- In all communities provision of *health services, drinking water* and *education* had expanded considerably since 2003 bringing many benefits.
- Ideal households were still *patriarchal* although men's authority over women and youth had declined and in some households greater female economic participation was paralleled with greater male domestic participation.
- *Malaria* regularly caused deaths in the majority of communities.
- Stigma meant that researching *HIV/AIDS* was impossible.
- *Very poor people* could not afford to use health and education services and use by poor people was restricted.
- In all communities there were *strong social networks* and numerous *community-initiated organisations*; informal social protection involved neighbours, relatives and wider kin, friends and in some places Protestant churches and/or clan/lineage structures.
- Religious identity was an increasing focus for organisation; *youth interest in religion* had increased.
- *Cultural entrepreneurs* potentially bringing new beliefs, knowledge, norms and values into the communities included *wereda* officials, school teachers and extension workers, opposition party followers, organisations associated with ethnic identities, religious leaders and missionaries, returned ex-soldiers, international and urban migrants, and media actors.

In all communities *government-community relations* were influenced by people's appreciation of new infrastructure, improved security and services, particularly education and health, and some community-specific interventions. However, there were also instances of violent conflict, refusal to co-operate, foot-dragging, and resentful conformity.

6.8.2.2   The Stage 1 and Stage 2 communities: looking to the future

In Stage 2 we took forward a *prospective diachronic approach* introduced in Stage 1 which identified potential future trajectories for each community focusing on a few key internal and local parameters. Of the fourteen Stage 1 and Stage 2 communities eleven were drought-prone and aid-dependent while the others were in areas of good economic potential.[18] Figures 6.10 and 6.11 divide them into communities which were experiencing the pre-cursors of big structural change and those which continued to reproduce structures which had been in place for some time.

Eight sites, seven of which were drought-prone and aid-dependent (Figure 6.10), were on *the edge of change* as a result of changes either externally driven or related to an internal control parameter.

The cities of Lalibela and Haramaya were expanding towards Shumsheha and Adele Keke, and increasing numbers were migrating to South Africa from Aze Debo'a and to Saudi Arabia from Harresaw, while the good irrigation potentials in Gelcha, Do'oma, and Korodegaga were likely to be more fully exploited in the next few years. The site of good agricultural potential, Turufe, was doing relatively well in 2010 exporting potatoes and grain to Shashemene and Addis Ababa, but Shashemene city was expanding very fast and already a piece of land at the edge of the *kebele* had been incorporated into Kuyera town which itself had recently become a suburb of Shashemene.

Three of the six communities with *no strong signs of structural change* (Figure 6.11) were experiencing good economic growth: Yetmen (good agricultural potential) and Girar (*chat*, eucalyptus and considerable urban migration) in early 2010 and Gara Godo (coffee, diversification, and small urbanization) at the end of 2011. In Dinki and Luqa there had been little growth. In 2010 remote Dinki's farming livelihood potential seemed to be fully exploited and there were no local off-farm opportunities and, while in late 2011 there were small moves in Luqa towards more agriculture, a little livestock fattening, and a small roadside settlement, the core pastoralist livelihood had not changed. The Geblen

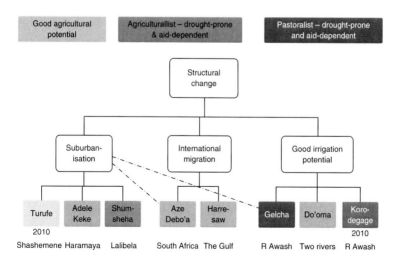

Figure 6.10 Communities on the edge of a structural change process

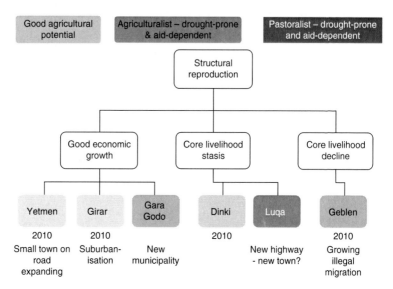

Figure 6.11   Communities involved in a process of structural reproduction

economy was in decline early in 2010 as a result of repeated severe droughts and while there was some (growing) illegal migration to Saudi Arabia it was not associated with the level of remittances and diasporic links found in Harresaw in late 2011.

6.8.3   Substantive theory

Looking ahead to the end of the Growth and Transformation Plan period in 2015 and beyond we have identified some wider less predictable forces for change with the potential to affect the WIDE communities. On the economic front there may be commercial investment in large-scale farming, small- and large-scale industrial investment, and formalization of the informal sector aimed at increasing the tax base. There is uncertainty in the political arena with, on the one hand, the prospect of further state/party penetration of communities, the private sector and civil society, and on the other, the pursuit by a growing class of rural-based relatively wealthy farmers, traders, and businessmen of a market-led route to prosperity, and the possibility that organizations with local roots, including religious and ethnic networks, will get more active in the political arena. As a result of increasing education and greater participation in income-generating activities women's voices should grow stronger within the household and, in the first instance, in economic and social domains, while the responses of the growing group of more and less educated youth to their difficult economic prospects may include a desire for political change. Illegal international migration is likely to increase exponentially creating diasporic linkages to some very different cultures.

Given this wider uncertain future we are theorizing that conditions in four main areas will govern community trajectories: (1) what we are calling "place," (2) the evolving state of the local economy, (3) the evolving state of the local political settlement, and (4) what is going on in the wider context. Table 6.4 shows ten parameters falling within these four areas, all of which are important for community trajectory continuity and change. We argue that a *big* change in one parameter could rapidly knock the system on to a new trajectory, or *incremental interacting changes in a number of parameters* could move the system in a chaotic direction opening up the possibility of structural change.

Place

"Place" encompasses two aspects. The first, *terrain, settlement, climate*, responds to the question "How (relatively) easy is it to grow crops, keep livestock and live here?" The question for the second, *remoteness*, is "How easy is it to access people outside the community, markets, services, etc?"

The state of the local economy

This has three aspects. The *farming system* question is "What crops and livestock are produced and how well do they work with the *place*?" The question relating to *agro-technologies* is "What agricultural technologies are currently used and how well do they work with the *place*?" The third question is about *livelihood diversification*: "What off-farm work opportunities are there and how do they fit with the *place*?"

Local political settlements

The first aspect is *community fault-lines*: "Considering identity group differences,[19] gender relations, adult-youth relations, and rich-poor relations how integrated is the community?" The question related to *society-government relations* is "How strong is the political settlement between the community and the government and what is it based on?"

Wider context

Here we introduce three aspects of the wider contexts of the communities. Considering *relations with neighbours* the questions are "What is the state of relations with wider identity groups (friends and enemies)

Table 6.4 Parameters guiding rural community trajectories

Place	The state of the local economy			Political settlement		Wider context		
Terrain, settlement, climate	Remoteness	Agri-technologies	Farming system	Livelihood diversification	Community fault-lines	Govt – society relns	Relations with neighbours	Cultural imports	Strategic location

in the neighbourhood? and How dangerous are potential or existing resource conflicts?" The question about *cultural imports* is "What are the consequences of incoming religious and political ideologies and new ideas from diasporas, towns, and elsewhere?" Finally in relation to *strategic location* we ask "What economic plans does the government have for the wider area?"

This new theory was developed towards the end of the Stage 2 analysis and has not yet been brought into dialogue with the existing data; we plan to do this for all twenty sites at the end of Stage 3.

6.8.4 Methodological reflections

While we have been concerned to maintain comparability across WIDE1, WIDE2, and WIDE3, and the three WIDE3 stages by focusing on the same topics we have revised the research protocols before each new project to take account of learning from previous projects. WIDE3 Stage 1 built on WIDE1 and WIDE2 but was still exploratory in many areas. We learned a lot about the communities, the usefulness of theoretical frameworks, and some things that were right and wrong about our fieldwork planning, research instruments, analysis process, and write-up plan. Nevertheless Stage 2 was also somewhat exploratory while generating notably better data, a deeper understanding of how Ethiopia's rural communities were working and where they might be heading, and a number of new ideas.

In both Stages 1 and 2 fieldwork Phases 1 and 2 were of equal length with Phase 1 seen partially as an initial "recce" of the communities to be used to inform the design of Phase 2. The write-ups of the community reports followed the completion of all fieldwork. In Stage 3 using our improved understanding some of our modules and questions are more focused and most of the fieldwork is being conducted in one long phase, following which we will use the data to write draft community reports. We will then return for a shorter fieldwork phase to fill gaps and follow-up on community-specific issues. Following completion of Stage 3 we will be exploring the use of new case-based modes of analysis for synchronic and diachronic comparisons of all twenty WIDE communities.

6.8.5 New directions

Until the closing stages of the Stage 2 analysis the cases our research focused on were complex systems: the communities, and their key subsystems of households and people. The first attempt to compare important features of the fourteen Stage 1 and Stage 2 communities suggested it would be interesting and useful for policymakers to consider some of these as cases to be compared. In this new enterprise we started with six important constituents of three of the parameters in Table 6.4:

Under *Place-> Remoteness* we selected (1) the case of **roads and bridges** and (2) the case of **urbanization**.

Under *The state of the local economy->Agri-technologies* we selected (3) the case of **irrigation** and under *The state of the local economy* (4) the case of **livelihood diversification**.

Under *Wider context->Cultural imports* we selected (5) the case of **migration links** and under *Wider context->Strategic location* (6) the case of **loss of community land**.

The case of irrigation is given as an example here. Nine communities had notable irrigation. As Figure 6.12 shows water sources and technologies varied considerably though there had been no studies of water potential and government was only involved in some promotion of irrigation in two of the communities.

6.9   Rhetoric and praxis

From the beginning of WIDE3 we have tried to engage with donors based in Ethiopia, the Ethiopian government, academics and NGOs in Ethiopia, non-resident academics with an interest in Ethiopia, and UK-based academics with an interest in methods for development-related research. Our main vehicles have been regular small workshops and meetings with Addis-based donors and government officials, Rapid

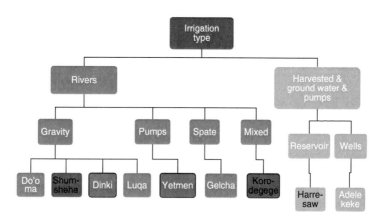

Figure 6.12   The case of irrigation – communities with potential

Briefing Notes emerging during the project, the Final Report and academic papers and presentations. We have also regularly sent workshop powerpoints, briefing notes, the Final Report, and academic papers to the WIDE3 "worknet" which in 2013 had around 100 members including donor and NGO employees, academics, and consultants. We invented the term "worknet" in the hope that members would get involved in the project and contribute comments and ideas in workshops and via email and this has increasingly been happening. However we face three major problems: very high turnover of overworked donor and NGO employees; a dearth of academics with time and/or inclination to get involved in this kind of research; and a disconnect between donor and government mental models which has made dialogue between them very difficult. All these can be seen as symptoms of a dysfunctional "dynamic open complex international development system."

Acknowledgement

Thanks to Laura Camfield for helpful comments on earlier drafts.

Notes

1. Ethiopian Rural Household Survey: http://www.ifpri.org/dataset/ethiopian-rural-household-surveys-erhs. The WIDE1 research was financed by the UK Overseas Development Administration and the lead researchers were myself and Alula Pankhurst.
2. WIDE2 fieldwork was conducted for a month in each site under the aegis of the 2002–2007 ESRC-funded Wellbeing in Developing Countries (WeD) Research Programme at the University of Bath http://www.welldev.org.uk/. As part of this programme in 2004/5 fieldworkers researched a range of topics in four of the WIDE communities over a period of 17 months in a project known as DEEP (in-Depth Exploration of Ethiopian Poverty). The lead researchers in WIDE2 were myself and Pankhurst.
3. The donors are DFID, CIDA and the Dutch and the project is managed by the World Bank. The lead researchers are myself, Pankhurst and Catherine Dom.
4. This chapter was written in spring 2013 so is describing a work still in progress.
5. The framework was used by Sumner and Tribe to structure a book on theories and methods for research and practice in international development studies (2008).
6. For more on this see Bevan 2010a and 2010b.
7. The handbook edited by Byrne and Ragin contains examples of a range of case-based methods and techniques including explanatory typologies in qualitative analysis, cluster analysis, correspondence analysis, classifications, Bayesian methods, configurational analysis including Qualitative

Comparative Analysis (QCA), fuzzy-set analysis, neural network analysis, choice of different types of cases for comparison (e.g. most different cases with a similar outcome; most similar cases with a different outcome), computer-based qualitative methods, ethnographic case studies, and a systems approach to multiple case study.

8. "The process by which a theory, lesson, or skill is enacted, practised, embodied, or realised. 'Praxis' may also refer to the act of engaging, applying, exercising, realizing, or practising ideas" (*Wikipedia*).
9. *Kebeles* are the smallest unit of government in Ethiopia. The next level up is the *wereda*, often translated as district. Each *wereda* is made up of 20–30 *kebeles* and there are now almost 1000 *weredas* in Ethiopia.
10. Process-tracing is a method used regularly by American political scientists to trace the sequencing and importance of trends and events in the lead up to an outcome of interest.
11. In variable-oriented research gender and age are seen as independent causal variables which have separate independent effects on whatever the outcome under consideration. When the focus is on cases gender and age taken together describe different kinds of people with different kinds of bodies, minds and aspirations: for example what old women, adolescent boys, and five-year-old girls do and their relations with other kinds of people in many respects are different.
12. The first government plan, the Sustainable Development and Poverty Reduction Programme 2003–2005, was followed by the Plan for Accelerated and Sustained Development to End Poverty 2005–2010 and the Growth and Transformation Plan 2010–2015.
13. In Section 8, Research Answers, under "New Directions" I describe how we have started to use the data to analyse control parameters and sub-parameters as cases.
14. Most of these topics were covered in the 1995 Village Studies (WIDE1) and a large number of them in WIDE2 in 2003.
15. Available on request.
16. In Stage 1 the programme was only used with data from two sites.
17. In Stage 2 Rebecca Carter, Catherine Dom, Alula Pankhurst and myself were each community leads for two sites.
18. The six sites being studied in Stage 3 are all in areas of good potential.
19. The six sites being studied in Stage 3 are all in areas of good potential.

References

Allen, P., S. Maguire, and B. McKelvey (eds) 2011 *The Sage Handbook of Complexity and Management* London: Sage.
Archer, M. S. 1995 *Realist Social Theory: The Morphogenetic Approach* Cambridge: Cambridge University Press.
Bevan, P. 2007 "Researching Well-being across the Disciplines: Some Key Intellectual Problems and Ways Forward" in I. Gough and J. A. McGregor (eds) *Wellbeing in Developing Countries: From Theory to Research*. Cambridge: Cambridge University Press.

Bevan, P. 2009 "Working with Cases in Development Contexts: Some Insights from an Outlier" in Byrne and Ragin (eds) *The Sage Handbook of Case-Based Methods* London: Sage.

Bevan, P. 2010a "Tracing the 'War against Poverty' in Rural Ethiopia since 2003 Using a Complexity Social Science Approach" Chronic Poverty Research Centre International Conference, Manchester. www.chronicpoverty.org/publications/details/tracing-the-war-against-poverty-in-rural-ethiopia.

Bevan, P. 2010b "The MDG-ing of Ethiopia's Rural Communities 2003–10: Some Meso, Micro and Macro Consequences." Symposium on "Promoting social inclusion in South Asia: policies, pitfalls and the analysis of welfare/insecurity regimes" University of Bath. www.bath.ac.uk/cds/events/sym-papers/Bevan2.pdf

Bevan, P. and A. Pankhurst (eds) 1996 *Ethiopian Village Studies*. http://www.csae.ox.ac.uk/evstudies/main.html.

Bevan, P., S. Urkato, and S. Neda 2012 "A Comparison of Two Diverse Food-Insecure Sites In North Omo. Where Have They Come from and Where Might They Be Heading?" Paper presented at the *18th International Conference of Ethiopian Studies*, Dire Dawa.

Bevan, P., R. Carter, and C. Dom 2013 "A Tale of Two Productive Safety Net Programme Sites" in A. Pankhurst, D. Rahmato, and G-J. V. Uffelen (eds) *Food Security, Safety Nets and Social Protection: The Ethiopian Experience* Addis Ababa: Forum for Social Studies.

Bowker, G. and S. Starr 1999 *Sorting Things Out: Classification and its Consequences* London: The MIT Press.

Byrne, D. 1998 *Complexity Theory in the Social Sciences* London: Routledge.

Byrne D. 2001 "Complexity Science and Transformations in Social Policy," *Social Issues Issue 2*. www.whb.co.uk/socialissues.

Byrne, D. 2002 *Interpreting Quantitative Data* London: Sage.

Byrne, D. 2011 *Applying Social Science: The Role of Social Research in Politics, Policy and Practice* Bristol: The Policy Press.

Byrne, D. and C. Ragin (eds) 2009 *The Sage Handbook of Case-Based Methods* London: Sage.

Carter, R., and E. Yihdego 2012 "How Are Urbanisation and Irrigation Affecting Food-Deficit Communities in Rural Ethiopia? A Comparison of Two *kebele*s near Lalibela and Harar." Paper presented at the *18th International Conference of Ethiopian Studies*, Dire Dawa.

Cilliers, P. 1998 *Complexity and Postmodernism* London: Routledge.

Cilliers, P. 2005 "Complexity, Deconstruction and Relativism," *Theory, Culture and Society* 22: 205.

Coveny, P. and R. Highfield 1995 *Frontiers of Complexity: The Search for Order in a Chaotic World* London: Faber and Faber.

Dom, C. 2011 *The Role of the "Government Go-Betweens" in Changing Rural Ethiopia: A WIDE3 report for DFID Ethiopia, mimeo* available from the author on request.

Dom, C. 2012 "Where are Ethiopian Communities Heading? Youth, Education and Migration in Two Food-deficit Communities in Eastern Tigray and Kambata." Paper presented at the *18th International Conference of Ethiopian Studies*, Dire Dawa.

George, A. and A. Bennett 2005 *Case Studies and Theory Development in the Social Sciences* London: MIT Press.

Hirschman, A. O. 1967 *Development Projects Observed* Washington: The Brookings Institution.

Mouzelis, N. 1995 *Sociology: What Went Wrong?* London: Routledge.

Pain, A. and P. Cantor 2010 "Understanding and Addressing Context in Rural Afghanistan: How Villages Differ and Why?" Afghanistan Research and Evaluation Unit. http://www.refworld.org/docid/4d09e5812.html.

Pankhurst, A. 2011 *Changing Inequalities in Rural Ethiopia: Differential Impacts of Interventions and Exclusions: A WIDE3 report for DFID Ethiopia, mimeo* available from the author on request.

Pankhurst, A. 2012 "Agropastoralism in Transition: Comparison of Trajectories of Two Communities in Oromia and Southern Region." Paper presented at the *18th International Conference of Ethiopian Studies*, DFID Ethiopia Dire Dawa.

Pawson, R. 1989 *A Measure for Measures: A Manifesto for Empirical Sociology* London: Routledge.

Pawson, R. and N. Tilly 1997 *Realistic Evaluation* London: Sage.

Ramalingam, B. 2013 *Aid on the Edge of Chaos: Rethinking International Co-operation in a Complex World* Oxford: Oxford University Press.

Ramalingam, B. and H. Jones with T. Reba and J. Young 2008 "Exploring the Science of Complexity: Ideas and Implications for Development and Humanitarian Efforts," *ODI Working Papers Issue 285.*

Room, G. 2011 *Complexity, Institutions and Public Policy: Agile Decision-Making in a Turbulent World* Cheltenham: Edward Elgar.

Sayer, A. 2000 *Realism and Social Science* London: Sage.

Sumner, A. and M. Tribe 2008 *International Development Studies: Theories and Methods in Research and Practice* London: Sage.

Tefera Goshu and Aster Shibeshi 2012 "Social Change: Impact of Development Interventions in the Gelcha Community of the Karrayu Pastoralists of the Upper Awash Valley of Ethiopia." Paper presented at the *18th International Conference of Ethiopian Studies, Dire Dawa.*

Tilly, C. 1985 *Big Structures, Large Processes, Huge Comparisons* New York: Russell Sage.

7
Patterns of Socio-economic Mobility in Rural Bangladesh: Lessons from Life History Interviews

Peter Davis

7.1 Introduction

In 2007 I led a team of researchers in conducting 293 life history interviews in eight districts of rural Bangladesh. While life history research is relatively new to Bangladesh, it is well established for poverty research in other countries (reviewed in Camfield and Roelen 2013). It also draws on a long tradition in social research which began with the Chicago School of sociology (see Thomas and Znaniecki 1958; Miller 2000, 2007; Dewilde 2003). The conceptual approach was also informed by multi-dimensional approaches to poverty research, as illustrated in studies of social exclusion, human development and capabilities, and participatory research methods (see Stewart et al. (2007) for a useful discussion of these approaches). Life histories also have potential for impact evaluation as they can include thought experiments concerning particular causes and effects where a "closest possible world" is imagined with or without the cause, i.e. the creation of a counterfactual. Counterfactual ideas are central to many philosophical ideas of causation. They are put into practice when we conduct qualitative life history interviews and discuss with a participant why a particular outcome occurred, whether the same outcome would have happened, or how the outcome would have differed, without the putative cause. For example in life history interviews in our study we ranked crises and opportunities according to the effect they had had on a person's present circumstances. In order to rank these we invited participants to think counterfactually, something we all do when we consider life trajectories and the effect of past events on present circumstances. When participants identified events or episodes that made a significant difference for their present situation we invited them to consider how things would be now if the particular event had not taken place. So for example a statement like, "if I hadn't got the job, I wouldn't have been able to afford medical care for my mother, and she would have died," contains information about circumstances which draws from an insider's perspective of the circumstances in which she lives and knows best. I return to the potential of life history methods within development at the end of the chapter.

Findings from this research have been published on methodological lessons learned (Davis and Baulch 2010), opportunities and challenges raised by mixing methods in poverty dynamics research (Davis and Baulch 2011), the impact of development interventions (Davis 2011a), exits from poverty (Davis 2011b), intergenerational transmission of poverty (Davis 2011c), social exclusion (Davis 2011d), the significance of assets (Davis 2011e), and how vulnerability is linked to poverty (Davis 2011f). This chapter presents key findings on socio-economic mobility, with a view to illustrating how life history methods can complement other approaches in the study of poverty, and thus make a contribution to development policy aimed at reducing chronic poverty.

7.2   Methods

The author led a team of researchers from Data Analysis and Technical Assistance (DATA) Ltd. in conducting 293 life history interviews in the eight districts given in Table 7.1 (below) between April and October 2007.[1] The households were selected as a subsample of a CPRC-IFPRI-DATA longitudinal study of poverty dynamics in rural Bangladesh, which covered 2,152 households (1,907 original households) from 14 districts.[2]

For the subsample of households selected for life history interviews (Phase 3[3] of the 2006–2007 research) eight of the original 14 districts were selected in such a way that a range of geographic and agricultural conditions typical of rural Bangladesh were represented. Sites were selected across a set of previous evaluation studies (Zeller et al. 2001; Ahmed 2005; Hallman et al. 2007; Kumar and Quisumbing 2009; Baulch 2010; Davis 2011a), and two villages per site[4] were selected in different unions. In each site, 20 households were selected from the original panel across two villages. Five households were then randomly selected from each of four poverty-transition categories,[5] which used per capita household expenditure calculated from the longitudinal quantitative survey (see Davis and Baulch (2010) for a more detailed explanation of these selection methods). This selection resulted in the following (Table 7.1) combination of districts and original intervention types.

Table 7.1   Locations of the life history research villages

Original intervention type	District	Number of villages	Number of life histories conducted
Microfinance	Manikganj	2	36
	Kurigram	2	39
Educational transfers	Nilphamari	2	38
	Tangail	2	39
	Cox's Bazar	2	32
Agricultural technology: household-based fish farming	Mymensingh	1	18
	Kishoreganj	1	19
Agricultural technology: group-based fish farming	Jessore	2	36
Agricultural technology: improved vegetables	Manikganj	2	36
	Total	16	293

In the life history interviews, one man and one woman were inter-viewed separately in each household. Research participants were often husband and wife, but in some cases, such as when a partner had died, only one parent and their son or daughter was interviewed. When an adult household member wasn't available – which was more often a man than a woman, especially during the main April–May rice harvest – or when there was only one adult household member, only one life his-tory interview was conducted in the household. We conducted 293 life history interviews overall in 161 households (133 men and 160 women) in 16 villages and eight districts. We found that interviewing two adult household members was ideal because it allowed immediate cross-checking, provided gender contrast, an alternative view of household dynamics, and allowed a mixed-sex team to work effectively, with men usually interviewing men and women interviewing women.

On the same day of each life history interview, interviewers wrote up the interview in Bengali in a format which had been devised in an ini-tial workshop and refined in field discussions including the author and the research team. In addition to the formal write-up of the life history interviews, interviewers wrote fieldwork diaries containing reflective impressions about the households and communities plus lessons-learned about methods. These diaries were translated and became a part of the qualitative dataset. When the author was with the team, he participated in interviews with both women and men.

Interviews and focus-group discussions were recorded, with permission of the research participants, with small unobtrusive digital voice recorders. We did not attempt to write full transcripts, but digital recordings were used for checking interviews for the initial same-day write-up of the life history narrative in Bengali, for later analysis, and for the final anonymized write-up in English.[6]

The life history was written as a chronological account of events, identifying causal mechanisms and drawing from discussions which had encouraged counterfactual thinking. The aim was to produce, as accurately as possible, the participant's perspective on her or his life trajectory, the causes behind improvement or decline in well-being, and to discuss how life could have been if events – both positive and negative – had not occurred.

During the initial days working in each village we also arranged a time for "knowledgeable people" to attend a focus-group discussion to be held on our last day in the village. This was usually held in a school building or in a near village leader's house. We tried to have a *Union Parishad* (Union Council) member and a number of elderly people in attendance.[7]

We spent about two weeks in each of the eight sites during the life history phase of the research and later revisited most of the households to check and discuss texts and diagrams with participants. As the principal analyst of the findings, I visited and discussed the research findings with participants in every household of the life history study.

During the life history interviews we used national and local historical markers, such as the 1971 war of independence or the 1988 floods, to pinpoint years of events described by the research participants. As an interview progressed, a chronological timeline of life events was built up. At the end of a life history interview, the researcher who had facilitated the interview, in discussion with the interviewee, drew a line depicting ups and downs in well-being in a trajectory, using this timeline of events. Then the interviewer reviewed the main points of the life trajectory and asked the interviewee to identify and rank the three or four most important sources of opportunity that had made the most difference for his or her long-term well-being. Similarly the three or four most important sources of downward pressure were also identified and ranked. These choices were recorded and used to generate frequencies of upward opportunities and downward pressures, as shown in Tables 7.3 and 7.4. At the end of the interview the interviewers and interviewee discussed the diagram and made adjustments together. The other researcher wrote the narrative-based life history from notes taken during the interview and the recording of the interview. Only two interviews were conducted per day by each pair of researchers to allow time for the diagram to be finalized and the interview to be written up in Bengali on the same day.

Life history diagrams were then traced, translated, and anonymized by the author and made available with the final anonymized, translated, and edited narrative life histories. The level of well-being (or "life condition" – *obosta* in Bengali) at different points in the life trajectory was indicated on the diagrams using a scale of one to five, using the categories described in Table 7.2 below. The diagrams allowed the well-being level to be estimated at any point in the trajectory. Levels were based on life conditions described by research participants, and cross-checked in the focus groups.

We intended for the line between Levels 2 and 3 (Table 7.2) to roughly correspond with the national poverty line used in our quantitative household assessments so that comparisons could be made with quantitative poverty assessments.[8] The five levels were defined by the qualitative research team in advance, and were applied consistently across villages. To minimize recall errors and other forms of misreporting, the well-being levels were verified by the focus-group discussion with local people who knew the households well, and then finalized in a round-table discussion of the qualitative research team at the end of fieldwork

Table 7.2 Qualitative well-being levels for individuals

Level	English	Bengali	Guideline
1	Very poor or destitute	*khub gorib, na keye chole*	Suffering tangible harm to health because of poverty, generally due to insufficient food. Tend to be landless or near landless.
2	Poor	*gorib*	Very vulnerable but eating reasonably well. Could easily move into Level 1 due to a common shock. If land is owned, it is equivalent to less than an acre for a medium-sized household.
3	Medium	*madhom*	A common shock would not result in tangible harm or going without food. Have household assets, or generate household income, equivalent to between one and two acres of land for a medium-sized household.
4	Rich	*dhoni*	Hold household assets or generate household income equivalent to that generated by two to ten acres for a medium-sized household.
5	Very rich	*khub dhoni*	Hold household assets or generate household income equivalent to that generated by ten acres or more for a medium-sized household.

in each village. In these meetings all information about households and members was used, and levels of well-being were agreed by consensus after discussion. These discussions were also digitally recorded for later reference. The various forms of data generated in this research were then coded and analysed using NVivo 8 by the author.[9]

7.3   Conceptualizing socio-economic mobility

We conceptualized a person's or a household's socio-economic status as a trajectory of well-being over time. In the interviews we explored a person's well-being most often expressed using the Bengali word *obosta*, which roughly translates as "life condition" or "situation" in English. We found this to be a useful way of referring in fairly general terms to how people describe improvements or declines in their well-being. People commonly use the word *obosta* to refer to a broad conception of well-being encompassing income and assets, health, social status, or prestige, having good social relationships, and a sense of security.

A person's *obosta* at one point in time can be seen as a set of endowments of tangible and intangible assets, plus other life-enhancing capabilities. These can be undermined by liabilities (negative assets) or disabilities (negative capabilities). Key assets, capabilities, liabilities, and disabilities all constitute current well-being and are instrumental in enhancing or undermining future levels of well-being. To explore well-being change over time, events – in the form of opportunities or downward pressures – impinge positively or negatively on people's endowments of assets, capabilities, liabilities, and disabilities. The ability to benefit from opportunities, or cope with downward pressures, depends on a person's existing set of endowments.

It is important to include negative assets (liabilities) and capabilities (disabilities) in conceptions of a person's well-being status. This side of well-being-determining endowments tends to be neglected in "asset-based approaches" to poverty research (see Davis 2011e). Liabilities and disabilities were seen to exacerbate the impact of downward pressures and undermine the ability to exploit upward opportunities. Using this conceptual approach the dynamics of socio-economic mobility for an individual trajectory can be examined. Figure 7.1 depicts this approach in a stylized way.

This conceptualization of the dynamics of well-being helps focus our enquiry on the interactions between endowments on one hand, and events creating either downward pressures or upward opportunities on the other.

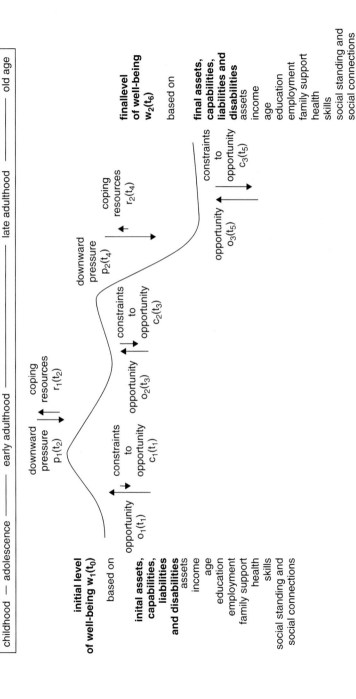

Figure 7.1 Conceptualizing socio-economic mobility within an ideal-typical trajectory

In order to operationalize this type of conceptual approach in investigating the causes of change in people's lives, a mixed-methods research strategy is likely to yield the best understanding. Quantitative panel surveys are able to track important trends in people's lives, such as changes in endowment levels, and relationships between these variables can be analysed statistically. However qualitative case-based research can complement this data by identifying causal mechanisms within individual trajectories and by exploring participant perspectives in more depth. Life history interviews are ideal because they allow a chronological exploration of events and causal mechanisms including respondents' interpretations (see Davis and Baulch 2010 for discussion on mixed methods and identifying of causation).

7.3.1   How endowments and events interact

7.3.1.1   Two illustrative examples

The conceptual approach described above provides a vocabulary for exploring how endowments and events interact to create mobility in particular cases. To illustrate I examine two life histories from our study: Ali (a pseudonym), a 45-year-old man from Tangail District, who lives in a village about three hours' drive north of Dhaka, and Amena (a pseudonym), a 54-year-old woman from Nilphamari District in the north-west of Bangladesh.

7.3.1.1.1   Ali: health-related crises leading to the intergenerational transmission of poverty.   Ali's trajectory diagram (Figure 7.2 below) shows how a series of health-related misfortunes (downward pressures) have long-term consequences – even crossing generations. The diagram shows how Ali's father's premature death undermined Ali's start in life, which in turn disadvantaged Ali's children. While Ali's trajectory improved slightly over his lifetime, the improvement was not enough for him to rise above the "poor" Level 2.[10] During this time opportunities to improve were not absent; but severe constraints (illness, poor education, etc.) throughout his family history undermined his ability to convert these opportunities into poverty-exiting life improvement.

Ali's father was an agricultural worker and earlier in his life had owned about 5 *bighas* of land.[11] He died from tuberculosis (TB) when Ali was a year old in 1963. Before he died the family had sold most of the land to pay for his treatment, leaving around 2 *bighas* remaining for the family to live on. Ali and his brothers were then forced from a young age to work as day labourers to keep the family going and all missed out on learning to read or write and other forms of elementary education.

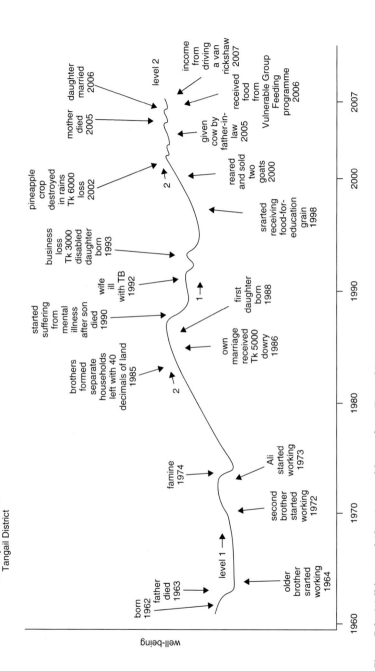

Figure 7.2 Well-being of Ali, 45-year-old man from Tangail District

Ali started work in 1973, when he was about 11. He worked for four different neighbours who fed, clothed, and housed him. He worked tending cows and earned about Tk 750 annually at first, but after seven years he was earning about Tk 4,500 annually. In 1980, at the age of 18, Ali returned home and started working as a regular agricultural day labourer. Ali's brothers formed separate households from Ali and his mother in 1985, but remained in the same neighbourhood. His brothers believed their situation would improve if they were separated. Ali said that his well-being was not affected much when his brothers separated, as at the time he was working and earning sufficiently to provide for his mother and himself. When his brothers separated, their 120 decimals of paternal land was split three ways, and Ali received 40 decimals – out of this, 16 decimals was public land (*khas jomi*).

Ali was married in 1986, a daughter was born in 1988, but his first son died as an infant from typhoid in 1990. The baby was treated by the traditional healer (*kobiraj*), which cost TK 400–500, but he was later taken to the local government hospital where he died the same day. The death of their son affected Ali and Hasina profoundly; Ali became mentally ill and Hasina suffered from depression.

Due to Ali's mental illness he spent several years wandering and sleeping rough. Ali considered that he had been possessed by a supernatural being (*jin*). He wandered around the district being fed by others, and being treated as a madman (*pagol*) with associated social stigma. He came home only occasionally. After seven years Ali began to suffer from abdominal pain for which he received extensive hospital treatment costing a total of Tk 20,000. This money was raised through the sale of pineapples grown on their small plot of land and with help from his father-in-law.

During this time his wife, Hasina, tried to survive without any income from Ali and as a result was forced to mortgage land and take loans in order to live. In 1992 Hasina contracted a fever and a cough and was later diagnosed by a doctor in a nearby town as having tuberculosis. She was first taken to the local government hospital for treatment and then was transferred to a specialist TB clinic in a hospital near Tangail. The treatment cost, Tk 1,500, was raised with help from Hasina's father. Hasina recovered after six months, but she had been pregnant with a daughter, born in 1993, who was born blind, partially deaf, and with severe learning difficulties.

A second son was born in 1995, and another son in 2000. The older son now attends primary school and has received the Primary Education Stipend (cash-for-education) for the last three years. Their eldest daughter also receives a stipend for attending secondary school. Most of this money is used to pay for the children's education and clothing expenses. Ali said that if he didn't receive this money they would need to cut back on food and eat only twice a day.

However their second daughter is unable to attend school because she is so disabled. Even though her condition is deteriorating, they have been unable to seek treatment for her because of the cost. They also worry for her future, as it is unlikely that they will be able to find a husband for her.

In recent years Ali has had medication for his mental condition and has returned home and has been working as a day labourer, driving a van rickshaw, and growing pineapples on their small plot of land. However without the various health problems and other pressures, which can be traced back to his vulnerability created by his father's illness and death, he and his family would be in a much stronger position today.

It is difficult to make linkages like this with absolute certainty; however the death of Ali's father caused the sale of assets and loss of income which increased Ali's vulnerability to downward pressures due to a resulting lack of assets or capabilities to cope – particularly after his son died. His "bad luck" is better seen as long-term vulnerability caused by a lack of coping resources.

In exploring Ali's trajectory the assets and capabilities that have been important are tangible, in terms of land and other assets such as livestock and cycle rickshaws. They are also intangible such as the relationship networks with his immediate family and relatives – particularly with his father-in-law who provided essential support. However Ali has had to cope with liabilities and disabilities both tangible in terms of monetary debt but also from poor health, learning difficulties, mental ill health, and social stigma. Thus his well-being can be understood in terms of initial endowments of assets and liabilities coming up against positive and negative events in a dynamic trajectory.

7.3.1.1.2 Amena: future insecurity due to an impending dowry and intermittent ill health. Amena (Figure 7.3) is a 54-year-old woman who lives in a village near the district town of Nilphamari with her two younger children – a son, aged 11, and a daughter, aged 16. She has two other sons who are married and live separately, although her second son, Entehar and his wife, Shuli, live in the same homestead area (*bari*), but keep a separate household (*khana* or *ghor*). The eldest son and his family live in a different district.

Amena's husband, Mafuz, died in 2006 after small injury on his foot became infected. He was ill for several months before he died. Before he died he had worked driving a bullock cart, and more recently, a van rickshaw.

152

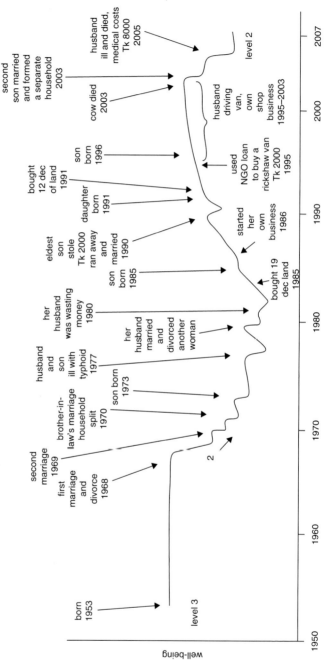

Figure 7.3 Well-being of Amena, 54-year-old woman from Nilphamari District

Amena now makes a living from a very small shop, selling everyday items such as soap and biscuits, beside her home. She also owns about an acre of land and a pond. Her second son, Entehar, works as a rickshaw driver in Dhaka some of each year, and the rest of the time does agricultural labouring work locally. He suffers from a bad back and so his trips to Dhaka, and income, are intermittent.

Amena has managed to slowly improve her situation through hard work and astutely running a small business, making use of loans from a range of different non-governmental organization (NGOs). However, at the time of the interview she was worried about arranging for her 16-year-old daughter's marriage. She told us a dowry of Tk 25,000 would be required for a groom from a family with a similar status as hers, or Tk 35,000 for a higher status groom. This was her main worry at the time of the interview.

Amena is vulnerable because she heads her small household alone and they have limited assets. One son is nearby and would help her in a crisis but his small family is also vulnerable because he suffers from an intermittent back problem which sometimes prevents him from earning an income. Amena's future prospects will depend of the balance of opportunities, enjoyed from her small shop business and living next to her son's family, and the downward pressures they will inevitably face – probably associated with raising a dowry for her daughter and any health problems that arise.

7.4 Findings

7.4.1 Overall patterns: endowments and events influencing improvement or decline

These illustrative cases show how two of the most frequent causes of crisis in our study (illness and dowry) can create severe downward pressure in life trajectories. They also show how assets such as livestock, land, and small businesses (sometimes supported by NGO-provided loans) provide opportunities. In order to widen the view of the types of opportunities and downward pressures that people face in rural Bangladesh, the tables below show frequencies of those most commonly reported using data from the 293 life history interviews conducted in this study. The life trajectories illustrate how endowments (assets, capabilities, liabilities, and disabilities) interact with life events (opportunities and downward pressures) to determine the direction of a life trajectory. They show how some people exploit opportunities or cope with crises, and are able to exit poverty, while others either stay in poverty or decline into poverty. The patterns observed can then help inform social and development policies to reduce downward pressures and their negative impacts and increase opportunities and people's ability to exploit them for long-term life improvement.

7.4.2   Positive endowments and opportunity

In order to explore patterns of improvement and decline, life histories showing improvement over the long term were separated from those declining. This was done by examining life history narratives, and our assessments of them, on a case-by-case basis. Seventy-nine life histories clearly showed an overall pattern of long-term improvement, and 71, clear long-term decline. Trajectories that could not be clearly classified either way, if a long-term (10 years or more) improving or declining trend was not clearly apparent from the life history interview, were placed in a "level" group, which contained 143 cases.

The life histories show that particular causes of improvement and decline occurred with differing frequency across the entire set of research participants (Tables 7.3 and 7.4). For example the categories: business activities – which usually involve accumulation of assets (such as shops, buildings, vehicles, machines, land, and livestock) – land, livestock, sons or daughters working, agriculture and fish farming, and help from relatives and inheritance, were most frequently cited as causes of improvement across the whole set of life histories.

We can reasonably conclude that these most frequently cited sources of opportunity are likely to be the most important for lifting people out of poverty. Other studies also support similar patterns of causes of improvement and decline in rural Bangladesh (see Sen and Hulme 2006; Quisumbing and Baulch 2009; Davis 2005, 2009).

When frequencies of citation of these causes discussed above are examined across the declining and improving trajectory groups (as in Table 5) the important causes of opportunity cited overall tend also to be those cited by people on improving trajectories: business (53.2 per cent), the accumulation of land (44.3 per cent), agriculture (26.6 per cent), livestock (26.6 per cent) and loans (24.1 per cent), inheritance and help from relatives (22.8 per cent), and salaried work (17.7 per cent). Thus asset-based sources of opportunity (such as land, business, agriculture and fish, livestock, and loans) and key capabilities (such as having salaried work) tend to be cited more frequently by those on long-term improving trajectories.

The pattern is slightly different for those on declining trajectories. While business is also the most commonly cited source of opportunity for this group (32.4 per cent), the number of opportunities reported overall is lower, and the ranking of the other opportunities is different: with benefits from official programmes (25.4 per cent), sons, or daughters working (22.5 per cent), the accumulation of land (19.7 per cent),

Table 7.3 Main causes of improvement in people's lives[12]

Cause	Number of life histories showing this as a main cause (of 293)	Percentage of life histories showing this as a main cause
Business activities	135	46
Accumulation or use of land assets	113	39
Income from livestock	80	27
Sons and daughters working	71	24
Income from agriculture and fish farming	69	24
Help from relatives or inheritance	65	22
Income from day labour	53	18
Benefits from microfinance	52	18
Benefits from all official programmes	49	17
Unspecified loans (including from neighbours and relatives)	47	16
Salaried work	42	14
Dowry receipt or favourable marriage	34	12
Household or property division	25	9
Official educational transfers	22	8
Domestic labour migration	21	7
Building a house	12	4
Benefits from irrigation	11	4
Benefits from having a united family	10	3

and help from relatives or inheritance (19.7 per cent), day labour (16.9 per cent), and livestock (16.9 per cent) appearing in that order.

Thus it seems that those on improving trajectories enjoy the key opportunities more frequently overall. This suggests that those declining may have less capacity to exploit key opportunities. They do benefit from some assets and capabilities, but these people tend to be less effective in exploiting the key areas of opportunity overall, and the opportunity categories they do enjoy are skewed towards less effective forms of improvement. These include the targeted official programmes (such as the Vulnerable Groups Development Programme, the Primary Education Stipend Programme, the Old Age Allowance Scheme, and the Allowance Scheme for Widowed and Distressed Women) and opportunities involving less-tangible assets linked to social capital of relatives (sons and daughters working, inheritance and family help) and/or less effective human capital (mainly day labour). This does not mean that these sources of opportunity are less effective in protecting people from further decline or not valued by this group, but it seems that they are not the most important causes of long-term improvement.

Table 7.4 Main causes of decline in people's lives

Cause	Number of life histories showing this as a main cause	Percentage of life histories showing this as a main cause
Illness and injury	220	75
Dowry and marriage	114	39
Death of family member	97	33
Household and property division	63	22
Theft or cheating	59	20
Litigation	56	19
Floods, cyclones, or storms	49	17
Crop damage	42	14
Violence, conflict, or physical insecurity	41	14
Family or village disputes	29	10
Death or illness of livestock	28	10
Disability	27	9
Unemployment or low income	26	9
Business loss	25	9
Sale or mortgage of land or house	25	9
Debt	21	7
Supernatural causes and superstition	20	7
Divorce and abandonment	19	6
Migration	19	6
Extortion corruption and harassment	17	6
Lack of food	12	4
Education and other expenses on children	11	4
Fire	10	3

7.4.2.1 Small businesses

Fourty six per cent of the 293 life histories cited involvement in small businesses as a significant source of opportunity, as did 53 per cent of the 79 improving trajectories. Of the 44 poverty exits identified, 26 life histories, or 59 per cent, also cited involvement in small businesses as one of the three or four most significant sources of opportunity in their lives. People with improving trajectories cited business involvement as a source of opportunity more often than people on declining trajectories, which suggests that that business involvement effectively supports poverty reduction, but mainly for those with the assets and capabilities which allow them to benefit from business activities.

Table 7.5 Frequency of causes of improvement or opportunity[13] (ranked according to difference in percentage)

Cause of improvement or opportunity	All life histories	Percentage	Improving trajectory	Percentage	Declining trajectory	Percentage	Per cent difference
Accumulation of land	113	38.6	35	44.3	14	19.7	24.6
Business activities	135	46.1	42	53.2	23	32.4	20.8
Agriculture or fish farming	69	23.5	21	26.6	7	9.9	16.7
Loans	47	16.0	19	24.1	7	9.9	14.2
Income from salaried work	42	14.3	14	17.7	3	4.2	13.5
All livestock production	80	27.3	21	26.6	12	16.9	9.7
Household or property division	25	8.5	9	11.4	2	2.8	8.6
Irrigation	11	3.8	6	7.6	2	2.8	4.8
Help from relatives or inheritance	65	22.2	18	22.8	14	19.7	3.1
Domestic labour migration	21	7.2	9	11.4	6	8.5	2.9
House building or improvement	12	4.1	4	5.1	2	2.8	2.2
Sons and daughters working	71	24.2	19	24.1	16	22.5	1.5
Dowry receipt or favourable marriage	34	11.6	10	12.7	8	11.3	1.4
Day labour	53	18.1	14	17.7	12	16.9	0.8
The benefits of a united family	10	3.4	0	0.0	5	7.0	-7.0
Benefits from official programmes	49	16.7	11	13.9	18	25.4	-11.4

Overall the forms of business that appeared in the life histories reflect the wide range of activities found in the rural economy of Bangladesh. The activities include references to other categories in the analysis, such as microfinance and livestock – when these were linked to businesses. Dealing in various agricultural commodities such as unprocessed rice, jute, other agricultural crops, and fruit and vegetables was common; as was dealing in building materials such as sand, timber, or bamboo. Livestock dealing (cows, goats, horses, and poultry) was also common, and was sometimes linked to livestock rearing or income from cow's milk sales. Some livestock also provided income from cultivation (e.g. bullocks or buffalo) or transport (such as horse-drawn carts). Other forms of transport provision included the very common use of cycle rickshaws, flat decked cycle van *garis*, or the person-powered *thelagaris*. A number of motorized forms of people and goods transport also formed the basis of transport-based businesses. Some of these vehicles were manufactured in local engineering workshops using modified agricultural engines.

A number of businesses were also linked to crop cultivation and processing: selling irrigation water from shallow tube wells (diesel or electric), power tillers, rice-husking machines, or running grain mill businesses. Various kinds of shops, market stalls, and door-to-door selling of produce were also common. Groceries, food snacks, dried fish, milk, and jewellery were typical items sold from a range of rural shops and stalls. Other services also formed the basis of small businesses such as hair cutting, money lending, and medical services (some involving traditional medical practices by traditional healers or *kobiraj*). A number of new types of business were also evident, such as hiring out mobile phones services or small businesses associated with servicing or trading in by-products of the mainly urban-based garments industry.

Some of the main features of small business activities are as follows: (1) Many households had complex portfolios of income-generating activities, for example combining rural businesses with agriculture, livestock, salaried work, and day labour; (2) if more than one household member was able to contribute to household income through business activities then improvements became more likely; (3) some businesses failed, causing decline and indebtedness; and (4) business activities which involved the accumulation of both protective and productive assets were particularly effective in supporting improvement and eventual exit from poverty.[14]

7.4.2.2   *The accumulation of land assets*

Of the 293 life histories, 113 or 39 per cent cited the accumulation of land as a significant source of life improvement. This category overlaps to some extent with other categories such as agriculture and fish farming (see 7.4.2.5 below) which often also reflect the benefits (protective and productive) of owning land. Also when land was inherited the event was also categorized as "help from relatives or inheritance" in my analysis.[15] Table 7.5 shows that many more people on improving trajectories cited the accumulation of land as a source of opportunity than those on declining trajectories.

7.4.2.3 Livestock

In the total of 293 life histories, livestock appeared as a significant source of opportunity in 80 life histories (27 per cent), although they were also the third most common cause of decline in Table 7.6. The majority of these were opportunities from cattle (67 life histories) followed by goats (19 life histories). Horses (5 life histories) and poultry (4 life histories) did not feature so strongly as significant sources of opportunity.

Livestock, and particularly cattle, are significant assets and cattle ownership was a very common step in paths of improvement involving the accumulation of even more valuable assets, such as land. Many stories of improvement show a pattern or small investment in livestock – starting with poultry or goats for example – which then allowed a larger investment – often in cattle – followed by the purchase of land. Cattle and land appeared as key resources: both assets are productive and feature strongly in stories of emergence from poverty. They are also important protective assets: they were often sold, and in the case of land there were a number of ways money was raised through mortgage arrangements – often with neighbours providing money in exchange for the use of the land as long as the funds are not returned – or leasing land.

7.4.2.4 Sons' or daughters' income

Of the 293 life histories, 71 (or 24 per cent) reported life-improving opportunities associated with children working and supporting the parent's household – either as part of the household or in the form of remittances sent from another place. These opportunities were almost exclusively from sons working. Only two life histories – a husband and wife from the same household – reported that their two daughters, who were working in a garments factory, provided them with one of three major life opportunities. There were numerous life histories where daughters were working (also commonly in the garments industry) but the contribution this made rarely translated into significant life improvements for their parents. The main reasons for this were that income-earning opportunities for young women in rural Bangladesh are still limited, with relatively low levels of remuneration, and rural

Table 7.6 Frequencies of causes of decline, comparing improving, and declining trajectories (ranked according to difference in percentage)

Responses or impacts	All life histories	Percentage	Improving trajectory	Percentage	Declining trajectory	Percentage	Difference in percentage
Loss of savings	23	7.8	10	12.7	3	4.2	8.4
Non-NGO loan	49	16.7	15	19.0	9	12.7	6.3
Other asset or crop sales	40	13.7	12	15.2	7	9.9	5.3
Psychological distress	46	15.7	15	19.0	10	14.1	4.9
Litigation	6	2.0	3	3.8	0	0.0	3.8
Loss of income	97	33.1	24	30.4	20	28.2	2.2
All loans	101	34.5	26	32.9	22	31.0	1.9
NGO loan	21	7.2	6	7.6	6	8.5	-0.9
Premature death	20	6.8	6	7.6	6	8.5	-0.9
No treatment of illness due to poverty	8	2.7	0	0.0	1	1.4	-1.4
Loss of education	11	3.8	2	2.5	3	4.2	-1.7
Money from business	14	4.8	4	5.1	5	7.0	-2.0
Non-specified loans	39	13.3	7	8.9	8	11.3	-2.4
Problems with property division or inheritance	8	2.7	1	1.3	3	4.2	-3.0
Going without food	16	5.5	2	2.5	4	5.6	-3.1
Women's extra labour	14	4.8	1	1.3	4	5.6	-4.4
Disability or chronic illness	28	9.6	3	3.8	6	8.5	-4.7
Family disputes	15	5.1	2	2.5	9	12.7	-10.1
Help from relatives or neighbours	58	19.8	12	15.2	19	26.8	-11.6
Sale of livestock	68	23.2	13	16.5	21	29.6	-13.1
Sale or mortgage of land	86	29.4	15	19.0	34	47.9	-28.9

women are commonly married quite young – especially if they have left school – and because marriage patterns are patrilocal their income rarely contributes to their parents' households.

The contribution that sons were making to parents' households was much more significant across the life histories. The jobs done ranged from day labour (e.g. agricultural, livestock, brick works, and road works) to small businesses (e.g. rickshaw or van owner-driving, dealing in food or agricultural raw materials, running various kinds of shops, irrigation businesses, furniture making, and tailoring) to salaried work in both private and public sectors (government departments, army, mills, presses, and factories). A small number of sons were also employed over-seas – mostly in the Middle East – sending remittances home.

7.4.2.5 Agriculture

Of the 293 life histories, 69 (23 per cent) had life-improving opportuni-ties linked to agricultural enterprises. Agriculture is a difficult category to delineate in rural Bangladesh as there are a wide variety of agricul-tural activities from arable crops (such as rice, jute, wheat, and maize) to a range of vegetables, fruit trees, pineapples, bamboo, spices, tree, and flower nurseries. Livestock and fishponds are also often linked into this production system. Machinery associated with agriculture, such as threshing machines, power tillers, and irrigation pumps, can also pro-vide an independent income in addition to their use on people's own land. There are also a wide variety of use and ownership arrangements of land from outright ownership, mortgage arrangements, leasing of land, and sharecropping of land, ponds, and livestock.

The relatively high frequency of agriculture as a source of opportu-nity demonstrates the continuing importance of these varied forms of income sources for rural households. Additionally these sources of income are also often accompanied by the accumulation of assets such as land, livestock, or machinery. As a result the stories of exit from poverty supported by agricultural enterprises tend also to be stories of gradual accumulation of assets. These stories generally show that hard work over the long term provides rewards, but the rewards are greater for those with initial resources to build on.

7.4.2.6 Salaried work

Of the 293 life histories, 42 (or 14 per cent) attributed significant life-improving opportunities to a household member or close family mem-ber gaining salaried work. Having salaried work in rural Bangladesh is usually referred to as having a *chakri*, sometimes literally translated as being "in service." The usual local distinctions are between having a relatively secure *chakri* on a monthly salary, less secure day labour (*din mojur*) paid at a daily rate, and being in business (*baebsha*).

The advantages of having salaried work are mainly in the regularity and security of income, but also other advantages such as having access to credit and savings in the form of salary advances or provident funds and pensions. Employers also act as patrons for their employees in asymmetric relationships which provide security in various forms for the employee in exchange for expected loyalty. The life history interviews show a wide range of salaried work and, when gained, it was commonly a source of long-term benefit for the employee and his or her family.

These jobs included work in public services, such as the army, police, and electricity department; public owned mills and factories; work in private companies ranging from small printing presses to petrol pumps, brick factories to larger sugar mills; packaging companies to steel mills; and a range of other private factories making: garments, cigarettes, cosmetics, and biscuits. Research participants also had salaried jobs teaching in schools and madrassas, or working as guards and drivers. A small number also had salaried jobs working in NGOs.

7.4.3   Negative endowments and vulnerability to downward pressures

The most frequently cited causes of downward pressure across the whole set of life histories in order of frequency were: illness and injury (75 per cent); dowry and wedding expenses (39 per cent); death of family members (33 per cent); division of household or property (22 per cent); theft or cheating (20 per cent); litigation (19 per cent); and weather-related events such as floods, cyclones, and storms (17 per cent). Such findings highlight the need for better quality, reasonably priced health provision as a poverty reduction measure in Bangladesh. They also draw attention to the serious impact – including the depletion of assets – dowry has on families with girls. Other life-cycle-related events such as the death of parents and household and property division seem to mark particularly risky times of life. Also adverse weather events causing damage to property and crops are significant causes of decline, as would be expected in Bangladesh where large numbers of people are dependent on crops (damaged by floods, hail, fog, wind, and drought) and livestock (floods and drought), and have houses that are vulnerable to floods, storms, etc.

Patterns of shocks and downward pressures between people on improving and declining trajectories were also seen to differ. When we compare frequencies of citation of the common downward pressures across the declining trajectory versus improving trajectory groups, we observe the most damaging sources of downward pressure overall being more frequently experienced by those in decline. Sale or mortgage of land, for example, was more often cited by the declining group. Also some events, such as household or property division, are more often sources of opportunity for those on improving trajectories, but more frequently a source of downward pressure for those declining. Also illness or injury – the most common and most serious sources of downward pressure overall – were more frequently experienced by those on declining trajectories. Thus those on improving trajectories were more likely to report the key forms of well-being-enhancing opportunity, while those in declining trajectories seem to experience the more serious causes of decline. The combination of these explains much socio-economic mobility. They also draw attention to the need for social programmes that, on one hand, protect and strengthen the endowment base (assets and capabilities) of vulnerable people, so that they can exploit opportunities, and, on the other, help them cope with downward pressures, without undermining their existing assets or capabilities.

7.4.4 Patterns of coping in crises

7.4.4.1 *Constructive and destructive coping*

Different forms of coping in crises also influence long-term chances of moving out of poverty. The life histories illustrate how destructive coping strategies – that is, strategies which undermine a family's endowments of productive assets or key capabilities – contribute to poor people being trapped in poverty. A comparison of the life histories of Monir and Zeehan (see Figures 7.4 and 7.5 below) illustrates the difference between the coping strategies of a person in long-term decline and those of someone on an improving trajectory.

Monir is a 46-year-old man who has been not-poor for most of his life and Zehaan is a 52-year-old woman who has declined from moderate poverty into extreme poverty in recent years. Both are from the same village in Nilphamari District in the north-west of Bangladesh and both have struggled with arranging marriages for an unusually large number of daughters. Monir married off his six daughters and paid hefty dowries to manage this, and Zehaan paid dowries for the marriages of seven daughters – with one more daughter yet to be married.

However the trajectory diagram illustrates how Monir and his wife were able to cope with these downward pressures and to continue to accumulate land assets despite the downward pressure of dowry expenses while Zeehan and her husband (Figure 7.4) were forced to sell land in order to arrange marriages. This difference is mainly because of Monir's (Figure 7.5) relatively larger holdings of land and other productive assets in the form of livestock and agricultural machinery and his reluctance to sell these assets to fund dowries. When Monir married, his father owned 20 *bighas* (6.6 acres) of land and they lived in an extended household with his parents and brothers. From the time of his marriage, he and his wife Bimola started to accumulate. The pattern of accumulation was from smaller livestock (goats and poultry) to larger livestock (cattle) and then to land. In the year following the death of Monir's father, the family's then 15 *bighas* homestead was divided and Monir received 8 *bighas*. Since then Monir and Bimola increased the amount of land they own to 16 *bighas* in 2007. Over the years Monir raised large dowries to arrange for suitable marriages for his six daughters, but each time he raised the money through the sale of crops or livestock, without selling any land.

Zehaan (Figure 7.5), on the other hand, started out with a smaller area of land, and then sold more each time one of her daughters was married. When Zehaan was married they owned and cultivated only 4 *bighas* (1.3 acres) of land. When their first daughter was married in 1981 they sold 16 decimals (0.16 acres) of this in order to raise the Tk 6,000 dowry. Then from 1996 to 2002 six other daughters were married and each time between 8 and 24 decimals of land was sold to raise the dowries of between Tk.6,000 and Tk. 18,000 for each marriage. In addition in 1989 Zehaan lost Tk. 60,000 which she had deposited with a bogus NGO – money which she got from some land her father had left her when he died. In the end Zehaan and her husband were left with only the small plot of land their house is built on. These differences lie behind the higher frequency of destructive coping observed among those on declining trajectories, as in Table 7.7. Our examination of individual cases suggests that destructive coping strategies commonly accompany long-term trajectories of decline. When a calamity befalls an individual or household with few coping assets available and/or liabilities present, then decline and destructive coping is often unavoidable creating a destructive downward spiral.

In order to explore patterns of coping, accounts of the four most frequently cited causes of downward pressure, or shock, were examined. Where the ways that the respondent coped was described in the life history narrative, the relevant sections were coded using the categories in Table 7.7. It was sometimes difficult to separate coping strategies from harmful impacts – as being harmed in various ways is sometimes the only form of coping able to be deployed by very poor people. For example, cutting down on meals is a coping strategy, but it can also be seen as

165

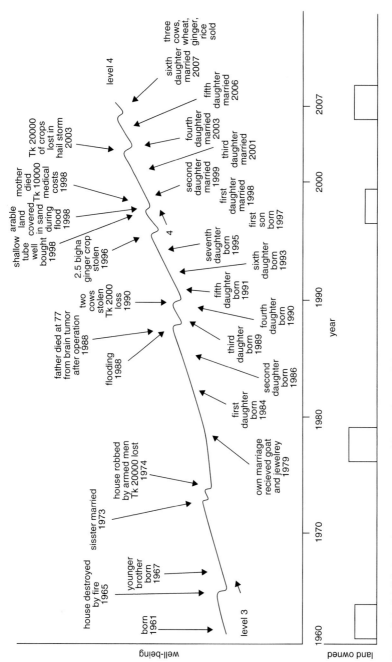

Figure 7.4 Well-being of Monir, 46-year-old man from Nilphamari District

166

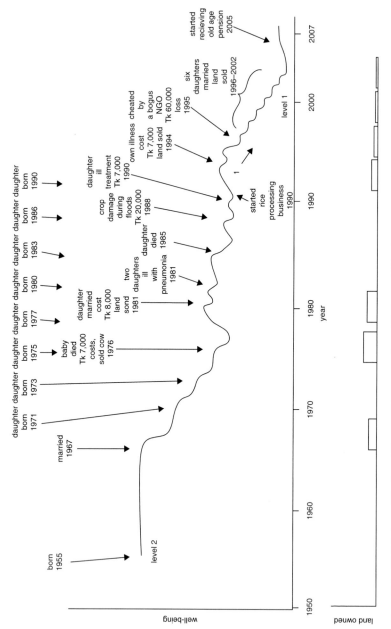

Figure 7.5 Well-being of Zeehan, 52-year-old woman from Niphamari District

constituting harm, as can withdrawing children from school. Some coping strategies damage social status, such as resorting to begging, which is socially stigmatizing in Bangladesh. Choosing to become socially stigmatized in this way in order to cope is thus a coping strategy and a form of harm. The four most frequently cited causes of downward pressure in the life histories were: illness, dowry, household or property division, and the death of relatives. Table 7.7 shows that loans of various kinds (e.g. NGO loans, informal interest-free loans from relatives and neighbours, and loans from moneylenders) were a very common form of coping with these crises. In many cases these were also subsequently paid off through the mortgage or sale of land and other assets. Many crises caused a loss of income – for example when business capital was used to cope, or illness led to a reduced capacity to work. We have already seen that those on declining trajectories cited the sale or mortgage of land as a cause of decline more frequently than those on improving trajectories. Here we also see the sale of land and livestock as a frequent means of coping. Help from relatives and neighbours – also often through loans – was also common, as was the sale of other assets such as crops, various stored commodities and food stuffs, trees, bamboo, building materials, rickshaws and bicycles.

Some differences in patterns of coping can be seen between improving- and declining-trajectory groups from this initial exploration (Table 7.7). For those declining, more destructive means of coping tend to be deployed more frequently. These involve the sale or mortgage of land, the sale of livestock, women's extra labour, and going without food. This also leads more often to illness and disability, and disputes. The only positive difference for those on declining trajectories was that they seemed to be helped more often by relatives or neighbours. This probably reflects moral economy (Scott 1976) norms of informal helping, and also their lack of other, more significant, forms of coping.

Tangible assets such as those linked to small businesses, land, livestock, and agricultural machinery are of key importance. The important intangible assets are in the form of family-based social capital which allows resources to be transferred across generations as inheritance, or as children supporting their parents via remittances, or in the form of general helping in crises. Human capital in the form of skills is also important while difficult to measure directly as they are not captured by educational outcomes. However the importance of salaried jobs, which invariably require special skills of educational qualifications, suggests that these kinds of human capital assets are important for socio-economic improvement.

The differences observed between people on improving trajectories compared with those on declining trajectories suggest that endowments

Table 7.7 Types of response to crisis events: comparing improving and declining trajectories (ranked according to difference in percentage)

Responses or impacts	All life histories	Percentage	Improving trajectory	Percentage	Declining trajectory	Percentage	Difference in percentage
Loss of savings	23	7.8	10	12.7	3	4.2	8.4
Non-NGO loan	49	16.7	15	19.0	9	12.7	6.3
Other asset or crop sales	40	13.7	12	15.2	7	9.9	5.3
Psychological distress	46	15.7	15	19.0	10	14.1	4.9
Litigation	6	2.0	3	3.8	0	0.0	3.8
Loss of income	97	33.1	24	30.4	20	28.2	2.2
All loans	101	34.5	26	32.9	22	31.0	1.9
NGO loan	21	7.2	6	7.6	6	8.5	-0.9
Premature death	20	6.8	6	7.6	6	8.5	-0.9
No treatment of illness due to poverty	8	2.7	0	0.0	1	1.4	-1.4
Loss of education	11	3.8	2	2.5	3	4.2	-1.7
Money from business	14	4.8	4	5.1	5	7.0	-2.0
Non-specified loans	39	13.3	7	8.9	8	11.3	-2.4
Problems with property division or inheritance	8	2.7	1	1.3	3	4.2	-3.0
Going without food	16	5.5	2	2.5	4	5.6	-3.1
Women's extra labour	14	4.8	1	1.3	4	5.6	-4.4
Disability or chronic illness	28	9.6	3	3.8	6	8.5	-4.7
Family disputes	15	5.1	2	2.5	9	12.7	-10.1
Help from relatives or neighbours	58	19.8	12	15.2	19	26.8	-11.6
Sale of livestock	68	23.2	13	16.5	21	29.6	-13.1
Sale or mortgage of land	86	29.4	15	19.0	34	47.9	-28.9

of assets *and* liabilities are important for understanding socio-economic mobility and the generation of inequality in rural Bangladesh. The assets providing opportunities for those on declining trajectories tended to be more protective – in terms of official social protection programmes, various forms of social capital, and day labour. However these assets were less likely to lift poor people permanently out of poverty than the key tangible assets such as business assets, land, and livestock – more enjoyed by those on improving trajectories.

It seems also that those on declining trajectories disproportionately suffer crises whose effects can become liabilities in the form of monetary debt, but also as ill health, poorer educated children, physical insecurity, lower social status, and other problems which offset the benefits of assets. Thus the poorest are likely to be held back in an asset *and* liability trap – rather than just one of low levels of asset endowments.

7.5   Concluding remarks: learning about poverty dynamics from life histories

The patterns of socio-economic mobility identified in this study draw attention to a number of areas in which social programmes could help reduce chronic poverty. In particular the research shows how ill health, dowry, and other kinds of pressures cause decline, and therefore how important social programmes aimed at reducing their impact may be. Affordable quality health services are key for poverty reduction, as are measures to reduce or eliminate dowry as a source of pressure on families with girls. In Bangladesh anti-dowry public policy needs to be seen as an anti-poverty imperative, in addition to a means of reducing oppression of women, and should be given more attention in national poverty reduction strategies.

Social protection programmes, which help poor people retain assets, or transfer assets to them, are also likely to reduce destructive coping leading to downward spirals. Livestock assets are key in stories of coping and improvement, as are a range of other business activities. While loans can be beneficial for those with the ability to succeed in business, the destructive capacity of debt for those who are not so able should not be ignored. In Bangladesh there has been a tendency to rely on micro-credit to reduce poverty while neglecting other measures that protect those not able to succeed in businesses supported by loans. Programmes are needed to reduce the impact of common downward pressures for the most vulnerable (including the prevention of destructive coping) while increasing the types of opportunities and people's ability to exploit opportunities.

The analysis provides evidence that individuals showing a long-term improvement in well-being tend to exploit a limited set of opportunity types. The most frequently cited types of opportunity were, in order of frequency across the set of all life histories: rural farm and non-farm-related businesses (some supported by loans); accumulation and production of assets such as land and livestock, and income derived from them; remittances and support from sons' and (to a lesser extent) daughters' incomes; crop and fish production (also linked to land); and help from relatives, inheritance, or a favourable division of family assets.

However, the frequency of appearance of types of opportunity showed a slightly different pattern in life histories of individuals enjoying long-term well-being improvement, compared with people on trajectories of long-term well-being decline. People on improving trajectories more frequently reported sources of opportunity associated with accumulation of land assets, benefits from business activities, agriculture and fish farming, use of loans, salaried employment, livestock, household or property division.

In contrast, those on declining trajectories more often cited official social protection and development programmes, such as the Vulnerable Groups Development Programme, or the Primary Education Stipend, as sources of opportunity – suggesting that these official programmes may be effectively reaching those who need help, but tend to protect from decline, rather than lift people out of poverty. The declining group also cited the benefits of having a united family more often than those on improving trajectories. Opportunities associated with day labour, dowry receipt or favourable marriage, and sons and daughters working did not show a marked difference in frequency of citation between those on improving or declining trajectories.

These findings support the view that work-related productive and asset-accumulating activities involving: land, businesses, agriculture, loans, livestock, and salaried work, are doing the "heavy lifting" of poverty reduction in rural Bangladesh, particularly for those with the resources and capabilities to exploit these routes out of poverty. Other forms of opportunity, such as official social protection programmes, seem to protect from further decline rather than function as a widespread cause of poverty exit.

The overall image of poverty reduction provided by household surveys can therefore be supplemented by life history interviews which provide a dynamic picture of how some people, with productive assets and capabilities (e.g. land, livestock, machinery, skills, access to salaried employment, and business ability), are able to both exploit opportunities and cope with crises, and thus improve their lives. However, at the same time they leave behind people who lack those key assets or capabilities – thus generating the observed increases in inequality in rural Bangladesh.

For poverty reduction policy, the findings provide implications for action, as well as for ways of thinking. Productive interventions such as those around business activities, livestock, land ownership, and production are likely to provide reductions in poverty, but unless these interventions enable productive assets to be transferred to the most vulnerable (represented by those on declining trajectories), it is likely they will help those already on improving trajectories, more than the most vulnerable. The approach and findings also provide support for the view that the amelioration of common downward pressures, and particularly the downward pressures that affect those declining, will also make an important contribution to poverty reduction. However, the effectiveness of these interventions should not be assessed solely on how many people they lift across the national poverty line (the reduction in headcount poverty). Attention should also be paid to the impact on the depth of poverty and the protective role these interventions have in preventing further declines, even when a poverty exit is not achieved.

The learning derived from examining life history trajectories does not replace what can be learned from household surveys with much larger sample sizes. However, a detailed examination of individual life histories provides a unique view of the complex dynamics of socio-economic mobility, and the way that a range of upward opportunities and downward pressures interact to create trajectories of well-being. This complements more quantitative variable-based research approaches in informing poverty reduction policy.

Notes

The Chronic Poverty Research Centre funded this research. It builds on collaborative work funded by the Department for International Development through the Economic and Social Research Council of the United Kingdom, HarvestPlus, and the World Bank. I acknowledge helpful discussions with, and comments from, Bob Baulch, Graham Brown, Agnes Quisumbing, and Andrew Shepherd. I also thank Zahidul Hassan and Md. Zobair of Data Analysis and Technical Assistance Ltd for managing the fieldwork team so efficiently, and Biswas Akhter, Rafiqul Haque (Shawpon), Dilara Hasin, Safia Satter (Sonia), Md. Abdul Aziz, and Anowara Begum (Nupur) for excellent research assistance. All errors or omissions are the author's.

1. Data Analysis and Technical Assistance Ltd., is a consultancy firm based in Dhaka with well-established expertise in conducting large-scale social surveys and other research activities.
2. The dataset from this study is publicly available at http://www.ifpri.org/dataset/ chronic-poverty-and-long-term-impact-study-bangladesh. Davis and Baulch (2010) provide a more detailed description of the methods used in this study.

3. The 2006–2007 study aimed to integrate and sequence quantitative and quali- tative methods, in three phases: Phase 1 involved focus-group discussions with four groups (of poor and better-off women, plus poor and better-off men) in each village. The focus groups aimed to elicit perceptions of changes, group members' perceptions of the interventions under study, and the degree to which these interventions affected people's lives (compared to other events in the community). Phase 2 was a quantitative survey of the original house- holds and new households that had split off from the original households but remained in the same district. The household survey took place from November 2006 to February 2007, the same agricultural season as the original surveys, with multi-topic questionnaires designed to be comparable across sites and with the original questionnaires from the evaluation studies. Phase 3 consisted of a qualitative study based on life histories of 293 men and women in 161 selected households in eight of the districts in the original quantitative study. The aim of this phase was to understand the processes and contexts which influence individual and household livelihood trajectories.

4. "Sites" refer to districts in all cases except in Mymensingh and Kishoreganj districts where the "site" and the two selected villages spanned the district boundary.

5. These categories are chronically not-poor, chronically poor, move up and move down with respect to the per capita expenditure national poverty line at the time of the baseline and 2006–2007 surveys.

6. Examples of these life histories are provided at http://www.sdri.org.uk/ bangladesh.asp.

7. In this chapter focus-group discussions refer to these exercises rather than a separate set of 116 focus-group discussions conducted in 2006 with findings reported in Davis (2007).

8. For more on comparing the quantitative and qualitative assessments see Davis and Baulch (2011).

9. NVivo is a qualitative data analysis software package developed by QSR International. See: http://www.qsrinternational.com.

10. Ali's household per capita expenditure rose from about half the poverty line in 2000, to just over it in 2007, in our quantitative assessment. However with household instability and health-related expenses, including Ali's ongoing mental illness, it is unlikely that the observed rise in household expenditure accurately reflected a corresponding rise in well-being for the same period. See Davis and Baulch (2011) for a discussion of disagreements of quantitative- and qualitative-based poverty assessment.

11. In this area there are 48 decimals per *bigha* or *pakhi* of land; there are 100 decimals in an acre of land. It is difficult to determine whether Ali's father would have been classified as poor or not poor earlier in his life before his illness from the life history interview. Five bighas of land was less productive in 1962 than in 2007, and an asset-based classification would need to account for this. Certainly once Ali's father became ill and land was sold to pay for treatment he would have been classified as poor using our qualitative criteria.

12. Categories with fewer than ten cases have been omitted. Events from each life history were coded to a list of categories: three or four events represent- ing opportunity were coded in each case, and any one event could be coded in several categories due to opportunities with multiple causes.

13. Causes of opportunity cited in fewer than ten life histories have been omitted.
14. Protective assets are those that can be sold in a time of crisis, such as jewellery or furniture, which may not appreciate or generate income. Productive assets can usually be sold but can also be used to generate income, such as land, trees, or livestock. Distress sales of productive assets can have damaging long-term consequences for poor families.
15. See Note 11 above for a breakdown of types of land accumulation or use associated with this category.

References

Ahmed, A. (2005) Comparing food and cash incentives for schooling in Bangladesh. Study commissioned by the United Nations University. Washington, DC: International Food Policy Research Institute.
Baulch, B. (2010) The medium-term impact of the primary education stipend in rural Bangladesh. Discussion Paper No. 976. Washington, DC: International Food Policy Research Institute.
Camfield, L. and K. Roelen (2013) and Household Trajectories in Rural Ethiopia: What Can a Mixed Method Approach Tell Us About the Impact of Poverty on Children? *Social Indicators Research*, 113(2), 729–749.
Davis, P. (2005) Power-resources and social policy in Bangladesh: A life-history perspective. Doctoral dissertation. Bath: University of Bath.
Davis, P. (2007) Discussions among the poor: Exploring poverty dynamics with focus groups in Bangladesh. Chronic Poverty Research Centre Working Paper No. 84. Manchester, UK: Chronic Poverty Research Centre. http://www.chronic poverty.org/uploads/publication_files/WP84_Davis.pdf
Davis, P. (2009) "Poverty in time: Exploring poverty dynamics from life history interviews in Bangladesh," in T. Addison, D. Hulme and R. Kanbur (eds) *Poverty Dynamics: Interdisciplinary Perspectives* (Oxford: Oxford University Press), pp. 154–182.
Davis, P. (2011a) "Exploring the long-term impact of development interventions within life-history narratives in rural Bangladesh," *The Journal of Development Effectiveness* 3(2), 263–280.
Davis, P. (2011b) Escaping poverty: Patterns and causes of poverty exits in rural Bangladesh. Chronic Poverty Research Centre Working Paper No. 194. Manchester, UK: Chronic Poverty Research Centre. http://www.chronic poverty.org/uploads/publication_files/WP194%20Davis.pdf
Davis, P. (2011c) Passing on poverty: The intergenerational transmission of wellbeing and ill-being in rural Bangladesh. Chronic Poverty Research Centre Working Paper No. 192. Manchester, UK: Chronic Poverty Research Centre. http://www.chronicpoverty.org/uploads/publication_files/WP192%20Davis.pdf
Davis, P. (2011d) Social exclusion and adverse incorporation in rural Bangladesh: Evidence from a mixed-methods study of poverty dynamics. Chronic Poverty Research Centre Working Paper No. 193. Manchester, UK: Chronic Poverty Research Centre. http://www.chronicpoverty.org/uploads/publication_files/WP193%20Davis.pdf
Davis, P. (2011e) The trappings of poverty: The role of assets and liabilities in socio-economic mobility in rural Bangladesh. Chronic Poverty Research Centre Working Paper No. 195. Manchester, UK: Chronic Poverty Research

Centre. http://www.chronicpoverty.org/uploads/publication_files/WP195%20 Davis.pdf

Davis, P. (2011f) Vulnerability in rural Bangladesh: Learning from life history interviews. Chronic Poverty Research Centre Working Paper No. 196. Manchester, UK: Chronic Poverty Research Centre. http://www.chronicpoverty.org/uploads/publication_files/WP196%20Davis.pdf

Davis, P. and B. Baulch (2010) Casting the net wide and deep: Lessons learned in a mixed methods study of poverty dynamics in rural Bangladesh. Chronic Poverty Research Centre Working Paper No. 155. Manchester, UK: Chronic Poverty Research Centre. http://www.chronicpoverty.org/uploads/ publication_files/WP155%20davis-baulch.pdf

Davis, P. and B. Baulch (2011) "Parallel realities: Exploring poverty dynamics using mixed methods in rural Bangladesh," *The Journal of Development Studies* 47(1), 118–142.

Dewilde, C. (2003) A life-course perspective on social exclusion and poverty. *British Journal of Sociology*, 54(1), pp. 109–128.

Hallman, K., D. Lewis and S. Begum (2007) "Assessing the impact of vegetable and fishpond technologies on poverty in rural Bangladesh," in M. Adato and R. Meinzen-Dick (eds) *Agricultural Research, Livelihoods, and Poverty: Studies of Economic and Social Impacts in Six Countries* (Baltimore: Johns Hopkins University Press), pp. 103–48.

Kumar, N. and A. Quisumbing (2009) Access, adoption, and diffusion: Understanding the long-term impacts of improved vegetable and fish technologies in Bangladesh. Discussion Paper No. 995. Washington, DC: International Food Policy Research Institute.

Miller, R. L. (2000) Researching life stories and family histories. London: Sage.

Miller, R. L. (2007) Using family histories to understand the intergenerational transmission of chronic poverty. Chronic Poverty Research Centre Working Paper No. 103. Manchester, UK: Chronic Poverty Research Centre. http://www. chronicpoverty.org/uploads/publication_files/WP103_Miller.pdf

Quisumbing, A. and B. Baulch (2009) Assets and poverty traps in rural Bangladesh. Chronic Poverty Research Centre Working Paper No. 143. Manchester, UK: Chronic Poverty Research Centre.http://www.chronicpoverty. org/uploads/publication_files/WP143%20Baulch-Quisumbing.pdf

Scott, J. C. (1976) *The Moral Economy of the Peasant: Rebellion and Subsistence in Southeast Asia*. New Haven: Yale University Press.

Sen, B. and D. Hulme (2006) Chronic poverty in Bangladesh: Tales of ascent, descent, marginality and persistence. Dhaka and Manchester: Bangladesh Institute of Development Studies/Chronic Poverty Research Centre.

Stewart, F., Saith, R. and Harriss-White, B. (2007) Defining poverty in the developing world (London: Palgrave Macmillan).

Thomas, W. I. and Znaniecki, F. (1958) The Polish Peasant in Europe and America, (New York: Dover) [first published New York: Knopf 1918–20].

Zeller, M., M. Sharma, A. Ahmed, and S. Rashid (2001) Group-based financial institutions for the rural poor in Bangladesh: An institutional- and household-level analysis. Research Report 120. Washington, D.C.: International Food Policy Research Institute. http://www.ifpri.org/sites/default/files/publications/ rr120.pdf

8
Household Surveys – Using Qualitative Data to Enhance Our Understanding of Household Dynamics over Time

Pamela Nasirumbi Muniina, Janet Seeley, and Sian Floyd

8.1 Introduction

Margo Russell suggested that the "household has become dangerously reified" (1993: 755). She had a point. As she and many commentators have explained, identifying "the household" in many African settings is not straightforward and, indeed, may be misleading because it fails to take account of linkages across a wider kinship or familial group (Guyer and Peters 1987; Martin and Beittel 1987; and, more recently, Müller 2004; McEwan and Samuels 2006; Hosegood et al. 2007). However, as Coast, et al. (2009: 1) have recently stated, "Household surveys are the mainstay of micro-level data for developing countries" and while the use of the household as a unit for data collection has well-documented limitations the important place of "the household" in research as well as for national health surveillance surveys suggests that developing a better understanding of how to define households, and distinguish among different types, is a worthwhile exercise. Demographers such as Sara Randall and Ernestina Coast have undertaken extensive research to understand the use of different definitions of the household in survey and census data, and whether they reflect the household and family structures in Europe and Africa (see, for example, Randall et al. 2011), and this chapter builds on this existing body of work.

In this chapter we explain how qualitative data from a small number of households drawn from a large total-population cohort study in a defined geographical area in rural south-west Uganda, informed our understanding of household dynamics, social mobility, and impoverishment. At the same time it provided valuable insights into appropriate ways to categorize individuals and households in the cohort, and how to determine if a household remained intact or ceased to exist, which is necessary for large-scale quantitative analysis of how households change and evolve over time.

The chapter proceeds as follows. We first describe the population cohort and the methods used for data collection for both the total-population survey rounds and the qualitative study, before explaining briefly how households have been defined in the literature, and are defined in the cohort study. We then explore some of the problems raised by that definition, based on the findings from the qualitative research, and following from this we suggest "rules" for how to decide when a household has changed to the extent that it no longer exists as the same social group. We then apply these rules to the total-population cohort data to describe and better understand household dynamics at the population level.

8.2   Background to the General Population Cohort

The research is based in a rural sub-county in Kalungu District, in south western Uganda. The people living in the area are largely subsistence farmers who produce small amounts of cash crops such as bananas, beans, and coffee. The majority of the population is ethnically Baganda (75 per cent), but there is a large representation of immigrants from Rwanda (15 per cent). Just over 50 per cent of the population is under the age of 15, and the ratio of females to males for the total population is roughly equal.

The Medical Research Council/Uganda Virus Research Institute (MRC/UVRI) has studied the evolution of the HIV epidemic in a cohort of about 10,000 individuals living in 15 villages since 1989 and an additional 10,000, living in 10 neighbouring villages, since 2000. Annual demographic, medical and serological surveys have been carried out with the cohort since 1989. In 2012 the medical survey frequency became biennial but the demographic data collection (information on births, deaths, migration, and current household residents, for example) continues on an annual basis. Information on socio-economic status, based on house construction and a weighted asset index, is collected every four years.

Informing people in the study area of the forthcoming data collection is followed by mapping, then the census and medical survey. In 2008 hand-drawn maps were replaced by mapping using Geographical Positioning System technology for locating all dwellings and demarcating village boundaries and principal geographical features within the study area. A census questionnaire is administered to a household head or adult representative to collect individual demographic and household socioeconomic data. To assess the internal validity of the census data, repeat interviews are conducted in a random sample of 10 per cent of the households. Households and individuals are assigned identification numbers during mapping and census and the number of the individual is maintained irrespective of the individual relocating to another village or household. The background to the General Population Cohort (GPC) is explained in more detail in Asiki et al. (2013).

Members of the cohort also take part in other small studies from time to time. These have included an ethnographic study on the impact of HIV and AIDS on daily life carried out with 27 households from three of the cohort villages in 1991/1992 and repeated with 24 of those households 15 years later (2006/2007), and it is from these two studies that the qualitative data in this paper are drawn. The original 27 households were chosen purposively in 1990 to represent a cross-section of different household types (by sex and age of household head, as well as socio-economic status) with over-sampling of female-headed households because at the time we were concerned that these households were particularly vulnerable to the impacts of the HIV epidemic. In both 1991/1992 and 2006/2007, local people, trained in qualitative data collection methods, visited the household monthly for a year to gather information from residents (and their visitors) about changes in household composition as well as ways of making a living and other day-to-day activities.

8.3   Definitions of household and family

Despite being identified as a problematic concept (Niehof 2004), a household has been one of the commonest units used to obtain information on African families (Goody 1989). Households have been viewed as a "building block" for much data collection and subsequent analyses (Bolt and Bird 2003). However the term "household" is understood differently across disciplines and in different contexts with the definitions based on the specific needs and constraints of the research being undertaken. In fact the description of a household frequently overlaps and intersects with that of a family despite these concepts being distinct. Key literature on definitions of households and families is summarized below (Table 8.1):

Common elements of these definitions suggest that we may refer to a household as a co-residential unit that is usually family-based, and is characterized by a collective provision of essentials (food, shelter, etc.); geographical proximity; the sharing of activities (such as food production and child bearing); and the acknowledgement of one person as a head.

Table 8.1 Defining a household and a family

Year	Researcher	Defining a household
1967	Bender	A set of individuals that share the same residence or are living in close geographical proximity.
1973	United Nations	A reflection of the living arrangements of persons, individually or in groups, for providing themselves with food, shelter, and other essentials.
1975	Berkner	Co-residence under the same roof is not crucial; of more importance is whether the household members cook and eat together and the nature of their social and economic relations.
1979	Yanagisako	A set of individuals who share not only a living space but also some activities such as food production, food consumption, and child bearing.
1987	Ponnighaus et al.	A group of people living together and acknowledging one person as a head.
1997	Fine et al.	
2001	Urassa et al.	A group of people who regularly eat from the same pot.
1995	Rudie	A co-residential unit, usually family-based in some way, which takes care of resource management and primary needs of its members.
2006	Timæus	Residential groups (that need not comprise of family) defined using one or more of the following criteria: co-residence in the same dwelling; commensality (eating together); pooling resources together; and the acknowledgement of authority as an identified household head. One or more persons who share a dwelling and make common provision for food and other essentials for living.
2007	Wittenberg and Collinson	An individual qualifies as a member of a household if he/she spends an average of four nights per week in the household.
2008	Hosegood	Characterized by their shared economic basis; the household member recognition of a single household head, and a single place as primary residence (for some or all of the members).
2012	World Bank	A group of persons who: live, cook and eat together; share a common source of food and/or income; or have one person who they regard as the household head. Or a single person who lives alone and eats independently

Year	Researcher	Defining a Family
1967	Bender	A reflection of kinship and marriage.
1984	Jaenson and Hamsworth	Kin-based group of people living in a dwelling(s), occupying a single compound and including members temporarily resident elsewhere (temporarily dispersed for occupational, social, or political reasons), but recognizing a common household head.
2006	Timæus	Group of related individuals who live in the same household.
2008	Hosegood	Characterized by their relationships through kinship or marriage

8.4   "The household" in the GPC

It was decided in 1989 that for the purposes of the GPC a household was to be defined as a group of individuals that regularly eat from the same "pot" of food and either live together or live in close proximity to the main residence. To qualify as a member a person should have been resident for at least three months or be intending to stay for more than three months. Household membership is determined by the member or members of the household interviewed by the "mapper" when compiling the initial list of household members. These may be family members (that have a relationship through kinship or marriage) or non-family members such as tenants, or domestic workers. The household should not include family members that do not live in the same structure or compound and do not share food and other resources, but this is often difficult to determine when family members live in the same village or pay frequent visits. It is intended that this definition allows some flexibility to accommodate the fact that a household member may be resident in one building (hut or house), a number of buildings in a common yard, or in neighbouring buildings. The household members are also asked to provide the mapper and census team with the name of one person as the head. Also accommodated in this definition are household heads with more than one spouse residing either in the same building or in neighbouring buildings but regularly eating from the same "pot" as one household.[1] If the spouses did not eat from the same "pot," then these are considered as separate households. However, despite the fact that a man with multiple partners may not be a permanent resident in more than one of the households of his wives, in most of these cases the mapper gives the man as the household head in each of the homes. In other cases, the "spouse" will be considered as the household head because she states that she is married but does not include the person she is married to on the household member list; this may particularly be the case if the woman is getting little support from the man. An example from the 2006/2007 qualitative data illustrates this situation. In May 2006 Nabukenya, aged 47 years old, was living with her four children (aged 21 to 9 years old) and her one-year-old grandchild. She said she was the head of the household. Her husband had gone and she did not think he would come back. She said he had other wives. At the next visit we found he was back and from June until October he was living in the house, but by November he had gone again and had not returned by the time the monthly visits finished in April 2007. This thus makes the identification of polygamy in different households difficult. Of the 7,931 GPC households that participated in the study at least once between 1989 and 2008, 7.2 per cent had female household heads who were recorded as married but did not have their spouse on the household member list at least once between 1989 and 2008.

While the example above illustrates the challenge of defining the household head, a further example from the qualitative data illustrates the challenge for the mapper and census team in deciding when a household is or is not a separate unit for the purposes of the survey.

In 1991 Lydia and Sara lived with their husband Jacob then aged 71, who was the household head. Sara had had six children and Lydia eight. Jacob, Sara, and Lydia had seven grandchildren staying with them, five of whom had at least one parent still alive: grandsons aged 18, 14, 14, and 9 and granddaughters: one aged 15 years, one aged six months and one aged one month (she joined the household on the death of her mother, the wife of one of Jacob's son's who had died). Two great nieces of Lydia who were orphans were also taken in by the household during the year when their own grandmother who had been caring for them died. Their house was made of mud and wattle with an iron sheet roof. It had six rooms. There was another piece of land that Jacob owned in the village near the place that Sara used to stay before she was moved by Jacob in the 1970s into the same house as Lydia.

In 2006 Lydia and Sara lived with two boys, who they called grandsons (they were great-nephews, but in the Baganda kinship terminology they are referred to as grandsons), aged 11 and 6 years. The old house was still standing, although was in need of repair. A new structure made of bricks and iron-sheets had been put up in the large compound. This was built by one of Lydia's sons who had intended to come and live there to care for them, but he died before the house was complete. The two women had finished the building work and said that they were keeping that house ready for the children of the son if they should wish to come and live there.

It seems likely that when the house was being built Lydia and Sara had told the mapper that the new structure belonged to their son. The mapper and the census team assigned a new number for that structure on the basis that the son would live in a separate household there (as other family members did who also lived nearby, eating and sleeping in their own homes). In order to "guard" the property Lydia decided to sleep in the new structure each night with one of the grandchildren while during the day they took their meals in the main house. Sara and the other boy slept in the old structure. Lydia maintained her identification number linked to the old house and the grandson who slept in the new structure with her had been given a number linked to her as household head of the old structure. However, the census takers had divided the household items, used in the household index, across the two houses presumably based on where the two women told them the items were at the time of the census visit. So the radio, for example, was listed as being in the new structure (although in actual fact it moved between the two structures with Lydia). The socio-economic status of the household, calculated based on the index was, therefore, "diluted" by the spread of items across the two buildings.

This example is not an isolated case. The person doing the mapping, and the census takers, quite correctly based on experience and the accepted definition of a household, assigned a new number to a new house structure which a new household head was establishing (even though the new household head never came to live in the house). However, the actual usage of the structures was different and reflected the fluid nature of many living arrangements, particularly where other family members live close by.

8.5   Household creation in the Ganda society

The Baganda have been described by Nahemow (1979: 172) as having a "loose patrilineal structure." All children belong to their father's clan (Roscoe 1965 [1911]: 128). This system of descent does not mean that a father and his children, once they had grown up, live together: "While they have a patrilineal kinship system, [the Baganda] are nuclear in their households and generations are often residentially segregated by considerable distances" (Nahemow 1979: 172). This can partly be explained by the availability of fertile land on which new households could be established but also high rates of marital instability (Nabaitu et al. 1994) and residential mobility (for work or accessing land). The fostering of children and widows moving to live with adult sons have all contributed to variability in the living arrangements of many Baganda.

A new household among the Baganda is formed mainly through marriage, with the wife being much more likely than the husband to move location, and the husband assuming the headship. The ideal is for the new household to be established after marriage, which consists of ritualized negotiations and a transfer of bridewealth as well as a feast known as an "introduction" (Kwanjula) (Karlström 2004). The traditional ceremonies are sometimes followed by a religious or civil wedding.

However co-habiting is very common among the Baganda. The high cost of the marriage ceremonies and bridewealth are mentioned as reasons for not formalizing a partnership. The GPC does not differentiate between those that are co-habiting; those that have a traditional marriage; or those that have a religious marriage. All these are considered as married as long as the respondent acknowledges the marriage.

Polygyny persists among the Baganda, as in other parts of Uganda. The 2006 Uganda Demographic and Health Survey found that over a quarter of marriages in Uganda are polygynous. Occasionally wives share a compound (as in the case of Lydia and Sara above) but in the majority of polygynous marriages the women live in different places, with the husband moving from household to household (Seeley 2012).

Marital instability resulting in the separation of the couple is quite common especially when no marriage contract had been attained. When this happens a woman may move to stay with her parents or a brother, taking some or all of the children with her. The man may remain with older children (because they belong to his clan) or ask a relative (often his mother) to care for them. Separation may thus result in single adult households, at least for a time.

8.6   Tracing households

As noted above, the GPC like many other demographic health studies gathers and retains household information at the point in time when "the household" joins the cohort and is assigned an identification number based solely on the physical location of the household. That number continues to be used as long as the house structure remains occupied. The GPC was established in 1989 with the expressed purpose of examining the trends in prevalence and incidence of HIV infection and their determinants. There was no intention at that time to look at residential units and demographic change, beyond exploring where HIV infection may occur in relationships between particular men and women and children. It is therefore a challenge to adapt the database in order to trace the history of the households to identify their changes over time, something that has become of increasing interest as researchers have looked at the broader impact of HIV on communities, in addition to a broadening spectrum of research questions beyond HIV epidemiology which have come on to the agenda.

Another example from the qualitative data illustrates the changes that many households have undergone in the study area and the challenges we face in trying to find a way to categorize "the household" so that change might be charted across the whole GPC. Regina died in 1995, she was 34 years old. Regina had two sisters (Rose and Teddy) and a brother. Rose had died in 1990, her partner, a lorry driver, had died in 1986. When we first met Regina in 1990 she had been living with the

13-year-old daughter and eight-year-old son of her sister Rose and their five-year-old cousin (the brother's son). The family stayed in the house that had belonged to her father. Regina's father had left his land to his four children. Each of the girls had received four acres but the boy had received more. When Rose died her children inherited her land. When Regina died she had no children, and so her land was given to her sister Teddy. Teddy's son now lives on her portion of land to care for it, he says, for his mother. The bulk of the land is fallow because the son of Rose is in Kampala although it is possible that he might wish to come back and take up residence on his land at some point. His sister, who could have access to the land if she needed it, has married and moved to another village.

Again, this example is not an unusual case with different family members, and sometimes non-family members, coming in to use land and house structures which continue to be owned by absent members. As with Teddy's son, these residents may not claim ownership; they may move on after a few years, or may continue to stay on the plot, all the while referring to himself or herself as the custodian on behalf of someone else.

There is a larger structure beyond family to which each person belongs: the clan. A clan comprises a group of related (patri)lineages. However far away an individual and his or her immediate family have moved, a man and his children are bound to the clan. According to Karlström (1999: 107), this bond cuts "across geography, status and interest, and by virtue of mandatory exogamy [is] constantly creating localized interclan affiliations as well."

We now review the literature on the tracing of households across time, and then go on to present new thinking on how to do this for the GPC in rural Uganda.

It is therefore sometimes unclear whether a household is the "same," the second time it is seen during the census (which is updated annually), if the composition has changed or a new head has taken over. This is a problem for any household definition, although it has received little attention in the literature. Relatively few researchers have undertaken the task of tracing households over time, particularly in an epidemiological cohort. Key studies from sub-Saharan Africa include: the investigation of changes in household structure in rural South Africa over the period 1996–2003 (Wittenberg and Collinson 2007); the investigation of the impact of adult mortality on household dissolution and migration in the same dataset from rural South Africa between 2000 and 2002 (Hosegood et al. 2004); and the study of household dynamics in northern Malawi during the 1980s (Chirwa et al. 2004). The studies in rural South Africa determined the "same" household retrospectively by an overlap of at least one household member. However the researchers in Malawi took an approach to household definition that focuses on the head, and considers that all people who acknowledge a particular individual as "head" are members of the same household, regardless of where they actually live, and that the household was no longer the same if that head died or left. The definition used in the Malawi study accepted that a group of people living together may be recognized by themselves and by their community as a particular household and that it may still be considered the same household after changes of membership.

Guided by some of the criteria in these studies and the findings from the qualitative research, we decided that households in the GPC could also be traced retrospectively by following a principal household member, who would be the major determinant of the household's existence (rather than the building in which they lived). In most cases, this household member is the one acknowledged by the household members as the household head, but not always. Between two time points, a household can therefore: continue in the same or different location within the study area; relocate outside the study area (out-migrated); relocate to an unknown location (lost to follow-up); cease to exist (dissolved); and return to the study area after an out-migration or loss to follow-up (left and returned). In addition new households can be created. The principles we have established to trace these changes across the annual rounds of data collection in the GPC are summarized in Table 8.2.

A lot of detailed relational information is lost in groupings which relate all the household members to the household head.

In addition, it should also be noted that unlike most Demographic and Health Surveys that relate household members to their household head, not all household members in the GPC are related to the household head, but are instead coded with reference to the household member to whom they are most closely related. For example, children are coded in reference to their mother if resident; while a married woman is coded in reference to her husband. Thus to enable the clear identification of for example the "next-in-line" the relation codes needed to be modified to relate all the household members to the household head.

8.7   Tracing GPC households

We now apply the criteria, summarized in Table 8.2 above, retrospectively to the households in the GPC between 1989 and 2008. The distribution of the number of households between the "start" and "end" time points that are five or five years apart is shown in the table below (Table 8.3). They are categorized according to whether they continued,

Table 8.2   Tracing of households over two time points

Household head status between two time points	Household continuation status
Same household head	
In the same geographical location	Same household
In a different geographical location	Same (Relocated)
Divorce between household head and spouse	
Household head and spouse maintain co-residency	Same household
Household headed by the divorced household head	Same household
Household headed by the divorced spouse	New household
Death of the household head	
Next-in-line* takes over headship	Same household
Majority of the household head's children remain resident	Same household
No next-in-line* takes over headship	Dissolved
Loses household head status	
Another takes up headship of the household	Dissolved
Relocates to another household and doesn't retain headship (for example, household head returns to parental home)	Dissolved
Household head moves/relocates outside study area	Out-migrated
Household head moves to an unknown location	Lost to follow-up
Re-identified after a previous out-migration or loss to follow-up	Left and returned
Newly created households	
Product of an individual shifting from another household where he/she was not a household head	
Household head creating another household	
Product of in-migration (from outside the study area)	
Missed in previous time point	
By a person who was once a household head of a previously dissolved household**	

*Next-in-line determined by the hierarchy of the close relations to the household head (that is spouse, biological child, parent, sibling).
**Once a dissolution occurs, a household cannot be re-created. If the household head of a previously dissolved household forms a household in the study, it is considered as a new household.

dissolved, or out-migrated over the four to five years of time period, were newly created, or returned to the study area after an earlier out-migration. Those present at the "end" time point are those that:

- continue from the start to the end of the follow-up period
- temporarily out-migrate or are lost to follow-up after the start time point but return within the follow-up period

Table 8.3 Application of the criteria to the GPC households followed from 1989 to 2008

Survey time points			1989/90	1993/94	1998/1999	2003/04	2007/08
Number of households at the specific survey time points			1,894	2,019	2,153	3,489	3,628
Household survival between the two time points (the "start" and "end" time points) (Percentage relative to the "start" time point)	Survived	Same location or change location[1]	1,334 (70.4%)	1,366 (67.7%)	1,471 (68.3%)	2441 (70.0%)	
		Leave (out-migrated/lost to follow-up) after the "start" time point but return before the "end" time point[2]	75 (4.0%)	58 (2.9%)	73 (3.3%)	189 (5.4%)	
	Didn't survive	Dissolve[3]	158 (8.3%)	175 (8.7%)	214 (9.9%)	197 (5.7%)	
		Out-migrate (don't return by the "end" time point)[4]	264 (13.9%)	353 (17.5%)	306 (14.2%)	506 (14.5%)	
		Lost to follow-up (don't return by the "end" time point)[5]	64 (3.4%)	67 (3.3%)	90 (4.2%)	156 (4.5%)	
		Total of households at start point	1,894 (100%)	2,019 (100%)	2,153 (100%)	3,489 (100%)	

Newly created after the "start" time point and survive to the "end" time point (percentage relative to the "start" time point)[6]	610 (32.2%)	687 (34.0%)	1,874 (87.0%)[a]	862 (24.7%)
Newly created after the "start" time point and DO NOT survive to the "end" time point (percentage relative to the "start" time point)[7]	295 (15.6%)	337 (16.7%)	935 (43.4%)[b]	379 (10.9%)
Households that left in the previous time points and returned in the new time points (percentage relative to the "start" time point)[8]	–	42 (2.1%)	71 (3.3%)	136 (3.9%)

The number of households at "start" time point are obtained by adding together the number of households corresponding to labels 1, 2, 3, 4, and 5; number of households at "end" time point obtained by adding together the number of households corresponding to labels 1, 2, 6, and 8; and households not "seen" at the "start" and "end" time points are represented by the number of households corresponding to label 7 in the table.

[a]After 1998/1999, 1,874 households were newly created and continued to 2003/04. However 1,076 were in the new villages only included in the study in 1999/2000. Which means, 798 (37.1% in reference to the households at the "start" time point) were newly created in the villages included in the start time point.

[b]After 1998/1999, 935 households were newly created and do not continue to 2003/04. However 586 were in the new villages only included in the study in 1999/2000. Which means, 349 (16.2% in reference to the households at the "start" time point) were those newly created in the villages considered/included in the start time point.

- are newly created after the start time point and continue to the end of the follow-up period
- out-migrated or were lost to follow-up in previous follow-up periods and return in the follow-up period under consideration.

While those that are not present in the "end" time point are those that:

- out-migrate after the "start" time point and do not return during the follow-up period
- are lost to follow-up after the "start" time point and do not return during the follow-up period
- dissolve after the "start" time point
- are newly created after the "start" time point but do not continue to the end of the follow-up period.

As noted above additional villages were added to the GPC 1999/2000, which accounts for the increase in numbers of households. This increased number of households is reflected in the number of households in the survey time points 2003/2004 and 2007/2008; as well as the increase in the number of newly created households between 1998/1999 and 2003/2004.

With reference to the number of households at the "start" point in time (considering only the villages considered at the "start" time point in the follow-up period), and averaging between the four follow-up periods:

- Of the households that are represented at "start" points of the follow-up periods:
  - 69.1 per cent continue from the start to the end of the follow-up period.
  - 3.9 per cent temporarily out-migrate or are lost to follow-up start time point but return within the follow-up period.
  - 15 per cent out-migrate after the "start" time point and do not return during the follow-up period.
  - 3.8 per cent are lost to follow-up after the "start" time point and do not return during the follow-up period.
  - 8.1 per cent dissolve after the "start" time point.
- Of those that are not represented at the "start" but are "seen" in the "end" point (with the percentages in reference to the number of households at the respective "start" points)
  - 32 per cent are newly created after the start time point and continue to the end of the follow-up period.

o 2.3 per cent out-migrate or are lost to follow-up in previous follow-up periods and return in the follow-up period under consideration.
• And, 14.8 per cent are newly created after the "start" time point but do not continue to the end of the follow-up period.

8.8   Comparison of our findings with those of other studies

In research where tracing has been undertaken, household definition and/or household tracing criteria have been used that are different to those we have used in the GPC. This makes the comparison of our findings with other demographic health studies difficult, however we attempt a comparison with studies from South Africa and Malawi below.

In the investigation of the impact of adult mortality on household dissolution and migration in rural South Africa between 2000 and 2002 (Hosegood et al. 2004), the definition of a household is similar to that used in the GPC and the households are also traced retrospectively. In addition, the definition of household out-migration is similar, but differs slightly in the definition of household dissolution. Between January 2000 and October 2002 the study shows that 2 per cent of the households dissolved while 8 per cent of the households migrated out of the area. Comparing with the GPC between the annual survey round of 2000/2001 and 2001/2002, of the 3.408 households that were recorded in the GPC in 2000/2001, 2.7 per cent dissolved, while 5.1 per cent migrated out of the study area. The differences in household dynamics in these two studies may be attributed not only to the differences in the definitions but also to the differences in the rural South African and rural Ugandan settings.

In the tracing of the households in the study of household dynamics in northern Malawi, during the 1980s (Chirwa et al. 2004), a setting which is broadly similar to rural Uganda, the continuation of the households is largely determined by most of the members remaining together while in the criteria applied to the GPC the household continuation is mainly determined by the "status" of the household head, although this also takes into account the relationship between a new and previous household head. For example, for the household of Jacob, described above, where Lydia one of his wives took on the headship when he died, the household kept the same household number when the household head changed.

Of the households in Northern Malawi interviewed in the early 1980s and followed up over five years, more than 84 per cent of the households were considered to have maintained their identity over the five years, and an appreciable proportion did so despite changes in location (21 per cent) or headship (8 per cent), or even both (1 per cent). In comparison, in the GPC 73 per cent of households continued (including those that out-migrated or were lost to follow-up but returned in the study within the four to five years follow-up period). The difference in the continuation could be partly explained by the eight per cent headship change in Malawi where this was considered to be the same household while in the GPC this would sometimes be considered as a new household. In other words, despite the similarity in the Malawi and GPC study settings, the differences could be partly attributed to the methodological difference in household and household "continuation" definitions.

Clearly the GPC method of tracing still uses the household as the unit of analysis and does not allow for links between households to be shown but the strength of the approach is that it does help us to build up a picture of the comings and goings of households and their members across the cohort as a whole. By focusing on a "principal household member" and charting their movements rather than using the dwelling/house structure, as defining the household, we have been able to avoid categorizing a household as new simply because they built or moved to a new house.

Take the example of Kiwanuka. In 1991 he was living in house "100" in his village. That house fell down and he built a new one a few years later not far from the old one, but on a different plot of land that he owned. The mapper gave that house the number "610." While Kiwanuka retained his identity number linked to house "100" one of his children who came to live with him from outside the study area was given a new number linked to the new house structure "610." Using the categorization that we have chosen to use, this household would be recognized as being the same household, linked to Kiwanuka.

We have also been able to ensure that households which leave the study area and then come back again retain their previous number (and therefore also that the data across the rounds can be linked) rather than treating them as a new household.

Even though the concept of the household as a unit of analysis has been contested by many, its usefulness in data collection and analysis cannot be denied. Special care is needed not only in the definition of the household for a specific research aim but also to ensure that this definition is adequately enforced during the data collection, analysis and interpretation of the results, and that it is applied prospectively (rather than reconstructed retrospectively). In the GPC we are now able to follow households as social groups, following the definitions set out in this paper, while maintaining the use of the household as a unit for the purposes of the annual census rounds. The new approach allows us to study the social dynamics of the communities, looking at, for example social mobility, changes in poverty levels and changes in household livelihood strategies.

Since households are viewed as a set of social relationships geared towards a common purpose and jointly managing resources then it is appropriate to assume that these bonds will loosen when the members no longer experience or perceive this commonality of purpose. Thus if the household head dies or leaves the household, and remaining household members do not stay together, with some if not all of the individuals departing elsewhere (either becoming part of other households or "creating" new households), then the household no longer exists as the same social group. For those that do not completely "fall-apart" following the death or leaving of the household head, they may experience a change in their composition as measured by the age and gender of the household members, and in their generational structure.

With household information available over a period of many years, we have used the longitudinal data to describe how households can be traced over time and how they evolve, allowing us to explore overall household dynamics as well as providing important insights about the effect of HIV infection and adult mortality on this population. We can draw broader lessons for international development from this research. We can expect the household to remain an important unit not only for survey research but also for the delivery of some forms of government and non-government support. Understanding household dynamics over time and the links between household members and family members outside the immediate household can provide insights into social mobility as well as the intergenerational transmission of poverty, for example, and the targeting of interventions.

Note

This research was funded by the Medical Research Council (UK) and Economic and Social Research Council (UK) (grant RES-062-23-0051). We are grateful to an anonymous reviewer and the editor for their helpful comments and for the detailed suggestions of three anonymous reviewers. We are indebted to the field teams for their hard work and the participants in the annual GPC surveys and those who took part in the ethnographic study both in 1991/1992 and 2006/2007 for giving us their time and information. Thank you.

1. Of the 7,892 GPC households that participated in the study at-least once between 1989 and 2008, 2.6 per cent had household heads with more than one spouse resident in the same household at-least once between 1989 and 2008.

References

Asiki, G., Murphy, G., Nakiyingi-Miiro, J., Seeley, J., Nsubuga, R. N., Karabarinde, A., Waswa, L., Pomilla, C., Maher, D. Young, E. H., Kamali, A. and Sandhu, M. S. (2013) "Data Resource Profile: The General Population Cohort (GPC) in rural South-western, Uganda; a platform for communicable and non communicable diseases studies," *International Journal of Epidemiology*, in press.

Bender, D. R. (1967) "A refinement of the concept of household: Families, co-residence, and domestic functions," *American Anthropologist*, 69 (5): 493–504.

Berkner, L. K. (1975) "The use and misuse of census data for the historical analysis of family structure," *Journal of Interdisciplinary History*, 5 (4): 721–738.

Bolt, V., and Bird, K. (2003) "The intrahousehold disadvantages framework: A framework for the analysis of intra-household difference and inequality," *Chronic Poverty Research Centre Working Paper* (Manchester and London, UK: Chronic Poverty Research Centre).

Chirwa, T., Floyd, S., Ponnighaus, J., Malema, S., Kileta, S., Zaba, B., Bliss, L. and Fine, P. (2004) "Household dynamics in northern Malawi during the 1980s," *Southern African Journal of Demography*, 9 (2): 1–23.

Drinkwater, M., McEwan, M. and Samuels, F. (2006) "The Effects of HIV/AIDS on agricultural production systems in Zambia: A restudy 1993–2005," *IFPRI RENEWAL report*, New York.

Fine, P. E. M., Sterne, J. A. C., Ponnighaus, J. M., Bliss, L., Saul, J., Chihana, A., Munthali, M. and Wamdorff, D. K. (1997) "Household and dwelling contact as risk factors for leprosy in northern Malawi," *American Journal of Epidemiology*, 146 (1): 91–102.

Goody, J. (1989) "Futures of the family in rural Africa," *Population and Development Review* 15: 119–144.

Guyer, J., and Peters, P. (1987) "Special Issue: Conceptualizing the household: Theory and policy in Africa," *Development and Change*, 18 (2): 197–214.

Hosegood, V. (2008) "Demographic evidence of family and household changes in response to the effects of HIV/AIDS in Southern Africa: Implications for efforts to strengthen families," *Joint Learning Initiative on Children and HIV/AIDS (JLICA) Learning Group 1 – Strengthening Families*.

Hosegood, V., McGrath, N., Herbst, K. and Timæus I. M. (2004) "The impact of adult mortality on household dissolution and migration in rural South Africa," *AIDS* 18 (11): 1585.

Hosegood, V., Preston-Whyte, E., Busza, J., Moitse, S. and Timaeus, I. M. (2007) "Revealing the full extent of households' experiences of HIV and AIDS in rural South Africa," *Social Science & Medicine*, 65 (6):1249–1259.

Jaenson, C., and Hamsworth, J. (1984) *Uganda Social and Institutional Profile* (Jinja, Uganda: USAID).

Karlström, M. (1999) "Civil society and its presuppositions: Lessons from Uganda," in Comaroff, J. and Comaroff, J. (eds) *Civil society and the political imagination in Africa: Critical Perspectives* (Chicago IL, University of Chicago Press), pp. 104–23.

Karlström, M. (2004) "Modernity and its aspirants," *Current Anthropology*, 45: 595–619.

Martin, W. G., and Beittel, M. (1987) "The hidden abode of reproduction: Conceptualizing households in Southern Africa," *Development and Change*, 18 (2): 215–234.

Müller, T. R. (2004) *HIV/AIDS and agriculture in sub-Saharan Africa: Impact on farming systems, agricultural practices and rural livelihoods: An overview and annotated bibliography*, Vol. 1 (Wageningen: Wageningen Academic Publication).

Nabaitu, J., Bachengana, C. and Seeley, J. A. (1994) "Marital instability in a population in rural South West Uganda: Implications for the spread of HIV infection," *Africa* 64(2): 243–251.

Nahemow, N. (1979) "Residence, kinship and social isolation among the aged Baganda," *Journal of Marriage and the Family*, 41 (1): 171–183.

Niehof, A. (2004) "Why should households care," *MedischeAntropologie*, 16 (2): 282–289.

Ponnighaus, J. M., Fine, P. E. M., Bliss, L. Sliney, I. J., Bradley, D. J. and Rees, R. J. W. (1987). "The Lepra Evaluation Project (LEP) an epidemiological study of leprosy in Northern Malawi. I: methods," *Leprosy review*, 58 (4): 359–375.

Randall, S., Coast, E. and Leone, T. (2011) "Cultural constructions of the concept of household in sample surveys," *Population studies*, 65 (2): 217–229.

Roscoe, J. (1965) [1911] *The Baganda: An account of Their Native Customs and Beliefs* (London: Frank Cass and Co Ltd.).

Rudie, I. (1995) "The significance of eating: Cooperation, support and reputation in Kelantan Malay households," in Karim, W.J. (ed.) *"Male" and "Female" in Developing Southeast Asia* (Oxford and Washington DC: Berg).

Russell, M. (1993) "Are households universal? On misunderstanding domestic groups in Swaziland)," *Development and Change*, 24 (4): 755–785.

Seeley, J. (2012) "The changing relationships of co-wives over time in rural southern Uganda," *Journal of Development Studies*, 48: 68–80.

Timaeus, I. (2006) "Families, households and members," *Workshop II*: ALPHA Network (London: London School of Hygiene and Tropical Medicine).

United Nations (1973) *Manual VII: Methods of projecting households and families* (New York: Department of Economic and Social Affairs, United Nations).

Urassa, M., Boerma, J. T., Isingo, R., Ngalula, J., Ng'weshemi, J., Mwaluko, G. and Zaba, B. (2001) "The impact of HIV/AIDS on mortality and household mobility in rural Tanzania," *AIDS*, 15 (15): 2017–2023.

Wittenberg, M., and Collinson, M. A. (2007) "Household transitions in rural South Africa, 1996–2003," *Scandinavian Journal of Public Health*, 35 (69 suppl.): 130–137.

World Bank (2012) *Living Standards Measurement study (LSMS)*, http://go.worldbank.org/IFS9WG7EO0, [accessed 4 August 2013].

Yanagisako, S. J. (1979) "Family and household: The analysis of domestic groups," *Annual Review of Anthropology*, 8: 161–205.

9
Using Qualitative and Panel Data to Create Durable Measures of Child Poverty and Well-being across Childhood

Keetie Roelen

9.1 Introduction

The need for using more innovative combinations and applications of methods in development research has long been recognized (see Appleton and Booth 2001). Within the field of poverty measurement and analysis, the use of mixed methods, or so-called "q-squared" methods,[1] has seen a great expansion in the past decade (Shaffer 2012). Most commonly, this involves the use of a large-scale quantitative survey as an entry point with additional qualitative elements to verify or triangulate quantitative findings. A stronger mixing of methods is, however, scarce. This chapter aims to illustrate the value added of comprehensively combining the use of qualitative and quantitative panel data in the specific field of longitudinal and multidimensional child poverty. Case studies from Vietnam and Ethiopia will be used to build the argument.

Measuring poverty from a longitudinal rather than a static perspective is now commonly acknowledged to be important for gaining a more in-depth understanding of the processes underlying poverty outcomes (Hulme and Shepherd 2003; Clark and Hulme 2005; Addison et al. 2009) and formulating a more adequate policy response (Baulch and Hoddinott 2000; Clark and Hulme 2005; Moore 2005; Hulme and McKay 2008). Measuring poverty from a multidimensional perspective is also considered to have important merits in terms of gaining a more comprehensive understanding of what it means to be poor and what can be done about it (Alkire and Santos 2010). Analysing child poverty from a longitudinal and multidimensional perspective can be considered particularly pertinent; children have different basic needs to adults and a failure to meet those needs can lead to long-term adverse effects (Brooks-Gunn and Duncan 1997; Haveman and Wolfe 2005).

Despite these acknowledgements, the measurement of the dynamics of multidimensional child poverty remains largely unexplored (Roelen 2013). This can partly be attributed to data constraints, particularly in developing countries. Whilst the availability of panel data in developed countries has led to a number of notable studies on poverty dynamics (see Bane and Ellwood 1986; Layte and Whelan 2003; Maholmes and King 2012) and on moves in and out of child poverty (Bradbury et al. 2001), this is much less the case in developing countries. As cross-sectional data is more widely available, the body of research on multidimensional child poverty from a static perspective has expanded rapidly in recent years (Boyden and Bourdillon 2012; Minujin and Nandy 2012). Newly available panel data that include both quantitative and qualitative elements, with the Young Lives study being a prime example, give rise to new opportunities to analyse and study child poverty dynamics from a multidimensional perspective. This chapter argues that the combination of quantitative and qualitative methods will allow for making better use of those opportunities, and for overcoming challenges in measuring child poverty dynamics from a multidimensional perspective.

Two case studies are used in this chapter to illustrate the need for and value of mixed method approaches in the analysis of longitudinal and multidimensional child poverty. On the basis of a case study from Vietnam, this chapter argues for the need of complementing analysis of quantitative household survey data with qualitative data and methods to come to a deeper and more profound understanding of poverty outcomes and their dynamics over time. This is done by analysing longitudinal child poverty outcomes from both monetary and multidimensional angles. The case study from Ethiopia provides an illustration of how methods can be mixed in a bid to gain a more comprehensive understanding of movements in and out of poverty over time. Building on previous work (Camfield and Roelen 2011; Roelen and Camfield 2012), Young Lives quantitative and qualitative data are used to analyse the situation of children and their households in rural Ethiopia across a period of seven years. Qualitative and quantitative panel data are combined in an iterative process to provide a nuanced insight into poverty dynamics, what prevents children and their households from moving out of poverty, and how they perceive their experiences.

The remainder of this chapter is as follows: First, a brief overview of the use of mixed methods approaches in research on poverty and particularly poverty dynamics will be provided. Second, the case study of

Vietnam will be introduced and discussed, elaborating on the data and methodology used and on main findings. The case study of Ethiopia will consequently be discussed in a similar manner. Finally, this chapter concludes with a discussion and reflections.

9.2   Mixed method approaches in longitudinal and child poverty research

A number of reasons can be put forward for the importance of analysing the durational aspects of poverty, especially for children. From a social justice perspective, one could argue that there is a moral concern to prioritize help to households that have been living in poverty for the longest period of time (Clark and Hulme 2005; Addison et al. 2009). Especially in relation to children, the duration as well as the timing of experiences of poverty increases the likelihood of negative long-term consequences (Brooks-Gunn and Duncan 1997). An exclusively static perspective on poverty also limits our understanding of why people become or remain poor (Hulme and Shepherd 2003), which is crucial for being able to address poverty adequately through policy (Baulch and Hoddinott 2000; Moore 2005). This is particularly so given that the characteristics and needs of chronic versus transient poor are generally quite different (Günther and Klasen, 2009).

Since the beginning of the 2000s, the use of mixed methods such as wealth rankings and surveys to assess and understand poverty has gained considerable traction within debates over poverty measurement and policy analysis (Shaffer 2012). It is now widely acknowledged that the combined rather than exclusive use of quantitative and qualitative data can deepen our understanding of issues pertaining to poverty and deprivation (Kanbur 2003; Kanbur and Shaffer 2005). The combined use of quantitative and qualitative information has been and is being applied in various forms in an expanding body of research (e.g. Adato et al. 2004; Levine and Roberts 2007; Roelen and Gassmann 2011). Davis and Baulch (2011) point out that the different reflections of poverty offered by assessments based on either quantitative or qualitative information should be welcomed rather than cause alarm as, in combination, they offer profound insights into the complex reality that the situation of poverty presents.

Many of these methods can be considered quant-dominant, as opposed to "qual dominant" (Brannen 2005). Nonetheless, Addison et al. (2009) highlight the role of qualitative data in increasing understanding of poverty dynamics – over the life-course, across generations and between different social groups. Qualitative data can also play a role in expanding the scope of poverty measures to include non-material dimensions and/ or dimensions that are identified as important by the respondents themselves. The dimension of time, for example, in relation to agricultural seasons, key life stages such as pregnancy, or the duration of poverty, is acknowledged to be extremely important. Given the value added by different types of information, few scholars would now deny the importance of linking quantitative and qualitative data in studying poverty and movements in and out of poverty. Others, however, believe that the simple combination or integration of methods is not enough, and that a more profound linking of the metanarratives that underpin assumptions about poverty dynamics and chronic poverty is required (Du Toit 2009). To truly study the situation of chronic poverty and gain an understanding of what it is that prevents movements out of poverty, the approach needs to engage with the causal dynamics and processes that shape poverty dynamics (Du Toit 2009).

Mixed method research can prove particularly useful when analysing poverty and vulnerability amongst children. While we know something about their experiences and have some understanding of poverty (Camfield 2010), we know little about how they experience movements *in and out* of poverty. Dercon (2012) indicates that particular information gaps exist with respect to children's experiences of and responses to poverty, especially throughout early stages of childhood and adolescence. Following greater prominence of the Convention of the Rights of the Child and increased recognition of the role of child agency, the inclusion of children's perspectives in child poverty studies is now on the rise (Barnes and Wright 2012). Coupled with the growing availability of quantitative and qualitative panel data, this allows for giving more centrality to children's own perceptions rather than relying solely on adult's understandings of children's needs, the processes through which those needs are met or not, and the way in which a failure to meet such needs impacts on children.

The two case studies in this chapter illustrate the need for using both quantitative and qualitative methods when studying poverty dynamics for children and the households they live in. Holistic integration, as opposed to simple combination, of methods would be preferred, as would the inclusion of children's own perceptions and opinions about levels of poverty and movements in and out of poverty.

9.3   Monetary and multidimensional child poverty in Vietnam

Research in Vietnam on child poverty from a static perspective indicates that there is a considerable mismatch between children experiencing monetary poverty and children experiencing multidimensional poverty (Roelen et al. 2012). In other words, those children living in households with monetary means below the poverty line are not necessarily the same as those children not having safe drinking water or unable to go to school. Such a poverty mismatch in a static context has been found in other contexts as well, including developed countries. Alkire and Roche (2012) show how the use of different poverty indicators rearranges the ranking order of regions in Bangladesh, whilst Roelen and Notten (2011) find that income- and non-income-related indicators capture different groups of children as being deprived in four countries in the European Union. Building on this cross-sectional research, the panel data from Vietnam are used to replicate the cross-sectional analysis from a longitudinal perspective and argue for the need of qualitative methods to allow for a more comprehensive understanding of findings.

9.3.1   Data

The data used for this study are taken from the Vietnam Households Living Standards Survey (VHLSS) conducted in 2004, 2006, and 2008. The VHLSS has been conducted every second year from 2002 onwards by the Government Statistical Office (GSO) following the World Bank's Living Standards Measurement Survey (LSMS) methodology. The VHLSS survey samples from 2002 to 2010 are drawn from a master sample, which is a random sample of the 1999 Population Census enumeration areas and includes a rotating panel section (GSO 2004). The surveys provide micro-data at the level of the household and their individual members on a range of issues related to children's well-being and poverty as well as social protection. A notable limitation of the VHLSS is its sampling method, which causes unregistered, recent, or temporary migrants in the society to be omitted from the sample and subsequent data (see Edmonds and Turk 2004; Pincus and Sender 2006, 2008; Evans and Harkness 2008; VDR 2008). The omission of these groups is not only an important issue to point out because of its suspected significant size but even more so because of the denial of social and public services they experience due to their status. The structural exclusion of the unregistered migrant group from the data will most likely lead to underestimations for (child) poverty.

Table 9.1 displays the sample sizes and distribution over demographic groups for the VHLSS datasets for 2004, 2006, and 2008 in comparison to the panel component. The total number of observations and distributions over demographic groups refer to the child population aged 0–15 inclusive. As children under the age of four in 2008 were not yet born in 2004, they are obviously not included in the panel sample, posing a limitation to the analysis of child poverty dynamics. A comparison of the sample distribution over different demographic groups between the cross-sectional samples and panel sample does not point toward significant changes in the representation of groups, given the exception of age groups. Previous studies using the VLSS data did not find any attrition bias either (Baulch and Masset 2003) and assumed an unbiased sample (Günther and Klasen 2009). The use of panel data means that cross-sectional weights can no longer be used. Panel weights are not available (Baulch and Masset 2003; GSO 2004), calling for caution when interpreting findings at the national level and decomposed for different demographic groups. Considering that the data only span a period of four years, the study does not distinguish cohort effects (see Moore 2005).

Table 9.1 Sample size and distribution of VHLSS panel data

	2004	**2006**	**2008**	**Panel (2008)**
Total	12154	10696	9960	1054
Gender				
Male	52.1	50.9	51.1	52.1
Female	47.9	49.1	48.9	47.9
Area				
Urban	19.6	20.1	21.7	17.1
Rural	80.4	79.9	78.3	82.9
Region				
Red River Delta	16.5	16.4	17.2	17.7
North East	14.3	14.3	14.6	14.1
North West	6.8	6.9	7.2	5.1
North Central Coast	12.5	12.4	11.3	13.9
South Central Coast	9.3	9.4	9.3	10.6
Central Highlands	9.6	9.9	9.6	10
South East	12.8	12.5	12.4	12.4
Mekong River Delta	18.3	18.1	18.4	16.1
Ethnicity				
Kinh/Chinese	78.6	77.2	77.4	79.5
Other Ethnicity	21.5	22.8	22.6	20.5
Age group				(age in 2008)
0–2	11.6	13.2	15.5	0
3–4	9.1	8.9	10.5	4.6
5	4.5	4.9	5.2	6
6–10	31.8	29.4	27.8	35.9
11–14	34.5	34.2	31.4	42.2
15	8.5	9.3	9.7	11.4

Source: Author's own calculations from VHLSS 2004, 2006, and 2008.

9.3.2 Results

Children were firstly identified as being either chronically poor, upwards transient poor, downwards transient poor, or non-poor. A spells approach was adopted for measuring poverty dynamics (see Hulme and Shepherd 2003; Günther and Klasen 2009), implying that we consider the periods of time during which a child's outcome with respect to the monetary or multidimensional indicator falls below the poverty line. Children that are classified as chronically poor find themselves below that threshold across all three time periods, whilst children that are considered upwards transient poor will have moved out of poverty from 2004 to 2008 and children that are referred to as downwards transient poor will have fallen into poverty.[2] A simple tabulation of poverty groups based on poverty status across the three survey rounds according to the monetary and multidimensional poverty measures (Table 9.2) shows that despite considerable overlap, there are also groups of children that are identified differently when using different poverty measures.

The groups that hold the largest proportions of children are the group of children that were non-poor across all rounds according to both measures and the group of children that was non-monetary poor and moved out of multidimensional poverty, respectively capturing 41 per cent and 14 per cent of all children. These results are not surprising given large size differences between monetary and multidimensional poverty outcomes in a cross-sectional context (with rates of multidimensional child poverty being almost twice as high as rates of monetary child poverty),

Table 9.2 Longitudinal poverty groups: monetary and multidimensional poverty

		Multidimensional poverty				
		Non-poor	*Chronically poor*	*Downwards transient poor*	*Upwards transient poor*	*Total*
Monetary poverty	*Non-poor*	40.99	3.61	5.22	13.85	63.66
	Chronically poor	1.42	7.4	2.09	4.93	15.84
	Downwards transient poor	2.28	1.9	1.04	1.52	6.74
	Upwards transient poor	4.65	3.13	1.61	4.36	13.76
	Total	49.34	16.03	9.96	24.67	100

and the large drops in poverty from 2004 to 2008 (see Roelen et al. 2012 and Roelen 2013). Findings indicate that 7 per cent of all children are chronically poor and ultra-poor; they were classified as poor according to both the monetary and multidimensional poverty measure. Despite this overlap and converging trends, one can also observe a mismatch in outcomes when using a monetary and multidimensional measure to capture longitudinal child poverty. Respectively 4 per cent and 5 per cent of all children in Vietnam were chronically multidimensionally poor or fell into multidimensional poverty despite being non-poor in monetary terms across the entire time period. Similarly, 5 per cent of all children found themselves below the monetary poverty line from 2004 to 2008 but moved out of multidimensional poverty in that same period.

More disaggregated information about these poverty groups illustrated more clearly how the use of different poverty measures indeed points towards a different picture of poverty. Table 9.3 presents the proportions of children classified as chronically poor, downwards transient poor and upwards transient poor by region according to the monetary and multidimensional poverty measure. In addition, the ranking of regions according to those proportions are reported.

When considering the regional rankings based on the monetary and multidimensional poverty outcomes vis-à-vis each other respectively for chronic poverty, downwards, and upwards transient poverty, it becomes apparent that the two different measures rearrange the rank order of regions. The most notable examples are the Mekong River Delta and North West regions. Whilst the Mekong River Delta performs badly in terms of the proportions of children being monetary chronically poor and having moved into monetary poverty, it is one of the best performers in terms of the proportions of children being chronically multidimensionally poor or having dropped into poverty in multidimensional terms. Similarly, whilst the North West holds one of the smallest proportions of children having moved out of monetary poverty, it still holds one of the largest proportions of children having moved out of multidimensional poverty. In other words, it is not necessarily the case that those children being locked into monetary poverty are the same children that are locked into multidimensional poverty and vice versa.

Although these findings provide an interesting insight into the complexity of poverty dynamics, future research is required to unpack these findings further. Particularly the situation of those groups of children that are classified differently by both poverty measures requires further examination. This includes the calculation of entry and exit rates, a consideration of group sizes of "mismatch" groups as a proportion of

Table 9.3 Poverty estimates and rankings by region

	Chronic poverty				Downwards transient poverty				Upwards transient poverty			
	monetary poverty		multidimensional poverty		monetary poverty		multidimensional poverty		monetary poverty		multidimentional poverty	
Red River Delta	2.14	2	3.21	1	3.74	1	6.95	5	18.18	8	12.83	5
North East	12.75	5	20.13	6	12.75	6	1.9	1	28.86	2	16.11	3
North West	61.11	8	66.67	8	11.11	4	4.79	3	20.37	7	18.52	2
North Central Coast	9.59	3	16.44	5	6.85	2	8.05	6	25.34	5	23.97	1
South Central Coast	1.79	1	9.82	3	8.04	3	5.56	4	27.68	3	10.71	6
Central Highlands	22.86	6	32.38	7	14.29	8	10	7	31.43	1	15.24	4
South East	12.21	4	10.69	4	11.45	5	10.71	8	20.61	6	6.87	8
Mekong River Delta	33.53	7	7.06	2	14.12	7	3.82	2	25.88	4	8.82	7

other poverty groups, the disaggregation of multidimensional outcomes by domain, and an analysis of micro-determinants of group classification. More fundamentally, qualitative research is required to understand the processes that lie underneath the mismatch and overlap of monetary and non-monetary outcomes for children. More information is needed to be able to assess how it is that children that remain poor in monetary terms for a prolonged period of time are able to move out of multidimensional poverty and vice versa. Similarly, what are the processes that cause children that are not poor on the basis of monetary indicators to have fluctuating experiences in terms of non-monetary outcomes? Whilst a more detailed investigation of the quantitative data can provide insight into whether these children find themselves just above or below the poverty line, and thus whether any mismatch is primarily due to measurement error, other types of information are required to tease out the mechanisms that lead to different outcomes. This would include issues around intra-household distribution, attitudes towards children and their educational, health, nutrition and other developmental needs as well as perceptions about and access to public services.

9.4 Chronic child poverty in rural Ethiopia

This second case study illustrates how quantitative and qualitative data and methods can be combined in a bid to gain more profound understandings of child poverty from a longitudinal perspective. It builds on previous research as published in Roelen and Camfield (2012) and Camfield and Roelen (2011, 2013). Based on three rounds of panel data and life histories collected by Young Lives, a longitudinal study of childhood poverty and qualitative and quantitative information has been used in an iterative process to develop a taxonomy of child poverty, analyse movements in and out of poverty, and investigate what prevents children and their households in rural Ethiopia from escaping chronic poverty.

9.4.1 Data

The analysis uses data from Young Lives, a study of childhood poverty in four countries (Peru, India, Vietnam, and Ethiopia), with the specific purpose of analysing the context of children's life trajectories. Three rounds of data are now available for analysis and enable researchers to follow the same two cohorts of children over a period of seven years. The first round of quantitative data collection took place in 2002 when children in the cohort under consideration for this analysis were 7–8 years of age. The second round of quantitative data collection took place in 2006 when the children were 11–12 years old and the third in 2009 when they were 14–15 years old. The Young Lives Ethiopian sample covers 20 sites in the ethnically based regions of Amhara, Oromia, SNNP (Southern Nations, Nationalities and Peoples), and Tigray, as well as in the capital, Addis Ababa. Together, these five regions cover different geographical characteristics, levels of development, urban/rural locations, and population characteristics (Outes-Leon and Dercon 2008). Thirteen of these sites are classified as rural and it is these that form the basis of our analysis. There were 570 children in the sample in Round 3 (see Table 9.4), thereby determining the sample of the panel dataset.

Qualitative data were collected from children in 3 of the 13 rural sites in 2007, 2008, and 2009 (the latter was for a sub-study on social protection, vulnerability, and social mobility). Table 9.5 provides full details of these data.

As the collection of Young Lives qualitative data was not designed to classify households as poor or non-poor, the information gathered does not allow for a poverty analysis in purely qualitative terms. The data do, however, contain valuable information about what children and adults think constitutes poverty and what is required to move out of this situation or prevent a fall into vulnerable conditions. In addition, it holds information about people's life histories which is important in order to contextualize, understand, and explain movements in and out of poverty over time.

9.4.2 Findings

A first step in this multi-stage and iterative investigation consisted of the development of a taxonomy that allowed for classifying children and the households they live in as ultra-poor, poor, near-poor, and

Table 9.4   Sample size and composition in each survey round (%)

	R1	R2	R3
Boys	52.1	51.9	52.5
Girls	47.9	48.1	47.5
Amhara	25.0	24.5	24.7
Oromia	24.9	24.7	24.6
SNNP	25.0	25.2	24.9
Tigray	25.0	25.7	25.8
Total (n)	599	584	570

Table 9.5 Description of qualitative data

Respondents	Study/stage	Focus of research/method	Villages[a]	Regions
Children aged 13–14, n = 20 (one focus group per site, with five participants)	2008 general qualitative fieldwork	Characteristics of poor and non-poor families; how families become poor or non-poor ("poverty tree" used as a visual aid)	Leki, Tach-Meret, Zeytuni	Amhara, Oromia, and Tigray
Children aged 11–15, n = 40 (two focus groups per site, with five participants)	2008 IDRC-funded study on the impact of social protection on children	Perceived fairness and relevance of criteria for wealth or poverty status in relation to inclusion within Productive Safety Net Programme (PSNP);[b] whether and how PSNP supports social mobility	Enkoy, Lomi, Weyn, and Gomen	Amhara, Oromia, Tigray, and SNNP
Adults, n = 80 (four focus groups per site, with five participants)	2008 IDRC-funded study on the impact of social protection on children	Perceived fairness and relevance of criteria for wealth or poverty status in relation to inclusion within PSNP; whether and how PSNP supports social mobility	Enkoy, Lomi, Weyn, and Gomen	Amhara, Oromia, Tigray, and SNNP
Adults, n = 28 (one focus group per site, with seven participants).	2009 sub-study on social protection, vulnerability and social mobility	How households move out of chronic poverty, which expenditures are the first to be made, and how these affect children in the household. Asked to identify a poverty threshold and discuss this in relation to criteria for PSNP entry and "graduation"	Leki, Tach-Meret, Zeytuni, and Buna	Amhara, Oromia, and Tigray

[a] All names are pseudonyms.
[b] The PSNP, which was introduced in 2005, aims to reduce household vulnerability, improve resilience to shocks, and decrease dependence on food aid. The programme has over eight million participants and provides food or cash for work such as digging ditches, and direct support to a smaller number of households with no adult labour.

non-poor. The concept of "Stages of Progress" as developed by Krishna (2007) was used to translate the qualitative information available about what children and adults associate with poverty or a good standard of living into a taxonomy of child poverty. This taxonomy consequently allows for a grouping of children and households using quantitative survey data. Table 9.6 presents the proportions of children in the different poverty groups across the three rounds of data collection.

Estimates indicate that many children experienced an improvement in their living conditions. Whilst half of all children were identified as being poor in Round 1, in addition to those children living in ultra-poverty, this proportion reduced to less than 20 per cent in Round 3. Households have largely followed the stages of progress as identified in the taxonomy as estimates point towards a shift from poverty to near-poverty from Round 1 to Round 2 and from Round 2 to Round 3. One out of three children is no longer living in poverty in Round 3, compared to only 1 out of 13 in Round 1. In terms of the underlying indicators, the majority of these shifts can be attributed to the growing availability of draught animals in the household and improvements in dwelling conditions, particularly the roof. Further quantitative analysis of the movements in and out of poverty shows that whilst more than half of all children experienced an improvement in their living conditions, there is a persistent and hard-to-reach group of chronically poor and ultra-poor children and families (Camfield and Roelen 2011).

A mixed method analysis then allows for an in-depth investigation of characteristics and factors of transient children and households (i.e. those experiencing shifts across the poverty categories over time) and those that are locked into ultra-poverty and poverty. An assessment of the quantitative data (see Camfield and Roelen 2011) suggests that there were no significant differences between male and female children in relation to their likelihood of moving out of poverty across the rounds. However, region of residence was a significant factor with households in Young Lives sites in Oromia, which typically have better

Table 9.6   Percentage of children in different poverty groups

Category	Round 1 (%)	Round 2 (%)	Round 3 (%)
Ultra-poor	7	8.6	8.4
Poor	49.8	24	17.2
Nearly poor	35.6	55.5	41.8
Not poor	7.7	12	32.6
Total	100	100	100

access to markets, being more likely to move out of poverty, while the more remote rural sites in Tigray which have fewer economic opportunities were more likely to have remained stable (see also Woldehanna et al. 2008). Children in female-headed households were more likely to experience downwards movements whilst children in male-headed households are more likely to move out of poverty. Eight case studies of children born in 1994 or 1995 were selected to further explore poverty movements and their underlying dynamics. They include boys and girls across three regions – Amhara, Oromia, and Tigray and two types of sites – near-rural and remote. They were purposively sampled from potential 20 cases where a full qualitative dataset was available as they presented the greatest range of experiences for analysis. Table 9.7 presents their basic characteristics from the quantitative panel data as well as their movements across the taxonomy over time. The last two columns provide an indication of the mobility across the different rounds, suggesting that the downwards mobility for Miniya, Gabra, and Naomi was a fluctuating rather than a linear process.

The analysis of these case studies shows that characteristics of chronically poor households are different from transient ones. It is often the multitude of vulnerabilities and cumulativity of shocks that moves or entrenches a household in poverty. For example, Gabra whose household has dropped into ultra-poverty has a female household head, land that is sharecropped-out[3] and subsists on piece work carried out by the whole family. Degife, whose household is transiently poor, may only have a small landholding, but also has four educated siblings likely to provide support in the future. Ephrem and his household have maintained near-poor status across all three rounds, largely due to the availability of livestock and participation in Ethiopia's Productive Safety Net Programme, but the multiplicity of recent shocks may cause a drop into poverty in the near future. These include crop failure, the sale of his family's livestock for little money, and outstanding credit.

Across the various case studies, downwards trajectories can largely be attributed to lack of oxen or male labour which led to the sharecropping-out of land. They were often exacerbated by exclusion from the Productive Safety Net Programme. Other factors were more specific to individual households; for example, imprisonment, illness, and the cost of medical treatment (see also Krishna 2010). Stable or upward trajectories were linked to factors such as agricultural diversification, non-farm activities such as selling stone, and remittances from relatives. The case studies also reveal that there is often a trade-off between the prosperity of the household and the well-being of children within that household;

Table 9.7 Case study characteristics

Name	Sex	Region	Site	Transition	Transition from R1 to R2	Transition from R2 to R3
Rising or stable						
Masresha	Boy	Amhara	Tachmeret	Upwards	Near-poor to non-poor	Non-poor to non-poor
Legesse	Boy	Amhara	Tachmeret	Upwards	Poor to non-poor	Non-poor to non-poor
Degife	Boy	Oromia	Leki	Upwards	Poor to poor	Poor to non-poor
Ephrem	Boy	Tigray	Semhal	Stable	Near-poor to near-poor	Near-poor to near-poor
Declining						
Miniya	Girl	Tigray	Semhal	Downwards	Near-poor to ultra-poor	Ultra-poor to poor
Gabra	Girl	Amhara	Tachmeret	Downwards	Poor to non-poor	Non-poor to ultra-poor
Naomi	Girl	Oromia	Leki	Downwards	Poor to near-poor	Near-poor to ultra-poor
Dibaba	Boy	Oromia	Leki	Downwards	Near-poor to near-poor	Near-poor to poor

Legesse, Degife, and Ephrem were all excluded from full-time education as they were required to support their household's economic activities. The upwards mobility of Legesse and his household was at the expense of his health as he is performing hard physical labour.

This study of child poverty in Ethiopia clearly illustrates the value of combining quantitative and qualitative methods in an iterative process. The use of qualitative information to inform the quantitative taxonomy ensured the inclusion of indicators that were identified by children and adults to denote progress out of poverty. In addition, the inclusion of children's perspectives allowed for giving more centrality to children's needs in the quantitative taxonomy. The consequent qualitative and quantitative analysis of poverty groups and movements across groups over time allowed for verification on one hand, and a more nuanced perspective on the other hand. The quantitative analysis allows for identification of characteristics that differ across the sample as a whole, while the qualitative data allow for a more profound insight and acknowledgement of the complex dynamics underlying such movements. In particular, it allows for the identification of multiple factors and the contradiction between child well-being and household welfare.

9.5   Discussion and conclusion

The combined use of qualitative and quantitative data and methods can help deepen our understandings of child poverty trends and dynamics. The Vietnam case study shows that although a lot can be learned from analysing quantitative panel survey data, namely the fact that monetary and non-monetary indicators point towards different pictures of child poverty both cross-sectionally and over time, a lot of questions remain that can best be answered using qualitative information. The Ethiopia case study illustrates how mixed methods research can indeed unpack child poverty dynamics and its underlying factors.

Beyond deepening our understandings, mixed method approaches to studying child poverty can also prove useful in at least two other ways. Firstly, it ensures that children's and adults' perceptions about what constitutes poverty and vulnerability are reflected in concurrent measures. A true integration of quantitative and qualitative methods ensures that child participation moves beyond being tokenistic, but the inclusion of their voices in child poverty measurement makes their needs and wishes even more visible. Secondly, the use of mixed methods can also improve the robustness of poverty measures and analyses by triangulation and verification. In the Ethiopian study, the findings from life histories were used to triangulate the classification of households following the mixed method taxonomy and their movements in and out of poverty over time.

With all this said, it has to be acknowledged that challenges remain in the use of mixed method approaches towards studying child poverty, particularly in a dynamic context. Notwithstanding the importance of reflecting children's perceptions and opinions, the highly dynamic nature of the period of childhood calls for caution when including them in poverty analysis over time. Children's perceptions and opinions will change over time as children grow older and move from infanthood to adolescence. Comparative analysis based on changing concepts of what it means to be poor, and especially the integration of those concepts in quantitative measures, requires careful consideration. A related issue is the fluidity of household composition over time and concerns about how to incorporate these changes in the analysis. Children and adults may leave or enter the household, which might have far-reaching consequences for the situation in terms of poverty as well as the way in which this situation is experienced and perceived. Panel studies should thus aim not only to track all individuals to the best extent possible, thereby limiting the level of attrition, but also to make changes in household composition and the way in which it affects living conditions and perceptions thereof an integral part of the analysis. Finally, a particular challenge pertains to the use of secondary data. This means that quantitative and qualitative data may not have been collected in conjunction with each other, or that data have been collected with a different purpose in mind. The Vietnam case study illustrates how the first issue may pose challenges for future research; the sampling framework and questionnaire of the VHLSS has been designed without considering the possibility of qualitative data collection using the same sample or for complementing the survey questionnaire. The Ethiopia case study shows how the second issue is a challenge in that the qualitative data have not been collected for the purposes of informing a taxonomy using quantitative data. More research needs to be done to address these concerns, and particularly in reference to the methodological challenge of how to combine secondary quantitative panel data and primary qualitative data.

Notes

1. The term "q-squared" was coined by economist Ravi Kanbur: http://www. kanbur.aem.cornell.edu at a workshop in 2001 on combining Qualitative and Quantitative Approaches in Poverty Analysis.
2. A detailed discussion about the classification of children and their households in different poverty groups on the basis of moves in and out of poverty can be

found in Roelen (2013). This article also details the methodology for measuring multidimensional child poverty from a longitudinal perspective.
3. "Sharecropping-out" refers to the practice of allowing others to cultivate the land in return for a share of the harvest, in this case because there is too little labour capacity to cultivate the land on their own.

References

Adato, M., Lund, F., and Mhlongo, P. (2004) "Methodological Innovations in Research on the Dynamics of Poverty: A Longitudinal Study in KwaZulu-Natal, South Africa." Paper presented at *Q-Squared in Practice: A Conference on Experiences of Combining Qualitative and Quantitative Methods in Poverty Appraisal*, University of Toronto, 15–16 May.
Addison, T., Hulme, D., and Kanbur, R. (2009) "Poverty Dynamics: Measurement and Understanding from an Interdisciplinary Perspective," in Addison, T., Hulme, D. and Kanbur, R. (eds) *Poverty Dynamics – Interdisciplinary Perspectives* (New York: Oxford University Press), pp. 3–28.
Alkire, S. and Roche, J. M. (2012) "Beyond Headcount: The Alkire-Foster Approach to Multidimensional Child Poverty Measurement," in Ortiz, I., Daniels, L. and Engilbertsdóttir, S. (eds) *Child Poverty and Inequality: New Perspectives* (New York: UNICEF), pp. 18–22.
Alkire, S. and Santos, M. E. (2010) "Acute Multidimensional Poverty: A New Index for Developing Countries," *OPHI Working Paper No. 38* (Oxford: OPHI).
Appleton, S. and Booth, D. (2001) "Combining Participatory and Survey-based Approaches to Poverty Monitoring and Analysis." Background paper prepared for Uganda workshop, 30 May–1 June.
Bane, M. J. and Ellwood, D. T. (1986) "Slipping into and out of Poverty: The Dynamics of Spells," *The Journal of Human Resources*, 21(1): 23.
Barnes, H. and Wright, G. (2012) "Defining Child Poverty in South Africa," in Minujin, A. and Nandy, S. (eds) *Global Child Poverty and Well-Being* (Bristol: The Policy Press), pp. 135–154.
Baulch, B. and Hoddinott, J. (2000) "Economic Mobility and Poverty Dynamics in Developing Countries," *Journal of Development Studies*, 36(6): 1–24.
Baulch, B. and Masset, E. (2003) "Do Monetary and Nonmonetary Indicators Tell the Same Story About Chronic Poverty? A Study of Vietnam in the 1990s," *World Development*, 31(3): 441–453.
Boyden, J. and Bourdillon, M. (eds) (2012) *Childhood Poverty. Multidisciplinary Approaches* (Basingstoke: Palgrave Macmillian).
Bradbury, B., Jenkins, S., and Micklewright, J. (2001) *The Dynamics of Child Poverty in Industrialised Nations* (Cambridge: Cambridge University Press).
Brannen, J. (2005) "NCRM Methods Review Papers, NCRM/005. Mixed Methods Research: A discussion paper." Downloaded from http://eprints.ncrm.ac.uk/89/, [Accessed 18 October 2012].
Brooks-Gunn, J. and Duncan, G. (1997) "The Effects of Poverty on Children," *The Future of Children*, 7(2): 55–71.
Camfield, L. (2010) "Even if She Learns, She Doesn't Understand Properly. Children's Understandings of Ill-being and Poverty in Five Ethiopian Communities," *Social Indicators Research*, 96 (1): 85–112.

Camfield, C. and Roelen, K. (2011) "Household Trajectories in Rural Ethiopia – What Can a Mixed Method Approach Tell us about the Impact of Poverty on Children?," *Working Paper 34, DEV Working Paper Series* (University of East Anglia, UK: The School of International Development).

Camfield, C. and Roelen, K. (2013) "Chronic Poverty in Rural Ethiopia through the Lens of Life histories," *Journal of Human Development and Capabilities'.* 14(4), pp. 581–602.

Clark, D. and Hulme, D. (2005) "Towards a Unified Framework for Understanding the Depth, Breadth and Duration of Poverty." Paper presented at The Many Dimensions of Poverty, Brasilia, Brazil, 29–31 August 2005.

Davis, P. and Baulch, B. (2011) "Parallel Realities: Exploring Poverty Dynamics Using Mixed Methods in Rural Bangladesh," *Journal of Development Studies,* 47(1): 118–142.

Dercon, S. (2012) "Understanding Child Poverty in Developing Countries: Measurement and Analysis," in Boyden, J. and Bourdillon, M. (eds) *Childhood Poverty. Multidisciplinary Approaches* (Basingstoke: Palgrave Macmillan), pp. 52–69.

Du Toit, A. (2009) "Poverty Measurement Blues. Beyond 'Q-squared' Approaches to Understanding Chronic Poverty in South Africa," in Addison, T., Hulme, D. and Kanbur, R. (eds) *Poverty Dynamics – Interdisciplinary Perspectives* (New York: Oxford University Press), pp. 225–246.

Edmonds, E. and Turk, C. (2004) "Child Labor in Transition in Vietnam," in Glewwe, P., Agrawal, N. and Dollar, D. (eds) *Economic Growth, Poverty and Household Welfare in Vietnam* (Washington DC: World Bank), pp. 505–550.

Evans, M. and Harkness, S. (2008) "Social Protection in Vietnam and Obstacles to Progressivity," *Asian Social Work and Policy Review,* 2(1): 30–52.

GSO (2004) *Vietnam Household Living Standards Survey (VHLSS), 2002, 2004,* Basic information (Hanoi: GSO).

Günther, I. and Klasen, S. (2009) "Measuring Chronic Non-Income Poverty," in Addison, T., Hulme, D. and Kanbur, R. (eds) *Poverty Dynamics: Interdisciplinary Perspectives* (New York: Oxford University Press), pp. 77–101.

Haveman, R. and Wolfe, B. (1995) "The Determinants of Children's Attainments: A Review of Methods and Findings," *Journal of Economic Literature,* 33(4): 1829–1878.

Hulme, D. and McKay, A. (2008) "Identifying and Measuring Chronic Poverty: Beyond Monetary Measures?," in Kakwani, N. and Silber, J. (eds) *The Many Dimensions of Poverty* (New York: Palgrave Macmillan), pp. 187–214.

Hulme, D. and Shepherd, A. (2003) "Conceptualizing Chronic Poverty," *World Development,* 31(3): 403–423.

Kanbur, R. (ed.) (2003) *Q-Squared: Qualitative and Quantitative Methods of Poverty Appraisal* (India: Permanent Black).

Kanbur, R. and Shaffer, P. (2005) "Epistemology, Normative Theory and Poverty Analysis: Implications for Q-Squared in Practice," *Q-Squared, Working Paper No. 2* (Toronto: Q-Squared).

Krishna, A. (2007) "Subjective Assessments, Participatory Methods and Poverty Dynamics: The Stages-of-Progress Method," *CPRC Working Paper 93* (Manchester: Chronic Poverty Research Centre).

Krishna, A. (2010) *One Illness Away: Why People Become Poor and How They Escape Poverty* (Oxford: Oxford University Press).

Layte, R. and Whelan, C. (2003) "Moving In and Out of Poverty," *European Societies* 5(2):167–191.

Levine. S. and Roberts, B. (2007) "A Q-Squared Approach to Pro-Poor Policy Formulation in Namibia," *Q-Squared Working Paper No. 49* (Toronto: Q-Squared).

Maholmes, V. and King, R (2012) *The Oxford Handbook of Poverty and Child Development* (Oxford: Oxford University Press).

Minujin, A. and Nandy, S. (eds) (2012) *Global Child Poverty and Well-Being. Measurement, Concepts, Policy and Action* (Bristol: The Policy Press).

Moore, K. (2005) "Thinking about Youth Poverty through the Lenses of Chronic Poverty, Life-course Poverty and Intergenerational Poverty," *CPRC Working Paper No. 57* (Manchester: Chronic Poverty Research Centre).

Outes-Leon, I. and Dercon, S. (2008) "Survey Attrition and Attrition Bias in Young Lives," *Young Lives Technical Note No. 5* (Oxford: Young Lives).

Pincus, J. and Sender, J. (2006) *Quantifying Poverty in Vietnam: UNDP* (London: School of Oriental and African Studies).

Pincus, J. and Sender, J. (2008) "Quantifying Poverty in Viet Nam: Who Counts?," *Journal of Vietnamese Studies*, 3(1): 108–150.

Roelen, K. (2013) "Multidimensional Child Poverty in Vietnam from a Longitudinal Perspective – Improved Lives or Impoverished Conditions, Child Indicators Research," DOI: 10.1007/s12187-013-9221-7.

Roelen, K. and Camfield, C. (2012) "A Mixed-method Taxonomy of Child Poverty: A Case Study from Rural Ethiopia," *Young Lives Working Paper No. 76* (Oxford, UK: Young Lives).

Roelen, K. and Gassmann, F. (2011) "How Effective can Efficient be? – Social Assistance in Kosovo and What It Means for Children," *Journal of European Social Policy*, 21(3): 238–252.

Roelen, K. and Notten, G. (2011) "The Breadth of Child Poverty in Europe: An Investigation into Poverty Overlap and Accumulation of Deprivation," *Innocenti Working Paper 2011–04* (Florence: UNICEF Innocenti Research Centre).

Roelen, K., Gassmann, F., and de Neubourg, C. (2012) "False Positives or Hidden Dimensions – What Can Monetary and Multidimensional Measurement Tell us about Child Poverty?," *Journal for International Social Welfare*, 21(4): 393–407.

Shaffer, P. (2012) "Beneath the 'Methods Debate' in Impact Assessment: Baring Assumptions of a Mixed Methods Impact Assessment in Vietnam," *Journal of Development Effectiveness*, 4(1): 134–150.

VDR (2008) *Vietnam Development Report 2008: Social Protection* (Hanoi: Joint Donor Report to the Consultative Group Meeting).

Woldehanna, T., Alemu, T., and Mekonnen, A. (2008) *Young Lives: Ethiopia Round 2 Survey Report* (Oxford: Department for International Development).

Section III
Analysis and Representation

10
Epistemology and Ethics in Data Sharing and Analysis: A Critical Overview

Joanna Bornat

10.1 Introduction

This chapter has developed from discussion of and practical experience in the re-use of archived qualitative data. As an oral historian I am fortunate that the research methodology I adopt means that I cross over the disciplinary boundaries between history and sociology, engaging with researchers who often work in parallel and quite separately, exploring and developing approaches to the same problems but coming from different directions. This can lead to fascinating and stimulating learning opportunities as well as much debate. Re-use, or as it is also known, secondary analysis, is a well-known approach amongst researchers who work with large data sets of quantitative data. However, until fairly recently data sharing had not been identified or much adopted amongst qualitative social science researchers or oral historians. It has been carried out even less frequently by development researchers due to additional concerns relating to interest, time, quality, and translation. In what follows I will be exploring where resistance to data sharing lies, how methods of data sharing have subsequently developed, and what the outcomes have been for research practice. In particular I will discuss the nature of re-used data and their epistemological status, and will consider some ethical issues arising from the use of archived data. I will be drawing on experience from being a part of the Timescapes Programme[1] which sought, as one of its central features, to embed re-use in its activity as an ongoing generator of research data and as a repository of data to be shared and re-used by others (Neale et al., 2012). An early document promised that the consortium of Timescapes:

> will develop, facilitate and showcase secondary analysis of data from the Timescapes archive. In order to ensure that the dataset does not

atrophy but remains a vibrant, growing and useable resource, we aim to advance methods for analysis, data sharing and re-use, and establish a community of users, as well as develop new theoretical and substantive insights arising from the synthesis of the Timescapes data. Secondary Analysis is central to the work of the consortium, being a core part of the remit of each project and an area ripe for development in qualitative work. (Neale, 2012: 39)

These intentions were realized through programme activities such as visits between projects and a project conference which focused specifically on re-use. This resulted in many and various outputs produced by the Timescapes collaborators as they carried out their projects.[2] In such ways, the Timescapes programme during its lifetime provided a laboratory for exploring and developing the theory and practice of data sharing.[3]

Alongside my experience with Timescapes, I was also involved in a quite different project. With colleagues Parvati Raghuram and Leroi Henry I was investigating the contribution of overseas-trained South Asian doctors to the development of the geriatric specialty in the UK.[4] Central to our research methodology was the secondary analysis of archived interviews which we analysed in parallel with a new set of interviews (Bornat et al., 2012).

In their very different ways, these two projects inform the discussion developed in this chapter and I am grateful to my co-researchers for the many insights and learning opportunities which ensued.

10.2   What do we mean by secondary analysis, re-use, or sharing?

The literature which has built up around the practice of re-using data has grown rapidly, in the UK at least, from first beginnings in the mid-1990s. The founding of Qualidata, the ESRC Qualitative Data Archive Resource Centre, in 1994 at the University of Essex, was a major step forward in acknowledging the need for a funded qualitative data archive, a "clearing house and an action unit, its role being to locate and evaluate research data, catalogue it ... (and) organize its transfer to suitable archives across the UK" (Corti and Thompson, 2004: 330). The idea that data needed to be rescued from neglect, or worse, had been developed principally by Paul Thompson who had himself created a number of large oral history data sets which today are amongst those most consulted by Qualidata users.[5] With funding council support, the idea that qualitative research data should be preserved for later use was now established. ESRC-funded projects were expected to make their data available by depositing with Qualidata.

There had been earlier examples of archived research data and collections of papers prepared for re-use as Corti and Thompson (2004) point out, some based in individual institutions, others bringing together collections of material from various sources. The Mass Observation Archive at the University of Sussex is perhaps the oldest established archive-based resource and includes diaries and questionnaire replies recording different aspects of everyday life in Britain. Operating from 1937 to 1951, it was revived in 1981 when a new generation of contributors was recruited who began writing in from all over Britain and now welcomes bona fide researchers interested in using the collections of materials (Sheridan, 2000).

Despite the fact that much survey data had been preserved for re-use, a pilot study carried out in 1991 by Paul Thompson had shown that 90 per cent of qualitative research data had been lost and also that the 10 per cent which had been archived were not being preserved under conditions which permitted re-use (Corti and Thompson, 2004: 330). Urgent action was needed to avert this "extraordinary" situation (Hammersley, 1997: 137) and this resulted in the founding of Qualidata in 1994.

Despite such high-level support for re-use, what different researchers mean by data sharing varied. Janet Heaton defines secondary analysis as "a methodology for doing research using pre-existing data" (Heaton, 2004: 1). Other researchers, both enthusiasts and critics have identified re-use as a more complex process that is still in development. Indeed sharing has origins and traditions which differ between disciplines. Historians, as Corti points out, are accustomed to re-using a variety of texts:

> Unlike the sociologist, the historian will not be daunted by the concept of re-use of material that is unfamiliar to them. Historians have had to deal with the challenges of assessing provenance and veracity for many hundreds of years – take the Dead Sea Scrolls, Testaments and many other critical texts. (Corti, 2006)

In literary studies too, the idea that texts and their interpretations can be read and re-read is part of normal practice. Biographers use and re-use the same set of resources as new documents are added to archived collections when diaries and letters are rescued or revealed (Bornat, 2003). Amongst anthropologists, open use of predecessors' fieldnotes is a well-established practice, though not without controversy. Given that most diaries are not intended for publication and function as private opportunities for reflection and critical self-evaluation it could be argued that as such they should not be subjected to re-use or public perusal This was Raymond Firth's opinion when he reluctantly agreed to Malinowski's widow's request that he write an introduction to her late husband's diary when this was first published in 1966. He later revised his view and in a new introduction to the reissued book, 20 years later he counterposed different interpretations and valuations that anthropologists put on the diary. He is critical of James Clifford's textually based literary comparison of the diary and Malinowski's fieldnotes and remarks on his own uneasiness at being involved in the publication of a document as personal as a diary. He is also concerned at the criticisms of Malinowski which some anthropologists, notably Clifford Geertz, drew when comparing the private diary with Malinowski's published accounts of his time with the Trobriand islanders. However, Firth's later conclusion in his introduction to the second edition of the diaries is reassuring as he comes back to reflect on this particular publishing experience. He has shifted in his views, pointing out that "the concept of ethnography has altered and widened, and the book has accordingly moved over to a more central place in the literature of anthropological reflection ... it is a highly significant contribution to the understanding of the position and role of a fieldworker as a conscious participator in a dynamic social situation" (Firth, 1989: xxxi).

The process of "appropriating someone else's fieldnotes" is chronicled in Robert J. Smith's account of publishing the journal of Ella Wiswell, who worked in Japan with her anthropologist husband in the late 1930s. She gave him her "journal" (Smith switches between this term and "fieldnotes" without distinguishing one from the other) together with her husband's papers, following Smith's own fieldwork in a Japanese village after the Second World War. They decided to publish her journal jointly and he describes his struggle as he tried to "make the journal mine" yet sought a way to ensure the immediacy and personal nature of the author's writing. Between them were the voices of the Japanese villagers, the "subjects" who he says "should never be forgotten ... always more interesting than their authors."Though, "In the end, the blend of voices in our composition will always be uneven" (Smith, 1990: 369).

Ella Wiswell's journal and Bronislaw Malinowski's diary became available for others to use only after Wiswell gave her late husband, John Embree's, papers to Robert Smith and Valetta Malinowska decided that her father's diary should be published. Both had a close attachment to the papers but wanted them to be shared by others. Fortunately their dilemmas were resolved through publication and archive deposit by anthropologists such as Pat Caplan, Mary Douglas, Raymond Smith, Jack Goody, and Raymond Firth. Following in the footsteps of earlier anthropologists and ethnographers, using their fieldnotes and diaries is seen as a valuable part of training and preparation for field research, even one of the "rites of passage" of the emergent fieldworker (Lutkehaus, 1990: 313). This can be a challenging experience but nonetheless invaluable, as sociologists and oral historians were to discover once they also began to explore possibilities for re-use and began entering the world of previous researchers.

Issues of ownership, the ethics of re-use, and the reputation of the original researcher continue to feature whenever secondary analysis is undertaken or debated as I will later go on to discuss. At this point I want to pursue ideas of what researchers understand by secondary analysis with three rather different definitions or emphases.

Writing in 2000, Thompson mentions the "strange silence at the heart of the qualitative research community," arguing that qualitative researchers have "simply ignored the possibilities" of earlier research data and that although such researchers enjoy meeting and hearing each others' ideas "we are considerably less at ease about sharing our material" (2000). He goes on to reflect on what he learned from re-using his own data, for example he was able to compare solicited and unsolicited responses in two data sets covering similar topics and was able to extend his knowledge of relationships between grandparents and grandchildren and of relations between generations by combining evidence from the earlier and later data set (2000). He concludes with a call for a shift in attitudes and "respect for ... different research traditions" seeing in this the possibility of returning to the accounts and stories of research participants as the proper focus of sociological enquiry (2000). While he emphasizes the contribution which secondary analysis is able to make to knowledge, the thrust of his argument is as much moral as academic: sharing is what qualitative researchers ought to be doing.

Martin Hammersley, an educational researcher, has written extensively on the philosophy of research methodologies and has discussed the epistemological and methodological possibilities and limitations of re-use. In a review of debates over the previous decade in 2007, rather than focusing on problems in re-use he prefers to set out what re-use means in terms of what we understand research to be. While agreeing that the boundaries between use and re-use are not clearly delineated he identifies differences as well as similarities. Thus while re-use means working with data that another researcher has generated it may also have a variety of purposes and be carried out in different ways. He also points out to critics who argue about such problems as lack of fit and insufficient knowledge of context that these are aspects that can also apply to primary research (Hammersley, 1997).

While none of the approaches to secondary analysis outlined by Thompson and Hammersley is unique, each carries a certain emphasis. Thus Sarah Irwin and Mandy Winterton's definition brings a focus on outcomes: "The (re)using of data produced on a previous occasion to glean new social scientific and/or methodological understandings" (2011: 2). They point out the advantages which re-use can bring, for example extending the use of the data beyond the remit or resources of the original project and benefiting from the economy of re-use when funding is scarce. However they also point out that re-use is not necessarily time-saving and that it can require great effort and creativity on the part of the secondary researcher (Irwin and Winterton, 2011: 2–3).

In the next section I consider different reasons and strategies for re-using qualitative data. In so doing I rely on a useful listing developed by Irwin and Winterton.

10.2.1   Why engage in the re-use of "old" data?

Researchers have different reasons for making use of data generated by others as Heaton and Hammersley, amongst others, point out (Heaton, 2004: 8–10; Hammersley, 2010: 2–3). In a Timescapes Working Paper, Irwin and Winterton identify six different reasons. I follow their categorization, agreeing that none should be viewed as mutually exclusive. This will be evident from examples I have chosen as illustration.

One reason for considering earlier studies dealing with similar topics or populations might be to see if findings from a current project may provide some kind of guide or pilot or a basis for generalization (Hammersley, 1997: 137). Thompson provides an example from his own research where he and his research partner were about to embark on a study of Jamaican trans-national families. Going back to an earlier project by Chamberlain and Goulbourne provided them with a pilot stage which helped them to draw up and later refine their interview guide (Thompson, 2000). A second reason might be to use data from an existing study to further develop a research topic by identifying missing or neglected aspects, as in a study of the experiences of pediatric oncology nurses described by Hinds et al. (1997). Kelder's account of analysing data from an earlier project on weather forecasting as she developed a separate study of her own was, she demonstrates, adopted for pragmatic reasons related to the time available to her (2005).

A third category could be research which goes back to earlier studies, mining them for rich descriptive historical or sociological information. Libby Bishop's examination of convenience food as part of a study of the changes in domestic eating habits, for example, went back to Blaxter's 1982 study, *Mothers and Daughters* and Thompson's 1970–1973 study, *The Edwardians*, (Blaxter, 1982; Thompson, 1975) because, as she explains, "re-analysing existing data seemed a useful starring point, akin to an in-depth literature review" (2007). Data collected by Margot Jefferys for a study of doctors who pioneered the development of the geriatric specialty are rich and detailed in accounts of health services before and after the founding of the National Health Service (NHS) in 1946 (Bornat, 2005).

A fourth reason for going back to an earlier study is to gain methodo-logical insights by reflecting on research strategies undertaken. Natasha Mauthner et al. (1998), for example, discuss the implications of going back to their own work and from this develop a critical approach to re-use based on awareness of the significance of context and temporality when interpreting archived qualitative data. Mike Savage (2005a) in his investigation into archived materials from Elizabeth Bott's classic 1957 *Family and Social Network* study shows how the methods adopted by a research project may be typical of a particular era, sociologically, and how a ground-breaking outcome was the result of failure to achieve originally set project goals. Johnson et al. went back to Peter Townsend's 1959 landmark study of residential care for older people, *The Last Refuge*, following up his methods and in so doing contrast his positivist assumptions with their more "reflexive approach" (2010: 59).

A fifth category of reasons for engaging with archived data is to generate new findings by asking new questions. Rosemary Elliot (2001) drew on Thompson's "Families, Social Mobility and Ageing, an Intergenerational Approach, 1900–1988" (a study of 100 families across the British Isles) to study smoking habits during the 20th century. The interviews took a life history approach, exploring attitudes and lifestyles. Smoking was not a topic directly addressed in the original interview schedule, yet it was present in accounts of ill health, family finances, and teenage transitions. Smoking thus appeared serendipitously as a new finding (Elliot, 2001). A similarly serendipitous outcome came following a search of the Jefferys data for references to South-Asian overseas-trained doctors. In this case, a re-evaluation of the development of the geriatric specialty, in relation to the careers and contribution of these doctors, was able to be developed. Where previously their presence had been marked in passing, by generating a set of interviews with South Asian geriatricians, the Jefferys data were re-interrogated with the result that the role of medical migration was added to an understanding of the development of the geriatric specialty. With this, links between the UK and the Indian sub-continent became evident in ways that had not been previously perceived in the original study (Bornat et al., 2012).

Comparing data between two of the Timescapes projects, "The Oldest Generation" and "Men as Fathers," produced an interesting contrast in the way different generations of men talked of fatherhood. For the younger "Men as Fathers" sample, fatherhood was expressed in terms of choice and timing. For the older generation, such words were absent from accounts which presented fatherhood in terms of inevitability within what appeared as more structured life course trajectories. This opened up new ways of thinking about The Oldest Generation data. It also led us, as researchers, to re-consider how we had approached interviewing men over the age of 75 about intimate matters particularly when other members of the family were also involved in the project (Irwin et al., 2012: 72).

Finally, researchers may turn to the data created earlier when the population they want to engage with is hard to reach. Gladstone et al., in a study of children's mental health, asked new questions of their own data because as they explain "this is a benefit to researchers working with sensitive, vulnerable, or hard-to-reach populations because it limits the overall burden placed on particular participants, especially to 'talk' more" (Gladstone et al., 2007: 440). Fielding and Fielding argue, following their re-study of Cohen and Taylor's book, *Psychological Survival*, which had investigated the effect of long-term imprisonment following research with prisoners in Durham gaol, that secondary analysis is appropriate where research topics are sensitive and participants are hard to reach and where there are likely to be obstacles to obtaining access. In such cases "extracting the maximum from studies" would seem to be a valuable strategy (Fielding and Fielding, 2000: 678).

So far I have presented an uncontroversial account of re-using qualitative archived data. In fact what makes this whole area of work interesting are the debates which have accompanied and also spurred developments. It is to these that I now turn.

10.3   Debates in re-use

Debate on the pros and cons of re-using qualitative research data has ranged over various issues and has varied between direct opposition to exploratory discussion. To simplify and focus on what I consider to be the most illuminating areas so far I am dividing the debates up under three headings: whether secondary analysis results in new data or new knowledge; the knowability of the context of the original research; and ethical issues.

10.3.1 New data or new knowledge?

Engaging with data generated in an earlier study, one's own or another researcher's, involves a process of understanding and reframing, arriving at new knowledge. The question arises as to the basis of this new knowledge: have the data been changed in some way, through re-use, or do they remain untouched? This was one of the arguments taken up by Natasha Mauthner and her colleagues in an article which challenged secondary analysis enthusiasm. Going back to examples of their own research completed some years earlier, they conclude that, "our data were a product of the dynamic, dialectical and reflexive nature of a particular research encounter which both described and delimited the meaning of the data" (1998: 736). They contrast their past and present selves and focus on the role of reflexivity in generating data, arguing that the emotional and intellectual engagement made by the earlier researcher render those data virtually unknowable by anyone else coming later. Data are socially constructed, they argue, created in a particular set of conditions and relationships. Moreover, they argue that researchers who use those data without considering these "epistemological issues" are "unwittingly serving to reify the data by hoodwinking us into believing that they are entities without concomitant relations" (Mauthner et al., 1998: 743).

Niamh Moore's challenge to this argument is to say that "the data in fact are not 'out there' at all, that the data are here and now, being constructed in the process of a new research project" (Moore, 2007). She accuses Mauthner and her colleagues of being "almost as realist as those they critique" (Moore, 2007: 33) and of having limited ideas as to possibilities for re-use. She goes further, criticizing a view of reflexivity which has the effect of fixing a research project and its various participants in some past, historical, point in time. Citing Adkins (2002), she warns against assumptions in-built in this approach which have the effect of creating earlier researchers, themselves or others as less aware, even "naïve" (Moore, 2007). She concludes by calling for researchers to leave their "comfort zones (to develop) ... a more creative, and even messy, approach" (Moore, 2007). Thus she embraces what she sees as the methodological and substantive creativity of re-use in the face of increased bureaucratization and professional strait-jacketing of academic research, as well as fear of methodological novelty. Moore's enthusiasm has been shared by many involved in secondary analysis and her engagement with the debate has provided a valuable contribution not only to this particular arena but to sociological and historical research more generally. One effect of re-use is to bring research methodologies and research practice under much closer scrutiny as people seek to understand not only other data and analyses but also the mindsets and approaches of earlier researchers. I will come back to this point later in the chapter.

However, one aspect of her argument has been reined in by Hammersley who takes a critical view of the idea that re-use means that researchers are engaging in creating new data. In advocating re-use he distinguishes between data when given or collected and data being analysed or being used to draw inferences. The latter he prefers to call "evidence" (Hammersley, 2010) He sees this as a process rather than two exclusive categories as data move in and out of view and are added to or selected as research proceeds thus being "given as well as constructed" (Hammersley, 2010). Those original data have an existence which is established in the sense that we are limited by what we can and cannot infer from them. They were socially constructed, but they exist. This can be true of both primary and secondary research. Thus, for example by going back to interviews with the pioneers of geriatric medicine we were able to find evidence that several had connections with the Indian sub-continent, six had been born there and another six had worked there at some point in their careers. This led us to a reconceptualization of the Jefferys data in terms of coloniality and professional migration, reinforced when we also discovered that Margot Jefferys had been born in India where her family had connections which went back two generations.

Reconceptualization brought the two data sets, the Jefferys' and the interviews with South Asian overseas-trained doctors, more closely into connection in ways that we had not originally anticipated. Those data were there in the original study, but only drawn out as we worked on them, turning them into evidence relating to the investigation we were engaged in (Bornat et al., 2012).

In secondary analysis such analysis is complicated, some argue it is impossible, by distance from the original research setting and conditions under which the data were created. It is to this issue of context which I turn to now.

10.3.2   Knowability of context

Sceptics regard the knowability of context as the main obstacle to the re-use of archived qualitative data. As Heaton points out, qualitative research typically relies on methods which allow for subjective, reflective ways of working and tend to mean that the researcher's own viewpoint, networks, and sources are inextricably tied into the creation of data (Heaton, 2004: 60–61). However Mauthner et al. simply argue that ensuring data are accompanied by sufficient information on deposit, for example materials which provide details of how a project was funded, what its aims were, its chosen methods, and what was found, is not enough. Nor, they argue, can deficits in the original data be made up for with more contextual information from new evidence and interpretation. Data are produced in "interpersonal, social, cultural, political and historical conditions" and raise "ontological and epistemological" questions for those who attempt to re-use them (Mauthner et al., 1998: 736).

Hammersley points to such contextual issues as cultural assumptions', "theoretical presuppositions," and differences in purpose, which can, of course, be true when working with one's own or another's data (Hammersley, 1997: 138–139). He also refers to what he calls the "cultural *habitus*" that a researcher develops, the latter he sees as particularly significant in ethnographic research where immersion in the field will inevitably change perceptions and outlook. However, though warning of limitations he also questions why there has not been more archiving of research data and materials, pointing to strategies which can help in making an archived project more understandable to subsequent researchers (Hammersley, 1997: 133)

Others have responded to Mauthner and her colleagues, suggesting that the position they take has its own realist qualities (Moore, 2007), that rejecting re-use could lead to the stifling of research endeavour (Bornat, 2003), that it is helpful to have insights into the development of research careers through accounts of dilemmas and negotiation (Moore, 2005), and that context itself may become reified if it is perceived as an unknowable entity (Moore, 2006). Moore cites Libby Bishop's re-use of Blaxter and Thompson's data in her study of convenience food as an exemplar of an approach to considering context and one which includes reflexivity as a part of the process. Bishop describes herself as being new to food research, so began by looking at earlier published studies in the sociology of food, from this drawing up some research questions. She used a computer software package, Atlas.ti 5.0, to search the Blaxter study, which included 46 grandmother interviews where food was mentioned. She devised coding categories such as types of food, mentions of tinned food, discussions of good food, cooking techniques, etc. and thus arrived at statements which she rated as negative or mixed, under headings such as "too expensive," "home made more nourishing," etc (reproduced in Bishop, 2007). For the Thompson study, she analysed answers to questions which she drew from 10 per cent of the collection, building a sample which allowed for a range of occupations and regions and which had mentioned food and eating. She used a binary coding scheme so that answers to the question "Did the family sit at the table for the meal?" were coded as "Yes" or "No" and by occupation. From this she could see that, across the occupational range, most families ate together, but that the semi-skilled manual were evenly divided and that most families made little use of tinned food, with those least likely being amongst the poorest and the most affluent. She sees her approach to context as being "a recontextualisation process," working with two contexts, the time of the original research and the time of her later analysis. Within each there are, she argues, three levels of context, "the interaction, the situation and the cultural/institutional" (Bishop, 2007). Both studies, it turns out, had good supporting documentation or metadata. She was able to find out, for example, that the interviewers in the Blaxter study were "two educated, white women" and that the grandmothers had been interviewed by someone who lived in the same area. She was also able to get some idea of how well Blaxter and her colleagues had got to know their research participants. Bishop includes historical context in her review of the research, noting that what might have been perceived as good food in the 1980s when the research was carried out was likely to be different in 2005 when she carried out her analysis of the data. This she says she took into account, along with other differences as she looked at the data (Bishop, 2007).

The Thompson study was from an earlier era, and so did not have any explicit mention of convenience or processed foods. The transcripts also showed that replies to questions about food and eating were short and unelaborated. However, these oral history interviews had what she describes as "an emotional intensity," which survived transcription as this excerpt, which she quotes, shows:

> 3G: Now my man now, he disnae [does not] believe in tinned food ... he disnae believe in that either. He says there's nae [no] nourishment in that, you're better wi' your own. Even though you got a bone you could mak' a pot o' soup. A bone, you're getting' the goodness off a bone, the marrow, oot a bone. (Bishop, 2007)

As with Elliot (2001) she points to the effect of serendipity. Her interest was in convenience foods so that the references she found in the answers can be valued for their independence, given that there was no likelihood that the original researcher, or herself, could have had any influence (Bishop, 2007). She concludes that "co-construction of data" is a part of secondary analysis, though not in any reflexive way at the time the data were originated, but with the forms in which they are preserved, in transcription, as an audio file and with the materials which are deposited in support (Bishop, 2007).

The rich complexity of reconceptualisating and exploring context is developed by Irwin and Winterton who point out the multiplicity of levels of contextual information which are "embedded" (2012) in research drawing on the Timescapes programme's focus on re-use. They point to the historical contexts of research methodologies and their socially determined characteristics. These will have affected, as we have seen from Bishop's study, which topics are identified as appropriate or suitable for research and also what sense is made of them at the time, and later at re-study. They also point out how the theory will have played a part in the identification of what were seen as appropriate indicators of behaviour by previous researchers. An example from my own research may be helpful here. Early on in my PhD research I interviewed a retired wool textile worker about her experiences as a young millworker in the Colne Valley of West Yorkshire. I was interested in the relationship between work, home, and trade union membership. I was disconcerted when, with much emotion, she turned the interview towards an experience she had as a young child, listening to the Messiah. She wanted to talk about social rejection to tell me how, hearing "He was rejected" sung at a local performance of Messiah, resonated with her own hurt feelings of social rejection as the child of unmarried parents. I wanted to hear about mill life and deflected her account. I later used this exchange many times as an example of bad practice in oral history interviewing. Coming back to that interview I realized that my theoretical take on life in the industry before the First World War had been narrowly framed in terms of the economy of the wage relationship; in particular I was not interested to hear talk of religious experiences. I had excluded a broader understanding of the nature of working-class culture in those communities which might have been helpful. Though overall my views and ideological standpoint had not changed when I came back to look at those earlier data, my explanations and wider sources of referencing had shifted (Bornat, 2010).

The temporality of re-use is exposed when contexts are brought into contact as this last example suggests. Going back with a changed 'cultural habitus' (Bornat, 2006) opens up data to transformation and exploration by the later researcher. Biographical and historical time for both researcher and researched provide opportunities for rich re-contextualizations as well as having implications for current research and archiving practice, as I shall go on to discuss in the next section. Time is both a challenge and an opportunity and is always present in whatever research we do, as Sheila Henderson et al. point out:

> The fact that we can never "go back" and re-experience the moment of data collection/production is a consequence or our positions as researchers *in time*, rather than a "problem" of secondary analysis or "old data." Whether the gap is a week or 10 years we are always revisiting data and analysis within successive historical moments. (Henderson et al., 2006: 55)

10.3.3   Ethical issues

However we view them, ethical protocols are now central to research practice. Indeed they are required to be, but may also be critically discussed. (Hammersley and Traianou, 2012; Erdos, 2013). Secondary analysis debates have played an important role in the development of ethical awareness highlighting issues which might be overlooked and bringing certain others into closer focus. Seeking to establish the certainty of informed consent and guaranteeing wishes for confidentiality and anonymity have been seen as impossibilities for some critics of re-use.

Barriers may be impassable simply because data were not created at a time when re-use was ever considered or when guidance then in operation was not sufficiently developed to allow for the protection of research participants. Kelder (2005) describes how the extent of her re-use of another researcher's data was limited because only four of the people previously interviewed were contactable. She outlines the elaborate procedures which were put into place in order for her to be able to use their original transcripts, including generating new consent forms and preservation of anonymity at all stages and concludes that "a better paradigm should be developed which allows for control to be given to research participants to be flexible in how they participate as the research progresses" (2005).

Mauthner et al. were similarly concerned about problems of participant anonymity and preserving confidentiality. Calls for more background information in order to make archived data more understandable would only create more problems, they argue (1998: 734). They were also concerned with issues of copyright and ownership in interviews as these have legal implications for researcher and researched (Parry and Mauthner, 2004).

Organizations such as Qualidata at the UK Data Archive and the Oral History Society have established protocols for re-use, specifically with interviews in mind;, these work with the codes of ethics of professional bodies such as the British Sociological Association and the British Association of Social Workers.[6] All point to the need to protect from harm, guarantee consent, and maintain conditions of confidentiality in accordance with the wishes of research participants. All suggest ways to maintain these codes, with both digital and non-digital data. As Kelder's (2005) experience suggests, care in all these aspects is of importance to any subsequent researcher who wants to consult archived data and is also important for archivists who are likely to be keen that collections are easily managed and as self-contained and clearly explained as possible.

As an archivist, Bishop's response to critics such as Parry and Mauthner who consider the complexity of anonymization amongst other things (2005) is to point to procedures which allow for varied levels of anonymity and of access to archived qualitative data arguing that transparency in procedures for preserving and depositing data for re-use is helpful to researchers and funders alike (Bishop, 2005). While the evolution and fixing of such bureaucratic practices are to be welcomed, they may encourage overcautious responses from researchers. Awareness that one's research may be of interest to others may mean that researchers edit fieldnotes, redesign methods, or hold back on reflection as ways to protect themselves from future scrutiny and judgement (McLeod and Thomson, 2009: 134).

While there has been much concern expressed about the security of research participants, the reputations and biographies of researchers have been equally a focus for critical discussion. Thompson asks why qualitative sociologists may be reluctant to deposit their data, wondering if this is due to inhibition or perhaps the fear that to use someone else's data is perhaps less worthy as an endeavour (2000). In the end he makes a moral and scientific case for data deposit but even so there are still ethical issues of a collegial nature which I now go on to explore.

Research data and findings are inextricably linked to the biography of individual researchers, close enough in some circumstances that "the researcher often becomes the research instrument and cannot be separated from the practice" (Goodwin and O'Connor, 2003). Evidence of the effect of social class, historical context, and cultural assumptions is visible in the interactions preserved in interview exchanges, fieldnotes, and other data. Secondary researchers have noted, for example, Dennis Marsden's sometimes pejorative and often detailed descriptions of the homes of the lone mothers he interviewed in the 1960s (Evans and Thane, 2006). Less personally perhaps, Savage points out how differences between researchers and researched in ways of talking and understanding what was meant by class led to a particular theory of class identity emerging from the Affluent Worker study of Goldthorpe and Lockwood, a theory which on going back to the original research data he now re-assesses (Savage, 2005b).

How to treat the work of the researcher whose data one is using was something that came up very soon in the study of South Asian geriatricians that I have already mentioned more than once in this chapter. We, the secondary researchers with our parallel set of interviews (Bornat et al., 2012), were ever mindful of the debt we owed to Margot Jefferys. Her archived data had, after all, given rise to our own research project. Had it not been for the references which her respondents made to "my Indians" (for example) the idea for our study might not have occurred to us. On the other hand, we were also aware that neither Jefferys nor her research partners and participants had considered the contribution of overseas-trained doctors as a topic in its own right. They appear only in passing within the transcripts. Nor, of course, had she or they considered framing their presence within any kind of explanation in terms of race, racism, or colonial and post-colonial networks, as we were interesting in doing.

Beyond our rather different approaches there was evidence in the tone of the interview dialogues, and we focused on one in particular, which seemed to suggest that Jefferys' reputation as a fair-minded, progressive member of the research community might be at risk. In an exchange with Professor John Brocklehurst where they discuss the period of the 1960s and 1970s when South Asian doctors were being recruited in large numbers to work in the NHS with many arriving in the new specialty of geriatric medicine, she talks about "deficits," difficulties," and "problems." So for example, when asking him how he built his department at Withington Hospital, Manchester the exchange develops as follows:

> All the junior staff I had were trained in India or Pakistan. Many of them had come over; they were junior, their knowledge of medicine was very limited in relation to British medicine, many of them had language problems and so it was a matter of educating them too. And, on the whole, they were very nice people who were keen to learn but it did mean that it was a constant … when you had an English person. English-trained doctor life became much simpler I must say.
> *Yes, because of the deficits both due to cultural differences.*
> Yes, and particularly in professional knowledge and the way in which they would go about writing up cases and all the rest of it. So it was a matter of teaching Asian doctors most of the time, and many of

them went on, I mean most of these doctors stayed in this country, many went into general practice, quite a few went into geriatrics in fact as the time went by.

What were the most difficult things? Was it to get them to see problems as broadly as you wished them to?

Yes, I think to take an overall view of a case and not get involved in one diagnostic aspect because old people do suffer from various things and they all contribute to their problems. And to have a sort of ordered writing up of the cases and to be able to tell you exactly what was happening the next day or the next week. These were all difficulties.[7]

What we gained from the Jefferys data was detailed pictures of the NHS during its early years and specifically the response which was developed to provide effective treatment for older people: the resourcing of the geriatric specialty. We also learned that this was not an area of work which home-grown doctors were interested in working in and hence the NHS had to rely on overseas-trained doctors. However, what we also see from the exchange is how a difficult and contentious issue was recalled at a time, the early 1990s, and in a way that was more measured than during the times that were being recalled, evident from contemporaneous documentary documents which were more directly discriminatory in their expression (Bornat et al., 2012). As we have suggested elsewhere (Bornat et al., 2012) it could be that both Jefferys and Brocklehurst were seeking ways to discuss such issues knowing that their words might later be scrutinized at a later date. With this in mind, the exchange might be read as an exploration of a known area of rapid change within the specialty and the NHS more generally rather than to judge the words as spoken in problematic ways. This layering of temporalities helps to redress any assumptions we might have been developing as to Jefferys' perceptions and, with the benefit of an interview from one of the South Asian doctors, we heard an account of Brocklehurst which presented him as a benign and helpful senior who encouraged overseas-trained doctors:

> Professor Brocklehurst had a wide range. He was a very kind man. If you wanted anything he will say "Why don't you see me in my office?" And he will talk to you very patiently, advising you "Is there anything I can do about you. Do you need some help?" Just like your parents. Oh yes. I wish there were more people like Professor Brocklehurst.[8]

In revisiting the Jefferys data it had always been our intention to promote her achievement and to draw attention to the richness of the interviews she and colleagues had conducted. However, this has also meant that her approach and methods, as well as the resulting data, have been subjected to different forms of scrutiny which she might not have expected or intended. We cannot know what she would have thought of our re-use (sadly she died before the project was initiated) and are aware of course that in carrying out our study in parallel we are opening up our own work to similar investigation. In going back to another's research we were mindful of the ethics of what we were attempting and of the temporalities at work in the process, in our case seeking ways to maintain the reputation of a researcher whose work we continue to hold in great respect.

10.4   Conclusions

Throughout this chapter I have ranged over various debates in relation to the re-use of archived qualitative data with the intention of presenting this development as a dynamic and creative area of research. I have also drawn on the findings of research to show what results have followed from turning to another or one's own earlier research. Researchers' motivations for re-using data may vary, curiosity surely being the strongest reason, as in any research endeavour. The opportunity to walk in the footsteps of a previous researcher, perhaps someone eminent, controversial, or original in his/her thinking and findings, is also irresistible, as I hope I have managed to convey. It is an added advantage that researchers dispute the nature and means of creating knowledge through re-use or find that ethical questions pose challenges to ways of working. Engagement with re-use or secondary analysis helps to widen the understanding of what researchers do and leads to researchers examining their own practice as reflection inevitably accompanies work with archived data.

Notes

1. The seven empirical projects making up the ESRC-funded Timescapes Programme (RES-347-25-0003; 2007–2012) generated qualitative longitudinal data with a view to understanding family and close personal relationships over time and through the life course. This was the first-time major qualitative longitudinal research programme to be funded in the UK.
2. For a full listing see the Timescapes website at: http://www.timescapes.leeds.ac.uk. The empirical project for which I was co-researcher with Bill Bytheway was "The Oldest Generation."
3. In particular I am grateful to Libby Bishop, Sarah Irwin, Bren Neale, Bill Bytheway, and Mandy Winterton for the many insights and examples of practice which they generated and shared.
4. "Overseas-trained South Asian doctors and the development of geriatric medicine," ESRC grant reference number: RES-062-23-0514.

5. In October 2012 Qualidata was integrated into the ESRC-funded UK Data Service (http://www.esds.ac.uk) continuing with its role in depositing, processing, and accessing qualitative data but on a more selective basis, working with individual institutional repositories.
6. British Sociological Association statement of ethical practice: www.britsoc.co.uk/equality/Statement+Ethical+Practice.htm; British Association of Social Workers Code of Ethics: http://www.basw.co.uk/about/code-of-ethics/; Oral History Society: http://www.ohs.org.uk/ethics/index.php; and UK Data Archive: advice on consent and ethics: www.data-archive.ac.uk/create-manage/consent-ethics.
7. Professor John Brocklehurst interviewed by Margot Jeffery, 5 September 1991, Jefferys, ref C512/32/01-2.
8. Dr Suchel Bansal, interviewed by Leroi Henry, 4 July 2008, SAG, ref C1536/04, track 1.

References

Adkins, L. (2002) *Revisions: Gender and Sexuality in Late Modernity* (Buckingham: Open University Press).
Bishop, L. (2005) "Protecting respondents *and* enabling data sharing: Reply to Parry and Mauthner," *Sociology*, 39(2): 333–336.
Bishop, L. (2007) "A reflexive account of reusing qualitative data: Beyond primary/secondary dualism," *Sociological Research Online*, 12(3). Available at: http://www.socresonline.org.uk/12/3/2.html, [Accessed 30 November 2012].
Blaxter, M. and Patterson, E. (1982) *Mothers and Daughters: A Three Generational Study of Health Attitudes and Behaviour* (London: Heinemann Educational Books).
Bornat, J. (2003) "Revisiting interviews with a different purpose," *Oral History*, 31(1): 47–53.
Bornat, J. (2005) "Recycling the evidence: Different approaches to the reanalysis of gerontological data," [37 paragraphs]. *Forum Qualitative Sozialforschung/Forum: Qualitative Social Research*, 6(1), Art. 42. Available at: http://nbn-resolving.de/urn:nbn:de:0114-fqs0501424, [Accessed 30 January 2012].
Bornat, J. (2006) "Secondary Analysis of One's Own and Others' Data," paper given at: "*Practice and Ethics in Qualitative Longitudinal Research' ESRC seminar,*" 20 January, University of Leeds.
Bornat, J. (2010) "Remembering and reworking emotions: The reanalysis of emotion in an interview," *Oral History*, 38(2): 43–52.
Bornat, J., Raghuram, P. and Henry, L. (2012) "Revisiting the archives: A case study from the history of geriatric medicine," *Sociological Research Online*, 17(2): 11. Available at: http://www.socresonline.org.uk/17/2/11.html, [Accessed 30 November 2012].
Corti, L. (2006) "Editorial," *Methodological Innovations Online*, 1(2): 1–9. Available at: http://www.pbs.plym.ac.uk/mi/pdf/Volume%201%20Issue%202/1.%20Corti%20editorial%20-%20pp1-9.pdf, [Accessed 28 November 2012].
Corti, L. and Thompson, P. (2004) "Secondary Analysis of Archived Data," in Seale, C., Gobo. G., Gubrium, G. and Silverman, D. (eds) *Qualitative Research Practice*, London: Sage: 327–343.
Elliot, R. (2001) "Growing up and giving up: Smoking in Paul Thompson's 100 Families," *Oral History*, 29(1): 73–84.
Evans, T. and Thane, P. (2006) "Secondary analysis of Dennis Marsden's *Mothers Alone,*" *Methodological Innovations Online*, 1(2): 78–82. Available at: http://www.

pbs.plym.ac.uk/mi/pdf/Volume%201%20Issue%202/07.%20Evans-pp78–82. pdf, [Accessed 5 August 2013].

Erdos, D. (2013) "Freedom of expression turned on its head: Academic social research and journalism in the European Union's privacy framework," *Public Law*, 1: 52–73.

Fielding, N. and Fielding, J. (2000) "Resistance and adaptation to criminal identity: Using secondary analysis to evaluate classic studies in crime and deviance," *Sociology*, 34(671): 671–689.

Firth, R. (1989) "Second Introduction," in Malinowski, B. (ed.) *A Diary in the Strict Sense of the Term* (Stanford: Stanford University Press), pp. xxi–xxxi.

Gladstone, B., Volpe, T. and Boydell, K. (2007) "Issues encountered in a qualitative secondary analysis of help-seeking in the prodrome to psychosis," *Journal of Behavioural Health Services & Research*, 34(4): 431–442.

Goodwin, J. and O'Connor, H. (2003) "'They had horrible wallpaper': Representations of respondents and the interview process in interview notes," *ESRC Young Worker Project Research Papers, Research Paper 4* (University of Leicester: Centre for Labour Market Studies).

Hammersley, M. (1997) "Qualitative data archiving: Its prospects and problems," *Sociology*, 31(1): 131–142.

Hammersley, M. (2010) "Can we re-use qualitative data via secondary analysis? Notes on some terminological and substantive issues," *Sociological Research Online*, 15(1). Available at: http://www.socresonline.org.uk/15/1/5.html, [Accessed 28 November 2012].

Hammersley, M. and Traianou, M. (2012) *Ethics in Qualitative Research: Controversies and Contexts* (London: Sage).

Heaton, J. (2004) *Reworking Qualitative Data* (London: Sage).

Henderson, S., Holland, J. and Thomson, R. (2006) "Making the long view: Perspectives on context from a qualitative longitudinal (QL) study," *Methodological Innovations Online*, 1(2): 47–63. Available at: http://www.pbs. plym.ac.uk/mi/pdf/Volume%201%20Issue%202/05.%20Henderson-pp47-63. pdf, [Accessed 5 December 2012].

Hinds, P., Vogel, R. and Clarke-Steffen, L. (1997) "The possibilities and pitfalls of doing secondary analysis of a qualitative data set," *Qualitative Health Research*, 7(3): 408–424.

Irwin, S. and Winterton, M. (2011) "Debates in qualitative secondary analysis: Critical reflections," *Timescapes Working Paper Series No. 4*. Available at: http:// www.timescapes.leeds.ac.uk/assets/files/WP4-March-2011.pdf, [Accessed 28 November 2012].

Irwin, S. and Winterton, M. (2012) "Qualitative secondary analysis and social explanation," *Sociological Research Online*, 17(2): 4. Available at: http://www. socresonline.org.uk/17/2/4.html> 10.5153/sro.2626, [Accessed 3 December 2012].

Irwin, S., Bornat, J. and Winterton, M. (2012) "Timescapes secondary analysis: Comparison, context and working across data sets," *Qualitative Reserch*, 12(1): 66–80.

Johnson, J., Rolph, S. and Smith, R. (2010) *Residential Care Transformed: Revisiting "The Last Refuge"* (Basingstoke: Palgrave).

Kelder, J. (2005) "Using someone else's data: Problems, pragmatics and provisions," [56 paragraphs]. *Forum Qualitative Sozialforschung/Forum: Qualitative Social*

Research, 6(1), Art. 39. Available at: http://nbn-resolving.de/urn:nbn:de:0114-fqs0501396, [Accessed 30 November 2012].

Lutkehaus, N. (1990) "Refractions of reality: On the use of other ethnographers' fieldnotes," in Sanjek, R. (ed.) *Fieldnotes: The Makings of Anthropology* (New York: Cornell), pp. 303–323.

Mauthner, N., Parry, O. and Backett-Milburn, K. (1998) "The data are out there, or are they? Implications for archiving and revisiting qualitative data," *Sociology*, 32: 733–745.

McLeod, J. and Thomson, R. (2009) *Researching Social Change* (London: Sage).

Moore, N. (2005) "(Re)using qualitative data?, Thoughts from the CRESC qualitative research laboratory," *CRESC Methods Workshop*, 28 September, University of Manchester.

Moore, N. (2006) "The contexts of context: Broadening perspectives in the (Re)use of qualitative data," *Methodological Innovations Online*, 1(2): 21–32. Available at: http://www.pbs.plym.ac.uk/, [Accessed 5 December 2012].

Moore, N. (2007) "(Re)using qualitative data?," *Sociological Research Online*, 12(3). Available at: http://www.socresonline.org.uk, [Accessed 3 December 2012].

Neale, B. (2012) *Timescapes an ESRC Qualitative Longitudinal Study: Changing Relationships and Identities through the Life course. Study Overview*. Available at: http://www.timescapes.leeds.ac.uk/, [Accessed 28 November 2012].

Neale, B., Henwood, K. and Holland, J. (2012) "Researching lives through time: An introduction to the Timescapes approach," *Qualitative Research*, 12(1): 4–15.

Parry, O. and Mauthner, N. (2004) "Whose data are they anyway? Practical, legal and ethical issues in archiving qualitative research data," *Sociology*, 38(1): 139–152.

Savage, M. (2005a) "Revisiting classic qualitative studies," *Forum Qualitative Sozialforschung/Forum: Qualitative Social Research*, 6(1), Art. 31. Available at: http://nbn- resolving.de/urn:nbn:de:0114-fqs0501312, [Accessed 30 November 2012].

Savage, M. (2005b) "Working-class identities in the 1960s: Revisiting the Affluent Worker study," *Sociology*, 39(5b): 929–946.

Sheridan, D. (2000) "Reviewing mass-observation: The archive and its researchers thirty years on," [9 paragraphs]. *Forum Qualitative Sozialforschung/Forum: Qualitative Social Research*, 1(3), Art. 26. Available at: http://nbn-resolving.de/urn:nbn:de:0114-fqs0003266, [Accessed 5 August 2013].

Smith, R. J. (1990) "Hearing voices, joining the Chorus: Appropriating someone else's fieldnotes," in Sanjek, R. (ed.) *Fieldnotes: The Makings of Anthropology* (New York: Cornell), pp. 356–370.

Thompson, P (1975) *The Edwardians: The Remaking of British Society* (London: Weidenfeld & Nicholson).

Thompson, P. (2000) "Re-using qualitative research data: A personal account," *Forum Qualitative Social Research*, 1(3), Art. 27. Available at: http://nbn-resolving.de/urn:nbn:de:0114-fqs0003277, [Accessed 28 November 2012].

11
Replication of Quantitative Work in Development Studies: Experiences and Suggestions

Maren Duvendack and Richard Palmer-Jones

11.1 Introduction

Replication[1] is seen as a key characteristic of natural science (Collins, 1985; Jasny et al., 2011); observations, especially those employing complex instruments, and experiments need to be repeated, and statistical analyses be scrutinized, before results gain credibility. This is not the case in social sciences; social science data are seldom re-produced,[2] or re-analysed to check the original calculations, or analysed using alternative perspectives or frameworks.[3] Hence, it is not clear that quantitative social science can advance in the same way as natural science. Nevertheless, there have often been calls among quantitative social scientists for replication (Frisch, 1933; Dewald et al., 1986; King, 1995; Gleditsch and Metelits, 2003; McCullough and Vinod, 2003; Pesaran, 2003; Bernanke, 2004; Freeze, 2007; McCullough and McKitrick, 2009; Burman et al., 2010), especially of computational[4] studies (Peng, 2011). The proposed benefits include: full understanding of the computations[5] and estimations, including for pedagogy; credibility; a basis for further work either assessing the robustness of the study to alternative variable constructions, model specifications, estimation methods or software, or extending or building on it; and an audit function – to identify and deter fraud and/or over-interpretation of the data (McCullough et al., 2006).

As noted above, replication is not common in quantitative social science, including economics. Replication can be seen as a public good as it has low publication chances, involves considerable professional risks, and has additional sociological or organizational features which may not be conducive to the investment of time and effort in replication work (Dewald et al., 1986). Extrinsic rewards such as publications, citations, and promotions are generally seen as awarded to innovation; since replication seemingly involves repetition it is almost by definition not being first.[6] Replications may be considered to lack novelty if they largely confirm the original study; although given the frequency with which programming error can occur, this is still valuable (Pesaran, 2003). If they contest original papers they can provoke hostility, and make difficulties for journal editors.

We argue that there are important reasons to replicate development economics studies, not only because of the more general arguments advanced for replication in economics, but also because of the growing influence of development economics on development policy (Banerjee, 2005; Banerjee and Duflo, 2011).

In the next sections we introduce the motivations and incentives for replication, and discuss prominent examples to illustrate behaviour during the replication process. We argue that understanding replicatory exchanges requires understanding of both the extrinsic (or instrumental) and intrinsic values of the replicators, the journal editors who publish them, and original authors. Several replications which have been strongly contested by original authors show that replicators and journal editors who publish them have the same public interest motives as the original authors. However, the language and actions of original authors can appear aimed to deter replication, and to manage reputation, rather than to promote constructive engagement arising from legitimate concerns about the original work.

11.2 Experiences with replication in social sciences

Replication should be a part of everyday practice in economics, not consigned to graduate classes (cf. Glandon, 2010). It should be a prerequisite for making substantive contributions to an area of work, so that not only is the validity of previous relevant work established (or not), but the work is thoroughly understood. This is frequently not possible by reading the published version alone as there is not enough space to provide all the details of the computations and so on (Donoho, 2010) and writing practices are oriented towards making the strongest possible case. One example of this is the focus on finding statistical significance (Ziliak and McCloskey, 2008) rather than establishing epistemological robustness and evaluating the performance of the maintained position relative to relevant and reputable alternatives. Nevertheless, while one gets the impression that many people embark on replications, published replications are quite rare. In the next section we examine the incentives for replication, by exploring the motivations of replicators, original authors, and journal editors, and their costs as well as benefits.

11.3   Motivation for replication

Mirowski and Sklivas (1991) and Feigenbaum and Levy (1993) develop models of replication focusing on extrinsic values of replicators, original authors, and journal editors (the former include also "extenders" who build on without closely replicating the original contribution). They conclude that "it is highly unlikely that scientists will engage in replication behaviour" (1993: 146), and that "widespread preaching to econometricians about the virtue of sharing data will not be a particularly effective method of making data freely available [7]" (1993: 230). Original authors will assume that "the only apparent intention [of the replicator] is ... to falsify the original ... report" (Mirowski and Sklivas, 1991: 152), and will seek to make replication more costly by withholding data, or crucial details of computations and methods, which they may not even have bothered to document or preserve (Dewald et al., 1986; McCullough et al., 2006). On the other hand, "extension ... is much more attractive ... [because] it is [in] everyone's interest. ... [it] lends validity and importance to the initial research finding ... costs are lower, encouragements are ubiquitous (grants etc.) ... [and] journals must regard this work as ... a legitimate contribution ... because it cites reports already published ... legitimizing past editorial choices, and because its limited novelty renders it easier to evaluate" (Mirowski and Sklivas1991: 153). That replications are undertaken at all is surprising in this framework. Other motives for replication are adduced by original authors (e.g. Hoxby, 2007), or on their behalf (Hamermesh, 2007); these include political motives (Hoxby, 2007), and overthrowing the reputation of established authors to advance the replicator's own career (Mirowsky and Sklivas, 1991; Hamermesh, 2007). Attribution of these motives to would-be replicators may be a considerable disincentive.

While there have been several attempts to institute replicability in economics and related disciplines by encouraging authors to make raw data more available, these attempts have generally been half-hearted (Anderson et al., 2008; McCullough, 2009). One partial exception is the data policy of the American Economic Review, initiated in 2004 in response to McCullough and Vinod (2003) (Bernanke, 2004), which requires data and code deposition prior to publication. Econometrica introduced a similar policy on data and code in 2005, and it is increasingly common among quantitative social science journals (McCullough et al., 2008: 1407). This model is gaining adherence but is not universal, even among high-ranked journals.

As far as we can see there has been no great increase in the number of published replications, despite greater availability of data and statistical software which makes replication easier. Perhaps this is because the solutions focus on cost-benefit analysis in terms of extrinsic rewards and their material opportunity costs, and this is incomplete. Other factors may be relevant, and indeed a more thorough sociology of academic and professional economics similar to the sociology of science (Latour, 1987) and of the academy (Bourdieu, 1998) may be required to understand replicatory choices.

Perhaps the most common motivation for replication (other than to fulfil coursework tasks) lies in being "skeptical of the validity of the published results" (Feigenbaum and Levy, 1993: 217) and wishing to increase professional transparency and accountability. However, replication also offers what Gustin (1973) has termed the "charisma" or intrinsic pleasures of practicing science (or ideal academic pursuits more generally[8]). These intrinsic motivations are perhaps the main reasons people undertake replications even though they provide few extrinsic returns. Thus, a commitment to the ideal of science, combined with a realization of the pervasive presence of errors in complex computations (Hatton and Roberts, 1994; McCullough and Vinod, 1999; Merali, 2010) and the fragility of econometric methods (Leamer, 1983), provide intrinsic motivations. Additionally, learning how to accomplish, and understanding, sophisticated analyses can surely lead to states of "flow" (Csikszentmihalyi, 1990) and other psychic pleasures often ascribed to scientific activity.

Ironically, the attribution by original authors of hostile intentions to replicators, the motive that "dare not speak its name," is displayed by the disciplinary way in which replication is sometimes used in mainstream economics. Thus Wade argues in relation to research within the World Bank that: "if you come up with pro-free-market findings you can send off your paper to *The Economist* or present it at an International Monetary Fund (IMF) seminar straight away without anybody else checking the results; whereas, if you come up with contrary results you will be required by your managers to check them out with a panel of colleagues who may be asked to undertake independent replication while the paper is kept under internal wraps. The differential response sends a message to the researchers who are looking for cues as to how to come along and get along in the Bank" (Wade, 2002: 233; see also Broad, 2006).

Informal discussions of replication we have had suggest similar views are held by many economists, perhaps especially junior researchers.[9]

These discussions make it clear that reluctance to embark on replication or to share data reflects not only desire to benefit from the efforts invested, but also reluctance to expose the quotidian workings of econometricians, which may be characterized as data dredging[10] (Selvin and Stuart, 1966), or hypothesizing after the results are known – HARKing (Kerr, 1998; Ionnidis, 2005).

These disciplinary techniques can perhaps be understood in terms of the professionalization of economics and attempts to claim academic status through quantification and mathematization, for example, prioritizing the provision of a "scientific reading" (characterized by a neutral style, preferably mathematized) over the scientificity of what is read (Bourdieu, 1998). There is little doubt that the techniques of econometrics, and the mathematization of economics (and other social sciences which mimic or co-develop these techniques) serve as barriers to enter into influential and lucrative opportunities. Similar approaches are taken by groups with other forms of expert knowledge in professions such as the law, or medicine (Friedson, 1970, 2001; Abbott, 1988; Macdonald, 1995). The prestige allocated to work that manifests use of advanced quantitative methods serves to institutionalize the dominance of economists at powerful development institutions such as the IMF and World Bank (Mosse, 2011).

These techniques also serve as selection and socialization processes, inscribing attributes on the identities of those who succeed in them; they become the disciplinary doxa and intellectual habitus of the profession (i.e. the characteristics and outcome of social structures interacting with human agency) (Bourdieu, 1977[1972] 1991). These skills are hard to acquire but yield considerable material and psychic returns. Thus, education and apprenticeship in econometrics function not only to impart skills and expertise, but also to create hegemonic identities.

However, as Wade points out in relation to support for neoliberalism, being hegemonic can lead to the hegemon's dilemma, that "legitimacy-protecting collective rules may cause the organization to lose support of the hegemon, while doing what the hegemon wants may entail breaking the collective rules" (Wade, 2002: 217). Replication which results in challenges to results of econometric studies could undermine the authority that pertains to the expertise and the experts who conduct them, even if in the longer run replication leads to better practices, and hence to more reliable knowledge.

It is arguable that replications are more important in development economics because of the power western, especially economic, theory exerts in development policy (cf. Stokes, 1989); the moral element lying behind many people's engagement with development; and the lower likelihood of contestation that development economics may face due to greater power asymmetries between (expert) researcher and researched (client) than exist in developed country social science and policy analysis.[11] These dynamics are illustrated in the following section through examples of replication in economics.

11.4 Prominent examples in replication in economics

The relatively uncontentious experiences of replications in replication sections of economics journals (such as the Journal of Applied Econometrics and the Journal of Economic and Social Measurement) contrast with some, but not all, cases of replication in the main body of journals. In the latter the formal presentation of the results of replications often hint at a more conflictual, even dysfunctional underlying replication process, which may only be known to participants and insiders (although the "gory details" are becoming increasingly available through social media). The readily available documentary record may result from compromises mediated by journal editors (cf. Hamermesh, 2007) which mean that these records are not all that could or indeed should be known. Natural science provides some paradigmatic examples of replication which have, arguably, been partly dysfunctional. The debate around the "hockey stick" graph in the climate change arena, used prominently in the arguments for replication as "due diligence" put forward by McCullough and McKitrick (2009), illustrates the concerns raised by hostile replications (see US EPA, 2010; Mann, 2012). This is not to argue that replication is compromised by political motivations, although it can be, but, as noted by Dewald et al. (1986), replication may be demotivated and/or devalued, by existence and attribution of political or personal contrarian motives to replicators. In this section we identify a number of notable cases of replication that appear in mainstream economics journals.

In economics replications we have examined, several patterns may be discerned. One is where the replication elicits either no response or a friendly acknowledgement and constructive response, sometimes through further "conversation" between replicator and original author. A second is where the original author is hostile and combative without explicitly challenging the competence and/or provenance of the replication. In yet others the original authors, or others taking a supportive stance on their behalf, are confrontational, generally rejecting most of the arguments in the replication, and casting doubts on the probity or motivations of the replicator. In a number of cases replies are civil but in others become abusive or indeed threatening (as in the hockey stick case referred to above). In other cases, response and counter-response go beyond the material reported in the original journal, and may be published other than in the original journal.[12]

Hamermesh (2007) provides the example of a constructive response in Feldstein's response to Leimer and Lesnoy (1982, hereafter LL). This exchange is seen as clarifying a computational mistake; yet, even here Feldstein goes on to provide arguments casting "strong doubts about the appropriateness of these [LL's] modifications and to come to a sensible conclusion" (Feldstein, 1982: 630). In this and other cases[13] original authors accept mistakes, but deploy other data and analysis to maintain their original conclusions, which do not always leave readers with a clear "assessment of each side's merit" (Hamermesh, 2007: 725).[14]

Perhaps one of the most constructive replications in the arena of development has arisen from concerns with the impacts of aid on growth and development. According to Hansen and Tarp (2000) this reached its most recent phase with Burnside and Dollar's (2000: 847) claim that "aid has a positive impact on growth in developing countries ... but has little effect in the presence of poor policies." Numerous authors attempted to purely, statistically, and scientifically replicate this work, with varying outcomes, summarized and extended in Easterly et al. (2004).[15] The value of aid is evidently very important, and contentious for policy, since it seemingly has implications not only for professional (and popular) support for aid, but also for the allocation of aid between countries, the direction of aid (e.g. towards that which fosters "good policy"), and, potentially, for aid conditionality (allocation of aid conditional on adoption of good policy). Since "good policy" was defined by Burnside and Dollar as closely related to neoliberal post-Washington consensus, it is not surprising that there was a lot at stake, and the results were reported in the media (The Economist, 2002; Washington Post, 2002). The threat that replication may play out in the media is an additional concern for potential replicators and replicatees (Hamermesh, 2007), especially in cases where participants have taken a more combative approach.[16]

Hostility towards replicators may well in part derive from factors enumerated by Hoxby (2005b):

> In economics, a replication that confirms an existing study is virtually unpublishable; when another researcher confirms my findings, I might get the results, but that is the last I'll see of them. To get a publication, a replicator must find non-confirmatory results. This

situation creates perverse incentives. It also discourages interesting, original work since researchers who do such work can look forward to many hours working with replicators with nothing to show for them. Because economics students only end up reading non-confirmatory replications, they can become confused and think that they are being assigned to find flaws when they are assigned to do replication.

While perhaps untypical in publishing her views, Hoxby (2005b) may well reflect the views of many economists about replicators, when she suggests that Rothstein was so critical of her because of "self-interest and ideological bias" (Hernandez, 2005; Hoxby, 2005b). In the next section we discuss economists' models of replicatory behaviour, which we then contrast with a more sociological understanding using the recent replications of Pitt and Khandker's iconic 1998 paper on the impact of microfinance on the poor.

11.5 Modelling incentives for replication

The low level of replicatory activity among economists relative to other disciplines[17] is commonly taken to reflect low rewards: "[S]earching for errors in empirical research is more costly and, when successful, notably less rewarding than searching for them in theoretical research" (Kane, 1984: 3). The low level of rewards derives from the low probability of getting career-enhancing publications, and the high costs from the difficulties of putting together the data and reproducing the statistical results. Hamermesh points out that "one should remember that the replicating author usually views him/herself as on the attack. Usually, too, as noted above, the replicating author is more junior and sees the opportunity to make his/her reputation through discrediting a more senior economist's highly visible work. With these incentives it is all the more important to take a gentle, restrained, professional tone in the comment" (2007: 724).

In contrast to his discussion of the possibly suspect motives (and status) of replicators (see also Hamermesh, 2007), Hamermesh has little to say about the behaviour of original authors other than to assert that "[I]f a finding is specious, better to have its props knocked out from under immediately than have it chipped away at slowly," and "if one receives a request for one's data sets or code, one should comply fully and speedily and should make the data available in a readily usable fashion" (2007: 723), although he admits that this guidance is difficult to follow. He argues that authors are unlikely to welcome replication, if only because "the controversies implicit in them [replications] have gripped the attention of many members of the profession (appealing, perhaps, to the same prurient interest as mud wrestling)" (2007:722). "[P]ublishing a mistake has always left researchers open to general opprobrium from their fellows, and if the mistake is viewed as deliberate – as reflecting falsified data – can lead to the scholarly equivalent of Mennonite shunning (Kevles, 1998), including the loss of funding and position."

Journal editors face other disincentives, which Mirowski and Sklivas explain as follows: "strong disconfirmation always implicitly calls into question the refereeing competence of the journal, and also makes inordinate demands upon journal editors to adjudicate the inevitable controversy which ensues" (1991: 154). Given the importance of journal "impact factors" editors may also be deterred by the perceived low page hit rates of replications (Anderson et al., 2008; Pesaran, 2012: slide 9) and also, perhaps, because publishing corrections implies earlier editorial failures (McCullough, et al., 2006). Editors may also fear that requiring deposition of data and code (Anderson et al., 2008: 112), and publishing articles critical of those already published in their journal may reduce the attractiveness of their journal to authors (Kane, 1984; pace King, 1995). The real-life consequences of replication contrast with the strong support in principle for replication by editors of social science journals (Madden et al., 1995). For example, on its website, the *Journal Economic Development and Cultural Change* (EDCC) states that "EDCC publishes both papers with new insights as well as carefully executed replications that explore the robustness of results to different data, diverse model specifications, or ways of estimation"; however, EDCC reports no replications (see also, Footnote 12).

Nevertheless, until very recently, there has been little evidence of replication in development studies; which may reflect the overwhelming dominance of economics in development policy making, and the convenient flag of "beneficence" in which development workers can clothe their activities. This leads to questions as to why any replication occurs at all and whether behaviour during replications sheds further light on their paucity.

11.6   Replicatory behaviours[18]

Hamermesh reviews replicatory exchanges "with the sole purpose of providing instruction on how to behave in such situations" (2007: 723–724); "[R]eaders of each [replication and response] should have been able to take away from the exchanges an assessment of each side's merit" (2007: 725). However, reviewing the prominent examples discussed above, even readers with persistence can come away with the impression that they generate more heat than light, as original authors respond to replication in defensive or unhelpful ways. Hamermesh's discussion is not even-handed between original authors and replicators, and provides limited insight into combative or disputed replications. In the next section we describe one such exchange in which we have been involved, which we contend generates light as well as heat.

11.6.1 Replicating Pitt and Khandker

Replications of Pitt and Khandker's (PnK) iconic paper, which is widely known for establishing "the ... positive and highly significant effects of women's participation in microfinance" (Pitt, 2012a), provide examples of various behaviours (Morduch, 1998; Pitt, 1999; Chemin, 2008; Roodman and Morduch 2009, 2011; Chemin 2012a, b; Duvendack and Palmer-Jones 2012b, c, d; Pitt 2012a, b). What motivated Morduch's (1998) statistical replication of PnK is not clear. When discussing discrepancies in their results, Morduch suggests there is a "more complicated selection problem" than the method used in PnK accommodates, that requires "additional identifying assumptions." The reason for this is that PnK's method "will not control for features of peer networks that are specific just to target (functionally landless) households in program villages" (see also Roodman, 2012, Chapter 6).

Pitt responded to Morduch's critique in damning and abusive terms (Pitt, 1999), with a mass of econometric argument, exposition, and code; for example, [Morduch, 1998] "gives no justification for this, and indeed there is none" (4); "sheds no light" (5); "mischaracterizes the approach" (8); and "[is] just plain wrong" (17). This served to deter publication of both papers, and further attempts at replication of PnK by warning to would-be replicators what to expect from the original authors. According to Morduch's later collaborator, these "American academics sparred to a murky draw in 1999" (Roodman, 2012: 162). Nevertheless, Morduch apparently remained sceptical and eventually teamed up with Roodman to produce their first detailed pure replication of PnK in 2009 (RnM), which failed to confirm PnK's headline findings. In the meantime, Chemin (2008) produced a statistical replication of PnK using a different estimation method. Chemin does not comment on differences between his results and PnK's. We attempted to purely replicate Chemin, and failing to do so, proceeded to a statistical replication (Duvendack and Palmer-Jones, 2012a – DPJa). Simultaneously with our work (DPJa), Roodman engaged in debate with Pitt over RnM's pure replication (i.e. using the same raw data and estimation methods as PnK). It turned out that RnM made mistakes which were plausibly due to incomplete documentation in PnK, and unsatisfactory communication between Pitt and Roodman during the latter's replicatory work.[19] When these mistakes were corrected the results did indeed confirm the original findings of PnK, but turned out to be entirely dependent on a few outliers. When these were removed PnK's results disappeared.

We also remained sceptical of PnK, in part because of the tone of Pitt (1999), and embarked on replication of Chemin, who had come to conclusions somewhat at odds with PnK (DPJa). DPJa's replication also turned out to have mistakes, the most basic of which seems to have been due to misleading documentation in Chemin.[20] Pitt (2012a) responded to DPJa, which only indirectly addresses PnK since it uses a different estimation method. Pitt's original text (Pitt, 2012b) is again abusive. While correctly identifying errors in DPJa, Pitt's reply contains its own errors, and also turns out to lack robustness (DPJb, d), leading DPJb to conclude that "the authority awarded to PnK is fragile and not credible, which is not surprising given the strength of the assumptions and "leaps of logic" (Manski, 2011: 261) required" (1896).

This episode shows how combative exchanges can be seen to generate more heat than light. They clearly depart from the appearance of disinterestedness and neutrality that is supposed to characterize science, but, akin to what Manski characterizes as "dueling certitudes" (2011: F270), are likely revealing the motivations and behaviours of scientists. Ironically, Pitt's various interventions may have helped, bringing about just that result which he seems to have wished to avoid – raising doubts about the efficacy of Microfinance (MF).

11.6.2 Argument and persuasion

Making sense of these wrangles is not easy, or perhaps even possible, and it is not surprising that these exchanges result in confusion, and frustration in policy communities. What is needed is a way to generate more light and less heat (see also Hamermesh, 2007: 726–727). One idea would be to restrict discussion to pure replication rather than getting side-tracked into debate about data, estimators, and so on (McCullough, 2012, personal communication), unless this is done in such a way that the original author's work is not traduced. We are not sure that this is possible since, if the underlying objective of replication is to assess the scientific merits of a work, then problems with the data beyond simple problems such as errors in transcription or in estimation become important. These issues can – though probably should not – be taken as challenging the competence of the original author. Complex methods such as the "black box" of econometrics are likely to trump simpler methods because they are seen as more "scientific." Hence, there is a need for replications that test the correctness, robustness, and generalizability of reported econometric results.

We can make better sense of replicatory exchanges (comments-responses-rejoinders) and indeed of original papers, if we view them as rhetoric rather than demonstration (see also McCloskey, 1985). Arguments can be seen as having two dimensions, one rhetorical, seeking to persuade, and the other empirical, seeking to be right (Sen, 1982; Johansson, 1994). Viewed this way, arguments can be good to make (bring about the desired response), or good in the sense of being accurate, right, and true. As the discussion of motives (of replicators and original authors) suggests, it may well be that rhetorical aims dominate empirics. Given the low probability of replication, self-interest may dominate truth-seeking. The demonstrated occurrence of fraud in scientific texts means that this is certainly sometimes the case.

Hostility in comment, response, or rejoinder seems likely to inhibit greater understanding, and further research, by raising the stakes for participants; items in such exchanges often seem more designed to persuade rather than enlighten. Persuasion does not sit well with popular conceptions of science as the "value free" pursuit of knowledge, however, incentives to be persuasive can be strong, including career advancement, research funding, and support for ideological predilections. While realizing that an "objectivist" conceptualization of economic discourse is naive – all argument seeks to be persuasive and hence makes use of rhetorical practices – professional practice can impose constraints on the inappropriate use of persuasive techniques. One can learn, and be taught, to recognize persuasive practices, and hence to examine their messages in particularly critical ways.

To make this argument more convincing we can briefly mention some of the techniques of rhetoric and illustrate their occurrence in replication studies. Aristotle (1991) draws attention to the *Ethos, Pathos,* and *Logos* of an argument. *Ethos* refers to the pose of the argument – detached or engaged – and *pathos* to the identity of the audience, its views, and conceptions. *Logos* is the substantive argument using deductive and inductive methods. Both good arguments (ones which seek to be correct) and persuasive arguments may portray themselves as detached and in doing so use the same techniques. For example, a literature review that seeks to be perceived as expert, will present itself as panoptic and balanced. But the execution may differ in ways that are hard to detect without detailed (and time consuming) inquiry, and expertise to verify that the treatment is indeed comprehensive and balanced (or is suitably qualified) (Hammersley, 2009). To be effective, however, a text not only portrays itself as detached, but will appeal to the *pathos* of the audience and exhibit exemplary *logos* (or argument). The text will be more convincing if it identifies itself with an existing position or argument that carries considerable currency with the audience – for example, the powerful impacts of colonialism for ill (Banerjee and Iyer, 2005), or the malign effects of the Green Revolution (Boyce and Ravallion, 1991; Palmer-Jones, 1999), or, in the case of Hoxby (2000), the supposed merits of school "choice." Display of competence in *logos*, in the case of econometric studies, consists in reporting (arguably) appropriate specifications, results, and tests. Substantiation of these claims to expertise cannot be conclusively established by the text alone, for reasons given above, but requires replication by independent researchers.

It is not surprising then that original authors seek to inhibit, deter, or obfuscate replication, and the power to do this increases with the academic status and reputation of original authors. Until recently, few economists can have anticipated that their work would be replicated, leading to unsystematic approaches to replicability.[21] When replicated, the incentive to act as Hamermesh advocates – to "admit it honestly and immediately, and move on to set out the importance of the error for your fundamental conclusions" (2007: 725) – does not seem strong, if only because that is not what the original authors in these controversies do. Rather, even if they admit error, for example in coding or data, most original authors bring on new data and/or analysis which supports their original argument. This can often only be controverted by further replication, or, if neither side admits defeat, by the test of time. Further argument as to why replication exchanges may not seem productive is that they generally involve one or other party needing to change their minds. But we know that people do not change their minds readily because there is a "distinct tendency to persist in believing one's existing theories about the world even when faced with overwhelming contrary evidence" (Hadorn, 1996; see also Tversky and Kahneman, 1974; Kahneman et al., 1982; Goldacre, 2008), even in response to persuasive communication (see DellaVigna and Gentzkow, 2010).

However, this does not deter participants in these debates from attempting to persuade readers, and perhaps themselves, if not their antagonist. In doing so they may well recourse to the techniques of rhetoric; in which case it is well for readers to be aware of these techniques. In addition to those discussed above, we may find the following: demonstration of authority or expertise, obscuring or marginalization of counter-arguments, abuse of logic, spurious or misleading quantification, and so on. Hence, replication of the replication of the replication (and so on) becomes necessary.

11.7 Conclusions

Replication in economics has often been advocated but seldom practised, yet it holds considerable promise both to clarify the state of existing policy-relevant knowledge, and to build more robust methods and analyses. This is perhaps particularly important given the current turn to evidence-based policy in development, comprising rigorous impact evaluation, systematic review, and meta-analysis. Most evidence will remain based on observational studies (pace Banerjee and Duflo, 2011) which are vulnerable to bias, even when subject to more sophisticated analyses, or will be taking advantage of natural experiments. Even experiments using randomization in natural contexts often require complex primary data production and sophisticated analyses,[22] which are vulnerable to error and misinterpretation. The replications, responses, and rejoinders discussed above provide ample evidence that even highly policy-relevant studies (and their replications) can contain mistakes. When replicated the conclusions are no longer supported but in contentious cases original authors seldom concede these points, putting forward new evidence and arguments in support of their original positions. These texts reveal characteristics of rhetoric, and a lack of fairness and balance towards alternative accounts and evidence.

These rhetorical characteristics can be revealed by replication, and primary studies which are replication-ready, in terms of archived data and code, can contribute greatly to learning what we really know, and building a stronger evidence base. Replication is a key component of science practice and training. Collins (1985) points out that replication in science is not just repeating previous work following the instructions clearly laid out in the relevant documents, but an apprenticeship in which replicators struggle with the materials and methods to hopefully come to the earlier results. However, narrow (pure replication as opposed to statistical and scientific replication) and uncritical replication can lead to socialization into practices which reinforce the everyday habitus, or doxa, of this (dominant) branch of the economics profession. Economics lacks codes of ethical practice that constrain the use of rhetorical practices, including those embodied in expertise (for example in econometrics). As is quite clear from some of the examples described above, statistical and scientific replications are not easy tasks if they are carried out independently and critically (nor indeed is pure replication if original data and or code are not available).

There are strong disincentives to replication, both from the point of view of replicators who seem– rightly – to perceive costs in terms of their career, and of institutions such as journals which find replications do not meet their needs for high page hits and straightforward editorial processes. It would be desirable to develop professional ethics which encourage more open and critical debate. We also advocate promoting a culture of replicability, especially the practices (and skills) of data archiving and coding to a high standard (e.g. correct, complete, simple, and well-documented; see Nagler, 1995). We have suggested that there are a number of ways in which incentives to fund and undertake replications can be enhanced (see 3ie: International Initiative for Impact Evaluation's recent call for proposals to undertake replications), or disincentives reduced. However, it seems likely that replications will remain something of a public good, which means that there are roles for external enforcement, for example by professional bodies, and funding agencies. We note with approval the American Economic Association policy of data availability, although practice may not entirely live up to the precept. We point out that ethical responsibilities to society, funders and employers, and peers, characteristic of ethical statements of those social science associations that have them, can be interpreted as promoting replicability and replication. However, there is not yet any movement for economics associations to make explicit these ethical responsibilities, to parallel the recent adoption of practices of declaration of interest and avoidance of conflicts of interest.

Replication, the expectation that empirical work will be replicated, and facilitation of replicability, have an important role to play in the advancement of understanding in development economics. The behaviour of replicatees, as of replicators, needs to be characterized by "rigour, respect and responsibility" (Government Office for Science, 2007: 1); it is not clear that, hitherto, it has been.

Notes

1. It is helpful to set out some definitions. Replication covers any attempt to re-do a piece of scientific work in the broad sense of testing the theory and empirics involved. We broadly follow the schema set out by Hamermesh (2007). These are: *pure replication or "checking"* (strict re-analysis of the same data set using the same model and estimation methods – do the data and estimations produce the results reported?); *statistical replication* (use alternative strictly comparable data, variable constructions, statistical software, or

estimation methods – how robust are results to plausible alternative data, data manipulations, and estimation methods?); and *scientific replication* (how well does the study stand up to alternative theoretical or conceptual approaches?).

2. For example, by conducting a new survey.
3. One exception is behavioural economics, where laboratory experiments are frequently repeated in order to extend them. Social experiments in everyday life cannot be closely repeated due to uniqueness of time and place.
4. By computational studies we mean those whose intellectual merit lies primarily in the data manipulations and statistical estimation techniques. It will also include compilation of data from existing sources, and simulation methods.
5. "As virtually every good methodology text explains, *the only way to understand and evaluate an empirical analysis fully is to know the exact process by which the data were generated and the analysis produced*" (King, 1995: 444 [emphasis in original]).
6. Although it is quite possible that replication produces new findings. The perception that a study may be flawed – a common reason for undertaking replications – can be considered innovative. New methods applied to the same or new data, which are involved in statistical and scientific replication, can also be considered innovative.
7. Often a prerequisite of pure and statistical replication
8. See also Chandrasekar (1985) and Csikszentmihalyi (1990).
9. By their nature these discussions are not attributed, but the authors of this chapter have had similar conversations.
10. This refers primarily to running many (perhaps millions) of regressions which to some is data mining. Some authors are entirely frank about these practices (Sala-i-Martin, 1997; Hendry and Krolzig, 2004; Hamermesh, 2007).
11. There is a telling moment in a talk given by Michael Kremer at the 2009 NBER Summer Institute, where the speaker asks rhetorically "why conduct field experiments in developing countries," and Kremer answers "because you can." (http://www.streamingmeeting.com/webmeeting/matrixvideo/nber/index.html, downloaded 10/2012; Kremer Part 1).
12. For example, Journal of Development Effectiveness; Journal of Social and Economic Measurement; Statistics, Politics and Policy; and various Journals of Negative Results (O'Hara, 2011, refers to: "Journal of Negative Results in Biomedicine, the Journal of Negative Results – Ecology and Evolutionary Biology, and the Journal of Articles in Support of the Null Hypothesis ... Journal of Universal Computer Sciences .... PLoS ONE"; see also Schooler, 2011), and Retraction Watch (http://retractionwatch.wordpress.com/).
13. For example, Levitt (2002) in response to McCrary's (2002) replication of Levitt (1997); Donohue and Levitt (2008) in their response to Foote and Goetz's (2008) response to Donohue and Levitt (2001); Donohue and Levitt's response (2004) to Joyce (2004).
14. Other examples include Neumark and Wascher's (2000) replication of Card and Krueger (2000) and the latter's reply (Card, Katz and Krueger, 1994); Antonovics and Goldberger's (2005) replication of Behrman and Rosenzweig (2002) and their reply (Behrman and Rosenzweig, 2005).

15. Hamermesh (2007) singles out Easterly et al. (2004) as "[P]erhaps the best recent example of how to write a comment based on a replication" (724), although Arndt et al. (2011) suggest that this may have been at the expense of a definitive conclusion.
16. For example, Hoxby's (2005a) putative demolition of Rothstein's (2005) replication of Hoxby (2000) (see Rothstein, 2007a, and Hoxby, 2007 and Rothstein's unpublished response and replication materials: http://gsppi. berkeley.edu/faculty/jrothstein/hoxby/documentation-for-hoxby-comment and his unpublished rejoinder (2007b). See also Acemoglu et al.'s (2012) response to Albouy's (2012) comment on Acemoglu et al. (2001), which was a replication of Acemoglu et al.'s extremely influential paper on the supposed "colonial origins of comparative development"; see also Albouy (2004, 2008).
17. The situation for quantitative components of other social sciences is not so straightforward, but there have been calls for replication (and data archiving) in political science (King, 1995) and sociology (Freeze, 2007), as well as business (and marketing) studies (Easterly et al., 2000) and policy analysis (Burman et al., 2010).
18. In this section we do not give details of the original papers and the various comments and rejoinders, because these are often still under debate. What we try to set out is the argumentative process to make the case that they are likely to inhibit replications and to identify how they might be made less inhibiting to replicators. Details of the arguments of each side can be found in the references.
19. See documents linked at http://blogs.cgdev.org/open_book/2011/12/bimodality-in-the-wild-latest-on-pitt-khandker.php (accessed October 2012).
20. Interested readers are referred to Chemin (2012a, b), Pitt (2012a, b), and DPJ (2012a, b, c, d).
21. Preservation of an archive that enables ready replication.
22. And social experiments also require replication, of course.

References

Abbott, A. (1988) *The System of the Professions: Essay on the Division of Expert Labour* (Chicago: Chicago University Press).
Acemoglu, D., Johnson, S. and Robinson, J. A. (2001) "The colonial origins of comparative development: An empirical investigation," *American Economic Review*, 91: 1369–1401.
Acemoglu, D., Johnson, S. and Robinson, J. A. (2012) "The colonial origins of comparative development: An empirical investigation: Reply," *American Economic Review*, 102: 3077–3110.
Albouy, D. Y. (2004) "The colonial origins of comparative development: A reexamination based on improved settler mortality data," unpublished paper, University of California, Berkeley, July.
Albouy, D. Y. (2008) "The colonial origins of comparative development: An investigation of the settler mortality data," *The National Bureau of Economic Research* Working Paper No. 14130, Cambridge, MA.
Albouy, D. Y. (2012) "The colonial origins of comparative development: An empirical investigation: Comment," *American Economic Review*, 102: 3059–3076.

Anderson, R. G., Greene, W. H., McCullough, B. D. and Vinod, H. D. (2008) "The role of data/code archives in the future of economic research," *Journal of Economic Methodology*, 15(1): 99–119.

Antonovics, K. L. and Goldberger, A. S. (2005) "Does increasing women's schooling raise the schooling of the next generation? Comment," *American Economic Review*, 95(5): 1738–1744.

Aristotle (1991) *The Art of Rhetoric*, H. Lawson-Tancred (ed.) (London: Penguin Classics).

Arndt, C., Jones, S. and Tarp, F. (2011) "Aid effectiveness: Opening the black box," World Institute for Development Economic Research (UNU-WIDER). Available at: http://ideas.repec.org/p/unu/wpaper/wp2011-44.html, [Accessed 5 July 2012].

Banerjee, A. V. (2005) "'New development economics' and the challenge to theory," *Economic and Political Weekly*, 40(40): 4340–4344.

Banerjee, A. and Duflo, E. (2011) *Poor Economics* (New York: Public Affairs).

Banerjee, A. and Iyer, L. (2005) "Colonial land tenure, electoral competition and public goods in India," *American Economic Review*, 95: 1190–1213.

Behrman, J. R. and Rosenzweig, M. R. (2002) "Does increasing women's schooling raise the schooling of the next generation?," *American Economic Review*, 92(1): 323–334.

Behrman, J. R. and Rosenzweig, M. R. (2005) "Does increasing women's schooling raise the schooling of the next generation? Reply," *American Economic Review*, 95(5): 1745–1751.

Bernanke, B. S. (2004) "Editorial statement," *American Economic Review*, 94(3): 404.

Bourdieu, P. (1977[1972]) *Outline of a Theory of Culture* (Cambridge: Cambridge University Press).

Bourdieu, P. (1991) *Language and Symbolic Power* (Cambridge: Polity Press).

Bourdieu, P. (1998) *Practical Reason: On the Theory of Action* (Cambridge: Polity Press).

Boyce, J. K. and Ravallion, M. (1991) "A dynamic econometric model of agricultural wage determination in Bangladesh," *Oxford Bulletin of Economics and Statistics*, 53(4): 361–376.

Broad, R. (2006) "Research, knowledge, and the art of 'paradigm maintenance': The World Bank's Development Economics Vice-Presidency (DEC)," *Review of International Political Economy*, 13(3): 387–419.

Burman, L. E., Reed, W. R. and Alm, J. (2010) "A call for replication studies," *Public Finance Review*, 38(6): 787–793.

Burnside, R. J. and Dollar, D. (2000) "Aid, policies and growth," *American Economic Review*, 90: 847–868.

Card, D., Katz, L. F. and Krueger, A. B. (1994) "Comment on David Neumark and William Wascher, 'employment effects of minimum and subminimum wages: Panel data on state minimum wage laws,'" *Industrial and Labor Relations Review*, 47(3): 487–497.

Card, D. and Krueger, A. B. (2000) "Minimum wages and employment: A case study of the fast-food industry in New Jersey and Pennsylvania: Reply," *American Economic Review*, 90(5): 1397–1420.

Chandrasekar, S. (1985) *Truth and Beauty: Aesthetics and Motivations in Science* (Chicago: University of Chicago Press).

Chemin, M. (2008) "The benefits and costs of microfinance: Evidence from Bangladesh," *Journal of Development Studies*, 44: 463–484.

Chemin, M. (2012a) "Response to 'high noon for microfinance impact evaluation,'" *The Journal of Development Studies*, 48: 1881–1885.

Chemin, M. (2012b) "Response to 'high noon for microfinance impact evaluation'" (Montreal: Department of Economics, University of Quebec). Available at: http://matthieuchemin-research.mcgill.ca/research.html, [Accessed 3 June 2013].

Collins, H. M. (1985) *Changing Order: Replication and Induction in Scientific Practice* (Chicago: University of Chicago Press).

Csikszentmihalyi, M. (1990) *Finding Flow: The Psychology of Engagement with Everyday Life* (New York: Harper Row).

DellaVigna, S. and Gentzkow, M. (2010) "Persuasion: Empirical evidence," *Annual Review of Economics*, 2(1): 643–669.

Dewald, W. G., Thursby, J. G. and Anderson, R. G. (1986) "Replication in empirical economics: The Journal of Money, Credit and Banking Project," *American Economic Review*, 76: 587–603.

Donoho, D. L. (2010) "An invitation to reproducible computational research," *Biostatistics*, 11: 385–388.

Donohue, J. and Levitt, S. D. (2001) "The impact of legalized abortion on crime," *Quarterly Journal of Economics*, 116(2): 379–420. Available at: http://works.bepress.com/john_donohue/8/, [Accessed 19 June 2012].

Donohue, J. and Levitt, S. D. (2004) "Further evidence that legalized abortion lowered crime: A reply to Joyce," *Journal of Human Resources*, 39(1): 29–49. Available at: http://works.bepress.com/cgi/viewcontent.cgi?article=1011&context=john_donohue [Accessed 19 June 2012].

Donohue, J. J. and Levitt, S. D. (2008) "Measurement error, legalized abortion, and the decline in crime: A response to Foote and Goetz," *The Quarterly Journal of Economics*, 123(1): 425–440.

Duvendack, M. and Palmer-Jones, R. (2012a) "High noon for microfinance impact evaluations: Re-investigating the evidence from Bangladesh," *Journal of Development Studies*, 48(12): 1864–1880.

Duvendack, M. and Palmer-Jones, R. (2012b) "Reply to Chemin and Pitt," *Journal of Development Studies*, 48(12): 1892–1897.

Duvendack, M. and Palmer-Jones, R. (2012c) "What Mat[t]hleu really did: Rejoinder to Chemin, 2012a," Available at: http://www.uea.ac.uk/~nga07htu/Rejoinder_to_Chemin_Final.pdf

Duvendack, M. and Palmer-Jones, R. (2012d) "Wyatt Earp's high noon? Rejoinder to Pitt, 2012b," Available at: http://www.uea.ac.uk/~nga07htu/Rejoinder_to_Pitt_Final.pdf

Easterly, W., Levine, R. and Roodman, D. R. (2000) "'Doubts: A comment on Burnside and Dollar's," *American Economic Review*, 94(3): 781–84.

Easterly, W., Levine, R. and Roodman, D. (2004) "Aid, policies, and growth: Comment," *The American Economic Review*, 94(3): 774–780.

Feigenbaum, S. and Levy, D. M. (1993) "The market for (ir)reproducible econometrics," *Social Epistemology*, 7(3): 215–232.

Feldstein, M. S. (1982) "Social security and private saving: Reply," *Journal of Political Economy*, 90(3): 630–642.

Foote, C. L. and Goetz, C. F. (2008) "The impact of legalized abortion on crime: Comment," *The Quarterly Journal of Economics*, 123(1): 407–423.

Freeze, J. (2007) "Replication standards for quantitative social science: Why not sociology?" *Sociological Methods and Research*, 36(2): 153–172.

Friedson, E. (1970) *Profession of Medicine: A Study of the Sociology of Applied Knowledge* (Chicago: Chicago University Press).

Friedson, E. (2001) *Professionalism: The Third Logic* (Chicago: Chicago University Press).

Frisch, R. (1933) "Editor's note," *Econometrica*, 1: 1–4. Available at: http://www.jstor.org/stable/1912224, [Accessed 3 June 2013].

Glandon, P. (2010) "Report on the American Economic Review Data Availability Compliance Project." Available at: https://www.aeaweb.org/aer/2011_Data_Compliance_Report.pdf & https://209.197.108.139/aer/2011_Data_Compliance_Report.pdf, [Accessed 13 March 2014].

Gleditsch, P. N. and Metelits, C. (2003) "The replication debate," *International Studies Perspectives*, 4: 443–499.

Goldacre, B. (2008) *Bad Science* (London: Fourth Estate).

Government Office for Science (2007) *Rigour, Respect, Responsibility: A Universal Ethical Code for Scientists* (London: Government Office for Science) Available at: http://www.berr.gov.uk/files/file41318.pdf, [Accessed 13 March 2014].

Gustin, B. H. (1973) "Charisma, recognition and the motivation of scientists," *American Journal of Sociology*, 78(5): 1119–1133.

Hadorn, D. (1996) "The role of cognitive errors in the drug policy debate," *International Journal of Drug Policy*, 7: 166–171. Available at: http://www.druglibrary.net/schaffer/media/hadorn1.htm, [Accessed 13 March 2014].

Hamermesh, D. S. (2007) "Replication in economics," *Canadian Journal of Economics*, 40(3): 715–733.

Hammersley, M. (2009) "Against the ethicists: On the evils of ethical regulation," *International Journal of Social Research Methodology*, 12: 211–125.

Hansen, H. and Tarp, F. (2000) "Aid effectiveness disputed," *Journal of International Development*, 12: 375–398.

Hatton, L., and Roberts, A. (1994) "How Accurate Is Scientific Software?" *IEEE Transactions on Software Engineering*, 20(10): 785–797. doi:10.1109/32.328993.

Hendry, D. F. and Krolzig, H. -M. (2004) "We ran one regression," *Oxford Bulletin of Economics and Statistics*, 66: 799–810.

Hernandez, J. C. (2005) "Star Ec Prof Caught in Academic Feud," *The Harvard Crimson*. Available at: http://www.thecrimson.com/article/2005/7/8/star-ec-prof-caught-in-academic/, [Accessed 14 August 2012].

Hoxby, C. M. (2000) "The effects of class size on student achievement: New evidence from population variation," *The Quarterly Journal of Economics*, 115(4): 1239–1285.

Hoxby, C M. (2005a) "Competition among public schools: A reply to Rothstein (2004)," *National Bureau of Economic Research* Working Paper No. 11216. Available at: http://www.nber.org/papers/w11216, [Accessed 3 June 2013].

Hoxby, C. M. (2005b) "Hoxby: Article presents slant view of academic debate," *The Harvard Crimson*. Available at: http://www.thecrimson.com/article/2005/7/15/hoxby-article-presents-slanted-veiw-of/, [Accessed 5 August 2013].

Hoxby, C. M. (2007) "Does competitions among public schools benefit students and taxpayers? A reply," *American Economic Review*, 97(5): 2038–2055.

Ionnidis, J. P. A. (2005) "Why most published research findings are false," *PLoS Medicine*, 28: e124.

Jasny, B. R., Chin, G., Chong, L. and Vignieri, S. (2011) "Again, and again, and again ...," *Science*, 334(6060): 1225.

Johansson, S. R. (1994) "Food for thought: Rhetoric and reality in modern mortality history," *Historical Methods*, 27(3): 101–125.

Joyce, T. (2004) "Did legalized abortion lower crime?" *Journal of Human Resources*, 39(1): 1–28.

Kahneman, D., Slovic, P. and Tversky, A. (1982) *Judgement under Uncertainty: Heuristics and Biases* (Cambridge: Cambridge University Press).

Kane, E. J. (1984) "Why journal editors should encourage the replication of applied econometric research," *Quarterly Journal of Business and Economics*, 23(1): 3–8.

Kerr, N. L. (1998) "HARKing: Hypothesizing after the results are known," *Personality and Social Psychology Review*, 2(3): 196–217.

Kevles, D. (1998) *The Baltimore Case* (New York: Norton).

King, G. (1995) "Replication, replication," *PS: Political Science and Politics*, 28(3): 444–452.

Latour, B. (1987) *Science in Action: How to Follow Scientists and Engineers through Society* (USA: Harvard University Press).

Leamer, E. E. (1983) "Let's take the con out of econometrics," *American Economic Review*, 73: 31–43.

Leimer, D. R. and Lesnoy, S. D. (1982) "Social security and private saving: New time-series evidence," *Journal of Political Economy*, 90(3): 606–629.

Levitt, S. D. (1997) "Using electoral cycles in police hiring to estimate the effects of police on crime: Reply," *The American Economic Review*, 87: 270–290.

Levitt, S. D. (2002) "Using electoral cycles in police hiring to estimate the effects of police on crime: Reply," *The American Economic Review*, 92(4): 1244–1250.

Macdonald, Keith M. *The Sociology of the Professions*. Sage Publications Ltd, 1995.

Madden, C. S., Easley, R. W. and Dunn, M. G. (1995) "How journal editors view replication research," *Journal of Advertising*, 24: 77–87.

Mann, M. (2012) *The Hockey Stick and the Climate Wars: Dispatches from the Front Lines*, first edition (Columbia: Columbia University Press).

Manski, C. F. (2011) "Policy analysis with incredible certitude," *The Economic Journal*, 121: F261–F289.

McCloskey, D. N. (1985) *The Rhetoric of Economics* (Wisconsin: University of Wisconsin Press).

McCrary, J. (2002) "Using electoral cycles in police hiring to estimate the effect of police on crime: Comment," *The American Economic Review*, 92(4): 1236–1243.

McCullough, B. D. (2009) "Open access economics journals and the market for reproducible economic research," *Economic Analysis and Policy*, 39: 117–126.

McCullogh, B. D. and McKitrick, R. (2009) *Check the Numbers: The Case for Due Diligence in Policy Formation* (Fraser Institute), Available at: http://www.terry.uga.edu/~mustard/courses/e8420/Frasier.pdf, [Accessed 13 March 2014].

McCullough, B. D. and Vinod, H. D. (1999) "The numerical reliability of econometric software," *Journal of Economic Literature*, 37: 633–655.

McCullough, B. D. and Vinod, H. D. (2003) "Verifying the solution from a nonlinear solver: A case study," *The American Economic Review*, 93(3): 873–892.

McCullough, B., McGeary, K. A. and Harrison, T. D. (2006) "Lessons from the JMCB Archive," *Journal of Money, Credit and Banking*, 38: 1093–1107.

McCullough, B. D., McGeary, K. A., Harrison T. D. (2008) "Do economics journal archives promote replicable research?," *Canadian Journal of Economics*, 41(4): 1406–1420.

Merali, Z. (2010) "Computational science: ... Error," *Nature News*, 467: 775–777.

Mirowski, P. and Sklivas, S. (1991) "Why econometricians don't replicate (although they do reproduce," *Review of Political Economy*, 3: 146–163.

Morduch, J. (1998) "Does microfinance really help the poor? New evidence from Flagship Programs in Bangladesh," unpublished mimeo.

Mosse, D. (2011) *Adventures in Aidland: The Anthropology of Professionals in International Development* (Oxford: Berghahn Books).

Nagler, J. (1995) "Coding style and good computing practices," *Political Science & Politics*, 3(September): 488–492.

Neumark, D. and Wascher, W. (2000) "Minimum wages and employment: A case study of the fast-food industry in New Jersey and Pennsylvania: Comment," *American Economic Review*, 90: 1362–1396.

O'Hara, R. (2011) "Negative results are published," *Nature*, 470: 448.

Palmer-Jones, R.W. (1999) "Slowdown in Agricultural Growth in Bangladesh? Neither a Good Description nor a Description Good to Give," in Rogaly, B., Harris-White, B. and Bose, S. (eds) *Sonar Bangla? Agrarian Structure and Agricultural Growth in Bengal* (Thousand Oaks: Sage), pp. 92–136.

Peng, R. D. (2011) "Reproducible research in computational science," *Science*, 334: 1226–1227.

Pesaran, H. (2003) "Introducing a replication section," *Journal of Applied Econometrics*, 18(1): 111.

Pesaran, H. (2012) "An example of replication and data archiving in journal publications." Presentation at the Association of Learned and Professional Society Publishers (ALPSP), Seminar, Data Publishing, London, Available at: http://www.google.com.np/url?sa=t&rct=j&q=&esrc=s&source=web&cd=1&ved=0CCYQFjAA&url=http%3A%2F%2Fwww.alpsp.org%2FEbusiness%2FLibraries%2F1204DPB_-_Media%2F1204DPB_Pesaran.sflb.ashx%3Fdownload%3Dtrue&ei=-iwjU-LbJ4aNrQfTpIHQDg&usg=AFQjCNEpLX1unjgmTyyygvEyTDA1g5olsg&bvm=bv.62922401,d.bmk, [Accessed 13 March 2014].

Pitt, M. M. (1999) "Reply to Jonathan Morduch's 'Does microfinance really help the poor? New evidence from Flagship Programs in Bangladesh,'" Unpublished mimeo.

Pitt, M. M. (2011a) "Over identification tests and causality: A second response to Roodman and Morduch" (Rhode Island: Department of Economics, Brown University). Available at: http://www.pstc.brown.edu/~mp/papers/Over identification.pdf, [Accessed 3 June 2013].

Pitt, M. M. (2011b) "Response to Roodman and Morduch's 'The impact of microcredit on the poor in Bangladesh: Revisiting the evidence'" (Rhode Island: Department of Economics, Brown University). Available at: http://www.pstc.brown.edu/~mp/papers/Pitt_response_to_RM.pdf, [Accessed 3 June 2013].

Pitt, M. M. (2012a) "Gunfight and the Not OK corral: Reply to 'high noon for microfinance,'" *The Journal of Development Studies*, 48: 1886–1891.

Pitt, M. M. (2012b) "Gunfight and the NOT OK corral: Reply to 'high noon for microfinance' by Duvendack and Palmer-Jones (Uncut Version)" (Rhode Island: Department of Economics, Brown University). Available at: http://

www. brown.edu/research/projects/pitt/sites/brown.edu.research.projects.pitt/ files/uploads/faults6.pdf, [Accessed 3 June 2012].

Pitt, M. M. and Khandker, S. R. (1998) "The impact of group-based credit programs on poor households in Bangladesh: Does the gender of participants matter?," *Journal of Political Economy*, 106(5): 958–996.

Roodman, D. (2012) *Due Diligence: An Impertinent Inquiry into Microfinance* (Center for Global Development, Washington DC).

Roodman, D. and Morduch, J. (2009) "The impact of microcredit on the poor in Bangladesh: Revisiting the evidence," *Center for Global Development* Working Paper No. 174, June, Available at: http://www.cgdev.org/files/1422302_ file_Roodman_Morduch_Bangladesh.pdf, Center for Global Development, Washington DC, [Accessed 13 March 2014].

Roodman, D. and Morduch, J. (2011) "The impact of microcredit on the poor in Bangladesh: Revisiting the evidence." Available at: http://www.cgdev.org/ files/1422302_file_Roodman_Morduch_Bangladesh_2.pdf, Center for Global Development, Washington DC, [Accessed 13 March 2014]

Rothstein, J. (2005) "Does competition among public schools benefit students and taxpayers? A comment on Hoxby (2000)," *National Bureau of Economic Research* Working Paper Series No. 11215, Available at: http://www.nber.org/ papers/w11215, [Accessed 13 March 2014].

Rothstein, J. (2007a) "Does competition among public schools benefit students and taxpayers? A comment on Hoxby (2000)," *American Economic Review*, 97: 2026–2037.

Rothstein, J. (2007b) "Rejoinder to Hoxby" (New Jersey, NJ: Princeton University). Available at: http://gsppi.berkeley.edu/faculty/jrothstein/hoxby/documentation-forhoxby-comment/, [Accessed 3 June 2013].

Sala-i-Martin, X. X. (1997) "I just ran four million regressions," National Bureau of Economic Research. Available at: http://www.nber.org/papers/w6252, [Accessed 7 August 2012].

Schooler, J. (2011) "Unpublished results hide the decline effect," *Nature News*, 470: 437.

Selvin, H. C. and Stuart, A. (1966) "Data-dredging procedures in survey analysis," *The American Statistician*, 20(3): 20–23.

Sen, A. K. (1982) "Description as choice," *Oxford Economic Papers*, 32: 353–369.

Stokes, E. (1989) *The English Utilitarians and India* (Oxford: Oxford University Press).

The Economist (2002) "Help in the Right Places," *The Economist*, 16 March.

Tversky, A. and Kahneman, D. (1974) "Judgment under uncertainty: Heuristics and biases," *Science*, 185(4157): 1124–1131.

US EPA (2010) "Denial of petitions for reconsideration of the endangerment and cause or contribute findings for greenhouse gases under Section 202(a) of the Clean Air Act," *Climate Change Division*. Available at: http://epa.gov/ climatechange/endangerment/petitions.html, [Accessed 7 May 2012].

Wade, R. H. (2002) "US hegemony and the World Bank: The fight over people and ideas," *Review of International Political Economy*, 9(2): 215–243.

Washington Post (2002) "Does aid help," *Washington Post*, 9 February, A26.

Ziliak, S. T. and McCloskey, D. N. (2008) *The Cult of Statistical Significance: How the Standard Error Cost us Jobs, Justice, and Lives* (Ann Arbor: University of Michigan Press).

12
Replicating "Sources of Slow Growth in African Economies"

Graham Davis

12.1 Introduction

Economic analysis, even when buried in academic conference proceedings and journals, influences policy. In 2010 Reinhart and Rogoff found that economic growth drops off sharply once government debt exceeds 90 per cent of gross domestic product. Their paper, published as an unrefereed conference proceeding, was taken up en masse by deficit hawks and had a major influence on the 2012 Presidential election in the United States and on austerity programmes in Europe. A recent replication attempt challenges Reinhart and Rogoff's findings, setting off a firestorm of controversy led by Nobel Prize-winning economist Paul Krugman (Herndon et al. 2013; Krugman 2013; Pollin and Ash 2013; Reinhart and Rogoff 2013). In this chapter I show the value of replication to development researchers. Via replication I challenge the mainstream understanding of economic growth in Africa that was spawned in part by an influential 1997 paper by Sachs and Warner (1997a).

Between 1965 and 1990, the 40 Sub-Saharan African (SSA) countries for which we have data grew at an average real annual per capita rate of 0.80 per cent. If we exclude Botswana, which was the fifth fastest-growing developing economy in the world over that period, the rate drops to 0.67 per cent. The rest of the developing world, or at least the 48 countries for which we have data, grew at an average rate of 1.96 per cent annually over this same period.[1] Even if we exclude the seven fastest-growing economies outside of Africa from this mix, the rest of the group grew at 1.30 per cent annually.

Why did Africa grow so slowly? Was it unfortunate geography? Poor demographics? Poor government policies? Or was there some unaccountable factor unique to Africa, known as the Africa dummy? In a now classic 1997 paper published in the *Journal of African Economies*, Jeffrey Sachs and Andrew Warner (1997a) examine this question using a cross-sectional growth-regression methodology that was the mainstay of a suite of six of their papers investigating economic growth (Sachs and Warner 1997a, 1997b, 1997c, 1999a, 1999b, 2001). The *Journal of African Economies* paper uses approximately the same cross-country regression model as the 1997b paper, but with an expanded data set that has been subsequently used in other growth analyses (the indices of trade openness, institutional quality, and geography have been especially used).

Sachs and Warner (hereafter SW) (1997a) make four broad conclusions from their analysis:

1. Growth in Africa, and indeed in all countries, can be explained when using the appropriate set of conditioning variables. There is no need for an Africa dummy or to control for contagion effects resulting from slow growth in neighbouring countries.
2. Aside from convergence effects related to initial income levels, it is government trade policy, savings policy, and institutional quality that are the most important determinants of economic growth. The health of the population is the next most important determinant.
3. Had the average African country adopted the average trade policy, savings policy, and institutional quality levels of the seven fastest-growing developing economies outside of Africa from 1965 to 1990, its real per capita growth rate would have risen from 0.80 to 4.3 per cent per year.
4. Had the average African country adopted the average trade policy, savings policy, and institutional quality levels of the rest of the developing economies from 1965 to 1990, its real per capita growth rate would have risen from 0.80 to 1.4 per cent per year. This effect is larger than the effect of unfavourable geography on Africa's growth.

They conclude their paper by stating that "even with its natural disadvantages, Africa could have grown at over 4 per cent per year in per capita terms with appropriate policies" (1997a: 361). These are astounding findings given the changes in the current world order that such growth would have entailed.

I argue that SW's paper on African growth has had almost as strong an influence on development policy as Reinhart and Rogoff's did on fiscal policy. An early set of results, presented in *The Economist* (Sachs 1996), recommended that aid to Africa be conditioned on reforms towards trade openness. The *Economist* article has been cited 84 times, and the idea of trade openness quickly made its way into policy at the United States Agency for International Development (USAID 2003). The World

Bank currently believes that "better governance is critical to development" in Africa and other developing economies (World Bank 2012). In development economics in general, institutional capacity building has replaced the Washington Consensus. My contention about the paper's influence is buttressed by the fact that it is the most cited paper ever published in *Journal of African Economies*, and by a wide margin.[2] It is also prominently mentioned in two subsequent survey articles on Africa's growth (Collier and Gunning 1999a, 1999b).

Despite its importance, the SW paper has never been purely replicated (i.e., verified).[3] Temple (1998) tests the SW regressions for sample robustness (known as statistical replication, or validation), and reports that the diagnostic tests are "generally satisfactory."[4] Bloom and Sachs (1998), Easterly and Levine (1998), and Temple (1998) are related and well-cited contemporaneous papers that can be seen to be scientific replications (model extensions) of SW. Temple and Easterly and Levine agree with SW's finding that Africa's policy differences explain its poor growth performance, though Temple argues that policy is endogenous to initial social capital and also finds that the Africa Dummy remains negative and statistically significant, contrary to SW's Conclusion 1 above, when initial conditions are included in the regressions. Easterly and Levine find that the initial condition of ethnic fractionalization largely explains Africa's poor policy path. The findings of both Temple and Easterly and Levine suggest little room for policy improvement via multilateral intervention that helps nations choose better paths. Bloom and Sachs, on the other hand, use much of the same data as SW and find that poor policy choice is not what differentiates Africa; had Africa had Latin America and the Caribbean's trade policies and institutional quality, for instance, its annual growth would have been only 0.05 percentage points higher.[5] If Africa had East and Southeast Asian trade policies and institutional quality its annual growth would have only been 1.65 percentage points higher. From this Bloom and Sachs conclude that it is geography, demography, and public health, not deviations from standard policy practice, that caused Africa's poor relative growth performance from 1965 to 1990.

None of these papers begins with a pure replication of the SW work. Given that most economic research cannot be purely replicated (Davis 2013), it would be instructive to ask whether errors in SW's original findings are the reason for the differences in the scientific replications.[6] I answer that question with a pure replication of their paper, which Duvendack and Palmer-Jones (this volume) suggest is an essential precursor to treating econometric findings as evidence. I am able to replicate Conclusions 1 and 2 given above. The conclusion that Africa could have grown at 4.3 per cent per year is not replicable; the estimated growth is downgraded to 4.1 per cent in my replication. This is still a substantial policy boost and far larger than other estimates at the time.[7] The incremental rate by which Africa could have grown had it followed average other-developing-country policies is only 0.07 per cent in my replication, not 0.6 per cent. This corroborates Bloom and Sachs' (1998) recommendation that economists and donors make programmes that combat disease, improve health systems, and support infrastructure spending at least as important as building institutional quality in the region.

My inability to confirm Conclusion 4, with its profound policy implications, causes me to rate the replication 1 out of 5 on the Glandon (2011: 699) Replication Accuracy Rating System. A score of 1, "Serious Discrepancies," indicates that "an error in the analysis has probably led to incorrect conclusions" (2011: 699).[8] In this case the analysis by Bloom and Sachs appears to correctly reflect what the data are telling us.

In the remainder of the chapter I review the data and empirics in each of the sections of the SW paper. The only section I do not review is Evidence on Growth and Reform in Africa, since there are no computations in that section.

12.2   Data used to explain growth

The data are currently available at http://www.cid.harvard.edu/ciddata/ciddata.html. There is a readme text file, an Excel file, a DO file with the regressions in table 2 and Appendix table A1 of their study coded in STATA, and a STATA DTA file containing the data. I have based my replication from the Excel file. SW are to be commended for taking time to make their data and code available. Where such recordkeeping is not made mandatory by the journal publishing the paper, as is the case in *Journal of African Economies*, such records are seldom available. The availability of the date and code made the replication relatively effortless.

The innovation in SW's analysis of Africa's growth is to include trade openness, institutional quality, geography, and demography as explanatory variables.[9] SW present a summary of the data in their table 1, which I reproduce as Table 12.1 below.

The data are broken into three country groupings, which is important later for predictions about how Africa would have grown had it followed the policy choices of the other two country groups. SW explicitly mention the seven fastest-growing developing economies in their sample, and the data file has a dummy for SSA. Hence, the countries in these two country groupings are known, and I am able to replicate most

Table 12.1 Africa compared with other developing countries

	Africa	Fastest-growing economies	All other developing economies
Real growth per capita 1965–1990	0.80	5.83 [5.82]	1.76 [1.30]
Real GDP per economically active population 1965 (PPP $1985)	1,480 [1,766]	2,703 [3,053]	2,585 [4,185]
Openness to international trade	0.07	0.81 [0.96]	0.19 [0.17]
Fraction of land-locked countries	0.33	0.00	0.11 [0.09]
Life expectancy (circa 1970)	41.6 [41.9]	57.1 [57.7]	51.9 [53.7]
Central government savings	4.14	4.97	1.18 [2.46]
Fraction of countries in tropical climates	0.89	0.69	0.59 [0.61]
Institutional quality index	4.54	6.86	4.29 [4.49]
Natural resource abundance	0.18	0.09	0.12 [0.20]
Average annual inflation	149.07 [10.29]	54.69 [10.40]	91.79 [19.25]
Growth of neighboring economies, 1970–1989	0.50	3.81	1.80 [1.48]
Average national savings ratio 1970–1990	7.18	22.64	10.13 [12.79]
Index of ethno-linguistic fractionalization	64.54	42.86	32.44 [32.16]
Growth of economically active population – total population growth	–0.09	0.82	0.33 [0.34]

Note: Where my calculations differ, they are listed in square brackets.

of the entries in the first two columns.[10] The two notable differences between their calculations and mine are the initial GDP per capita figures and the inflation figures. SW's data file contains log GDP per capita, which they average and then anti-log. The correct procedure for calculating this average for a group of countries is to anti-log the data and then average them. The same mistake was made with the average life expectancy calculations. The inflation numbers SW present are incredible. The averages that I compute from the data set are reasonable.

The main failing of the data posting is not listing those countries included in the "Other Developing Country" grouping, and I spent considerable time trying to reverse-engineer the grouping based on the data SW produce in their table 1. I was ultimately unsuccessful, and ended up forming my own grouping based on country classifications given by the United Nations in their 2005 Human Development Report (United Nations Development Programme 2005).[11] This appears to be a different country set from that considered by SW, as evidenced by the fact that the data averages I compute in the last column of Table 12.1 are vastly different from the averages given for this country group in SW. Experimentation with the country list did not reveal a country grouping that produced their results; there is no single country that can be dropped to raise the average growth rate to 1.76, for instance. The differences in the SW values and my calculated values will be important, as they will affect the counterfactuals created when SW apply their regression results to the differences in country group averages. In particular, Africa was less resource-intensive than all other developing economies, not more resource-intensive, and had lower inflation than both other country groupings, not higher inflation.[12]

As a final note on the data, life expectancy is reported by SW to be circa 1970 and provided by Jong-Wha Lee. Lee published a paper in 1993 with Robert Barro (Barro and Lee 1993), and the National Bureau of Economic Research (NBER) maintains a data archive for the paper (http://www.nber.org/pub/barro.lee/ZIP/). Comparing the archive with the data set provided by SW, it is clear that the life expectancy data SW use is the average life expectancy at birth averaged over 1960–1964. In what will turn out to be especially descriptive of Africa as a continent, its life expectancy during that period is well below par. Also, the average national savings ratio is listed in the SW data appendix as being from 1970 to 1989, not to 1990 as listed in Table 12.1. The Excel file also codes the variable as being to 1989. I have not checked the original source file, which is a World Bank CD ROM that is no longer available, to see which of these is correct.

12.3   Theoretical background

SW then go into the theoretical background for their regression specification. One of their propositions is that the time path of income per worker converges to a steady state that is a function of the national savings rate. They propose that government savings and life expectancy help determine the national savings rate, and produce a regression in footnote 8 supporting this proposition. I am unable to replicate the reported regression results.[13] The regression results I obtain are:

$$\text{Saving/GDP} = -123 + 34 \text{ log(life)} + 1.04 \text{ government saving/GDP} \quad R^2 = 0.36$$
$$(6.5) \quad\quad\quad (4.8)$$

Their point about overall savings being determined by life expectancy and government savings remains intact, though the r-squared that they report for the relationship is significantly higher than that here. There are no other empirical results in this section.

12.3.1 Regression estimates

SW first conduct a test for influential data points using the DFITS test in STATA. They find five countries (Botswana, Gabon, Madagascar, Guyana, and Israel) that have DFITS statistics greater than 0.9 in absolute value, and remove these from their main regressions (they include the five countries in supplemental regressions in an appendix). The recommended sample-adjusted cut-off (Belsley et al., 1980) is actually $2\sqrt{12/84} = 0.76$, and by this criterion Zambia, Malaysia, and Niger could also have been removed. I have tested the first regression in their table 2 with these additional three countries removed and found that some of the coefficient values change dramatically, though none lose their statistical significance. I do not pursue the effect of these three influence points further, though the sensitivity of growth regressions to sample has been noted in recent research (Knabb 2005; Norman 2009).

The main regression results are given in SW table 2. I am able to replicate each of their first five regressions save for rounding errors in the second decimal place for three t-statistics. The final regression, in which inflation is added as a conditioning variable, is well off in coefficient results, t-statistics, and sample size. This may be related to the very different inflation averages that I obtained in Table 12.1. Table 12.2 below presents the SW results from regression six, and then my replication. The only major changes are that the coefficient on landlocked becomes statistically insignificant, the only regression in which this is the case, and the coefficient on the interaction term turns from insignificant to significant, as it is in all of the other regressions. Their conclusion here, "that average inflation does not add anything to the explanation of growth after controlling for our ten variables" (1997a: 351) still holds.[14]

In an appendix to their paper SW retest their regressions with the five influential countries added back in. The main difference in the appendix results is that the national savings rate becomes statistically significant

Table 12.2   Regression estimates, SW table 2 and appendix A1 regression 6, with replication results

	Table 2 results (five influence points removed)		Table A1 results (full sample)	
	SW	Replication	SW	Replication
Log of real GDP per economically active population in 1965	−1.71 (−8.05)	−1.64 (−7.43)	−1.50 (−5.97)	−1.45 (−5.45)
Openness times log real GDP per economically active population in 1965	−0.62 (−1.95)	−0.81 (−2.42)	−1.07 (−2.95)	−1.21 (−3.06)
Openness to international trade	7.21 (2.76)	8.77 (3.20)	10.76 (3.62)	11.93 (3.67)
Landlocked dummy variable	−0.60 (−2.71)	−0.47 (−1.94)	−0.53 (−2.00)	−0.49 (−1.74)
Log life expectancy circa 1970	47.85 (2.71)	43.87 (2.41)	41.23 (2.04)	36.79 (1.74)
Square of log life expectancy	−5.71 (−2.52)	−5.15 (−2.20)	−4.84 (−1.88)	−4.24 (−1.57)
Central government savings, 1970–1990	0.12 (5.30)	0.12 (4.85)	0.12 (5.22)	0.11 (4.56)
Dummy for tropical climate	−0.91 (−3.75)	−0.81 (−3.37)	−0.89 (−3.08)	−0.82 (−2.75)
Institutional quality index	0.28 (3.94)	0.26 (3.48)	0.32 (3.82)	0.29 (3.27)
Natural resource exports/GDP 1970	−3.36 (−3.45)	−3.38 (−3.44)	−4.11 (−4.08)	−4.10 (−3.99)
Growth in economically active population – total population growth	1.36 (4.14)	1.11 (3.24)	0.96 (2.66)	0.77 (2.11)
Average inflation 1970–1990	−0.0002 (−0.61)	−0.0044 (−0.88)	−0.0003 (−1.18)	−0.0051 (−0.82)
Adjusted R^2	0.89	0.88	0.85	0.83
Number of countries	77	74	81	79

Note: Dependent variable: growth per capita of PPP-adjusted GDP, 1965–1990. t-statistics in parentheses.

when added to the baseline regression, whereas SW make a point of noting in the main body text that it is insignificant and that such insignificance supports the idea that their nine variables are capturing differences in savings rates across countries (recall the argument earlier that life expectancy and government savings determine overall savings rates). The sensitivity of the coefficient on national savings rate to sample is consistent with the sample robustness findings by Temple (1998) mentioned in endnote 4.

I am able to replicate the results for the first five regressions in the appendix save for two differences in the reported t-ratios at the second decimal point. My replication of regression 6, which adds inflation as a control variable, is again widely off (see Table 12.2), probably due to an error in the inflation data that SW use. Many of the covariates are now statistically insignificant, as would be expected when adding back outlying data points. The coefficient on inflation remains statistically insignificant.

Once the regression results are listed SW explore their implications for growth, an examination of economic importance as opposed to statistical significance. They first note that the effect of openness is quite large. Given the coefficients in regression 1 of their table 2, SW state that the effect on growth of an average country moving from a completely closed to completely open regime is 2.21 percentage points per year "(= 8.48 − 0.77*8.05)" (1997a: 346). The correct computation of the quoted equation yields 2.28 percentage points, and at the full precision of the results yields 2.31 percentage points. SW note that this is a far larger growth impact than moving from being landlocked to open to the sea (0.58 percentage points) or moving out of the tropics (0.85 percentage points).

The discussion over the next few pages of the section involves the quantitative importance of the nine variables in their baseline regression. The quantification is replicable save for the following items. Their discussion on page 350 reports the impact of a one standard deviation change of each variable on growth in order to rank the variables by importance, reproduced in Table 12.3. In my replication of these

Table 12.3 Absolute percentage point impact on growth of a one standard deviation change in the variable, evaluated at the sample average

Variable	SW result	Replication result	Replication result with extended data sample
Openness	0.9	0.9	0.9
Life expectancy	0.7	0.6	0.8
Institutional quality	0.6	0.6	0.6
Central government savings	0.6	0.7	0.6
Resource abundance	0.5	0.5	0.4
Differential pop growth	0.4	0.4	0.5
Tropical climate	0.4	0.4	0.5
Landlocked	0.3	0.2	0.2

Note: Extended data sample uses the regression results in Table 12.5 below with 13 African countries added.

calculations life expectancy is associated with a 0.6 percentage point increase in growth (not 0.7 as reported), government savings with a 0.7 percentage point increase (not 0.6), and being landlocked is associated with a 0.2 percentage point decrease in growth (not 0.3).[15]

This downgrading of the impact of cross-country differences in life expectancy and being landlocked, and the upgrading of government savings, strengthens SW's second conclusion (listed above in the introduction) that policy variables like openness (0.9 percentage points), institutional quality (0.6 percentage points), and government savings (0.7 percentage points) are more important than geography and as important as health (0.6 percentage points) in effecting growth.[16] Life expectancy itself reflects to some degree public health policy, and so one might even conclude that the four most important variables impacting growth over the measurement period are related to policy.

SW then propose that their expanded list of regression variables obviates the need for a SSA dummy to explain Africa's slow growth, as was common in the literature at the time. To demonstrate this, SW's regression 2 in their table 2 adds a SSA dummy, on which the coefficient is statistically insignificant at a t-ratio of 0.05. They then argue that this is due to their modelling of trade openness and life expectancy: "if we start with regression 2 in Table 2 and simply drop the SOPEN variable, the t-ratio on the Sub-Saharan Africa variable rises to –2.2. If we do the same with the life expectancy variable, the t-ratio on the Sub-Saharan Africa variable rises to –1.4" (1997a: 351). Repeating their experiment, I find that omitting the openness variable from regression 2 causes the SSA dummy coefficient t-ratio to "rise" to –1.96, which is still insignificant at the 5 per cent level. Omitting the life expectancy variable causes the t-ratio to "rise" to –0.95, which is still far from significant. If openness and life expectancy are *both* removed, the dummy comes significantly into play at a value of –1.5 percentage points. This highlights the importance of modelling at least one of these independent variables when seeking to avoid the need for an Africa dummy, and indicates that what is special about Africa as a region is its trade policies (which tend to be closed) and life expectancy (which is lower than normal).[17]

SW also suggest via their regression 3 that the negative neighbourhood spill-over effects that some growth diagnosticians (e.g., Easterly and Levine 1995) need to use to explain Africa's slow growth are because of their omission of a trade openness effect. I can confirm that the absence of a negative neighbourhood effect in SW's regression 3 is because of the inclusion of the trade openness covariates; when these are removed the growth of neighbouring countries becomes statistically significant.

SW's analysis here has been criticized by some as replacing the Africa dummy with a tropics dummy and for that reason SW do not really get rid of an Africa dummy in their regressions. This criticism is unfounded on two fronts. First, the tropics variable is a continuous variable that can be non-zero for countries not in Africa. It is not a dummy variable specific to SSA. Second, if I remove the tropics dummy from regression 2 in SW table 2 the SSA dummy remains statistically insignificant.[18] In sum, I find that their first conclusion noted above in the introduction, that there is no need for an Africa Dummy or neighbourhood contagion effects when the appropriate set of conditioning variables are included in the regression, is correct. The policy implication is that reform need not be coordinated across Africa to be effective.

Since openness ranks quite highly in terms of its impact on growth, SW next explore why African countries had less openness than other developing countries. They argue that countries with a colonial past were more likely to pursue closed trade policies, and that this statistically dominates explanations relating closed policies to ethnic diversity.[19] On page 353 they regress openness on ethnic fractionalization and colonial origins. They find that the coefficient on colony is negative and statistically significant, while the coefficient on ethnicity (ethling) is negative but not statistically significant. When I replicate their regression with the restricted sample I obtain

$$\text{open6590} = 0.63 - 0.003 \text{ ethling} - 0.26 \text{ colony} \qquad R^2 = 0.20$$
$$(-1.97) \qquad\qquad (-2.72)$$

The coefficients on colony and ethling are substantially different from those reported in SW, as are the t-ratios.[20] The coefficient on ethling is now just barely insignificant, at 5.15 per cent. This weakens the claim that colonial origins were the main or only cause of closed trade policies.

While there are several computations in this section that could not be replicated, no finding is overturned, though some are modified. Policy is important, especially trade openness, which appears to be conditioned on colonial heritage. There is no need for an Africa dummy as long as the model includes *at least one of* the independent variables trade openness and life expectancy. Contagion neighbourhood effects also disappear once trade openness is included as an independent variable.

12.4 The problem of missing countries

The next section of the SW paper investigates possible bias from only having 23 of the 46 SSA countries in the baseline regression sample.

Perhaps SW's model only explains growth for African countries with good data. To investigate this they compare their growth predictions for the 23 SSA countries in their sample against growth predictions for an additional 13 SSA countries that are added to the sample after filling in missing data.

In their table 3 they compute the root mean squared error (RMSE) for the 23 SSA countries in their sample using regression 1 in Appendix Table A1. That regression sample includes the five influential points that were omitted in the previous analyses. It is not clear why they change to this sample here. The predicted growth data in SW table 3 are correct save for Cote D'Ivoire, which should be 0.02 rather than −0.02, and Madagascar, which should be 0.51 rather than 0.47. The averages calculated at the bottom of the table are not correct. The average for the actual growth of the 23 countries is 0.64, not 0.41, and the average for the predicted growth is 0.67, not 0.44. SW report the standard error for the 23 African countries listed in their table 3 to be 0.89. I calculate it to be 0.90 based on the data in their table, and 0.91 after correcting the predicted growth numbers for Cote D'Ivoire and Madagascar. Despite these errors, their statement that "predicted growth ... is close to actual growth ... for this subset of countries" (1997a: 353) is correct. Using the baseline regression that omits the five influential points, and thus excludes Botswana, Gabon, and Madagascar in this table, I compute the RMSE for the growth of the remaining 20 African countries to be even lower, at 0.68.

SW table 4 lists the 23 SSA countries that are listwise deleted from the baseline regression due to missing data. Thirteen of these were missing data for three or fewer variables, and SW replace these missing entries with the averages for all other African countries. In two cases I found that the reported number of missing data points was incorrect. These are noted in Table 12.4 below. SW then predict growth for these 13 countries using the regression results from a sample that presumably includes the five influence points. The predicted growth numbers that they report are not replicable using either this sample or the sample without the five influence points. To be consistent with SW table 3, I use the full sample baseline regression to generate the growth predictions in Table 12.4 below. SW report that the predicted growth for these 13 countries averages 1.02, quite a bit higher than the actual growth average of 0.67. The average predicted growth by my calculation is 0.93, which lowers the gap slightly.

SW then compare the performance of the growth predictions for SSA vis-à-vis the total sample. They report in the text that the standard error for the baseline regression with all regions of the world included is 0.67.

Table 12.4 Actual and predicted growth for African countries not in the regression sample, no influence points removed

Country	Actual growth	Predicted growth	Number of times that missing data were replaced by Africa averages
Angola			
Benin	–0.96	0.96 [0.70]	1
Burundi	1.39	2.15 [1.97]	1
Cape Verde Islands	3.63		
Central African Republic	–0.50	0.05 [–0.06]	1
Chad	–2.37	–0.60 [–0.66]	2
Comoros	–0.53		
Djibouti			
Ethiopia			
Guinea	1.36	1.75 [1.70]	1 [3]
Guinea-Bissau	0.49	1.26 [0.76]	2
Lesotho	3.45	3.16 [3.40]	3
Liberia			
Mauritania	–0.43	–0.49 [–0.81]	1
Mauritius	2.50	1.92 [1.80]	1
Mozambique	–2.03	–0.59 [–0.55]	2
Namibia	0.88		
Reunion			
Rwanda	3.05	2.07 [2.10]	1
Seychelles	4.39		
Sudan			
Swaziland	1.71	0.61 [0.59]	3 [2]
Togo	1.07	1.04 [1.11]	1
Average for 13 countries with 3 or fewer imputations	0.67	1.02 [0.93]	
RMSE	1.00 [0.94]		

Note: Where my calculations differ they are given in square brackets.

Since I am able to replicate that regression I test this directly and find that it is not correct. The standard error from the baseline regression is either 0.63 (with five influence points excluded), 0.77 (with five influence points included), or 0.82 (with five influence points included and the imputations for 13 missing African counties included). This is only slightly higher than the standard errors for the 23 countries in their table 3. They then refer to the standard error for the 13 countries in their table 4 as 1.00. I compute it to be 0.94 based on my replication growth results. SW conclude that "This figure is slightly higher than 0.67, but not tremendously higher when one considers the inevitable errors that arise from our data imputations" (1997a: 356).[21] They are comparing a RMSE of 1.00 for the 13 missing Africa countries with a RMSE of 0.67 for the sample as a whole, whereas the comparison should be between 0.94 and 0.77. This difference is smaller, strengthening their conclusions that the model performs well enough even for the 13 African countries with imputed data.

Something that SW don't do, but is of interest given the possibility that the listwise deletion of these 13 countries causes bias in the estimators (Firebaugh 2008), is to compare the baseline regression results in SW table 2 with the results after adding to the sample the 13 missing African countries in their table 4. Table 12.5 presents the regression results with and without the additional 13 African countries, but continuing to exclude the original five influence points. The results are not greatly changed by the addition of these 13 African countries. From the results in the second column I then recomputed the importance of the independent variables for determining growth, and the ranking in Table 12.3 remains roughly intact: openness is still the most important variable (0.9 percentage points), followed by life expectancy (0.8 percentage points), and then the policy variables government savings (0.6 percentage points) and institutional quality (0.6 percentage points). Tropics are now slightly more important (0.5 percentage points), and natural resources (0.4 percentage points) and being landlocked (0.2 percentage points) are slightly less important. In any event, the missing African countries were not biasing the finding that policy and health are more important determinants of growth than geography and demography.

12.5   Policy implications

In this section SW take into account differences in regional geographic, demographic, and policy variables and use the base case regression results to undertake a deconstruction of why Africa's growth was slower than the growth of the fast growers in Asia and the other developing economies. This type of analysis is important for its examination of where Africa lags. For, although policy may be the most important determinant of growth, if Africa's policies are actually superior to those of other developing countries the prospect for growth-improving policy in Africa is limited. On the premise of decreasing returns, one wants to search for the control variables that are furthest below the mean. Table 5 in their paper reports the results of this analysis. In what is the most damaging finding from the exercise, I am unable to replicate these results and hence unable to confirm their policy prescriptions.

Table 12.5 Regression estimates, SW table 2 regression 1, with original data set and with extended country sample that includes 13 additional African countries with imputed data

	Original data set	Extended data set
Log of real GDP per economically active population in 1965	−1.63 (−8.47)	−1.73 (−9.38)
Openness times log real GDP per economically active population in 1965	−0.77 (−2.54)	−0.69 (−2.19)
Openness to international trade	8.48 (3.44)	7.81 (3.03)
Landlocked dummy variable	−0.58 (−2.69)	−0.52 (−2.53)
Log life expectancy circa 1970	45.48 (2.60)	58.61 (3.30)
Square of log life expectancy	−5.40 (−2.41)	−6.98 (−3.04)
Central government savings, 1970–1990	0.12 (5.40)	0.11 (5.21)
Dummy for tropical climate	−0.85 (−3.64)	−0.99 (−4.32)
Institutional quality index	0.28 (3.95)	0.27 (3.74)
Natural resource exports/ GDP 1970	−3.26 (−3.41)	−2.33 (−2.56)
Growth in economically active population – total population growth	1.19 (3.82)	1.32 (4.21)
Adjusted R^2	0.89	0.87
Number of countries	79	92

Note: Dependent variable: growth per capita of PPP-adjusted GDP, 1965–1990. t-statistics in parentheses.

Recall that in Table 12.1 some of the covariate averages reported by SW are different from those I compute using their data. To begin, I use *their* values in Table 12.1 to confirm that my method of replication in this section is correct when I apply their base regression results to these values. Table 12.6 compares Africa's growth factors determined by geography, changing demography, and health of the population with the growth factors of all other developing economies. The replication is successful, with changing demography, geography, and health dealing SSA a 2.0 percentage point per year blow in growth compared with other developing economies. Table 12.7 then compares the impacts of policy differences. Here I impose on Africa the average policy levels that SW report in Table 12.1 for all other developing economies and then apply the baseline regression coefficients. The resulting growth differences due to policy cannot be replicated. SW's institutional quality impact is incorrect by inspection. Using SW's values in Table 12.1 the African index of institutional quality is better than that of other developing countries. It is therefore impossible to get a negative impact of differences in institutional quality on African growth, though SW indicate a negative impact of –0.0 in their table 5. In conclusion, using the results in base case regression 1 and the reported values in Table 12.1, had Africa followed the policy and institutional quality of all other developing economies it would have had *slower* growth than was observed.

How does this result change if I use my computations of the covariate averages listed in Table 12.1? Table 12.8 reproduces Table 12.6 given this change. The results for geography, demography, and public health are not greatly different. However, from Table 12.9, which reproduces

Table 12.6   Effect of differences in geography, changing demography, and public health on the rate of growth, in percentage points

Geography, changing demography, and health effect	SW estimate	Replication estimate
Tropics	–0.2	–0.25
Landlocked	–0.1	–0.13
Natural resource endowments	–0.2	–0.20
Growth in non working-age population	–0.6	–0.50
Life expectancy	–0.9	–0.90
Total	–2.0	–1.98

Note: Africa versus the average other developing economy using SW-reported averages for the levels of the independent variables in Table 12.1.

Table 12.7   Effect of policy and governance differences on the rate of growth, in percentage points

Policy and governance effect	SW estimate	Replication estimate
Trade openness	–0.9*	–0.35
Government saving	+0.2	+0.36
Institutional quality	–0.0	+0.07
Total	–0.7	+0.09

Africa versus the average other developing economy using SW-reported averages for the levels of the independent variables in Table 12.1. *Attributes the –0.1 policy impact of "catch up" in SW table 5 to openness.

Table 12.7 with the corrected covariate values, it is observed that if Africa followed the policies of the other average developing country it could have grown at 0.80 + 0.07 = 0.87 per cent, not 0.80 + 0.60 = 1.4 per cent as claimed by SW. From the results in Tables 12.8 and 12.9, the main difference in growth between Africa and the other developing countries was not due to overall policy but due to differing demography and public health (see the last two items of Table 12.8, which add up to a growth differential of 1.4 percentage points). These corrections put the SW results in line with those of Bloom and Sachs (1998). They also resolve Collier and Gunning's (1999a) mention of the exceptionally large impacts that SW attribute to trade policy, being landlocked, and resource dependence on African growth, at 1.2 percentage points per annum. Collier and Gunning suggest that 0.4 percentage points would be more typical. My replication in Tables 12.8 and 12.9 shows that the combined effect of these three factors in the SW analysis is 0.4 percentage points.

If I repeat this exercise by comparing Africa to the seven fastest-growing countries using my data from Table 12.1, I get the results shown in Table 12.10. Africa would not have grown at the 4.3 per cent

Table 12.8 Effect of differences in geography, changing demography, and public health on the rate of growth, in percentage points

Geography, changing demography, and health effect	
Tropics	−0.24
Landlocked	−0.14
Natural resource endowments	+0.07
Growth in non working-age population	−0.51
Life expectancy	−0.95
Total	−1.77

Note: Africa versus the average other developing economy using my calculated averages for the levels of the independent variables in Table 12.1.

Table 12.9 Effect of policy and governance differences on the rate of growth, in percentage points

Policy and governance effect	
Trade openness	−0.29
Government saving	+0.21
Institutional quality	+0.01
Total	−0.07

Note: Africa versus the average other developing economy using my calculated levels of the independent variables in Table 12.1.

Table 12.10   Effect of policy and governance differences on the rate of growth, in percentage points

Policy and governance effect	SW estimate	Replication estimate using my values in Table 12.1
Trade openness	−2.8[*]	−2.56
Government saving	−0.1	−0.10
Institutional quality	−0.6	−0.66
Total	−3.5	−3.32

Note: Africa versus average of seven fastest-growing non-African economies. [*]Attributes the −0.3 growth difference due to "catch up" in SW table 5 to openness.

claimed by SW if it had followed fast-growth policies; it would have grown at 4.1 per cent. SW's broad inferences about the impact of policy differences between Asia and Africa are correct even in the face of my inability to match their data in Table 12.1.

12.6   Concluding remarks

The concluding remarks of the SW paper state that poor economic policies have had a larger negative impact on Africa's growth rates than have geographic factors. This does not stand up to replication, at least in terms of explaining the growth differences between Africa and the developing countries other than the fastest-growing Asian economies. I calculate that growth in Africa over the sample period would only have been 0.07 percentage points higher had it had the policies and institutional quality of these other developing economies, not 0.6 percentage points as claimed by SW. Geography was responsible for a 0.3 percentage point growth lag, four times the impact of policy and institutional quality differences. Changing demography and poor public health were responsible for a 1.5 percentage point growth lag, 20 times the impact of policy and institutional quality differences. This is not to say that the SW regression results do not show policy to be an important determinant of economic growth. It is just that Africa's policies and institutional quality were on the whole not that different from other developing countries over the sample period, while its geography, changing demography, and public health were. In fact, SW come to a similar conclusion in that the final section of their concluding remarks notes the caveat that regardless of actions taken on the policy front Africa will continue to suffer from three structural conditions: being landlocked, having high natural resource dependence, and having low life expectancy. However, even here their conclusions are undermined by the inaccuracy of their analysis: a review of the revised averages in Table 12.1 shows that contrary to popular perception Africa is actually light on resource dependence compared with the rest of the developing world.

In conclusion, SW's widely heralded result, I would argue, erroneously directed development practice at institutions like the World Bank and USAID towards capacity building. The correct policy implication from this analysis is that infrastructure financing, public health financing, and efforts to control or eradicate major tropical diseases should have taken priority in any special development plan for Africa. This illustrates the value of replicating analyses *before* basing policy on them.

Notes

1. There is always the worry that the sample is biased due to poorer countries not being included in the analysis because they have missing data. Sachs and Warner address this problem, at least for Africa, and conclude that such bias is not affecting their results.
2. As of 5 May 2013 it had 1,013 cites according to Harzing's Publish or Perish software. The next most cited paper in the journal (Elbadawi and Sambanis 2000) had 246 cites.
3. See Hammermesh (2007) for a discussion of the different types of replication in economics. The need for, and the impediments against, purely replicating empirical economics research is nicely summarized in Anderson et al. (2008) and Tomek (1993). Davis (2013) provides the motivation for specifically replicating the series of Sachs and Warner papers on growth.
4. In the only noted exception, the average national savings ratio in table 2, regression 5, is insignificant but becomes significant at the 10 per cent level if China, the Congo, Egypt, Guatemala, and Syria are excluded from the sample.
5. See table 7 in Bloom and Sachs (1998). They do not report the counterfactual of following the average policies of all other developing economies or of the seven fastest-growing economies.
6. Ideally one would also want to replicate the Temple, Easterly and Levine, and Bloom and Sachs papers. A major impediment to replication is lack of data and code archives (Anderson et al. 2008). In preparing this paper I could only find data and code for the Sachs and Warner paper.
7. The growth gap between Africa and East Asia due to policy is estimated by Easterly and Levine (1998) to be 2.5 percentage points.
8. There is also the issue of whether the econometric technique used by SW is appropriate (e.g., see the comments by Collier and Udry in Bloom and Sachs 1998) and whether their independent variables are exogenous (Collier and Gunning 1999a, 1999b). Comment on this is beyond the scope of pure replication.
9. Trade openness is defined as the fraction of years during the period 1965–1990 in which a country is rated open. Institutional quality is an unweighted average of five indexes; a rule of law index, a bureaucratic quality index, a corruption in government index, a risk of expropriation index, and a government repudiation of contracts index.

10. The averages for each grouping are taken from the entire sample, and include all countries for which there is data. The country sample is therefore not consistent across rows.

11. The group of countries in the SW data set that I consider to be "other developing countries" and for which there is at least partial data includes Afghanistan, Algeria, Antigua and Barbuda, Argentina, Bahamas, Bahrain, Bangladesh, Barbados, Belize, Bhutan, Bolivia, Brazil, Brunei, Cambodia, Chile, China, Colombia, Costa Rica, Cuba, Cyprus, Dominica, Dominican Rep., Ecuador, Egypt, El Salvador, Equatorial Guinea, Eritrea, Fiji, Grenada, Guatemala, Guyana, Haiti, Honduras, India, Iran, Iraq, Jamaica, Jordan, Kiribati, Korea Dem. Rep., Kuwait, Laos, Lebanon, Libya, Maldives, Marshall Islands, Mexico, Micronesia, Mongolia, Morocco, Myanmar, Nepal, Nicaragua, Oman, Pakistan, Panama, Papua New Guinea, Paraguay, Peru, Philippines, Qatar, Sao Tome and Principe, Saudi Arabia, Solomon Is., Sri Lanka, St. Kitts and Nevis, St. Lucia, St Vincent and Grenadines, Suriname, Syria, Tonga, Trinidad and Tobago, Tunisia, Turkey, United Arab Emirates, Uruguay, Vanuatu, Venezuela, Vietnam, Western Samoa, and Yemen.

12. Inflation turns out to be a statistically insignificant variable in most of the regressions, and so this last detail is moot.

13. SW report Saving/GDP = $-102 + 29$ log(life) + 0.72 government saving/GDP $R^2 = 0.59$, with t-stats 10.6 on log(life) and 6.3 on government savings. I also cannot replicate their regression if I exclude the 5 influence points SW list in their footnote 9.

14. SW repeatedly reference the "ten" variables in their regression, apparently counting the square of life expectancy as an independent variable. There are 9 variables and 11 covariates. Once again the life expectancy variable in these regressions is an average from 1960 to 1964, and not circa 1970. Inflation is also reported to be from 1965 to 1990 in the data appendix, as opposed to from 1970 as listed in SW's table 2. The Excel file column header lists inflation as being from 1965 to 1990.

15. Initial level of income, which is another variable, has the strongest impact at 1.7 percentage points. SW do not compute this statistic for this variable.

16. Butkiewicz and Yanikkaya (2010) argue that the SW index of trade openness is poorly correlated with trade measures, and is instead a measure of the quality of overall institutions and economic policies. Rodrik (1998) suggests that Sachs and Warner are measuring macroeconomic adjustments and structural reforms. Butkiewicz and Yanikkaya find that openness to trade reduces the rate of economic growth in developing countries. Falkinger and Grossman (2005) provide a model of why this can be the case.

17. Neither Temple (1998) nor Easterly and Levine (1998) include these covariates in their regressions, and both find a statistically significant Africa dummy.

18. This is true if the landlocked dummy is also removed, and so it is neither being in the tropics nor absence of access to the sea that makes Africa special. This point has been previously made by Paul Collier in Bloom and Sachs (1998: 275).

19. A major theme in Easterly and Levine (1998) is that ethnic fractionalization is an economically large determinant of policy differences between Africa and East Asia.

20. SW report open6590 = 0.62 – 0.002 ethling – 0.32 colony, R^2 = 0.20, with t-stats –1.33 on ethling and –3.38 on colony. I also cannot replicate this when I test the regression using the full sample.
21. This method of imputation actually biases the RMSE downwards because constants are replacing variables (Firebaugh 2008).

References

Anderson, R. G., Greene, W. H., McCullough, B. D. and Vinod, H. D. (2008) "The role of data/code archives in the future of economic research," *Journal of Economic Methodology*, 15(1): 99–119.

Barro, R. J. and Lee, J. (1993) "Losers and winners in economic growth," NBER Working Paper Series No. WP4341 (April).

Belsley, D., Kuh, E. and Welsch, R. (1980) *Regression diagnostics* (New York: J. Wiley).

Bloom, D. E. and Sachs, J. D. (1998) "Geography, demography, and economic growth in Africa," *Brookings Papers on Economic Activity*, 1998(2): 207–295.

Butkiewicz, J. L. and Yanikkaya, H. (2010) "Minerals, institutions, openness, and growth: An empirical analysis," *Land Economics* 86(2): 313–328.

Collier, P. and Gunning, J. W. (1999a) "Explaining African economic performance," *Journal of Economic Literature*, 37: 64–111.

Collier, P. and Gunning, J. W. (1999b) "Why has Africa grown slowly?," *Journal of Economic Perspectives*, 13(3): 3–22.

Davis, G. A. (2013) "Replicating Sachs and Warner's working papers on the resource curse," *Journal of Development Studies*, 49(12): 1615–1630.

Easterly, W. and Levine, R. (1995) "Africa's growth tragedy: A retrospective, 1960–1989," Policy Research Working Paper No. 1503 (August), The World Bank.

Easterly, W. and Levine, R. (1998) "Africa's growth tragedy: Policies and ethnic divisions," *Quarterly Journal of Economics*, 112(4): 1203–1250.

Elbadawi, E. and Sambanis, N. (2000) "Why are there so many civil wars in Africa? Understanding and preventing violent conflict," *Journal of African Economies*, 9(3): 244–269.

Falkinger, J. and Grossman, V. (2005) "Institutions and development: The interaction between trade regime and political system," *Journal of Economic Growth* 10: 231–272.

Firebaugh, G. (2008) *Seven Rules for Social Research* (Princeton NJ: Princeton University Press).

Glandon, P. J. (2011) "Appendix to the report of the editor: Report on the *American Economic Review* data availability compliance project," *American Economic Review*, 101(3): 695–699.

Hammermesh, D. S. (2007) "Viewpoint: Replication in economics," *Canadian Journal of Economics*, 40(3): 715–733.

Herndon, T., Ash, M. and Pollin, R. (2013) "Does higher debt consistently stifle economic growth? A critique of Reinhart and Rogoff," Working Paper No. 322, University of Massachusetts Amherst.

Knabb, S. D. (2005) "The contribution of institutions, trade, and geography to the development process: How robust is the empirical evidence to variations in the sample?," *Empirical Economics*, 30(2): 393–409.

Krugman, P. (2013) "The Excel depression," *New York Times*, April 18.

Norman, C. S. (2009) "Rule of law and the resource curse: Abundance versus intensity," *Environmental and Resource Economics*, 43(2): 183–207.

Pollin, R. and Ash, M. (2013) "Debt and growth: A response to Reinhart and Rogoff," *New York Times*, April 29.

Reinhart, C. M. and Rogoff, K. S. (2010) "Growth in a time of debt," *American Economic Review: Papers & Proceedings*, 100(May): 573–578.

Reinhart, C. M. and Rogoff, K. S. (2013) "Debt, growth and the austerity debate," *New York Times*, April 25.

Rodrik, D. (1998) "Trade policy and economic performance in Sub-Saharan Africa," NBER Working Paper No. 6562.

Sachs, J. D. (1996) "It can be done: Growth in Africa," *Economist* (US) 29 June: 19+.

Sachs, J. D. and Warner, A. M. (1997a) "Sources of slow growth in African economies," *Journal of African Economies* 6(3): 335–376.

Sachs, J. D. and Warner, A. M. (1997b) Natural resource abundance and economic growth, Center for International Development and Harvard Institute for International Development, November.

Sachs, J. D. and Warner, A. M. (1997c) "Fundamental sources of long-run growth," *American Economic Review* 87(2): 184–188.

Sachs, J. D. and Warner, A. M. (1999a) "The big push, natural resource booms and growth," *Journal of Development Economics* 59: 43–76.

Sachs, J. D. and Warner, A. M. (1999b) "Natural resource intensity and economic growth," in Mayer, J., Chambers, B. and Farooq, A. (eds) *Development Policies in Natural Resource Economies* (Cheltenham, UK: Edward Elgar), pp. 13–38.

Sachs, J. D. and Warner, A. M. (2001) "The curse of natural resources," *European Economic Review*, 45: 827–838.

Temple, J. (1998) "Initial conditions, social capital and growth in Africa," *Journal of African Economies*, 7(3): 309–347.

Tomek, W. G. (1993) "Confirmation and replication in empirical econometrics: A step toward improving scholarship," *American Journal of Agricultural Economics* 75: 6–14.

United Nations Development Programme (2005) *Human development report 2005*, New York.

USAID (2003) Building trade capacity in the developing world, USAID Strategy Paper, March.

World Bank (2012) *Strengthening Governance: Tackling Corruption*, March 6, available at http://siteresources.worldbank.org/PUBLICSECTORANDGOVERNANCE/Resources/285741-1326816182754/GACStrategyImplementationPlan.pdf, accessed 26 August 2013.

13
Reflexive Relations and the Contested Creation of Epistemic Diversity in the Safe Motherhood Initiative

Dominique Béhague and Katerini Storeng

13.1 Introduction: denouncing "evidence-based advocacy"[1]

Over the past two decades, the demand for experimentally derived evidence of the impact and cost-effectiveness of proposed public health interventions has grown exponentially, often to the exclusion of other epistemological traditions within epidemiology and allied social science disciplines (Lambert et al., 2006). Epidemiologists who bemoan this development have argued that the shift towards impact research is undermining one of epidemiology's core defining features and strengths, namely the interest in multivariate understandings of the interconnected biological, social, political, and economic determinants of health (Davey Smith et al., 2001; Victora et al., 2004; McPake, 2006). Though experimental evidence theoretically provides definitive proof of the causal links between intervention and impact, critics note that the kinds of health interventions now being routinely proposed in global public health are becoming increasingly technocratic and divorced from known distal (social and economic) determinants of health in part *because of* the demand that they be experimentally trialled (Travis et al., 2004).

The recent demand for impact evidence has been partially attributed to the infiltration of neoliberal market principles in global public health over the past 20–30 years (Strathern, 2000; Mykhalovskiy and Weir, 2004). For major donors operating increasingly at a global level, impact evidence facilitates the calculation of the health returns on investments and provides a key mechanism for holding donor recipients (including governments) to account (Laurell and Arellanbo, 1996). The past ten years has thus witnessed a significant growth in global accountabil-ity mechanisms, such as the Millennium Development Goals (MDGs) initiative and monitoring framework (McCoy, 2004; Travis et al., 2004). In response, self-identified global "advocacy coalitions" have mush-roomed, as networks of experts realign their activities towards one main aim: that is, to keep their particular health issue on the agenda through the use of various tools that generate political priority (Shiffman, 2003).

Evidence production has become one of the most central of these tools. As we have noted elsewhere, subfields within global health that can base their policy recommendations on high quality experimental evidence, now deemed the gold standard method for evaluating virtu-ally all types of health programmes, are more readily prioritized and given funding by global agencies, and national governmental and non-governmental organizations (Béhague and Storeng, 2008). Public health experts who are openly critical of the excessive demand for impact evidence often feel powerless to counter the institutional structures that account for these developments. Some even find themselves (un)will-ingly producing impact research even when they do not deem it program-matically or epistemologically necessary (Béhague and Storeng, 2008). Those who have grown particularly frustrated with this process now use the term "evidence-based advocacy" rather than "evidence-based policy" to refer to the political and competitive uses of evidence in advocating for coalition-sustaining funds. For these experts, *evidence-based advocacy* stands in detrimental contradistinction to what *evidence-based policy-mak-ing* should be comprised of, namely, the use of evidence to better under-stand mechanisms of change and thus to engage with programmatic problem-solving (Storeng and Béhague, 2014).

This chapter draws on an ethnographic study of the evidence-based movement conducted on a continuous part-time basis from 2004 to 2009 to explore how these debates are playing themselves out in unu-sual and provocative ways in the Safe Motherhood Initiative (SMI) sub-field.[2] The SMI is exceptional in a number of ways: it is comprised of a unique demographic and geopolitical group of experts, many of whom see themselves as marginally situated vis-à-vis the broader field of global health. Indeed, as we began our fieldwork, we were surprised to learn that when maternal health was selected to be one of the eight MDGs, this represented a mixed blessing for many in the field. While the MDG demonstrated the long-awaited global recognition of the importance of maternal health, some feared that this added attention would come with additional pressures to produce evidence of impact within a time frame that would invariably only consider "quick-fix" interventions.

This critical perspective has permeated SMI practices from its inception. Perhaps the most notable of these practices can be found in the way SMI experts use historical case studies of naturally occurring mortality declines to subtly challenge dominant epistemic views and the more far-reaching neoliberal values of which cost-effectiveness frameworks are a part (Béhague and Storeng, 2013). As we will show, this type of evidence has enabled them to engage with the notion that health improvement is, at heart, an issue that requires commitment to equity and coordinated political and governmental action. By using historical insight, SMI experts have adopted a potentially stigmatizing evidence-production position that risks undermining their already fragile authority as policy-savvy scientists. Yet this type of epistemic diversity has not been wholly marginalized. Rather, it has emerged as an unlikely (if also indirect) source of empiric clout.

To theorize the social life of this epistemic diversity, we draw from works in the anthropology and sociology of science and consider the broader social, political, and institutional relationships in which epistemological convictions and practices take shape. Our contribution to the aims of this book lies in providing an account of how maternal health researchers have encountered the increasing salience of a cost-effectiveness impact agenda. We hope this chapter will inspire public health and development researchers to critically assess – perhaps even actively influence – the broader networks of social relationships that both constrain and inspire them. We recognize that insight on such broader contexts is difficult to develop from the perspective of the individual expert actor, both because it emerges from aggregate level insights and because the social forces at play, as highlighted by our informants, are not often explicitly articulated.

Ethnographic methods are particularly well suited to uncovering the tacit aspects of social life. Open-ended exploratory and in-depth interviews, and perhaps more importantly, participant observation, allowed us to gain access to an array of different kinds of informants, as well as to the more private and less explicitly articulated realms of experts' values and practices. We also conducted an extensive review of published and grey literature, including informal documents provided to us by our informants. A total of 72 experts were interviewed, identified opportunistically through professional networking, publications, and conference proceedings; 29 of these were from academic institutions, primarily in the UK, US, Belgium, and Norway, with a minority (6) from collaborating research institutions in Africa and Asia. Although most self-identified as maternal health experts, many had experience working in multiple domains of international public health. Participant observation was conducted within academic settings, as well as at 20 more public venues (conferences, workshops, institutional meetings, etc.). Of these, eight were not specific to maternal health but focused on general public health, and child, neonatal, or reproductive health (for details, see Béhague and Storeng, 2007; Béhague and Storeng, 2008; Storeng, 2010).

13.2 Roots of exceptionality

The SMI was launched in 1987 in an attempt to redress what experts had then identified as the marginalization of the "M" in Maternal and Child Health programmes, or the "neglected tragedy of maternal mortality" (Rosenfield and Maine, 1985: 83). Since then, a recognizable network of researchers, advocates, and policy experts has emerged. At approximately 200–300 people globally, the SMI is small relative to other prominent global health coalitions such as, for example, the Global Fund to Fight HIV/AIDS, TB, and Malaria.

The SMI's own self-reflective history is mired in what Storeng has called a "narrative of failure" that refers to both lack of global progress in maternal mortality (MM) decline and the SMI coalition's ineffective advocacy for funds and political will at the global level (Storeng, 2010). One could speculate, however, that it is *because of* the reflexive and public uses of this narrative of failure, developed in private meetings, commentaries, and editorials (AbouZahr, 2003), that the SMI has in fact managed to position itself strategically and with authoritative influence in global and national policy debates.

Such authority has been achieved through multiple and at times unconventional, even seemingly conflicting, pathways. When the SMI was launched the first item on their agenda was the so-called "measurement trap," a term used in a key 1992 article that highlighted the way in which lack of data is intricately linked to lack of prioritization (Graham and Campbell, 1992). While such a "trap" exists for all advocacy coalition, in maternal health, it is often said to be particularly acute, since MM is very complex to measure. Measurement was deemed essential for basic monitoring and advocacy and was also important for producing evidence of efficacy of interventions to reduce MM. This task was complicated by the fact that MM is of low-enough prevalence to make conducting experimental evaluations a veritable logistical challenge, even in high prevalence settings (Starrs, 2006). Several key leaders in the field have thus devoted the better part of their careers to devising innovative measurement techniques for estimating the MM ratio

(MMR) in data-poor developing country contexts. Their efforts were not prompted by a blanket conviction in measurement, but rather a pragmatic recognition of the political centrality of easy-to-standardize measurement techniques.

These very same actors have not become mere measurement "technocrats," however, losing sight of the specific socio-institutional contexts in which statistical indicators should be interpreted. Rather, some of the most prominent "measurement experts" have also been at the forefront of using in-depth historical case studies to understand the broader social contexts in which maternal mortality reduction has been observed to occur. In fact, these experts have at times been so "political" – at least relative to mainstream public health – that several informants from related subfields such as child and neonatal health claimed that the SMI has been a comparatively weak subfield because it has based its key policy decisions on "ideology rather than science." These informants noted, for example, that the first cohort of SMI experts was comprised largely of "feminist" demographers and epidemiologists whose ideological commitment to the politics of health have led them to endorse policies that are not always backed by rigorous epidemiological evidence of effectiveness. "Ideological" tendencies were also attributed to Francophone public health experts who have used historical evidence to argue that political change – including commitment to equity, social welfare, and professional accountability – is as crucial to MM reduction as specific medical interventions. The position of these experts is a clear departure from the emphasis on evidence-based science that, as one Francophone informant described, has been taken to dogmatic extremes in Anglophone contexts over the last 15 year.

13.3   Theorizing the boarders of normative epistemologies

To theorize the sources and effects of the SMI's geopolitical and epistemological diversity, we draw from a growing body of philosophically inspired literature in the history, sociology, and anthropology of scientific epistemic cultures, genres, or "styles of reasoning" (Hacking, 1992; Foucault, 1994 (1970); Cetina, 1999; Rose, 2007; Morgan, 2012). The rise of statistics and notions of risk, and of how statistics engenders powerful truth-values integral to the management of populations has been the topic of considerable attention (Daston, 1992; Porter, 1992; Rose, 1996). As authors have shown, it is precisely the assumption of neutrality and objectivity that gives science an autonomous and self-vindicating style of reasoning (Pickering, 1992; Hacking, 1992). This style of reasoning typically responds to unexpected observations not by engaging in fundamental reinterpretation, altering key research questions or even scrutinizing epistemological limitations, but by identifying such observations to be either "outliers" or artefacts of poor measurement technologies. Anthropologists and sociologists have now provided exceptionally insightful analyses of the centrality of this medico-scientific ethos in the global dissemination of template-based approaches to clinical and public health practice (Geissler, 2001; Timmermans and Berg, 2003; Adams, 2005; Lambert, 2006).

In studies of the global health arena, less attention has been given to how epistemic genres divide and multiply (Cetina, 1999). Our initial ethnographic research led us to wonder how it is that alternative epistemologies emerge not simply through highly polarized debates, but also on the marginalized fringes of normative epistemologies. We became intrigued by the everyday practices of influential scientists who are willing to seriously consider "aberrant" empirical observations that confront both their assumptions of the world and the normative epistemologies they use to understand it (Harding, 2008). As we will show, some researchers in the SMI do not adopt a self-vindicating style of reasoning. Rather, they reconsider the epistemological assumptions imbedded in their methodological approaches and actively shape a distinctly more interactive relationship with the unruly world they observe.

Holmes and Marcus have described practices such as these to be imbedded in "para-ethnographic" modes of reasoning that emerge from the "de facto and self-conscious critical faculty that operates in any expert domain as a way of dealing with contradiction, exception, facts that are fugitive, and that suggest a social realm not in alignment with the representations generated by the application of the reigning statistical mode of analysis" (Holmes and Marcus, 2008: 237). "Para-ethnographic" ways of knowing are normally relegated to the unscientific and less powerful realms of "anecdote and intuition." However, Holmes and Marcus point to the "sustained puzzles" that draw scientists to para-ethnographic observations and that compel (and empower) them to destabilize statistical forms of reasoning that tend towards simplification and the marginalization of contingency and "context" (2008: 238).

It is precisely this process of destabilization that interests us in this chapter. In exploring the broader dynamics that enable SMI actors to use historical and case study evidence as a destabilizing force, our ethnography alerts us to the importance of considering the social – and increasingly commodified – life of epistemic values and objects

(Appadurai, 1994). SMI researchers are uniquely reflexive not just about epistemology but also about how they themselves are situated within powerful institutional arrangements. As such, they work to modify not only their research questions and methodologies but also the broader relationships and contexts that constrain epistemic diversity. While numerous editorials and articles have been published over the last decade arguing against the rise of a dogmatically quantitative and accountability-oriented evidence-based movement, very little has changed.[3] In part this may be because divorcing epistemic debates from the social realms in which these debates take shape reifies the notion that scientific ways of reasoning are intrinsically cognitive rather than social, contextual, and thus prone to apparent contradictions (Young, 1981a; Young, 1981b). By grounding our argument in the experiences of a particular field, we thus seek to avoid facile interpretations about the growing salience of quantitative scientific values.

13.4   Early historical insight: the comprehensive agenda

The SMI was launched nine years after the 1978 Alma Ata Declaration, in which primary health care (PHC) was endorsed as a fundamental human right and as a cornerstone of development as a whole (Rosenfield and Maine, 1985). Alma Ata focused on creating conditions that would ensure maximum community and individual self-reliance in building a "comprehensive" approach to health improvement, which includes well-integrated multi-tiered health systems and partnerships with sectors outside of health, including education and civil society (WHO, 1978). In relation to maternal mortality, the Director-General of the WHO, a supporter of comprehensive multi-sectoral and political action in health, stated in 1987: "The roots of much MM lie in discrimination against women, in terms of legal status and access to education, financial resources and health care, including family planning" (Mahler, 1987: 668).

The post-Alma Ata era of the 1980s was typified by a recognizable split in public health ideologies, with a then-growing contingent of stakeholders arguing that comprehensive approaches were too expensive and lengthy to implement in poor countries and should be replaced by interim approaches based on "selective" PHC – such as the GOBI (Growth monitoring, Oral rehydration, Breastfeeding and Immunization) initiative in child health (Rifkin and Walt, 1986). Selective approaches such as GOBI became increasingly popular amongst donors and governments who, concerned with limited budgets, preferred the identification of targeted interventions that would (theoretically) impact on mortality quickly and cheaply (Cueto, 2004). Faced with the reality of donors' and governments' preference for selective interventions, many national safe motherhood programmes focused exclusively on the promotion of traditional birth attendants (TBAs) and the implementation of ante-natal care risk screening programmes – the two SMI components that aligned best with a focus on low-cost, community-based strategies.

Nonetheless, many maternal health experts either rejected selective approaches or felt uncomfortable endorsing them, even when these were explicitly justified as "interim" strategies that should not stand in contradistinction to longer term and more sustainable solutions. As one of the founding members of the SMI stated; "I think the maternal health field has suffered for always saying we need cheaper short term solutions. I think we've always gone for the ineffective things, like antenatal screening and TBA training." By the mid- to late-1980s, epidemiological trend data from those low-income countries where MM could be monitored supported this interpretation, for virtually no decline in the MMR could be detected despite the relatively significant investments that had been made into these two strategies (Goodburn and Campbell, 2001). However, strong epistemological views against accepting trend data as anything more than speculative or within the margin of "statistical error" were also beginning to take hold, particularly amongst those who felt it would be premature to throw the TBA "baby out with the bathwater." While some responded by calling for more rigorous experimental trials of community-based TBA training, others felt that experimental trials of TBA training would not answer the right question, since TBAs would in any event need to be embedded in a much broader multi-tiered health system approach.

To explore these questions with a broader empirical base than either observational or experimental data can provide, some researchers began to atypically reach out to the works of medical historians (Berridge, 2008).[4] Amongst the most well-known of these, read and cited by numerous SMI experts, was Irvine Loudon, a family doctor from Oxfordshire who retired in his fifties to pursue his interests in medical history. Systematically analysing mortality declines in late-19th and early 20th centuries European countries, Loudon was one of the first historians to note that maternal mortality declines were unlike the all-cause mortality decline that had occurred in most Western European countries with improvements in nutrition and socio-economic conditions. MM, he claimed, appeared to be "relatively insensitive" to broader social development, for it had remained high – as high as in many of today's developing countries – until well into the 20th century

(Loudon, 1986; Loudon, 1991). A group of Swedish public health obstetrician-researchers inspired by Loudon also showed that late-19th century Sweden appeared to have managed to reduce its MMR earlier than most other Western European countries, despite the fact it was amongst the poorest and most rural of nations in the region (Högberg et al., 1986).

Case study analyses of the two to three decades in which MM did eventually decline, first in Sweden and then in other countries, showed that it was not vast amounts of technological (medical) investment, nor overall socio-economic development that was required. Rather, successful early MM decline was attributed to a *synergistic* combination of clinical, public health, political, and economic factors. These included key clinical innovations (e.g. control of sepsis), improved therapeutic management of childbirth (including the curtailing of unnecessary medical interventions), the creation of a trained and fully accountable rural midwifery system, increased awareness of the problem through advances in statistical surveillance systems run by small monitoring committees responsible for a small locality, concerted coordination between primary and tertiary providers, and perhaps most importantly – sustained political and governmental attention to the problems of health and economic inequity (Van Lerberghe and De Brouwere, 2001b).

The main conclusions of these studies clearly supported a comprehensive PHC approach and not one based solely on targeted approaches. This fundamentally changed key stakeholders' ways of thinking. Several of our informants noted that reading Loudon's book *Death in Childbirth: An International Study of Maternal Care and Maternal Mortality, 1800–1950* (Loudon, 1992a) had constituted a life-changing moment in their careers and some went on to seek collaborative research links with him. Loudon, being an outsider to the field of safe motherhood as well as a medical doctor, occupied a uniquely authoritative and distanced position relative to those at the heart of the SMI. In his main monograph, published in 1992, his innovative methodological approach was made explicit, as was the fact that he situated his work, epistemologically, within a "moderate" empirically grounded but nevertheless critical, even politicized, position:

> Although some notable histories of maternal care have been confined to a socio-historical or feminist approach with scarcely a statistic, let alone a statistical evaluation in sight, I believe that without rigorous statistical analysis, the history of maternal care can easily become

impressionistic, unreliable and in the end unsatisfying. If there is a danger that a purely demographic approach may deflect attention from features of central important which are inherently unmeasurable ... there is also the danger that without statistical analysis large conclusion are often based on the shaky foundation of thin evidence and small unrepresentative samples. (Loudon, 1992a: 5)

While Loudon's methodological position may to some seem weighted against the "feminist approach," his simple acknowledgement of the pivotal salience of "unmeasurable" factors is noteworthy. What's more, the extent to which Loudon's research influenced the field is exemplified in the first WHO document to be devoted to SMI in developing countries, which made direct reference to Loudon's historical research (WHO, 1994). While focused on training of health personnel, this document importantly retained Loudon's broader messages regarding the role of effective management and government in ensuring equity (WHO, 1994).

13.5   The public health lens: identifying "modifiability"

Ironically, these early historical works gained circulation in the global public health and donor communities throughout the 1990s not because they pointed to the need for a comprehensive agenda, but rather because they demonstrated that health can improve in the absence of broader socio-economic development. As one key stakeholder explained, "these studies showed that public health action *can* make a difference ... through targeted health system action, MM *can* decline even while a country is still poor and largely rural, struggling with public health problems of the kind affecting many developing countries today." The popularization of this more "selective" interpretation of Loudon's work into mainstream public health became central to the creation of political momentum for the SMI as a whole. Not coincidentally, it was precisely during this time that MM in developing countries was reconceptualized as not just a "neglected tragedy" but a "preventable tragedy" that would require the urgent response from donors and the industrialized west (Rosenfield and Maine, 1985).

On that back of this momentum, a powerful contingent of the SMI began to challenge the view that historical case studies pointed to the importance of a comprehensive agenda. In fact, they used Loudon's work to buttress the exact opposite position – namely, that the history of MM decline had been, first and foremost, about improved treatment. Specifically, these experts endorsed access to emergency obstetric care – coined "EmOC" – as the single most important intervention for

MM reduction. Maine and Rosenfeld, probably the most influential of these researchers, argued in a highly cited 1999 editorial that of the many different subcomponents officially endorsed in the comprehensive safe motherhood agenda of the time, "only one – essential obstetric care – includes actions that can substantially reduce maternal deaths" (Maine and Rosenfield, 1999: 481).

At the heart of this technologically oriented interpretation of the historical record was a core concern with the political authority of the SMI itself, which many felt could only be bolstered if experts focused on identifying and intervening upon "modifiable determinants" (Pearce, 1996). EmOC was deemed more modifiable than equity and health systems strengthening. According to Maine and Rosenfield, the main reason the SMI had failed to either make a dent in the MMR of most developing countries or indeed to become a well-established global advocacy coalition was because, unlike the GOBI strategy adopted in child health, it "lacked a clear strategic focus" and endorsed an excessively broad approach that made policy-makers feel as though reducing MM "would require dauntingly vast efforts" (Maine and Rosenfield, 1999: 481). Though proponents of this position agreed that EmOC should ideally be implemented alongside other strategies, many also acknowledged that in resource-poor "countries with high MMR" leaders need to know "whether to give priority [either] to more skilled [and integrated] birth attendants (SBA) or to EmOC" (Paxton et al., 2005: 183).

Critics of the focus on EmOC were not hard to find, particularly amongst those who had originally read and been inspired by Loudon's works. Several of our informants told us that Maine and Rosenfield's position represented a "selective interpretation" of the historical evidence on MM decline that assimilated only the "technical" conclusions about treatment while ignoring the very important messages about political will, social momentum, and community accountability. These were precisely the statistically "unmeasurable" variables that Loudon had identified as being of "central importance." The ironies of this were highlighted repeatedly by some of our informants: the same historical analyses that had pointed to the importance of social and political factors were being used to justify the targeted focus on EmOC – a focus that, as one informant argued, "was at risk of becoming the new targeted panacea."

Despite these critical voices, there was a growing sense that it would be damaging to the field's reputation to demonstrate a lack of programmatic consensus by *not* endorsing EmOC. Here was a fresh new policy proposal that was attracting considerable interest from the donors. To criticize an EmOC strategy for being too "selective" and ignoring "complexity" or "context" was tantamount to repudiating donor support and undermining the field's international credibility. Even those informants who had been highly critical of Maine and Rosenfield's simplifications were keenly aware of their field's marginalized position in global health as a whole and of the fact that consensus around a single set of simple policy recommendations would hold more sway than any broader lessons about the importance of synergy between the political and the technical. Indeed, some EmoC supporters were purported to have taken a "with us or against us" attitude in presenting EmOC as *the* safe motherhood solution, not because they did not recognize the complexities that the historical record pointed to, but rather because they recognized the importance of simplicity in advocacy. To paraphrase several of our informants, better to keep the SMI alive and do *something* than to let it disappear. Such realism, according to some informants, is what eventually completed the policy shift from the mid- to late-1990s from an integrated comprehensive approach to a more exclusively curative approach focused on EmOC (only at times together with the provision of skilled birth attendance in primary care centres).

In many ways, however, this policy shift pertained more to the SMI's global public image than to the internal debates and tensions that continued to play themselves out in the more private realms of workshops, departmental meetings, and research programmes. Several of our informants who felt troubled by this shift confessed that they had played a "complicit" if inadvertent role in endorsing more "technocratic" interpretations of the historical record just by virtue of their failure to keep repeating Loudon's broader messages. Their concerns with the detrimental effects of the relative *absence* of a critically engaged relationship with historical insight only increased as cost-effectiveness rationales were pushed forward.

In the sections that follow, we look first at the growth in cost-effectiveness practices by experts who began calling for evaluations of selective intervention packages that would theoretically provide the greatest impact on mortality with the least economic investment. We then consider how and why historical case study research – which we take to be representative of para-ethnographic modes of reasoning – grew out of dissatisfaction with the way effectiveness models feed into the fragmentation of comprehensive approaches and the marginalization of broader social and political mechanisms of change. In returning time and again to observations of "fugitive facts" that do not conform to more technocratic assumptions of how health improves, many of our informants were effectively challenging the assumption that chance can be experimentally tamed (Hacking, 1990).

13.6   Cost-effectiveness and the search for political clout

Throughout the early- to mid-2000s, public denouncements of the lack of evidence for the SMI policy shift towards facility-based interventions such as EmOC came to a head. Informants recall this period as being one of increasing competition for power and funds between different advocacy coalitions. Child and reproductive health experts worried that the focus on professionalizing birthing care in secondary- and/or tertiary-level facilities would take attention and funds away from the community-based cadre of health workers they considered so integral to delivering child and reproductive health interventions. One prominent child health expert argued, for example, that this policy shift had been inappropriately based on no more than "observational epidemiology, quantitative history" and "dubious analyses of mortality trends." Such critical denouncements were common; several of our informants explained that the potential for biased use of historical research was reinforced by the "weak" nature of such evidence: the lack of generalizability, the inability to prove causality and thus, the propensity to be used as a tool for reinforcing non-scientific and ideologically driven policy preferences. One informant described cynically how "experts love to use this so-called ... evidence, but [history] is not evidence actually, but rather a robust interpretation of a given set of facts." The relative epistemological weakness of historical case study evidence became the *Achilles heel* of a broader safe motherhood agenda.

A small minority of SMI epidemiologists and demographers, being heavily influenced by these critiques, shifted into positions of leadership within the SMI. In doing so, they moved closer to cost-effectiveness rationales. Though a few had in previous years actually been keen supporters of Loudon's work, they came to publically endorse the view that the epistemological certainty provided by experimental evaluations should be a prerequisite for any and all kinds of safe motherhood interventions. This epistemological position was also seen as essential for rectifying the subfield's fragile position in global health. Even those who privately admitted that Loudon's work had revolutionized – even politicized – ways of thinking in maternal health argued for the more rigorous testing of his findings, if only to convince the broader international health community of the importance of investing in health systems strengthening (Graham et al., 2001). In a 2003 land-mark article entitled "Where is the E in maternal health" Miller and other prominent maternal health experts argued that the field would urgently need to over-turn the "inadequate tools to assess intervention effectiveness," including historical analyses that, as they claimed, "do not meet rigorous standards of causality" (Miller et al., 2003:13–14). Some of our informants went so far as to argue that "process evaluations," which many public health experts today argue are essential for understanding *how* interventions work and thus how/if they can be exported to other contexts, are not necessary. "As long as a given intervention is proven to work through a trial," said one such informant, "it can be faithfully recommended."

Such strict epistemological conviction was more frequent in the public consensus-building domains of publications and conferences. In private discussions, many of the population scientists and policy experts we spoke with did not question historical studies' truth value, particularly when reflecting on the broader mechanisms of long-term sustainable political and public health change that these studies highlighted. In fact, though the vast majority of our informants were involved in producing or using trial data, in private, most argued in favour of adopting a pluralistic epistemological approach that uses cost-effectiveness data together with insights from case-histories. As one senior researcher and policy advisor described, interdisciplinarity is essential for putting the "pieces of the jigsaw puzzle" together and drawing up a rational policy position that gives equal attention to the technical and accompanying social, professional, and political changes needed to reduce maternal mortality.

13.7   Defending epistemic flexibility

Moderate positions favouring epistemic flexibility are, of course, easier to sustain in the world of ideas and ideals than in the world of social relations and power. In practice, cost-effectiveness and case study designs have become polar opposites of one another. The growing entrenchment of antagonism towards cost-effective paradigms amongst some of our informants can be partially accounted for by their informal observations that, in the world of budgets, priorities, accountability, and monitoring, the interim solutions delineated by cost-effectiveness trials are often preferred over investment into sustainable health systems initiatives and broader socio-political engagement.

In looking more closely at the professional lives of our informants who sustained a more vocal critique of cost-effectiveness models, we came to realize that their critical insight was nurtured through the relationships that many of them developed with colleagues not in the global arena of expertise but in the specific country contexts in which many of them have been working for the better part of their careers. As we will demonstrate below, we contend that it is partially because of their more "intimate" experiences in these contexts that they have developed an interest in contingency, context and case-study methodologies. Such professionals thus demonstrate a willingness to confront the limitations of evidence-based policy and an interest in interpreting newly emerging "fugitive" facts about maternal mortality reduction through what we believe is a para-ethnographic inductive lens.

The most notable of these "para-ethnographic" experts are Belgian: two public health medical doctors, de Brouwere and Van Lerberghe, working in a country much less permeated by the evidence-based movement and at an institution known for its commitment to public health implementation (the Prince Leopold Institute of Tropical Medicine in Antwerp). In a series of articles published in Anglophone journals, these authors have interpreted Loudon's research for a policy audience and furthered his method by including a broader number of countries to explore differences in the rates of MM decline in the industrialized countries of the early 20th century.

One such publication features an impressive graph of maternal mortality at the beginning of the 20th century in which the US, New Zealand, and Scotland stand out as having MMRs that are three to four times the rate found in Sweden, Denmark, and the Netherlands. "It was really striking to see these [contrasting] curves," described one informant, "because the countries were [broadly] equivalent by standard measures of socio-economic development." In analysing the reasons that might account for such dissimilar MMRs trajectories, these publications lent support to the issues of equity and governance originally identified by Loudon. Importantly, they also highlighted that professional conflicts between obstetricians and midwives, in some situations fuelled by the privatization of maternity care, contributed to the marginalization of midwives and thus to reduced access to skilled attendance as a whole (De Brouwere et al., 1998; Van Lerberghe and De Brouwere, 2001a). Related to this, authors found that obstetricians' poor use of medical technology was actually contributing to maternal deaths. The authors note:

> The history of these relative successes and failures is to a large extent a history of different approaches to the professionalisation of delivery care, even before technology-assisted hospital delivery

became the norm ... Those countries that managed to get doctors to co-operate with a midwifery-based policy fared relatively well. Where doctors won the battle for professional dominance – and for their share of the market – women died." (Van Lerberghe and De Brouwere, 2001b: 11–18)

Having a greater and more diverse empirical base with which to work than Loudon's, these researchers outlined an "evidence-informed" model of effective delivery care that specified the "synergistic" technical *and* political ingredients deemed essential for any country to achieve large-scale MM reductions. In fact, one of the key authors of these publications told us that the focus on synergy between the technical and political was so important and yet so neglected that he felt compelled to devote much of his career to repeating this message in all his publications, from editorials to think-pieces to original research papers.

In undertaking this strategy, these authors were directly challenging the politically expedient and more reductionist interpretation of Loudon's work focused on EmOC only (see above). Rather than supporting the view that the history of MM had fundamentally been about treatment, this body of literature argued that the introduction of medical technologies *cannot* ensure sustained MM decline *without* concomitant socio-economic, professional and political developments relating to health system functioning and equity. As one such researcher explained,

> I think Loudon got it wrong, I think he got the "necessary," but not "sufficient" bit. I think he was right that the medical technologies were necessary – that they came into place and made a big difference – so in that sense he was right. But, what I think he didn't look at was the health systems and political context in which that happened. Whereas I think Vincent's [de Brouwere] work does that."

Along similar lines, another informant pointed out that Loudon had in fact showed that MM does not respond *spontaneously* to socio-economic development, but this should not be taken to mean that it does not require resources. Prompted by this informant's views, we returned to Loudon's original works and found that Loudon had indeed been careful to state that "mortality was relatively insensitive to social and economic determinants *except* in so far as these determine the type and quality of birth attendants" (Loudon, 1992b: 1560). MM decline, he emphasized, depended on the convergence of "a large number of factors, therapeutic, educational, and administrative" (Loudon, 1992b: 1560).[5]

Importantly, what the informant cited above claiming that Loudon "got it wrong" was highlighting is a subtle distinction in Loudon's writings which demonstrates the distinct positions he adopted in his research, depending on his audience and intent. While his monograph certainly emphasized the synergy of socio-political and therapeutic factors, his articles written for a global health audience called more simply for better access to trained personnel and medical technology in contemporary low-income countries (Loudon, 2000).

13.8   Interest in "context"

The reworking of the early historical evidence in these ways sparked renewed interest in multivariate influences and the debate about the relative value of investing in interim (selective) strategies versus more long-term (comprehensive) strategies to improve maternal health. Van Lerberghe and De Brouwere's publications effectively set the stage for the production of a series of additional case studies of natural declines in MM occurring, this time, from the mid-20th century in low- to middle-income countries. These studies were, once again, conducted not by historians but by population scientists (epidemiologists and demographers).

The core hypothesis proposed by these researchers was that there might be not just one solution for most countries but rather different "contexts" and models of health service organization that could foster mortality decline. Importantly, this hypothesis emerged informally (and inductively) from a key observation that several of our informants made in their respective research sites: since the global policy shift-away from TBA training occurred in the 1990s, many countries began striving for institutionalization of births in hospitals, often emphasizing attendance by physicians rather than by the midwives identified in historical studies as so crucial to large-scale maternal mortality decline. As one such informant noted, "there have been notable increases in skilled attendance around the world, [but] every single bit of that increase is due to the use of a physician ... [and not midwives]." In highlighting the "age-old" but somewhat neglected issue of professional conflicts between midwifery and obstetrics, this informant was also flagging the issue of quality of care, since in many settings, hospitals and secondary-level facilities have not been adequately equipped to deal with a rapid increase in numbers of patients.

To explore different contexts for and mechanisms of MM decline, population-level MM reductions in Malaysia, Cuba, Costa Rica, and Sri Lanka from the 1950s onwards were studied, together with more recent if less substantial improvements in Honduras, rural China, Zimbabwe, Bolivia, Egypt, Indonesia, and Jamaica (Koblinsky et al., 1999; Koblinsky and Cambell, 2003; Pathmanathan et al., 2003; Liljestrand and Pathmanathan, 2004). Rather than discerning universally applicable lessons or intervention packages, these authors used observational case study material to analyse MM declines in relation to the variability in service delivery "models" that can be found in most developing countries today. These models range from home delivery by a non-professional (such as a TBA or a relative) to SBA in secondary-level facilities to near-total population coverage of deliveries in a referral facility (hospital) with comprehensive essential obstetric care by a professional SBA (such as an obstetrician or a midwife) (Koblinsky et al., 1999).[6]

Results showed that although some countries had experienced MM reductions with the first model (home delivery by a non-professional), improvements appeared to stagnate once MMRs reached 100 or so per 100,000 live births, still well above the ratio found in most developed countries. However, in the presence of strong referral mechanisms, countries that had introduced a more skilled cadre of birth attendant in low-level facilities had witnessed significant mortality reductions. The studies also controversially showed – reaffirming the finding from earlier studies that medical technology can actually do more harm than good – that persuading all women in a given population to birth in hospitals does not necessarily lead to significant mortality decline and may even contribute to high MM levels, especially where there is poor quality of care (Koblinsky and Cambell, 2003).

This body of research led several researchers to actively reject what they argued had become an artificial and unproductive dichotomy between community-based and facility-based approaches (or indeed even more reductionistically between SBA and EmOC) and push for greater attention to the policy and health system contexts of specific countries. As one of the co-authors of the above-cited studies explained,

> The work that had been done in Sweden, etc … it is now being criticized, because people are saying, oh, that is 19th century. So we set out to say, ok, let's examine a few success stories from 20th century. What did they do, did they go for, obstetric emergencies or did they go for skilled attendants? … Of course they did both.

The key to success thus appeared to be neither SBA or EmOC, nor even the rapid adoption of facility-based births, but rather an incremental and pragmatic approach to ensuring equitable access to good quality skilled attendance and coordination between different levels of care. This process should, in turn, be underpinned by strong political support, accountability of local officials and providers for their performance, and perhaps most importantly, the elimination of financial barriers that structural adjustment programmes of the 1980s and 1990s have created in many countries (Koblinsky et al., 1999). Several informants even referred to these new case studies as additional evidence of the inaccuracy of the overly technocratic interpretation of Loudon's original work that had emerged in the 1990s.

By defining different models for the organization of delivery care for countries with different epidemiological profiles and health system capabilities, countries were encouraged to reject universal blueprints and identify solutions that would be better adapted to each country's health system and socio-economic context (Koblinsky and Cambell, 2003). Indeed, several of our more policy-oriented informants repeatedly highlighted the "operational" value of these studies. The case study method, explained one, is "strongly grounded with the stakeholder at the country level and it looks toward country-level and regional-level success as a guiding principle in its learning." Recent attention to the success story provided by Bangladesh, which has reduced its MMR over the past 30 years *despite* low coverage of SBAs and high levels of home birthing, is perhaps the most significant recent example of the openness with which SMI experts are adopting new and quite flexible epistemological practices. In-depth analyses of the Bangladeshi data suggest that MM decline can be attributed to a range of factors, including a fall in abortion-related deaths, better access to EmOC, and community-based delivery care systems in case of emergencies, as well as key policies that expand women's access to education and more affordable health services (Chowdhury et al., 2009). Those involved in these studies do not believe that the Bangladesh case study invalidates the general importance now attributed to SBAs or facility-based birth. Rather, they argue that "MM reduction is much more complex than [just training and] putting in skilled birth attendants."

At the close of the first decade of the 21st century, SMI experts have thus found themselves repeating a message they have been focusing on for more than two decades: that health change is not simply about training workers to scale up intervention but involves engagement with health systems, politics, equity, and government.

13.9   The ethics of epistemological power

In reflecting on the issues raised in this chapter, and specifically on the difficulties of keeping epistemic diversity on the agenda, some of our informants used ethical arguments that we (to make our own position clear) empathize with and support. Key amongst these is the way political and advocacy uses of cost-effectiveness evidence marginalize other forms of evidence, including not just case study approaches, but also basic monitoring data, which tend to be either of poor quality or under-utilized (Gabrysch et al., 2011). In fact, as historians such as Loudon highlighted, one key ingredient in national-level success stories like that of Sweden relates to the careful and locally empowering documentation of MM. In contrast to collecting statistics for the purposes of global and national accountability, data collection at the local level appears to be essential for generating political will and for developing localized pragmatic action over the long term (for similar debates in the field of health systems and broader development, see Mills, 2012 and White, 2009, respectively).

However, so powerful have experimental designs become that some of our informants from developing countries felt that investing in randomized controlled trials over other forms of evidence production would make their countries "advanced" and governed in more "cost-efficient" ways (Béhague et al., 2009). Yet, as several of our informants pointed out, industrialized countries reduced MM well before the popularization of experimental epistemologies. Some of our informants further argued that the health system fragmentation induced by the cost-effectiveness ethos has been positively detrimental. "I am convinced that our over-emphasis on evidence and numbers has basically slowed safe motherhood down," a demographer active in both academia and an NGO stated, "if we only focus on small things that go on within facilities or small things that affect women's behaviour without looking at the political and social environment in which policy decisions are made, we can't really hope to get very far." Similarly, a prominent epidemiologist and policy-advisor argued,

> If you look at the UK over the last 100 years, we have developed, reduced mortality, etc … by putting all the pieces together … but …. I don't think we are doing this in developing countries. I'm always a bit surprised and concerned when agencies think, well, if we just focus on this [technical component], we'll get it right. But we've never done that in any developed country. We've always had all of it, together.

For researchers such as these, the combined weight of observational studies, historical research, and both clinical and managerial common sense should be considered sufficiently conclusive to make further experimental study into the effectiveness of targeted interventions unjustifiable and indeed unethical.

A less explicit but no less important ethical dilemma raised by our informants relates to the extent to which the tenets of objective and neutral science have dampened open and transparent debate about the politics of health, particularly when evidence is used in the service of a neoliberal cost-saving agenda that promotes a narrow clinical focus. In fundamental ways, historical case study analyses have pointed to the importance of the political processes that account for improved health, and specifically, the role of a welfare-oriented government and publically funded services in ensuring health equity (Van Lerberghe and De Brouwere, 2001b). Though few of our informants were willing to discuss the role of politics beyond simply highlighting the importance of equity, our analysis indicates that this remains a key, if implicit, perspective within the SMI.

The issues raised by these critical SMI actors are key ingredients in what was previously known as "social medicine" and is now characterized as the movement for "social justice" in global health (Marmot et al., 2012). Though the aims of social justice are quite clear – "to reduce unfair differences in health between social groups within a country and among countries" (Marmot et al., 2012: 27) – what is perhaps less well defined is how to politicize health in the current evidence-based climate. Recognizing the sensitivities that being overtly political entails for epidemiologists and public health experts more generally, the SMI case study might be read as providing researchers in public health and development with inspiration for reflecting on their own practice. Given the long-standing geopolitical challenges and lessons of development (Escobar, 1995), it may be worth considering whether producing large impact studies of targeted interventions – or even qualitative studies demonstrating the suffering of the poor, for that matter – may have less utility than in-depth and theoretically informed case studies on societal and political mechanisms of sustainable change.

Notes

1. This chapter draws upon and extends arguments put forward in Behague and Storeng (2013).
2. We would like to thank all our informants for being such forthright and helpful participants in this research. We also like to thank colleagues in the Maternal Health Group at the London School of Hygiene and Tropical

Medicine (LSHTM) for their feedback, and Drs Laura Camfield and Richard Palmer-Jones, who invited us to present this research at the Research Ethics in Economic and Social Research workshop at the University of East Anglia. The Economic and Social Research Council (RES-000-22-1039) and the Research Council of Norway funded this research. From 2005 to 2010, a Postdoctoral Fellowship from The Wellcome Trust (GR077175MA) supported D. Béhague. Since 2010, a Postdoctoral Fellowship from the Research Council of Norway has supported K. Storeng. The funders were not involved in determining the study design, and the collection, analysis, and interpretation of data, or in writing this chapter. The LSHTM ethics board approved the study.

3. If anything, the evidence-based movement has progressively appropriated a greater array of non-statistical methodologies – named variously narrative, qualitative, operational, or participatory research – not for in-depth critical analysis of health change, but for the very same purposes of advocacy and accountability to which quantitative data have been increasingly put (Lambert, 2006).

4. In turning to history, SMI experts were also partially attempting to address the debilitating "measurement gap" by learning from countries that had instated accurate statistical surveillance systems already in the mid-1850s.

5. Not surprisingly, these authors contributed to a growing position that emerged in the mid-2000s to press donors and governments to eliminate the user-fees that had been instated in the 1980s in many countries, at least when it came to emergency maternity care.

6. By considering countries with socio-epidemiological profiles that are allegedly more similar to contemporary developing country contexts, these authors' explicit aim was also to address an emerging critique that questions the applicability of universalizing "lessons learned" from the industrialized West to countries across the globe.

References

Abouzahr, C. (2003) Safe motherhood: A brief history of the global movement 1947–2002. *British Medical Bulletin*, 67: 13–25.

Adams, V. (2005) Saving Tibet? An inquiry into modernity, lies, truths, and beliefs. *Medical Anthropology*, 24: 71–110.

Appadurai, A. (1994) Commodities and the politics of value. In: Pearce, S. (ed.) *Interpreting Objects and Collections* (London: Routledge), p. 76–91.

Béhague, D. and Storeng, K. (2007) Final report: An ethnography of evidence-based policy-making in international maternal health. Grant number Res-00-22-1039. Economic and Social Research Council. http://www.esrc.ac.uk/my-esrc/grants/RES-000-22-1039/outputs/Read/feda13d7-980b-4328-b0bc-8da0e1dcfeb0

Béhague, D. and Storeng, K. (2008) Collapsing the vertical-horizontal divide in public health: Lessons from an ethnographic study of evidence-based policy making in maternal health. *American Journal of Public Health*, 98(4): 644–649.

Béhague, D., Tawiah, C., Rosato, M., Somed, T. and Morrison, J. (2009) Evidence-based policy-making: The implications of globally-applicable research for context-specific problem-solving in developing countries. *Social Science & Medicine*, 69: 1539–1546.

Béhague D. P. and Storeng, K. T. (2013) Pragmatic politics and epistemological diversity: The contested and authoritative uses of historical evidence in the Safe Motherhood Initiative. *Evidence and Policy*, 9(1): 65–85.

Berridge, V. (2008) History matters? History's role in health policy making. *Medical History*, 52: 311–326.

Cetina, K. K. (1999) *Epistemic Cultures: How the Sciences Make Knowledge* (Cambridge: Harvard University Press).

Chowdhury, M. E., Ahmed, A., Kalim, N. and Koblinsky, M. (2009) Causes of maternal mortality decline in Matlab, Bangladesh. *Journal of Health, Population and Nutrion*, 27: 108–123.

Cueto, M. (2004) The origins of primary health care and selective primary health care. *American Journal of Public Health*, 94(11): 1864–1874.

Daston, L. (1992) Objectivity and the escape from perspective. *Social Studies of Science*, 22: 597–618.

Davey Smith, G., Ebrahim, S. and Frankel, S. (2001) How policy informs the evidence: Evidence based thinking can lead to debased policy making. *British Medical Journal*, 322: 184–185.

De Brouwere, V., Tonglet, R. and Van Lerberghe, W. (1998) Strategies for reducing maternal mortality in developing countries: What can we learn from the history of the industrialized west? *Tropical Medicine & International Health*, 3: 771–782.

Escobar, A. (1995) *Encountering Development: The Making and Unmaking of the Third World* (Princeton: Princeton University Press).

Foucault, M. (1994 [1970]) *The Order of Things: An Archaeology of the Human Sciences* (New York: Vintage).

Gabrysch, S., Zanger, P., Seneviratne, H., Mbewe, R. and Campbell, O. (2011) Tracking progress towards safe motherhood: Meeting the benchmark yet missing the goal? An appeal for better use of health-system output indicators with evidence from Zambia and Sri Lanka. *Tropical Medicine & International Health*, 16: 627–639.

Geissler, P (2001) Introduction: Studying trial communities: Anthropological and historical inquiries into ethos, politics and economy of medical research in Africa. In: Geissler, P. and Molyneu, C. (eds) *Evidence, Ethos and Experiment: The Anthropology and History of Medical Research in Africa* (Oxford: Bergahn).

Goodburn, E. and Campbell, O. (2001) Reducing maternal mortality in the developing world: Sector-wide approaches may be the key. *British Medical Journal*, 322(7291): 917–920.

Graham, W., Bell, J. and Bullough, C. (2001) Can skilled attendance at delivery reduce maternal mortality in developing countries? *Studies in Health Services Organisation and Policy*, 17: 97–130.

Graham, W. and Campbell, O. (1992) Maternal health and the measurement trap. *Social Science and Medicine*, 35: 867–977.

Hacking, I. (1990) *The Taming of Chance* (Cambridge: Cambridge University Press).

Hacking, I. (1992) Statistical language, statistical truth, and statistical reason: The self-authentification of a style of scientific reasoning. In: McMullin, E. (ed.) *The Social Dimension of Science* (Notre Dame: Notre Dame Press).

Harding, S. (2008) *Sciences from Below: Feminisms, Postcoloniatialies, and Modernities* (Durham, NC: Duke University Press).

Högberg, U., Wallb, S. and Broströmc, G. (1986) The impact of early medical technology on maternal mortality in late 19th century Sweden. *International Journal of Gynecology & Obstetrics*, 24: 251–261.

Holmes, D. and Marcus, G. (2008) Cultures of expertise and the management of globalization: Toward the re-functioning of ethnography. In: Ong, A. and Collier, S. (eds) *Global Assemblages: Technology, Politics, and Ethics as Anthropological Problems* (Oxford, UK: Blackwell Publishing Ltd).

Koblinsky, M. and Cambell, O. (2003) Factors affecting the reduction of maternal mortality. In: Koblinsky, M. (ed.) *Reducing Maternal Mortality: Learning from Bolivia, China, Egypt, Honduras, Indonesia, Jamaica, and Zimbabwe* (Washington DC: The World Bank).

Koblinsky, M., Campbell, O. and Heichelheim J. (1999) Organizing delivery care: What works for safe motherhood? *Bulletin of the World Health Organization*, 77: 399–406.

Lambert, H. (2006) Accounting for EBM: Contested notions of evidence in medicine. *Social Science and Medicine*, 62, 2633–2645.

Lambert, H., Gordon, E. and Bogdan-Lovis, L. (2006) Introduction: Gift horse or trojan horse? Social science perspectives on evidence-based health care [special issue on evidence-based medicine and practice]. *Social Science and Medicine*, 62: 2613–2620.

Laurell, A. and Arellanbo, O. (1996) Market commodities and poor relief: The World Bank proposal for health. *International Journal of Health Services*, 26: 1–18.

Liljestrand, J. and Pathmanathan, I. (2004) Reducing maternal mortality: Can we derive policy guidance from developing country experiences? *Journal of Public Health Policy*, 25: 299–314.

Loudon, I. (1986) Deaths in childbed from the eighteenth century to 1935. *Medical History* 30: 1–41.

Loudon, I. (1991) On maternal and infant mortality, 1900–1960. *Social History of Medicine*, 4: 29–73.

Loudon, I. (1992a) *Death in Childbirth: An International Study of Maternal Care and Maternal Mortality, 1800–1950* (Oxford: Clarendon Press).

Loudon, I. (1992b) The transformation of maternal mortality. *British Medical Journal*, 305: 1557–1560.

Loudon, I. (2000) Maternal mortality in the past and its relevance to developing countries today. *American Journal of Clinical Nutrition*, 72: 241s–246s.

Mahler, H. (1987) The safe motherhood initiative: A call to action. *The Lancet*, March 21: 668–670.

Maine, D. and Rosenfield, A. (1999) The safe motherhood initiative: Why has it stalled? *American Journal of Public Health*, 89: 480–482.

Marmot, M., Allen, J., Bell, R. and Goldblatt, P. (2012) Building of the global movement for health equity: From Santiago to Rio and beyond. *The Lancet*, 379: 181–188.

Mccoy, D. (2004) Pushing the international health research agenda towards equity and effectiveness. *The Lancet*, 364: 1630–631.

McPake, B. (2006) Recognising patterns: Health systems research beyond controlled trials. *Health Systems Discussion Group* (London: London School of Hygiene and Tropical Medicine).

Miller, S., Sloan, N., Winikoff, B., Langer, A. and Fikree, F. (2003) Where is the "E" in MCH? The need for an evidence-based approach in safe motherhood. *Journal of Midwifery and Women's Health*, 48: 10–18.

Mills, A. (2012) Health policy and systems research: Defining the terrain; identifying the methods. *Health Policy and Planning*, 27: 1–7.

Morgan, M. (2012) *The World in the Model: How Economists Work and Think* (Cambridge: Cambridge University Press).

Mykhalovskiy, E. and Weir, L. (2004) The problem of evidence-based medicine: Directions for social science. *Social Science and Medicine*, 59: 1059–1069.

Pathmanathan, I., Liljestrand, J., Martins, J., Rajapaksa, L., Lissner, C., Silva, A. D., Selvaraju, S. and Singh, P. (2003) *Investing in Maternal Health: Learning from Malaysia and Sri Lanka* (Washington, DC: World Bank).

Paxton, A., Maine, D., Freedman, L., Fry, D. and Lobis, S. (2005) The evidence for emergency obstetric care. *International Journal of Gynecology and Obstetrics*, 88: 181–193.

Pearce, N. (1996) Traditional epidemiology, modern epidemiology, and public health. *American Journal of Public Health*, 86: 678–683.

Pickering, A. (1992) From science as knowledge to science as practice. In: Pickering, A. (ed.) *Science as Culture and Practice* (Chicago: University of Chicago Press).

Porter, T. (1992) Objectivity as standardization: The rhetoric of impersonality in measurement, statistics and cost-benefit analysis. *Annals of Scholarship*, 9: 19–59.

Rifkin, S. B. and Walt, G. (1986) Why health improves: Defining the issues concerning "comprehensive primary health care" and "selective primary health care." *Social Science and Medicine*, 23: 559–566.

Rose, N. (1996) Governing "advanced" liberal democracies. In: Barry, A., Osborne, T. and Rose, N. (eds) *Foucault and Political Reason: Liberalism, Neoliberalism, and Rationalities* (Chicago: University of Chicago Press).

Rose, N. (2007) *The Politics of Life Itself: Biomedicine, Power, and Subjectivity in the Twenty-First Century* (Princeton: Princeton University Press).

Rosenfield, A. and Maine, D. (1985) Maternal mortality—a neglected tragedy: where is the M in MCH? *The Lancet*, 2(8446), 83–85.

Shiffman, J. (2003) Generating political will for safe motherhood in Indonesia. *Social Science and Medicine*, 56: 1197–1207.

Starrs, A. M. (2006) Safe motherhood initiative: 20 years and counting. *The Lancet*, 368: 2–4.

Storeng, K. (2010) Safe motherhood: The making of a global health initiative (London: University of London.)

Storeng, K. and Béhague, D. (2014) Playing the "numbers game": Evidence-based advocacy for safe motherhood. *Medical Anthropology Quarterly*, DOI: 10.1111/maq.12072.

Strathern, M. (ed.) (2000) *Audit Cultures: Anthropological Studies in Accountability, Ethics, and the Academy* (New York: Routledge).

Timmermans, S. and Berg, M. (2003) *The Gold Standard: The Challenge of Evidence-based Medicine and Standardization in Health Care* (Philadelphia: Temple University Press).

Travis, P., Bennet, S., Haines, A., Pang, T., Bhutta, Z., Hyder, A. A., Pielemeier, N. R., Mills, A. and Evans, T. (2004) Overcoming health-systems constraints to achieve the millennium development goals. *The Lancet*, 364: 900–906.

Van Lerberghe, W. and De Brouwere, V. (2001a) Of blind alleys and things that have worked: History's lessons on reducing maternal mortality. *Studies in Health Service Organization and Policy*, 17: 7–33.

Van Lerberghe, W. and De Brouwere, V. (2001b) Reducing maternal mortality in the context of poverty. *Studies in Health Services Organisation & Policy*, 17: 1–33.

Victora, C., Habicht, J. and Bryce, J. (2004) Evidence-based public health: Moving beyond randomized trials. *American Journal of Public Health*, 94: 400–405.

White, H. (2009) Theory-based impact evaluation: Principles and practice. *Journal of Development Effectiveness*, 1: 271–284.

WHO (1978) Primary health care: A joint report by the directorate-general of the who and the executive director of the United Nations children's fund on the international conference on primary health care (Alma-Ata, USSR: WHO).

WHO (1994) Mother-baby package: Implementing safe motherhood in countries (Geneva: World Health Organization).

Young, A. (1981a) The creation of medical knowledge: Some problems in interpretation. *Social Science and Medicine*, 15(3): 379–386.

Young, A. (1981b) When rational men fall sick: An inquiry into some assumptions made by medical anthropologists. *Culture, Medicine and Psychiatry*, 5: 317–335.

14
Conclusion

Laura Camfield

In the concluding chapter I briefly review the challenges faced in key areas for research in international development,[1] such as understanding and measuring poverty and well-being and studying poverty over time; identify the main international organizations, institutions, and programmes working in this field (see Tables 14A.1 and 14A.2 in the Appendix); and discuss the lessons that can be drawn from the preceding chapters.

14.1 Defining and measuring poverty

Within development economic measures of poverty and development such as the World Bank's "dollar a day" predominate (Sumner, 2007). Methods of calculation are hotly debated by economists and sociologists who argue that the monetary poverty lines which guide resource allocation ignore the multifaceted nature of human deprivation and can lead to misidentification of the poor (Saith, 2005; Deaton, 2010; Roelen, this volume). There is a growing emphasis on multidimensional measures such as the Multidimensional Poverty Index (Alkire and Santos, 2010) which was included in the United Nations Development Programme's 2010 Human Development Report. These measures go beyond income and the subset of dimensions captured by the widely used Human Development Index (income, literacy and life-expectancy) although by increasing the number of dimensions they create challenges in relation to their weighting. The recognition that survey measures cannot currently capture everything that is important to poor people, fuelled in part by the growth in research using "participatory" methods (White and Pettit, 2004; Chambers, 2007), has caused economists to look for reliable measures of "missing dimensions" such as shame and agency (Alkire, 2007). This quest has not been wholly successful due to the culturally and historically specific nature of these concepts (Christopher, 1999) and the public nature of survey adminis- tration which reduces the accuracy of responses to sensitive questions. However, simple and more complex measures of subjective well-being (for example, the "general happiness question" or the "ladder," see http://worlddatabaseofhappiness.eur.nl/) are widely used in household and national surveys in developing countries (Camfield and McGregor, 2009; Graham, 2009). There is also growing interest in influences on people's behaviour (Coulthard et al., this volume) such as their psy- chosocial competencies (Dercon and Krishnan, 2009) and aspirations (Ray, 2006; Bernard et al., 2011). However, the emphasis on individual resources characteristic of purely subjective approaches is seen by some as a way to "support" people's movements out of poverty without changing prevailing economic structures (cf. Green and Hulme, 2005).

Many of the challenges faced by researchers trying to measure poverty and well-being were discussed in the Introduction; I briefly recap here, drawing on questions raised in the preceeding chapters. The first chal- lenge is defining poverty in a way that is measurable, comparable, and true to the understandings and priorities of the people the definition is being applied to. As Roelen (this volume) explains, this is far from easy, and may result in a mismatch between concept and indicator (e.g. the UNICEF (2007) global report card uses "liking school a lot" as its indicator of subjective well-being). A second challenge is capturing the multidimensional nature of poverty, something Coulthard et al., Bevan. and P. Davis also explore (this volume), and using relevant contextual knowledge or other explicit criteria to decide how these dimensions should be weighted. A third challenge is in the area of relationships – how can one establish the importance and often dual-edged nature of relationships and capture sensitive dimensions such as alcohol-related violence, something Coulthard et al. touch upon in their chapter. Fourthly, as Roelen explains in relation to children, measures are being applied to a moving target and both the content and the salience of different dimensions change over time. Finally, as both Bevan and Nasirumbi et al. outline, poverty has different impacts on different household members, which cannot necessarily be captured using a conventional household survey method.

14.2   Studying poverty over time[2]

A second area of interest is the impact of poverty throughout the life course and at moments of physiological or social vulnerability (for example, during the first two years of life while the structure of the brain is developing, or at the start of primary school) (see also Roelen, this volume). Greater attention is being paid to the "early years" (age 0–4), expressed in the growth of Early Childhood Development programmes and cash transfers targeted at the mothers of this age group, and to the effects of early-life experiences in adulthood. There is also a growing recognition that the majority of elderly people live in low- or middle-income countries (Lloyd-Sherlock, 2010) and that making cash transfers to elderly people often benefits their grandchildren as well (e.g. Duflo, 2003). The use of cash transfers connects to another area of research on chronic poverty and poverty dynamics through the attention paid to arresting the intergenerational transfer of poverty (Shepherd et al., 2011; P. Davis and Roelen, this volume).

Research into poverty dynamics seeks not only to map trends, but also to understand the processes behind these trends, namely what moves people out of or into poverty and why people remain poor.[3] While practitioners are interested in the characteristics of the chronically poor (Eyben, 2007), recent research in this area is more concerned with the role of politics and relationships in keeping people poor (Mosse, 2010, Van Dijk, 2011, Coulthard et al., this volume). In this section I summarize some of the challenges of research in this area, for example, operating at the micro as well as the macro level and recognizing the importance of history and political economy, as Bevan and P. Davis describe in their chapters. Within longitudinal research the "gold standard" is considered to be repeated surveys of a representative panel of households or cohort of individuals (DFID, 2012), or, on a much smaller scale, sustained ethnographic engagement. This imperative is challenging for a field that essentially lives in the present as setting up panels takes time and money and few funders are prepared to commit funding for at least five years. Secondly, there are obvious risks and costs associated with panel construction in fragile states or with highly mobile populations where the need for data is greatest (Nasirumbi et al., this volume). Thirdly, and related to this, household panels cannot capture the experiences of migrants and those living outside or in unregistered households, which is an increasingly common experience in urban areas. Fourthly, as Roelen argues in her chapter, respondents and settings are continually changing so the initial site selection or questionnaire design will not continue to capture what the study was set up to reflect, even if the questionnaire expands exponentially. Perhaps related to the increasing burdensomeness of the research, attrition is a continual problem (Taylor et al., this volume), including attrition of the research team. The fission and reformation of households present additional challenges (Nasirumbi et al., this volume). Finally, there is often a shortage of expertise in panel data analysis, as Duvendack and Palmer-Jones and Behague and Storeng (this volume) argue in relation to econometrics and experimental methods. This limits the involvement of researchers' in-country in the analysis of this data, leading to curiously context-free conclusions.

14.3 Generating evidence

Greater attention is being paid to research design and data generation within development (e.g. Smith, 2007; Laws et al., 2013). However, analysis and representation often represent a black box where even the most experienced authors appear to make interpretive leaps from thin or ambiguous data to conclusive recommendations. This is a problem because as Simpson (2007: 162) notes, "ethical concerns in social science research do not begin and end with the construction of a methodology, but rather are a fundamental part of data analysis, and the knowledge claims we purport to make." The third section of the book explored some of the assumptions underpinning this process, for example, the role played by different epistemologies, and looked at how evidence is actually used (or ignored[4]), drawing on the examples of growth in Africa and the global maternal health movement (G. Davis and Behague and Storeng respectively, this volume). The challenges researchers face relate firstly to the fact that most development research is secondary or even tertiary analysis (Temple et al., 2006), but this is rarely acknowledged and data are not approached with the caution shown by Bornat, G. Davis or Palmer-Jones and Duvendack (this volume). Secondly, as Palmer-Jones and Duvendack, G. Davis and Behague and Storeng separately confirm, there are hierarchies of evidence and some types of analysis and messages are more acceptable than others. Thirdly, in evaluating the strength of evidence behind claims, it is often far from clear how the data were produced which argues for greater transparency and more detailed methodological accounts (cf. the examples provided by P. Davis and Bevan, this volume; see also Shaxon's (2005 in Bakewell, 2007) five criteria for robust evidence). Finally, as Crow and Taylor et al. imply, our representations may fail to do justice to others' realities or be simultaneously effective and respectful.

14.4 Cross-cutting issues

In this section, I draw out the cross-cutting issues raised by the different chapters, which have been loosely grouped under mismatched understandings of research; informed consent; research relationships; researchers' positionality and the value of emic understandings; case-based research; strategies for studying change over time; capturing fieldworkers' insights and sharing research; responsibilities to peers; and analysis, evidence, and replication.

14.4.1 Mismatched understandings of research

Many of the chapters highlighted different understandings of the meaning and purpose of research among different stakeholders (for example, problem-solving, communication, and advocacy). Participants may not understand the limitations to preserving anonymity in a community study, or even think that this is desirable – in Taylor et al. NGO participants saw anonymization as a disadvantage because they could not use their participation in funding bids or publicity materials. There is an inherent tension between the researcher's interest in contradictions between what is said and done[5] and participants' need for consistent self-presentation (Taylor et al., this volume), and avoidance of washing "dirty linen" in public (Srinivas in Crow, this volume). For example, Young and Wilmott's work in Bethnal Green was accused of lack of rigour because they tried not to create "discord" by asking awkward questions. The imperative for research to be palatable was noted by Warwick and Littlejohn (in Crow, this volume) who ask whether "a community study [can] ever be a negotiated product in which sociologists are not the only definer of the situation?" Evidence from the other chapters suggests that much development research is negotiated in this way; however, participants are rarely the most powerful voices.

While in some cases participants are keen to have their views heard, or communicate their needs to a service provider, there is "respondent burden" in terms of both time and the potentially unreasonable expectation of researchers that participants will expose their internal processes to external scrutiny to an extent that most researchers would not feel comfortable with. Crow notes that community dissatisfaction with Gallaher's research on Plainville was expressed in the language of trust, a point also made by Arvidson. Experiences of trust betrayed may partially arise from different understandings of what researchers will use data for. This presents a particular problem in obtaining informed consent for data archiving as data are likely to be used in a way that even the original researchers could not have anticipated (for example, Bornat describes her own use of archived data on the history of geriatrics to explore the racialized experiences of South Asian doctors working in the newly formed UK National Health Service).

14.4.2   Informed consent

The mismatch between researchers' and participants' expectations questions the meaning of *informed* consent – to what extent is it genuinely informed, given that it may be hard to describe all the implications of participation? And who can grant it for an organization, especially when that organization is in a state of flux? Taylor et al. observe that dynamics of consent vary for different organizations, which is an important point to bear in mind when "studying up," as some may be vulnerable in ways that are not immediately apparent. She recommends moving to a process-based understanding of consent (see also Arvidson, this voulme), which is not about formal consent but about "creating access" – "educating, familiarising and even selling the research to staff who are prospective participants." The research implications of this are obvious as in a comparative, case-based study, differential levels of access, or changes in access across rounds after the departure of a gatekeeper, reduce comparability.

14.4.3   Research relationships

A processual understanding of consent directs attention towards the emotional labour of creating and maintaining relationships to ensure continued access – where intimacy between researchers and respondents is effectively used as a research "tool" (Arvidson). The use of the word "tool" alerts us to a potential problem which is that developing instrumental relationships with informants will invariably leave them feeling "sore" and used (Srinivas in Crow). Combining an ethical and instrumental motivation for creating intimacy may entail cognitive dissonance as "while the building of rapport and intimacy are primarily interpreted as ethically informed approaches, they have become commodified, professionalized, and are now part of any sociologist's toolkit" (Arvidson). Even though one of the commonplaces of guides to development research is the need to build trust and demonstrate genuine interest through revisits, perhaps we should be more concerned about the ethics of "faking friendship" if identities and boundaries are not clearly maintained. Arvidson raises a further question of whether intimacy always generates good data (see also Simpson, 2007) and describes the advantages of more formal approaches, both in terms of the quality of the analysis (some distance may be necessary for analysis to have credibility) and the relationship with participants (interviewing them rather than conversing with them may make them feel respected). She asks whether it always good practice to try to blend into the background and avoid conflict, which can be productive in exposing perspectives and practices that might otherwise have remained hidden (Taylor et al., this volume). Owning your status as a researcher – and therefore by definition an outsider – may avoid blurring of boundaries in longitudinal research which exacerbates clashes between different ethical realms, for example, research, friendship, and community norms. There is a clear tension between research ethics, which Arvidson characterizes as passive and vague (what does it mean to "protect all those involved in the research"?) and the ethics of community interaction. A further consideration in relation to interaction is the choice of gatekeeper, which can be seen as a dimension of a researcher's positionality that needs be explicitly acknowledged, as it affects how researchers are perceived, the relationships they can form, and the information they can access.

14.4.4 Researchers' positionality and the value of emic understandings

One of the implicit themes of this volume is the way biographical and historical time provides alternative contexts for research (for example, researchers' interests – often shaped by organizational affiliations and disciplines, their values, their gender, and their age). Crow describes how Goran Djurfeldt and colleagues returned to India 25 years later to find that their setting and even their previously collected data looked very different because they were no longer framing it in dependency theory – "25 years is almost half the working life time of a researcher, and it is not only the village and the villagers that have changed but so have we." Bornat identifies a similar lacuna in her earlier interviews with mill workers where because her research focus was the wage relationship she saw one respondent's discussion of a religious experience as an irrelevant digression, neglecting the importance of religion in working-class culture at that time. Bevan also emphasizes the importance of being conscious of and transparent about where you are coming from as a researcher. She outlines a nine-fold "Foundations of Knowledge Framework" which looks at the domain of interest, values, ontology, epistemology, theory, research design, research answers (evidence), rhetoric (dissemination), and praxis (implications for policy). She shows how domain of interest, theory, and methodology interact to generate a research design, fieldwork, data, and evidence, which loop back to inform the original domain of interest, theory, and methodology. The process Bevan describes is similar to Behague and Storeng's concept of "para-ethnographic reasoning" which highlights the way epistemological assumptions embedded in particular methodologies shape our understandings of the world. Behague and Storeng argue that researchers should acknowledge that methodological reasoning is social and contextual rather than purely cognitive, which means that methods cannot be arbitrarily "mixed" without understanding the meta-narratives that underpin assumptions about the topic being researched (Roelen, this volume). If knowledge is contingent and provisional and pertains to a certain context, this affects what we can know, including the forms of analysis we can do and claims we can make. Nonetheless, Bevan and P. Davis argue separately that it is possible to "generalize to theory" by identifying patterned similarities and common processes and mechanisms rather than universal laws.

Foregrounding context acknowledges the importance of time (the past is also responsible for the current state of a complex system) and of the social relationships and structures which influences people's behaviours, as Coulthard et al. explain in relation to fishers. Chronology and relationality are encompassed within a three-dimensional well-being approach which Coulthard et al. see as beneficial to development research because it offers a deeper former of "social impact assessment." It does this by capturing the social and psychological implications of fisheries decline and increasing understanding of fishers' behaviour. This is especially important where people's behaviour does not appear (economically) rational, and forms part of an ethical commitment to understanding that even people living in dire circumstances are conscious of how they are doing in life and have some capacity to achieve well-being as they perceive it. For example, P. Davis describes an emic concept of well-being in Bangladesh, "Obosta," which encompasses "income and assets, health, social status or prestige, having good social relationships, and a sense of security." However, he argues that researchers need to include liabilities and disabilities as well as assets and capabilities to get a rounded picture of people's lives. Roelen and Coulthard et al. draw similarly on local understandings of thresholds at which people would be considered poor or in need and use information from other studies to critically evaluate the cut-offs for their measures.

Definitions present a perennial problem for measurement within development research, as discussed in the first part of the Conclusion. Nasirumbi et al. describe the challenges of defining households in a way that respects local understandings and recognize the implications of different definitions in capturing change over time. For example, an apparent rise in female-headed households may be due to defining households with migrant or polygynous partners as single-headed, and an apparent fall in assets may be due to the spreading of assets over two compounds, which are actually part of the same household. Nasirumbi et al. argue that studies need explicit and complex decision rules when tracking households to decide whether they are in fact the same, especially given the high mortality and marital instability in the Ugandan context in which they are working. Without these it is not possible to compare results across studies as they may have different understandings of what constitutes a household and/ or a household's continuation over time that have not been made explicit.

14.4.5 Case-based research

While not a criteria for inclusion in this volume, most of the empirical studies are case-based and use a mix of purposive and stratified random sampling to create comparative "cases" at different levels, e.g. agricultural systems and vulnerable households. Bevan and P. Davis highlight the value of comparative case-based research as a way of identifying causal mechanisms within individual trajectories and the interaction of endowments and life events in shaping these trajectories. This enables the identification of points of intervention for social and development policy (see also Coulthard et al.), for example, assets identified by poor people tend to be protective, e.g. government assistance, rather than developmental, e.g. land acquisition, which suggests the limited nature of government/ development assistance in moving people out of poverty. Bevan suggests that it is also possible to identify "control parameters" as a potential site for intervention because these act to inhibit change and ensure that systems reproduce themselves. One advantage of case-based analysis is that its method of classification fits with the way that people think, for example, their use of stereotypes to guide their responses. For this reason, Behague and Storeng suggest that it is particularly accessible to country policymakers because it is grounded in particular contexts and focuses on success at country and regional level.[6]

There are multiple different approaches within case-based research as cases can be analysed in terms of their internal dynamics and location within a larger system or compared to find diversities or regularities. Bevan's focus is on "variates" (traces of complex systems) rather than "variables" as the latter terminology tends to reify measurements such as years of schooling. Reification turns them from indicators into causal factors, forgetting that "what exists are complex systems ... what we measure are traces of the systems that make up reality." One example of a complex system in development research is the household and Nasirumbi et al., Davis and Roelen employ various strategies to understand what goes on within households and cross-check information, for example, monthly visits, interviews with senior males and females, and focusing on child outcomes.

14.4.6   Strategies for studying change over time

In-depth understanding of contexts needs to be combined with an understanding of how these change over time, hence the common concern as to the lack of longitudinal quantitative and qualitative data sets in developing countries (DFID 2012). This lack inhibits many of the beneficial practices discussed in this volume such as longitudinal analysis (Roelen), secondary analysis (Bornat, Crow), and replication (G. Davis and Duvendack and Palmer-Jones). The establishment of the Qualidata archive (described in Bornat) was prompted by a study in 1991 which estimated that due to lack of archival facilities 90 per cent of qualitative data had been lost and the 10 per cent that remained was not preserved under conditions that enabled re-use. The absence of reliable longitudinal data causes researchers to adopt a synchronic perspective, which reduces understanding of why people remain poor, especially as the characteristics of the chronic and transient poor and those who are income poor and poor in multiple dimensions are usually different (P. Davis, Roelen). It also reduces understanding of children's well-being as their needs and aspirations change over time (Roelen). Arguably the same is true of adults who also progress through defined life stages, albeit in a non-linear and dynamic way, and may adapt to better or worse circumstances and change aspirations accordingly – hence Coulthard et al.'s emphasis on the subjective. The need for a diachronic perspective is one reason why Bornat advocates secondary analysis as it offers opportunities to broaden the temporal and spatial lens of a study, as well as raising useful questions around the status, production, and ownership of knowledge.

14.4.7   Capturing fieldworkers' insights and sharing research

The role of embedded knowledge in interpretation was discussed in the Introduction and the following chapters described strategies used by different researchers to ensure this is included in analysis. For example, Bevan describes debriefing workshops with fieldworkers and P. Davis requested fieldwork diaries which were then translated and became part of the qualitative data set. The way the fieldwork is structured is clearly important as doing a smaller number of interviews each day gave fieldworkers time to reflect and record their reflections. P. Davis also visited every household in the sample to check his interpretation of their accounts and discuss emerging findings.

Bevan emphasizes the importance of sharing findings as soon as possible and describes efforts to engage policymakers, local officials, and donor and NGO staff through "rapid policy briefings" and an online "worknet" (this shared workshop powerpoints, briefing notes and reports). However, she also notes – as discussed in the Introduction – that the appetite for research is reduced by the high turnover of NGO and donor staff and disconnects between the mental models of donors and government (see also Bakewell, 2007).

14.4.8 Responsibilities to peers

In the Introduction I outlined responsibilities to multiple groups "as well as the subject" (the title of the seminar series where many of these chapters were developed). In relation to peers, data sets can be seen as training resources in the same way that returning to the fieldsites of supervisors, guided by their notes and diaries, was once seen as a rite of passage for young anthropologists (Bornat). Nonetheless, engaging with other people's data, whether qualitative or quantitative, is not a "short cut" as it requires considerable effort and creativity to understand the context of the study (cf. G Davis's battle with Sachs and Warner's data sets). Drawing on earlier research might, however, be an important part of a pilot stage, e.g. in developing an interview schedule for piloting. Even revisiting one's own data from a different life stage or theoretical perspective can be illuminating (cf. Djurfeld and Mauthner et al. in Crow and Bornat respectively), and this opportunity would have been enjoyed by anthropologists such as Mead who maintained long relationships with the communities they studied. There is a question of whether it is ethically appropriate to ask new questions of data as this may not be what the respondents signed up for (cf. Bornat's geriatricians) and may be misleading if, for example, a study of access to water is used to draw conclusions about awareness of human rights (Bakewell, 2007). While to some extent data are constructed through analysis (Mauthner), they have a prior existence (Hammersley) that limits the conclusions that can be drawn from them – "data is given as well as constructed" (Hammersley in Bornat).

14.4.9 Analysis, evidence, and replication

The final lessons to be drawn relate to the process of analysis and how this can best be shared (for example, by using Qualitative Data Analysis software and then archiving the analysed files as well as the raw data as P. Davis and Bevan have done). Of course, this may be assuming a commitment to openness on the part of researchers that doesn't currently exist, as Bornat and Duvendack and Palmer-Jones outline in relation to qualitative and quantitative researchers respectively.

The broader context to the interest in the "black box" of analysis within development is the growth of medical models of evidence-based policy and the increasing influence of development economics on development policy. The increase in influence of (selected) development research makes its quality even more important – as G. Davis observes, we need to demonstrate that analyses are replicable before basing policy on them. However, G. Davis and Duvendack and Palmer-Jones also note a lack of enthusiasm for replication that borders on hostility, despite its role in highlighting error and over-interpretation. Replication also has an important teaching role, although uncritical replication can socialize students into practices that reinforce the doxa of economics, and replication can be used as a disciplinary tool when findings do not fit with prevailing orthodoxy.[7] Nonetheless, in the same way that students of international development are encouraged to review other studies before embarking on their own, replicating existing studies should be a prerequisite to further work in an area.

14.5   Conclusion

The concluding points relate to the ways in which development researchers establish their credibility and persuade others of their conclusions. In the same way that qualitative researchers claim that only they can establish the rapport and intimacy required to hear the "voices of the poor," economists use quantification and mathematization as "barriers to entry to influential and lucrative opportunities" offered by development actors (Duvendack and Palmer-Jones). The status of these techniques is challenged by unsuccessful replications, hence the lack of enthusiasm for replication at a disciplinary level. Behague and Storeng find similarly that competition by health advocacy coalitions for the large amounts of philanthropic funding available within global health reduces opportunities for (public) critique as "to criticize an EmOC strategy ... was tantamount to repudiating donor support and undermining the field's international credibility." Despite these powerful disciplinary mechanisms, they identify a small group of epidemiologists, many of whom have worked extensively in developing countries, who use a marginalized form of evidence – historical case studies – to argue for a broader and more political understanding of the determinants of change over time.

Duvendack and Palmer-Jones identify "persuasive practices" within the reporting of research, for example, identifying oneself with a popular pre-existing position (see also Behague and Storeng) and using rhetorical devices such as "demonstration of authority or expertise, obscuring or marginalization of counter-arguments, abuse of logic [and] spurious or misleading quantification." Here, as with the maternal health specialists described in Behague and Storeng, development researchers are advised to "keep it simple" as this makes for effective advocacy. It also provides new development actors such as private philanthropists with the "low hanging fruit" that results-based organizations such as the Gates Foundation prefer to target. Nonetheless, as Behague and Storeng and others have identified, this can have perverse effects[8] and directing attention away from the "interconnected biological, social, political and economic determinants of health [or poverty]" to please prospective funders may not be the most ethical course of action for development researchers. As Cowen (2011) argues in relation to the US education system, international development may now be eating all the "low hanging fruit" and future development researchers will have to wrestle with "difficult obstacles ... and highly uncertain returns" in addressing problems of increasing inequality, persistent and patterned poverty, and the differential impacts of climatic change. These "wicked problems" require a sophisticated understanding of the complex, dynamic, and politically sensitive contexts in which they are embedded and a constructively critical appraisal of the interventions put forward to address them.

Appendix

Table 14A.1 International organizations, institutions, and programmes working on the measurement of poverty and well-being

- Oxford Poverty and Human Development Initiative (Multidimensional Poverty Index and "missing dimensions")
- World Bank (Living Standards Measurement Survey and International Comparison Programme)
- Gallup (World Values Survey)
- Globalbarometer network (e.g. Latinobarometer and Afrobarometer)
- Child poverty – UNICEF (Innocenti Report Card, State of the World's Children). See also Townsend Centre for International Poverty Research, Multidimensional Indicator Cluster Survey, and Global Study of Child Poverty and Disparities.
- International Society for Quality of Life Studies, Child Indicators Research
- OECD (Measuring Well-being and Progress, including child well-being, Better Life Initiative)
- New Economics Foundation (happy planet index)
- Demographic and Health Surveys
- Robert Chambers and the Participation, Power and Social Change group at the Institute for Development Studies
- Individual studies such as Pathways to Poverty and Well-being in Developing Countries ESRC Research group

Table 14A.2 International organizations, institutions, and programmes studying poverty over time

- Chronic Poverty Research Centre (2001–2011)
- Prof. Stefan Dercon (e.g. ICRISAT, Ethiopian Rural Households Study, and Young Lives)
- World Bank – Living Standards Measurement Survey, which is starting to develop panels, and repeated cross-sections to capture seasonality
- International Food Policy Research Institute (IFPRI)
- Longitudinal epidemiological survey, e.g. Matlab Survey Network, International Centre for Diarrhoeal Disease Research, Bangladesh (ICDDR,B); MRC Uganda Virus Research Institute Research Unit on AIDS
- Panel surveys and cohort studies summarized in Baulch (2011)

Notes

1. Impact evaluation is an increasingly important area for research, however, I do not have space to address this here.
2. See also Baulch, 2012; Narayan and Petesch, 2007; Bird, 2011; and Shepherd et al., 2011.
3. See also Hickey et al.'s special issue on the government of chronic poverty, Journal of Development Studies, 2010.
4. According to Bakewell (2007: 226), the Swedish International Development Agency receives 10,000 pages of reports each year from which they prepare a 1.5-page summary for their annual report.
5. Crow describes how Cornwell's study of understandings of health was improved by her presentation of public and private accounts of responsibility for health, with the latter noticeably more judgmental.
6. Nonetheless, some country informants preferred experimental techniques as they felt these would make their country appear more "advanced."
7. Behague and Storeng describe the attribution of "ideological" motivations to Francophone health experts who drew on historical rather than experimental evidence.
8. Paul Farmer, quoted in an LA Times critique of this approach published in December 2007, says that while "it doesn't surprise me that as someone who has made his fortune on developing a novel technology, Bill Gates would look for magic bullets in vaccines and medicines, if we don't have a solid delivery system, this work will be thwarted. That's something that's going to be hard for the big foundations [to understand]. They treat tuberculosis. They don't treat poverty."

References

Alkire, S. (2007). The Missing Dimensions of Poverty Data: An Introduction. OPHI Working Paper Series No. 00. Queen Elizabeth House, Oxford University, Oxford.

Alkire, S. and Santos, M. (2010). Acute Multidimensional Poverty: A New Index for Developing Countries. OPHI Working Paper Series No. 38. Queen Elizabeth House, Oxford University, Oxford.

Bakewell, O. (2007). "Breaching the Borders between Research and Practice: Development NGOs and Qualitative Data," in M. Smith (ed.) *Negotiating Boundaries and Borders*, Studies in Qualitative Methodology, Volume 8 (UK: Emerald Group Publishing Limited), pp. 217–238.

Baulch, B. (2011). Household Panel Data Sets in Developing and Transition Countries. Chronic Poverty Research Centre technical note. Chronic Poverty Research Centre, Manchester University, Manchester.

Baulch, B. (2012). *Why Poverty Persists: Poverty Dynamics in Africa and Asia*. Cheltenham and London: Edward Elgar Publishing.

Bernard, T., Taffesse, A., S. and Dercon, S. (2011). "Beyond Fatalism: An Empirical Exploration of Self-Efficacy and Aspirations Failure in Ethiopia." International Food Policy Research Institute Discussion Paper No. 01101. July 2011. International Food Policy Research Institute, Washington D.C.

Bird, K. (2011). Life histories: A resource pack. Chronic Poverty Research Centre technical note. Chronic Poverty Research Centre, Manchester University, Manchester.

Camfield, L. and McGregor, J. A. (2009). Editorial. Quality of Life and International Development Policy and Practice. *Applied Research in Quality of Life*, 4(2), 129–134.

Chambers, R. (2007). From PRA to PLA and Pluralism: Practice and Theory. IDS Working Paper No. 286. Institute of Development Studies, Sussex.

Christopher, J. C. (1999). Situating Psychological Wellbeing: Exploring the Cultural Roots of Its Theory and Research. *Journal of counselling and development*, 77, 141–152.

Cowen, T. (2011). The Great Stagnation: How America Ate All the Low-Hanging Fruit of Modern History, Got Sick, and Will(Eventually) Feel Better. Dutton, 9 June 2011. ISBN 0525952713.

Deaton, A. (2010). Price Indexes, Inequality, and the Measurement of World Poverty. Unpublished paper. Published in *American Economic Review*, 100(1): 5–34.

Deneulin, S. and McGregor, J. A. (2010). The Capability Approach and the Politics of a Social Conception of Wellbeing. WeD Working Paper Series No. 9, University of Bath, Bath.

Dercon, S. and Krishnan, P. (2009). Poverty and the Psycho-Social Competencies of Children: Evidence from the Young Lives Sample in Four Developing Countries. *Children, youth and environments*, 19(2), 138–163.

DFID (2012). Understanding Poverty and Wellbeing: A Note with Implications for Research and Policy. Unpublished report. http://www.odi.org.uk/sites/odi.org.uk/files/odi-assets/publications-opinion-files/7654.pdf, downloaded 07/02/2014.

Duflo, E. (2003). Grandmothers and Granddaughters: Old Age Pensions and Intrahousehold Allocation in South Africa. *World Bank Economic Review*, 17(1), 1–25.

Eyben, R. (2007). "Labelling People for Aid," in J. Moncrieffe and R. Eyben (eds) *The Power of Labelling. How People Are Categorised and Why It Matters* (London: Earthscan), pp. 33–47.

Graham, C. (2009). *Happiness around the World: The Paradox of Happy Peasants and Miserable Millionaires*. Oxford University Press, USA

Green, M. and Hulme, D. (2005). From Correlates and Characteristics to Causes: Thinking about Poverty from a Chronic Poverty Perspective. *World Development*, 33(6), 867–879.

Hickey, S. (ed.) (2010). Special Issue: The Government of Chronic Poverty. *The Journal of Development Studies*, 46(7), 1139–1326.

Lloyd-Sherlock, P. (2010). *Population Ageing and International Development: From Generalisation to Evidence*. UK: Policy Press.

Laws, S., Harper, C., Jones, N., Marcus, R. (eds.). (2013). *Research for Development: A Practical Guide*. Second Edition. SAGE Publications.

Mosse, D. (2010). A Relational Approach to Durable Poverty, Inequality and Power. *Journal of Development Studies*, 46(70), 1156–1178.

Narayan, D. and Petesch, P. (2007). *Moving Out of Poverty, volume 1. Cross-Disciplinary Perspectives on Mobility*. World Bank, Washington.

Ray, D. (2006). "Aspirations, Poverty, and Economic Change," in A. V. Banerjee, R. Bénabou and D. Mookherjee (eds) *Understanding Poverty* (Oxford, UK: Oxford University Press), 409–22.

Saith, A. (2005). Poverty-lines versus the Poor: Method versus Meaning. ISS Working Paper series No. 420. International Institute of Social Studies, Hague, Netherlands.

Shepherd, A. et al. (2011). Tackling Chronic Poverty: The Policy Implications of Research on Chronic Poverty and Poverty Dynamics. Chronic Poverty Research Centre final report. Chronic Poverty Research Centre, Manchester University, Manchester.

Simpson, K. (2007). "Hearing Voices? Negotiating Multiple Ethical Commitments in Development Research," in M. Smith (ed.) *Negotiating Boundaries and Borders, Studies in Qualitative Methodology*, Volume 8 (UK: Emerald Group Publishing Limited), pp. 155–173.

Smith, M. (ed.) (2007). "Negotiating Boundaries and Borders," in M. Smith (ed.) *Studies in Qualitative Methodology*, Volume 8 (UK: Emerald Group Publishing Limited), 155–73.

Sumner, A. (2007). Meaning versus measurement: why do 'economic' indicators of poverty still predominate? *Development in Practice*, 17: 4–13.

Temple, B., Edwards, R. and Alexander, C. (2006). Grasping at Context: Cross Language Qualitative Research as Secondary Qualitative Data Analysis. *FQS*, 7(4) art. 10.

van Dijk, T. (2011). Livelihoods, Capitals and Livelihood Trajectories: A More Sociological Conceptualisation. *Progress in Development Studies*, 11: 101–117.

White, S. and Pettit, J. (2004). Participatory Approaches and the Measurement of Human Well-Being. WeD Working Paper No. 8 (Bath: Wellbeing in Developing Countries (WeD) Research Group).

Index

Printed and bound in the United States of America